ACADEMY AWARD™ WINNERS

ACADEMY AWARD WINNERS ™

RONALD BERGAN·GRAHAM FULLER·DAVID MALCOLM

This book is neither authorized nor endorsed by the
Academy of Motion Picture Arts and Sciences.

Crescent Books
New York

This book was devised and produced by
Multimedia Publications (UK) Ltd

Project Editor: Richard Rosenfeld
Editor: Robyn Karney
Research Editor: Dan Millar
Production: Karen Bromley
Design: Bob Burroughs
Picture Research: Pauline Simcock and Joel Finler

1986 edition published by
Crescent Books, distributed by
Crown Publishers Inc.

ISBN 0 517 60467 1

Typeset by Rapidset
Origination by Imago
Printed in Italy by Sagdos, Milan

hgfedcb

ENDPAPERS *Robert Redford directs Donald Sutherland
and Mary Tyler Moore in* Ordinary People *(1980)*
HALF-TITLE *Claudette Colbert and Clark Gable in* It
Happened One Night *(1934)*
TITLE PAGE *Charlton Heston as* Ben-Hur *(1959)*
ABOVE *Jack Nicholson as Randle P. McMurphy in* One
Flew Over The Cuckoo's Nest *(1975)*
Wilfrid Hyde White and Audrey Hepburn in My Fair
Lady *(1964)*

CONTENTS

Introduction and essays from 1927/8
– 1947 by Ronald Bergan · 1948-1968 by
David Malcolm · 1969-1985 by Graham
Fuller

Acknowledgements
The editor would like to record her special appreciation
and thanks to Tammy Collins, Peter Cartwright, Brian Rooney,
Graham Fuller, Michelle Sewell, Melanie Downing, and the staff of
The Kobal Collection for their invaluable assistance in
the preparation of this book

INTRODUCTION

THE ACADEMY OF Motion Picture Arts and Sciences was first dreamed up by powerful mogul Louis B. Mayer in order to lend respectability and status to the movie industry, the reputation of which was tarnished during 'The Roaring 20s'. It was formed on May 4, 1927, to "raise the cultural, educational and scientific standards" of film, a statement calculated to placate those who saw the movies as having a corrupting effect on American morals and ideals.

Composer and musicals producer Arthur Freed, the Academy's president from 1963-1967, has been quoted as saying that the awards "honor artistic achievement, with little regard for popularity, box-office success or other yardsticks applied by the critics or the general public." Despite many controversial judgments, and occasional submissions to "other yardsticks", the Academy, as a whole, has maintained the standards set at its beginnings. Yet, at the same time, it has seldom cut itself off from public taste, and has managed to acknowledge Hollywood's greatest strength: the manufacture of sup-

erbly crafted mass entertainment. Perhaps that is why people are more comfortable using the affectionate but slightly disreputable nickname of 'Oscar' to describe the Academy Award.

Until 1931, the 13½ inch tall, eight-pound figure of a man with a crusader's sword standing thoughtlessly on a reel of film was known merely as The Statuette. Legend has it that the Academy librarian, Margaret Herrick, chanced to remark on studying it, "Why, he looks just like my

BELOW LEFT *Multimillionaire, charity worker, golfer, and internationally famous comedian Bob Hope, with Lana Turner, at the 1966 Awards at which he was the Master of Ceremonies. Hope was Oscar's MC on 16 occasions, and the Academy honored him with a plaque in 1940, a life membership (1944), a statuette (1952) and a gold medal (1965)*
BELOW *Movie mogul Darryl F. Zanuck was the first recipient of the Irving G. Thalberg Award, instituted in 1937 to honor MGM's 'boy wonder' who died at the tragically early age of 37. Zanuck won twice more before the practice of giving the award to the same person more than once was discontinued*

©A.M.P.A.S.®

uncle Oscar!" Just as likely is the claim that Bette Davis named it after her first husband, Harmon Oscar Nelson Jr. Whatever the truth behind its christening, the name stuck forever. Double Oscar-winning scriptwriter Frances Marion once described the figurine as "a perfect symbol of the picture business; a powerful athletic body clutching a gleaming sword, with half of his head, that part which held the brains, completely sliced off."

'Oscar' was designed in a few minutes on a tablecloth at Hollywood's Biltmore Hotel by MGM art director Cedric Gibbons (an 11-times recipient of his own creation), executed by sculptor George Stanley, and manufactured by the Dodge Trophy Co. of Crystal Lake, Illinois. The value of the gold-plated statuette is around $180, but all winners pledge never to sell it except back to the Academy who will pay $10 for it. But its value at the box-office is inestimable. So important is it as a means of increasing business that the major studios spend in the region of $300,000 publicizing their nominated properties.

One of the first functions of the 36 charter members of the Academy, who included Douglas Fairbanks, Mary Pickford, Cecil B. DeMille, Irving Thalberg and Raoul Walsh, was to organize the annual achievement awards. Until 1934, the awards were based on seasonal not calendar years (1927/1928, 1928/1929 and so on). To be eligible, a film must be shown in the Los Angeles area for a least a week during the previous year. (Charles Chaplin only received his award for Best Original Dramatic Score for **Limelight** in 1972, 20 years after the picture had been released in the USA, but not in Los Angeles.) An exception to this rule is the Foreign Language movie, which only needs one showing in the States.

For the first nine years, only Academy members determined the awards, but in 1937 voting was extended to some 15,000 people in the movie industry, although the nominations were limited to Academy members. Later the procedure was reversed, with the industry at large selecting the nominations, and the Academy the winners. From 1957 to the present day all voting is confined to the Academy. The latter is divided into several branches, the acting branch, the writing branch and so on. These decide on the five nominees for their particular category, although all branches select the Best Picture nominees. The honorary and special awards such as the Irving G. Thalberg Memorial (instigated in 1937) and the Jean Hersholt Humanitarian (begun in 1956) are chosen by the Academy's Board of Governors. The unglamorous but essential scientific and technical awards are voted by the Scientific or Technical Awards Committee. The Best Foreign Language Film, an honorary award until 1956, is

BELOW *The elegant and sensitive English director, Edmund Goulding (seated foreground left), had the task of controlling the clashing temperaments of the all-star cast of MGM's Best Picture,* Grand Hotel *(1931/32). Here, he rehearses on set with Wallace Beery and Joan Crawford*

selected by the entire Academy membership. Any country can submit films, but only one per nation can be nominated in a particular year. For the record, France has been favored more often than other countries with Italy coming a close second.

The winners at the first award-giving ceremony, held at Hollywood's Roosevelt Hotel on May 16th, 1929, had been known for three months before the banquet. During the following years, prizes were announced a week prior to the presentations until, in 1941, the policy of sealed envelopes, opened to accompanying squeals of surprise, was introduced. As the event became more popular and prestigious, so the venues increased in size. From various Hollywood hotels, it moved to Grauman's Chinese Theatre in 1944, then to the larger Shrine Auditorium in 1947, and on to the RKO Pantages Theatre from 1950 to 1959. The Santa Monica Civic Auditorium was the site until 1969 when it moved to its present home, the Dorothy Chandler Pavilion at the Los Angeles County Music Center.

Over the years there have been variations in designations of awards and increases in categories due to changes in techniques and attitudes, but the general lines laid down for the reward of excellence in the motion picture industry have remained. The Academy Awards came into being simultaneously with the birth of sound, so that the very first honors represented a valedictory homage to the silent cinema while paying tribute to **The Jazz Singer** (1927), the "outstanding talking picture

TOP *The most famous ape in the world,* King Kong, *failed to win any awards. This can only be put down to the fact that, in 1933, the year of his birth, no categories had yet been introduced to acknowledge special visual effects*
ABOVE *Producer David O. Selznick (left), who had the foresight to purchase the rights to* Gone With The Wind *and film it in 1939, chats to his Scarlett O'Hara (Best Actress Vivien Leigh), and his Oscar-winning director Victor Fleming during a break in filming*

which has revolutionized the industry." By the second year, the award for Title Writing had disappeared and a musical, **Broadway Melody** (1929), was named Best Picture. The following year a Sound Recording category was added, and the Best Song and Best Score were first recognized in 1934. The immense triumph of **Gone With The Wind** (1939), led to the introduction of separate color and black-and-white Oscars for cinematography and interior decoration. Despite the fact that the 30s saw the acme of fashion in Hollywood, costume designers had to wait until 1948 to get their statuettes. The ceremony was in its ninth year before the important contri-

board, **It Happened One Night** (1934) gave Columbia, a hitherto Poverty Row studio, a major boost and gained fame for its director, Frank Capra, who became President of the Academy from 1935 to 1939.

The outbreak of war in Europe in 1939 changed the character of Hollywood films and the flavor of the award ceremony. After Pearl Harbor, formal attire was banned from the evening event, the banquet was renamed a dinner, and the searchlights that played outside the venue were switched off until peace returned. Six-Oscar winner **Mrs Miniver** (1942) and Special Award winner **In Which We Serve** (1942) helped create a wave of pro-

ABOVE *Judy Garland was perhaps the most vibrantly gifted all-round performer the screen has known. Generally remembered as a musical star, she was a Best Supporting Actress nominee in 1961 for her dramatic portrayal of a homely German* hausfrau *in* Judgment At Nuremberg

bution of supporting players was acknowledged by the Academy.

Mainly, however, the story of 'Uncle Oscar' reflects the development of American cinema, and the trends, tastes, and events in society as a whole. When the movies thrived as great escapist entertainment during the Depression – a case of breadlines and circuses – the annual awards were the cherry on the top. By sweeping the

British sentiment in America, while **Since You Went Away** (1944) showed how Americans were bearing up on the home front. After the world conflict, Hollywood and the Academy emerged with new maturity. In three successive years, Best Picture Oscars were given to films that contained a strong social message – **The Lost Weekend** (1945) about alcoholism, **The Best Years Of Our Lives** (1946) on the problems of returning veterans, and **Gentleman's Agreement** (1947) dealing with anti-Semitism.

Although audience figures had already begun to decline in 1947, the main cause for drastic reductions in cinema admissions was soon laid at the door of television, the one-eyed monster that was proliferating in the

LEFT *Ace cinematographer Freddie Young (left) lines up a shot for* Ryan's Daughter *(1970) with director David Lean. Five-times nominated, Young won the Cinematography Oscar for all three of his David Lean films –* Lawrence Of Arabia *(1962) and* Doctor Zhivago *(1965) were the others*

ABOVE *Veteran director John Huston photographed during the filming of his Oscar-nominated* Prizzi's Honor *(1985), which starred Jack Nicholson (left), Kathleen Turner (2nd left), and Huston's daughter, Anjelica (right), who won for Best Supporting Actress*

USA in the early 50s. Billy Wilder, Oscar-winning director of **The Lost Weekend** and, later, the last black-and-white Best Picture **The Apartment** (1960), remarked that "it used to be films that were the lowest form of art. Now we have something to look down on." The industry reacted by trying to attract the public to bigger, though not necessarily better entertainment. The Academy in the 50s, while recognizing the merits of spectacles like **The Greatest Show On Earth** (1952), **Around The World In 80 Days** (1956) and **The Bridge On The River Kwai** (1957), did not neglect realistic black-and-white films like **From Here To Eternity** (1953), **On The Waterfront** (1954) and **Marty** (1955), and the stamp of Oscar's approval helped these to gather large audiences.

In the 60s, despite the break-up of the studio system, there were enough blockbusters to bring in millions of dollars. Musicals such as **West Side Story** (1961), **Mary Poppins** (1964), **My Fair Lady** (1964) and **The Sound Of Music** (1965) earned vast amounts at the box-office, as well as a clutch of statuettes each. With the aid of the annual Oscar bonanza, exciting new young stars and directors emerged in the 70s with films like **The Godfather** (1972), **Rocky** (1976), **Annie Hall** (1977), **Star Wars** (1977), **The Deer Hunter** (1978) and **Kramer vs Kramer** (1979). Over 55 years after their inception, the Oscars still keep the excitement in movies alive, are still as sought after as they ever were, and Hollywood is still producing films worthy of the accolade.

Although the Academy makes financial contributions to the development of cinematic techniques, and supports a substantial film library, it is Awards night that lends the institution its glamor. Each year the glittering occasion, now seen on TV by over 70 million Americans and 350 million people in 54 countries, gives Hollywood a sense of community and a chance to honor its own. It is also the night when the rest of the world can enjoy the razzamatazz and share in Tinseltown's special glory.

Ronald Bergan

1927/8

NOBODY AT THE first Academy Award presentation on May 16, 1929 at Hollywood's Roosevelt Hotel could have guessed how important the awards would become. The banquet for 200 members of the movie industry was a low-key affair completely ignored by the media. William C. de Mille, elder brother of Cecil B. acted as chairman, and Douglas Fairbanks, the President of the Academy, handed out the statuettes in the record time of four minutes and twenty-two seconds. There was no suspense, since the winners had been announced three months previously on the back page of the Academy Bulletin. Janet Gaynor, the first Best Actress winner recalled, "Naturally, I was thrilled but, being the first year, the Academy Awards had no background or tradition. It naturally didn't mean what it does now. Had I known then what it would come to mean in the next few years, I'm sure I'd have been overwhelmed. At the time I think I was more thrilled over meeting Douglas Fairbanks."

The two Special prizes given at the first ever Academy Award ceremony reflected the dramatic change that was taking place in the motion picture business. One was presented to Charles Chaplin, the supreme clown of the silent screen, for "his genius and versatility in writing, acting, directing and producing **The Circus**", and the other was "To Warner Brothers for producing **The Jazz Singer**, the pioneer talking picture, which has revolutionized the industry." An indication of the impact the sound revolution was having was that the biggest sensation at the awards banquet was a short talker (as the first sound pictures were initially called) in which Douglas Fairbanks seen and *heard* having a conversation with Adolph Zukor, the producer of **Wings**, the Best Picture winner. It was to be the first and last time the nameless statuette, later dubbed Oscar, would be awarded to non-speaking movies (by then they all had synchronized music and sound effects) and their silent stars.

"To those young warriors of the sky whose wings are folded about them forever, this motion picture is reverently dedicated," was the way in which **Wings** director William A. Wellman introduced his movie in the program at its triumphant opening night. Wellman's experi-

RIGHT *One of the spectacular and authentic battle scenes which exemplify the superb pictorial qualities of William A. Wellman's World War I drama,* Wings. *The first winner of the Best Picture award, it was also the only silent film ever to win that honor*

ences as a much-decorated airman with the crack Lafayette Flying Corps in France during World War I, and later as a stunt pilot, lent authority to the spectacular aerial sequences, all filmed without faking or process shots. This was done by mounting cameras on the front of the planes, the actors going aloft with a pilot who would duck down as they struck the right heroic attitudes. The film was shot with the co-operation of the US government, which supplied thousands of soldiers, hundreds of planes, and pilots as extras. One of the stunt flyers ended in hospital with a broken neck after a crash. Besides being a worthy Best Picture winner, the picture also gained an award for Roy Pomeroy's 'Engineering Effects', the only time such a prize was given, until the institution of the awards for 'Special Effects' in 1940.

On ground, the simple tale told of the rivalry between two airmen pals, Richard Arlen (another flying veteran of the war) and Charles 'Buddy' Rogers (nine years later to marry Mary Pickford) for the affections of small-town girl Clara Bow. However, Paramount Studios was flooded

ABOVE *Demure Janet Gaynor (left) as the Parisian waif in* Seventh Heaven, *one of the three movies that gave her the first Best Actress Oscar. Charles Farrell (foreground center), Gaynor's sweetheart in ten movies, George E. Stone (background center), and Albert Gran complete the scene*

with fan letters for the young actor who played a pilot who leaves a half-eaten candybar before going to his death in the sky. On the strength of the reaction to his 20-second appearance, the studio offered Gary Cooper a contract. At the time, Cooper hit the headlines because of his affair with Miss Bow, which ended due to his jealousy and her refusal to settle for one man – not that, had she wished to give up her freedom, she could have counted on his fidelity. The attractive Cooper is documented as one of Hollywood's most famous studs!

In contrast to the 'It' girl (as Clara Bow became known) in **Wings**, petite Janet Gaynor was the embodiment of sweetness and innocence on screen. (In reality, she was an astute businesswoman.) She earned the honor of becoming the first actress to win an Academy Award not for one role, but three: her combined work in **Sunrise** (1927), **Seventh Heaven** (1927) and **Street Angel** (1928). The latter two were sentimental romances directed by Frank Borzage (the Best Director winner), in which Gaynor played waifs (French and Italian respectively) rescued from poverty and sin through the love of a man. The object of her affections in both (and nine other) films was the ineffectual Charles Farrell, who was prettier and had a higher voice than she, and together they became known as 'America's favorite lovebirds'. Far better was her poignant portrayal of the farmer's wife whose husband is egged on to drown her by a city woman in F. W. Murnau's poetic masterpiece, **Sunrise**. The husband (George O'Brien) thinks better of it, and the couple go on a second honeymoon to the metropolis. The most impressive sequence is the trip to the big city by trolley car, where she sits transfixed as the scenery passes by.

Janet Gaynor's closest rival for the award was Gloria Swanson, who had put her heart and soul into the role of Somerset Maugham's famous floozie **Sadie Thompson** (1927). Gaynor recalled some years later that 'Until I won that prize, I wasn't keen about being an actress. I was not stagestruck one bit. I didn't like to have to go around and ask for jobs.' The Academy Award made sure she would never have to do that again. She retired from the screen in 1939 after marrying MGM's top costume designer Adrian, though Hollywood gossip has always maintained it was a marriage of convenience.

While William Fox was trying to inject more class into his studio's productions by hiring famed German director F. W. Murnau to direct Gaynor in **Sunrise**, Paramount had managed to obtain the services of the great German actor Emil Jannings, star of Murnau's **The Last Laugh** (1924), **Tartuffe** (1925) and **Faust** (1926), all made in Germany. In order to allay any xenophobia, they announced that Jannings had been born in Brooklyn and

BELOW *The legendary Charlie Chaplin as an out-of-work clown in* The Circus, *shares a sandwich with his secret love, bareback rider Merna Kennedy. Chaplin's special Oscar honored this performance as well as his fourteen previous glorious years as actor, writer and director*

ABOVE *A poignant moment from F.W. Murnau's masterpiece* Sunrise *in which Janet Gaynor was the long-suffering wife of unfaithful but repentant farmer George O'Brien (both illustrated).*

was taken to Germany at the age of one. In fact, he was born in Rorschach, Switzerland, although Jannings himself perpetuated the lie in his autobiography. It was typical of the larger-than-life, 250-lb actor who lived in a huge copy of a Southern mansion on Hollywood Boulevard, surrounded by servants, pets and hangers-on.

The German star's popularity increased greatly after winning the Best Actor award for his efforts in his first two Hollywood films, **The Way Of All Flesh** (1927) and Josef von Sternberg's **The Last Command** (1928). In the former, made by Victor Fleming, future director of **Gone With The Wind** (1939), Jannings was typically cast as a respectable family man humiliated and destroyed by lust for blonde vamp Phyllis Haver. More impressively in **The Last Command**, despite excessive use of his eyes and

eyebrows, he was an exiled Tsarist general who winds up in Hollywood playing himself in a movie whose director (William Powell) had been a Russian revolutionary. The general, confusing reality and fiction, triumphs in the role before dying on the set.

Jannings' thick German accent put an end to his Hollywood career at the coming of sound, and he returned to Germany in 1929. There, he lent himself to the Nazi cause, making propaganda films for the regime. Although cleared by the War Crimes Commission, he was blacklisted by the Allied authorities after the war. Thus Jannings, the first actor ever to win an Oscar, never made another film, dying in disgrace in 1960. Another winner at that historic first Oscar ceremony, director Frank Borzage, was forced out of work for ten years in 1948 by the HUAC blacklist, proving that the aura of success an Academy Award confers on the recipient can be very short-lived.

WINNERS 1927/8

Awards Ceremony: May 16, 1929
Hollywood Roosevelt Hotel-Banquet

Best Picture
WINGS, Paramount

Actor
EMIL JANNINGS in *The Last Command*, Paramount
EMIL JANNINGS in *The Way Of All Flesh*, Paramount

Actress
JANET GAYNOR in *Seventh Heaven*, Fox
JANET GAYNOR in *Street Angel*, Fox
JANET GAYNOR in *Sunrise*, Fox

Directing
FRANK BORZAGE for *Seventh Heaven*

Comedy Direction
(Not given after this year)
LEWIS MILESTONE for *Two Arabian Knights*, UA

Writing
(Adaptation)
SEVENTH HEAVEN: BENJAMIN GLAZER
(Original Story)
UNDERWORLD, Paramount: BEN HECHT
(Title Writing – Not given after this year.)
THE FAIR CO-ED, MGM: JOSEPH FARNHAM
LAUGH, CLOWN, LAUGH, MGM: JOSEPH FARNHAM
TELLING THE WORLD, MGM: JOSEPH FARNHAM

Cinematography
SUNRISE: CHARLES ROSHER and KARL STRUSS

Interior Decoration
THE DOVE, UA: WILLIAM CAMERON MENZIES
THE TEMPEST, UA: WILLIAM CAMERON MENZIES

Artistic Quality of Production
(Not given after this year.)
SUNRISE

Engineering Effects
(Not given after this year.)
WINGS: ROY POMEROY

Special Awards
CHARLES CHAPLIN for versatility and genius in writing, acting, directing and producing *The Circus*. (statuette)
WARNER BROS. for producing *The Jazz Singer*, the pioneer outstanding talking picture, which has revolutionized the industry. (statuette)

For the First Awards only, all nominees who did not win Oscars were given Honorable Mention awards.

1928/9

"THE DEVELOPMENT OF talking pictures has made individual achievement of artists more difficult to judge," said Academy secretary Frank Woods. "Sound has brought a new element to screen art and a host of new people." The problem of assessing the winners was so great that the second Annual Academy Awards were given eight months after the eligibility period of August 1st, 1928 to July 31st, 1929. Although no special distinction was made between sound and silent movies, talking pictures swept the board at the banquet held at the Ambassador Hotel on April 3rd, 1930. All the awards were presented by William C. de Mille, Cecil B. DeMille's elder brother (Cecil B. adopted his own spelling of the family name), and for the first and last time the honors were distributed evenly with no picture winning more than a single prize. The only silent film among the five nominees for Best Picture, Ernst Lubitsch's **The Patriot**, didn't stand a chance. In the year following the first award ceremony, everybody was climbing onto the sound bandwagon, each studio claiming to have produced "the first 100% all-talking drama filmed outdoors", "the first all-Negro, all-talking film" or "the first 100% talking, singing college picture". Meanwhile, many stars who had emoted magnificently but mutely were destroyed by the microphone, while others had the faces plus the voices to relish the talkies. It was an era wittily re-created in the great MGM musical, **Singin' In The Rain** (1952).

Several of the Arthur Freed-Nacio Herb Brown songs featured in the latter movie, including 'You Were Meant For Me', were first heard in **The Broadway Melody**, the first sound film and therefore the first musical to win the Best Picture award. The Hollywood musical, the only new cinematic genre to be born with the coming of sound, was a mere two years old when it received the American cinema's highest accolade. The "100% all-talking, all-singing, all-dancing" movie introduced a theme that was to dominate the genre, on and off, for decades to come—the 'backstage' musical. As *Motion Picture News* trumpeted, "MGM have stolen a march on all their competitors in the talkie production field by being the first on the market with a combination drama and musical revue that will knock the audiences for a goal."

Audiences today may be less likely to be "knocked for a goal" by the static numbers and tenuous tale involving two small town vaudevillian sisters (Bessie Love and Anita Page) who both fall for the same Broadway song 'n'

dance man (Charles King). As the sister who loses out in the end, Bessie Love, whose career began back in 1916 and stretched into the 1980s, was nominated for an Oscar. She recalled that, "at this period, the sound equipment was being improved almost week to week, so that the end of **The Broadway Melody** sounded much better than the beginning." The movie also contained a number, 'The Wedding Of The Painted Doll', filmed in two-color Technicolor (red and green). MGM used the title tag for the **Broadway Melodies** of 1936, 1938 and 1940.

Warner Baxter's most famous role would come three years later in **42nd Street** (1933), the quintessential backstage musical in which, as the slave-driving producer, he inspires nervous stand-in Ruby Keeler, getting her big chance when the lead breaks a leg, to "go out there a youngster and come back a star." But Baxter's Best Actor award in 1928/1929 can also be put down to

BELOW *Previous year's Oscar winner, Emil Jannings, as Tsar Paul the First in Ernst Lubitsch's* The Patriot, *prepares for death. The silent film's only Oscar went to its screenwriter Hans Kräly, who had come over to Hollywood from Germany with Lubitsch in 1923*

an accident. Raoul Walsh, who was directing (and playing the Cisco Kid) in **In Old Arizona**, was driving home one night from location shooting when a rabbit, frightened by the headlights, jumped up and crashed through the windshield, permanently blinding Walsh in one eye. Unable to continue the assignment, Walsh handed over the task of directing to Irving Cummings, and the central role to Warner Baxter.

The handsome Baxter, with the pencil-thin moustache, had been in pictures for ten years but had made little impact. Now, as the guitar-strumming, singing, devil-may-care outlaw, pursued throughout by army sergeant Edmund Lowe, he shot into the top money earning

RIGHT *Charles King (center) with Anita Page on his left and Bessie Love on his right in* The Broadway Melody, *the first musical to win the Best Picture award and the first MGM movie to do so. The modest feminine chorus line of twelve would soon multiply ten-fold in future musicals.*
BELOW *Warner Baxter displays his Oscar-winning ways as the amiable singing Mexican bandit The Cisco Kid in* In Old Arizona, *serenading senorita Dorothy Burgess. The unassuming Western was nominated in almost every category*

bracket where he remained until the late 30s. He reprised the role of the western Robin Hood in **The Arizona Kid** (1930), **The Cisco Kid** (1931), and **The Return Of The Cisco Kid** (1939). In the next decade he suffered a decline and a nervous breakdown, but continued working in 'B' pictures until his premature death of pneumonia at the age of 57 (in 1951), following a lobotomy to relieve a painful arthritic condition.

Although Baxter had keen competition from Chester Morris (**Alibi**), Paul Muni (**The Valiant**) and George Bancroft (**Thunderbolt**), few disputed the choice. More controversial was Mary Pickford's Academy Award as Best Actress for **Coquette**, creating the first of many heated debates about the winners that was to become part of

almost every annual selection thereafter. One critic, who thought Ruth Chatterton in **Madame X** and Jeanne Eagels in **The Letter** more deserving, wrote, "It gives the impression that the Academy is handing out cups on a political or social basis." Pickford, of course, was the wife of Academy President Douglas Fairbanks, and also an active member in the organization. She was also known to have entertained the judges lavishly at 'Pickfair', the Fairbanks' celebrated Hollywood mansion. This was probably why the balloting, in which only a handful of voters took part, was extended in following years to the entire Academy membership.

Aside from any suggestion of "friendly persuasion" on

her part, Pickford's Oscar seemed to have been given in recognition of one of the longest and most successful careers in motion pictures, rather than for her speaking debut in **Coquette**. However, she coped well enough with the challenging role (played on stage by Helen Hayes) of the spoiled Southern flapper who lies in court to save her father from being charged with the murder of her lover. But despite cameraman Karl Struss' "wrinkle eradicator" light below the lens, the 35-year-old star seemed a trifle mature for the part of the college girl. Ironically, her age had never been an obstacle when she played curly-headed little girls in short frocks, not even when she was in her 30s. No attempt was ever made to hoodwink audiences into believing they were seeing a real child in films such as **Pollyanna** (1920) and **Little Annie Rooney** (1925), only a phenomenal child impersonator. At one stage in her career she protested, "I hate these curls. I'm in a dramatic rut eternally playing this curly-headed girl. I loathe them! I loathe them!" Unfortunately for her, the public was only interested in paying to see their beloved 'Little Mary', and not a mature actress.

For **Coquette**, Pickford set out to create a new screen persona, and photos of her having her curls cut off and her hair bobbed were published around the world. But, in becoming modern, she lost her uniqueness and set herself up as a rival to dozens of other 'Jazz Babies' who were filling the screens in 1929. Despite the Oscar, Pickford made only three more films before devoting her time to the vice-presidency of United Artists, the company she helped found, and the Mary Pickford Cosmetics Company. In 1975, four years before her death, she received an Honorary Academy Award for her 'contributions to the industry'.

ABOVE *An example of Cedric Gibbons' Oscar-winning art direction for* The Bridge Of San Luis Rey, *set in 18th-century Peru. The Donna in the spangled Spanish costume is Lili Damita, the future Mrs Errol Flynn. It was the first of eleven Academy Awards won by the designer of the statuette*

Other winners at that year's ceremony, broadcast for the first time by a local radio station, were Cedric Gibbons, the designer of the Oscar statuette, for his art direction on the silent **The Bridge Of San Luis Rey**, and Frank Lloyd, future director of **Mutiny On The Bounty** (1935), nominated for no less than three films as Best Director, for **The Divine Lady**, a title which referred to Emma Hamilton as well as the beautiful 'Orchid Lady', Corinne Griffith, in the role. Curiously, in spite of the dominance of sound, the Best Writing award went to Hans Kraly for the non-talking **The Patriot**, and the cinematography of Clyde De Vinna caught the judges' eyes in the silent film, **White Shadows In The South Seas**. Apparently silents were still golden to some.

WINNERS 1928/9

Nominations Announced: October 31, 1929
Awards Ceremony: April 3, 1930
Ambassador Hotel-Banquet

Best Picture
BROADWAY MELODY, MGM

Actor
WARNER BAXTER in *In Old Arizona*, Fox

Actress
MARY PICKFORD in *Coquette*, Pickford/UA

Directing
FRANK LLOYD for *The Divine Lady*, First National

Writing
(Achievement)
THE PATRIOT, Paramount: HANS KRALY

Cinematography
WHITE SHADOWS IN THE SOUTH SEAS, MGM: CLYDE DE VINNA

Interior Decoration
THE BRIDGE OF SAN LUIS REY, MGM: CEDRIC GIBBONS

"THE LEAGUE OF Nations could make no better investment than to buy the master print and reproduce it in every language for every nation to show every year until the word "war" is taken out of the dictionaries," wrote one critic about **All Quiet On The Western Front**, the year's Best Picture winner, and a milestone in anti-war movies. Based on Erich Maria Remarque's bestseller, it followed seven German boys who leave school in 1914, full of patriotic fervor, to fight for their country. Their enthusiasm is soon dampened when they are thrown into the horror of trench warfare. Particularly effective were the tracking shots of soldiers attacking the enemy lines and the counterattacks with appalling deaths on both sides. Skilful use was made of the single track sound system, crane shots and music. So realistic were the battle sequences that some of them have often been incorporated into documentary films of World War I. The bleak message, that war is hell for both sides, led to both Germany and France banning the film for many years for fear it would have a demoralizing effect on their armed forces. The most moving moment is when one of the young German soldiers finds a Frenchman in a shell-hole, stabs him, and then agonizes over what he has done. The famous last scene, where the only surviving boy (Lew Ayres) is killed by a sniper's bullet while stretching towards a butterfly, was shot some months after the film's completion, using director Lewis Milestone's own hand – the same hand that received the Best Director's award.

The film was a brave venture in a world mainly at peace but going through a depression. At the first preview, audiences laughed when ZaSu Pitts, then making a name as a comedienne, appeared as the boy's mother. Her dramatic role, therefore, had to be reshot with actress Beryl Mercer. **All Quiet On The Western Front** had been planned by Universal Pictures producer Carl Laemmle Jr as a silent movie but, when talking pictures began to dominate the industry, he quickly switched it to all sound on the western front. The transitional period between the silents and the talkies in Hollywood was over. The novelty of sound was no longer enough to attract audiences who now expected quality as well. A new Academy Award was

RIGHT *The 'War is Hell' message of Lewis Milestone's* All Quiet On The Western Front *was seldom stronger than in this scene where German boy Lew Ayres (left) is forced to kill a French soldier (Raymond Griffith, right) in a shell hole*

thus introduced to honor Sound Recording. The first winner was Douglas Shearer for his work on the grim prison drama **The Big House**, a nominee for Best Picture. Shearer was to win a further 11 Oscars during his 40-year career as head of the MGM sound department.

Norma Shearer, Douglas' sister, was the rather surprising winner of the Best Actress award for her performance in the glossy but heavy-handed soap opera **The Divorcee**. (She was also up for another soapy offering, **Their Own Desire**.) It was widely believed that Greta Garbo, nominated for **Anna Christie** ("Garbo Talks!" ran the celebrated publicity line) and **Romance**, would – and, indeed should – carry off the glittering prize. Garbo's first words ever spoken on screen were, "Gimme a visky with chincher ale on the side and don't be stingy, baby." But the Academy was certainly stingy, for this most famous of screen actresses never won an award for a single one of her films. In 1954, 13 years after her last picture, the star belatedly received a special award "for her unforgettable screen performances."

Garbo was originally offered the starring role in **The Divorcee**, but she turned it down because she was offended by the story, and Joan Crawford was chosen. But Norma Shearer was reputed to have said to her husband, MGM production chief Irving Thalberg, "Irving, the public is getting tired of me being the lady in every picture. I've got to play something more daring." Thalberg gave way and Crawford lost the part, which led to her oft-repeated comment, "How can I compete with Norma when she sleeps with the boss?" In the film, the slightly squint-eyed, aquiline 'First Lady of the Screen', as MGM billed her, played a liberated woman (at least in the context of Hollywood at the time) who seeks revenge on her philandering husband (Chester Morris) by taking two lovers of her own (Robert Montgomery and Conrad Nagel). In the end, amidst tears, she takes back her chastened mate. The flattering camerawork, favoring her left profile, and the stunning Adrian gowns, gave her a certain allure, enough for the *New York Sun* to write that "Norma Shearer is the American beauty rose of the MGM nurseries." She never won another Oscar, but was nominated a further five times before her retirement from the screen in 1942. After Thalberg's death from pneumonia in 1936 aged 37, Shearer's appearances were rare, and her judgement wobbly. She turned down both Scarlett

BELOW *So authentic were the World War I battle scenes depicted in the Best Picture,* All Quiet On The Western Front, *that many of them were later used in documentary films of the conflict. Lewis Milestone won the Best Director Oscar*

ABOVE *Best Actress Norma Shearer, wife of MGM production chief Irving Thalberg, dances with Theodore von Eltz in The Divorcee, the first of many wayward wives she would portray. She got the part by persuading her husband to allow her something more daring than her previous roles*

O'Hara in **Gone With The Wind** (1939) and **Mrs Miniver** (1942) – her loss but the cinema's gain.

Many distinguished and vastly contrasting performers were up for the Best Actor award in 1930. Debonair Ronald Colman, whose attractive, and impeccably English, voice was a boon to sound movies, was nominated for the witty **Bulldog Drummond** and for **Condemned**; the rakish Maurice Chevalier, whose French accent was as broad as the Champs-Elysées, was singled out for his part in Ernst Lubitsch's first talkie **The Love Parade**, and for **The Big Pond**. Gravel-voiced plug-ugly Wallace Beery had hopes of winning for his powerful portrayal of a bullying convict in **The Big House**, and Metropolitan Opera baritone Lawrence Tibbett, making his screen debut in **Rogue Song**, proved he could act as well as belt out an aria. The winner, however, was probably the least 'cinematic' actor of them all. George Arliss, making his sound debut at the age of 61 as **Disraeli**, became the first British star to win an Oscar.

Arliss had made his reputation on stage in the same role in 1911, and repeated it in the silent film version of 1921. He was seen so often in the part that an American lady

LEFT *Veteran English actor George Arliss as Disraeli, one of his many impersonations of great men, helps Joan Bennett with an affair of the heart in between dealing with affairs of state – and wins a Best Actor Oscar at the same time*

opportunity to use his excellent if rather mannered voice.

Mr George Arliss, as Warner Bros. respectfully billed him, had a hammy old time playing the British Prime Minister, spending as much of his energy matchmaking for a young couple (Joan Bennett and Anthony Bushell) as outwitting the Russians and acquiring the Suez Canal for Queen Victoria. Arliss made a speciality of portraying actual historical personages such as **Alexander Hamilton** (1931), **Voltaire** (1933), Nathan Rothschild in **The House Of Rothschild** (1934), Wellington in **The Iron Duke** and **Cardinal Richelieu** (1935), giving exactly the same urbane performance each time except for changes of costume. He retired from the screen in 1937 after his wife, Florence, who appeared with him in three films, lost her sight. He died in London in 1946 aged 77. Their son, Leslie Arliss, became known as the director of two popular Gainsborough melodramas, **The Man In Grey** (1943) and **The Wicked Lady** (1945), both starring James Mason and Margaret Lockwood.

By honoring 'The First Lady' and 'The First Gentleman' of the screen, a serious war film, an investigative prison drama (Frances Marion won the Best Writer award for **The Big House**), and the cinematography of Joseph T. Rucker and Willard Van Der Veer for their work on the documentary **With Byrd At The South Pole**, the Academy was able to convince its guests, including the puritanical Will H. Hays, President of the Motion Pictures and Distributors organization, at the $10-a-plate banquet at the Ambassador Hotel, of its high moral tone, as well as its ability to give praise to a range of styles and subjects.

tourist in Westminster Abbey remarked, on seeing the monument to Benjamin Disraeli, "My, what a lovely statue of George Arliss!" The gaunt, monocled figure, who made his first film when already in his 50s, had been rather dismissive of the movies until sound gave him the

---

WINNERS 1929/30

Nominations Announced: September 19, 1930
Awards Ceremony: November 5, 1930
Ambassador Hotel-Banquet

Best Picture
ALL QUIET ON THE WESTERN FRONT, Universal

Actor
GEORGE ARLISS in *Disraeli*, Warner Bros.

Actress
NORMA SHEARER in *The Divorcee*, MGM

Directing
LEWIS MILESTONE for *All Quiet On The Western Front*

Writing
(Achievement – Not given after this year.)
THE BIG HOUSE, MGM: FRANCES MARION

Cinematography
WITH BYRD AT THE SOUTH POLE, Paramount: JOSEPH T. RUCKER and WILLARD VAN DER VEER

Interior Decoration
KING OF JAZZ, Universal: HERMAN ROSSE

Sound Recording
(New Category)
THE BIG HOUSE: DOUGLAS SHEARER

1930/1

GLAMOR WAS VERY much on display among the nominees for the Best Actress award at the fourth annual Academy Award beanfeast held at the Biltmore Hotel. There was German star Marlene Dietrich, who had made a sensational debut in her first Hollywood picture, **Morocco**, cool blonde Ann Harding for **Holiday**, patrician beauty Irene Dunne for **Cimarron**, only her second film, and the previous year's winner and wife of MGM production chief Irving Thalberg, Norma Shearer, nominated for **A Free Soul**.

But they were all pipped at the post by an overweight, frumpish, five-foot-seven-inch tall 61-year-old. Shearer presented the award to Marie Dressler for her performance in **Min And Bill** with the words, "to the grandest trouper of them all—the grand old firehorse of the

screen." Dressler was a popular winner, even with her younger, more attractive rivals, who might have felt jealousy if any of their contemporaries had won.

It was not the year for glamor in the Best Actor category either. Fifty-three-year-old stage and screen veteran Lionel Barrymore carried off the gold statuette for **A Free Soul** from under the noses of his juniors, Richard Dix (**Cimarron**), Fredric March (**The Royal Family Of Broadway**), Adolphe Menjou (**The Front Page**) and 10-year-old Jackie Cooper (**Skippy**). The latter fell asleep on Miss Dressler's ample bosom during the long speeches. One of them was delivered by America's Vice President, Charles Curtis, sent as an emissary from Washington by President Herbert Hoover to "pay my respects to the creative minds of the world's greatest and most influential enterprise – the motion picture."

It was ironic that Marie Dressler was now hobnobbing with the Vice-President and his sister Mrs Dolly Gann, as well as being feted by the 1800 guests, after her years of oblivion. "I feel so important," she said, "I think Mrs Dolly Gann should get up and give me her seat." Dressler was a top vaudevillian when she made her screen debut oppo-

BELOW *Monocled George Arliss (seated left), the previous year's Best Actor, watches as Norma Shearer (center right), the previous year's Best Actress, congratulates Marie Dressler, while Lionel Barrymore contemplates his own victory*

site Charlie Chaplin in Mack Sennett's **Tillie's Punctured Romance** (1914), but her film career failed to take off. Her stage career also suffered when she was blacklisted by theatrical impresarios for taking a dominant part in the chorus girls' strike of 1917. She was forced to work in France, and contemplated suicide at one point, all revealed in her frankly titled autobiography, *The Life Story Of An Ugly Duckling*. Thanks to her friend, screenwriter Frances Marion, she made a comeback in 1927, and scored a triumph as Marthy in Garbo's first talkie **Anna Christie** (1930). In the mid-1920s, she had contracted the cancer that was to kill her three years after her finest hour at the 1931 awards ceremony.

In **Min And Bill**, Dressler played the boozing, battle-axe landlady of a run down waterfront hotel who carries on a love-hate relationship with a crude, beer-bellied fishing boat captain (Wallace Beery). With her homely face and his gross features, they made an unusual and dynamic duo (a partnership they memorably renewed in **Tugboat Annie**, 1933). In one scene in which she finds Beery flirting with another woman, she literally throws everything she can lay her hands on at him. But comedy turns to pathos when she kills the dissolute mother (Marjorie Rambeau) of the foundling (Dorothy Jordan) whom she has brought up, when the woman returns after many years to reclaim the child.

Lionel Barrymore was the older brother of Ethel and John Barrymore, and, from the mid-1930s onwards, the best known of the three to cinemagoers. Before being offered the part of the heavy-drinking, free-thinking criminal lawyer in **A Free Soul**, he had vowed never to act again, only to direct. But he couldn't resist the challenge of the role, and the resultant Oscar plus a life-long MGM contract given to the ever-broke actor, finally settled his future. The film itself was a pretty ponderous affair (remade in 1953 as **The Girl Who Had Everything** with Elizabeth Taylor and William Powell) in which Barrymore is called upon to defend his spoiled daughter's fiance when the latter kills a gangster the girl has fallen for. The highlight of the picture was the lawyer's impassioned speech to the jury in which he blames himself for his daughter's upbringing. "There is only one breast that you can pin the responsibility for this murder on . . .", and then he falls dead. Knowing of Barrymore's theatrical background, director Clarence Brown got him to rehearse the scene in one non-stop take. The actor flung himself into the speech with so much energy that after the run-through he informed Brown that he was too exhausted to do it again for the cameras that day. Brown then revealed that he had had three cameras turning during the performance, and that is the take that was printed and that won Barrymore his Oscar.

RIGHT *The wonderful battle-axe Marie Dressler (right), in her Best Actress role as Min, looking daggers at Wallace Beery as Bill, whom she has caught flirting with Marjorie Rambeau in the waterfront comedy-drama* Min And Bill. *Dressler died four years later at the peak of her career*

The cast of **A Free Soul** also included Norma Shearer as the daughter, British import Leslie Howard as the fiance, and a little known contract player named Clark Gable as the racketeer, who actually got to slap 'The First Lady of the Screen' around. As Shearer commented, "he made villains popular. Instead of the audience wanting the good guy to get the girl, they wanted the heavy to win her." The part was the breakthrough Gable needed, and he was immediately cast opposite Greta Garbo and Joan Crawford in his next movies. Coincidentally, it was Lionel Barrymore who had directed Gable's disastrous screen test for MGM back in 1926. In 1936, Barrymore, already stricken with arthritis, had an accident in which he fractured a hip and broke his kneecaps. Thereafter he acted on crutches and later from a wheelchair, although this did not prevent him from being extremely active in films, often playing the crippled patriarch, until his death in 1954. Once asked if he ever considered retiring, he replied, "I've never given the matter much thought. I'll make pictures as long as I can wiggle."

A Free Soul's director Clarence Brown, Garbo's favorite, was up for the Best Director award in the company of Josef von Sternberg (**Morocco**), Lewis Milestone (**The**

RIGHT *Best Actor winner Lionel Barrymore, the eldest of the famous acting family, as the drunken lawyer in* A Free Soul, *between James Gleason (left) and Clark Gable as a brutal underworld leader. The film provided a boost for Barrymore and a breakthrough for Gable*
BELOW *Richard Dix, Douglas Scott (center) and Irene Dunne as the pioneering Cravat family in the celebrated Land Rush scene from* Cimarron, *surprisingly, the only Western ever to win the Best Picture Oscar*

Front Page), Wesley Ruggles (**Cimarron**) and Norman Taurog (**Skippy**). It is rather surprising from today's perspective that it was journeyman director Taurog who got the judges' nod. It seems that he not only had the knack of getting child actors to do what he wanted, but had a way with members of the Academy as well. But there is no way that the direction of **Skippy**, a pleasant family entertainment with a predominantly child cast, could be compared with the baroque wonders of **Morocco**, nor the snappiness of **The Front Page**, the film that initiated the kind of rapid-fire, wisecracking dialogue that became a conspicuous ingredient of many high grade 30s comedies. The latter also had the strongest claim among the Best Picture nominees. That honor, however, went to the epic RKO Western **Cimarron**.

Cimarron (kept off TV screens by MGM's pale 1960 remake) was an ambitious saga, based on Edna Ferber's novel, covering the rise of Oklahoma from early pioneer days to statehood. The make-up department had their work cut out as the film followed a period of 40 years in the life of homesteaders Yancey and Sabra Cravat (Richard Dix and Irene Dunne), who help turn an overnight camp into a respectable town. The most impressive scene came near the start of the 130-minute movie, showing the spectacular land rush, with homesteaders in wagons and on horseback racing to capture part of the vast territory released by the government to first comers. The film gathered two other awards, for Howard Estabrook's adaptation and for Max Ree's interior decoration.

Astonishingly, **Cimarron** remains the only Western in the history of the Academy Awards to date to win the Best Picture prize. No, not even **Stagecoach** (1939), **High Noon** (1952), **Shane** (1953) or **Butch Cassidy And The Sundance Kid** (1969), the finest examples of that most American (and cinematic) of genres, won it.

WINNERS 1930/1

Nominations Announced: October 5, 1931
Awards Ceremony: November 10, 1931
Biltmore Hotel – Banquet

Best Picture
CIMARRON, RKO Radio

Actor
LIONEL BARRYMORE in *A Free Soul*, MGM

Actress
MARIE DRESSLER in *Min And Bill*, MGM

Directing
NORMAN TAUROG for *Skippy*, Paramount

Writing
(Adaptation)
CIMARRON: HOWARD ESTABROOK

(Original Story)
THE DAWN PATROL, Warner Bros. – First National: JOHN MONK SAUNDERS

Cinematography
TABU, Paramount: FLOYD CROSBY

Interior Decoration
CIMARRON: MAX REE

Sound Recording
PARAMOUNT STUDIO SOUND DEPARTMENT

1931/2

O N NOVEMBER 18, 1932, eight days after Franklin D. Roosevelt's landslide victory in the US Presidential election, staunch Republican Louis B. Mayer was at least certain his candidate Wallace Beery would win the Best Actor Academy Award for his role as the boozing ex-prizefighter in MGM's **The Champ**. However, at the ceremony at the Ambassador Hotel, Fredric March was announced the winner for **Dr Jekyll And Mr Hyde**.

Furious, 'Hollywood Rajah' Mayer barged into a back room and demanded to see the voting figures. On learn-

ing that March had defeated Beery by a single vote, he persuaded the Academy executives to announce a tie. They acquiesced because, under the rules at the time, duplicate trophies were to be given to any contenders who came within three votes of the winner in the final ballot. This unforseen happening caused a messenger to be sent out at speed to get hold of an extra statuette for Beery. It was the only occasion on which a tie was given in such circumstances. Under present rules, two Oscars for the same category are only to be handed out if the two finalists receive exactly the same number of votes. The fact that, besides March and Beery, there was only one other nominee for the award, meant that only Alfred Lunt, up for **The Guardsman**, went home empty-handed.

Actually, Fredric March should have received two statuettes to himself, one for each of his bravura performances in the dual roles of **Dr Jekyll And Mr Hyde**.

BELOW *Fredric March disguised under extraordinary make-up as the evil alter ego, Edward Hyde, of a respectable Victorian scientist in Rouben Mamoulian's* Dr Jekyll And Mr Hyde. *March shared this first of his two Oscars with Wallace Beery*

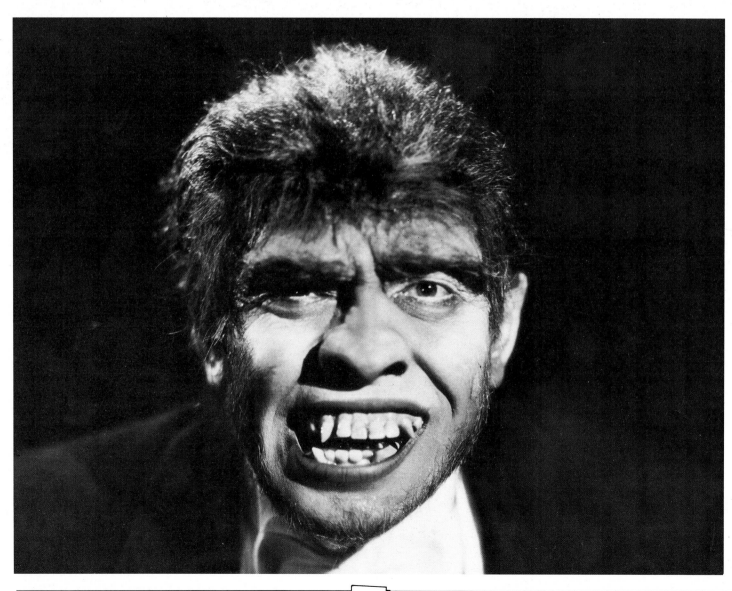

March followed John Barrymore's brilliant silent screen portrayal of 1920, after having earned himself an Oscar nomination impersonating Barrymore in **The Royal Family Of Broadway** the previous year. Others who have played Robert Louis Stevenson's renowned split personality creation were James Cruze (1912), King Baggot (1913), Sheldon Lewis (1919), and Spencer Tracy (1941). March had to spend over three hours each morning applying the heavy make-up, extra sets of teeth, a false nose and forehead, and ape-like hands. In order to avoid dissolves or cuts during the transformation by potion of the upright doctor into his evil *alter ego*, director Rouben Mamoulian devised a complex system of layers of colored make-up and filters. The whole conception came closest to Stevenson's thesis that the manifestation of Hyde was a

ABOVE *The heart-warming combination of Best Actor Wallace Beery (left) as* The Champ *and ten-year-old Jackie Cooper as his hero-worshipping son in the first of their four movies together. Cooper was still acting five decades later*

reflection of what happens to the psyche when emotions and desires are repressed, in this case by strict Victorian ethics. March was particularly successful in contrasting the prissy and stiff English gentleman with his liberated but bestial other self.

It might have been possible for the coarse-featured Wallace Beery to have played Mr Hyde to Fredric March's good-looking Dr Jekyll. But after years as a heavy, Beery became the cinema's most lovable slob in **The Champ**. Teamed up for the first of four films with child actor Jackie

Cooper, the tough-skinned but good-hearted old timer combined perfectly with the cocky but sensitive kid. The tearjerking tale (directed by Oscar-nominated King Vidor) told of ex-boxer Beery trying to scrape a living and bring up his small son in Tijuana, Mexico. Because of his son's hero-worship of him, he decides to make a comeback in the ring. The original cut of the film had him losing the fight, but it was reshot with him winning the championship. However, this was balanced by having him die of a heart attack, in his son's arms, in the dressing room after his triumph. Jackie Cooper recalled in later years how Beery resisted showing emotion off the screen. One day, after an especially well-played scene between them, 10-year-old Cooper threw his arms around Beery who pushed the boy away, causing him to burst into unrehearsed tears. Beery, who tried to live up to his reputation as one of Hollywood's rudest citizens and claimed "I have no art in my soul . . . I'm just plain me", died of heart failure in 1948, aged 68.

Wallace Beery was also one of the glittering array of stars in MGM's glossy showcase production **Grand Hotel**. (In 1973, MGM built the Grand Hotel in Las Vegas.) It gained the Best Picture award over undoubtedly superior contenders such as the Josef von Sternberg-Marlene Dietrich erotic-exotic masterpiece **Shanghai Express** (for which cinematographer Lee Garmes won a deserved prize), the two 'naughty' Ernst Lubitsch-Maurice Chevalier musicals, **One Hour With You** and **The Smiling Lieutenant**, the punchy Mervyn LeRoy-Edward G. Robinson newspaper drama **Five Star Final**, and the touching romance **Bad Girl** (for which Frank Borzage won his second Best Director Oscar). But **Grand Hotel** was vastly entertaining and the prototype for future all-star portmanteau pictures in which the lives of a disparate group of people intermingle in shared surroundings.

Staying at the plush Berlin hotel are a bored ballerina (Greta Garbo, uttering her immortal "I want to be alone!"), an impoverished baron (John Barrymore) after the

dancer's jewels, a dying bookkeeper (Lionel Barrymore) spending his last days in luxury, a crooked industrialist (Beery), and a stenographer (Joan Crawford) with whom the latter is having an adulterous affair. Within 48 hours, there is a murder, an attempted suicide, a birth, a romance and a Cinderella story, although the battle-scarred doctor (Lewis Stone) can only say, "Same thing every day . . . They come and go . . . Nothing ever happens."

The coming together in one film of some of the biggest stars in Hollywood proved to be a combustible experi-

BELOW: *Two of the most famous of screen profiles, those of Greta Garbo and John Barrymore, as the ballet dancer and the baron, glamorous guests at* Grand Hotel, *MGM's Best Picture winner*
RIGHT *Josef Von Sternberg's Oscar-nominated* Shanghai Express *lost out, but won the cinematography award for Lee Garmes, whose magnificent lighting and photography further glamorized the breathtaking Marlene Dietrich (illustrated with Clive Brook) and the exotic sets*

ence on the set. Firstly, none of them was keen to be in it. Garbo, self-conscious about her notoriously large feet, was not at all happy to play a ballet dancer; John Barrymore thought his role was that of a clotheshorse; his brother Lionel couldn't see the point of having so many stars in one movie like "zoo animals"; Beery thought his part "lousy. Lower than anyone I've ever played." Joan Crawford, fearing she would be upstaged by the others, entered the fray pugnaciously, declaring to the Barrymores, "Don't forget that the American movie public would rather have one look at my back than watch both of your faces for an hour." She also played Dietrich records incessantly to remind Garbo of her European rival. But director Edmund Goulding, known as 'The Lion Tamer', managed to keep the stars as much apart as possible. Not one of them gained an Academy nomination, although Miss Crawford, outacting her seniors, should certainly have been listed.

Of the three nominees for Best Actress, two—Lynn Fontanne (who co-starred with her husband Alfred Lunt in **The Guardsman**) and Helen Hayes – were far better known for their stage work. In fact, neither Fontanne nor Lunt ever acted in a film again, apart from a joint cameo in **Stage Door Canteen** (1943). Marie Dressler, the previous year's popular winner, was nominated for **Emma**, in which she was splendid as the down-to-earth housekeeper who marries her employer but is not accepted by his children. However, it was Miss Hayes who walked off with her first Oscar. (She won her second over 40 years

LEFT *Broadway star Helen Hayes, the Best Actress winner for* The Sin Of Madelon Claudet, *seen suffering romantically in the Parisian attic of her artist lover Neil Hamilton. Despite her Oscar, Miss Hayes' film career was sporadic*

later for her supporting role as an eccentric elderly passenger in **Airport**, 1970).

The Sin Of Madelon Claudet, for which Hayes won the award, was initially called *The Lullaby*. The leading lady's entry into talkies was not trouble free. During the shooting, the screenplay was found to be inadequate and Miss Hayes' husband, Charles MacArthur, was brought in to doctor it. New scenes were inserted, a prologue and epilogue added, and the title changed. Yet, only her performance as the self-sacrificial mother who works as a streetwalker and cleaning woman to put her illegitimate son (Robert Young) through medical school, salvaged the soppy melodrama, now faded into oblivion. More memorable was her shorter role as Ronald Colman's young wife who dies of bubonic plague in the same year's Oscar-nominated **Arrowsmith**.

It was also the year when short subjects were honored for the first time. Walt Disney captured an Oscar for his **Flowers And Trees**, the first Technicolor cartoon, and won a special citation for the creation of Mickey Mouse, then only four years old. The Best Comedy Short Subject award went to the Laurel and Hardy classic, **The Music Box**. Their gargantuan efforts to get a piano up a tremendous flight of stone steps did not go unrewarded.

WINNERS 1931/2

Nominations Announced: October 13, 1932
Awards Ceremony: November 18, 1932
Ambassador Hotel-Banquet

Best Picture
GRAND HOTEL, MGM

Actor (tie awards)
WALLACE BEERY in *The Champ*, MGM
FREDRIC MARCH in *Dr Jekyll And Mr Hyde*, Paramount

Actress
HELEN HAYES in *The Sin Of Madelon Claudet*, MGM

Directing
FRANK BORZAGE for *Bad Girl*, Fox

Writing
(Adaptation)
BAD GIRL: EDWIN BURKE
(Original Story)
THE CHAMP: FRANCES MARION

Cinematography
SHANGHAI EXPRESS, Paramount: LEE GARMES

Interior Decoration
TRANSATLANTIC, Fox: GORDON WILES

Sound Recording
PARAMOUNT STUDIO SOUND DEPARTMENT

Short Subjects
(New Category)
(Cartoons)
FLOWERS AND TREES, Disney/UA
(Comedy)
THE MUSIC BOX, Roach/MGM. (Laurel & Hardy)
(Novelty)
WRESTLING SWORDFISH, Sennett/Educational.
(Cannibals Of The Deep)

Special Award
WALT DISNEY for the creation of Mickey Mouse. (statuette)

1932/3

WILL ROGERS, POPULAR entertainer and crackerbarrel philosopher, caused two embarrassing situations at the sixth annual Academy Award ceremony held at the Ambassador Hotel. In announcing the Best Director's trophy, he spoke merely of "my good friend Frank." Nominee Frank Capra (for **Lady For A Day**) was on his way to receive the statuette, when Rogers added, "The winner is Frank Lloyd." Capra returned to his seat, a walk which he later described as "the longest crawl in history." (He was to be well compensated for his humiliation by winning the 1934, 1936 and 1938 Oscars.) Rogers then invited two of the three Best Actress

nominees, May Robson (**Lady For A Day**) and Diana Wynyard (in Lloyd's **Cavalcade**) to come to the speaker's table as if to signify a tie, as had been the case in the previous year's Best Actor category. He kissed them both, congratulated them on their "sparkling performances", and announced the absent 23-year-old Katharine Hepburn as the winner for *her* "sparkling performance" in **Morning Glory**. Nobody knew where the non-comformist Katie was, but Charles Laughton, the first actor to win an Oscar in a British film, Alexander Korda's **The Private Life Of Henry VIII**, was still in England, making it one of the rare occasions when both major acting winners were not present at the ceremony.

Charles Laughton's larger-than-life portrayal of the gluttonous King Henry VIII bulldozed away any challenge from the politeness of Leslie Howard in **Berkeley Square** (another Frank Lloyd-directed movie), and the stoicism of Paul Muni in **I Am A Fugitive From A Chain Gang**. The British actor, then 33 years old, had already made some

BELOW *Upstairs and downstairs meet in the parlour in Best Picture winner* Cavalcade. *Upstairs: Mr and Mrs Marryot (Clive Brook and Diana Wynyard – center right and left). Downstairs: Mr and Mrs Bridges (Herbert Mundin, left, and Una O'Connor, right)*

ABOVE *Charles Laughton, the first actor to win an Oscar in a British film, as the much-married monarch in* The Private Life Of Henry VIII, *with his real-life wife Elsa Lanchester. Miss Lanchester gave a splendid performance as the disappointingly homely Anne of Cleves, the royal wife imported from Germany. Here, she successfully entertains Henry with a late-night card game*
RIGHT *A Farewell To Arms, the first of Ernest Hemingway's novels to reach the screen, had the benefit of Charles B. Lang Jr's Oscar-winning cinematography. Gary Cooper and Helen Hayes played the lovers who meet during the Great War*

impression in a number of American movies before this Korda production made him an international star. The film, directed quickly and rather cheaply by Korda, achieved a success in America unprecedented in British cinema history. Laughton, in keeping with the film's witty and irreverent treatment of the past, superbly burlesqued his way through the story of five of Henry's six marriages. (Catherine of Aragon was omitted on the grounds of being far too respectable.) One of them, the homely Anne of Cleves, was played by Laughton's own wife, Elsa Lanchester. The scene in which Henry tears a chicken in two at the banquet table, and then proceeds to devour it hungrily before belching, was the most famous lesson in bad table manners for generations of moviegoers before **La Grande Bouffe** (1973).

Contrary to his screen persona, Laughton was a terribly insecure man. This was due, in part, to the strain of keeping his homosexuality a secret from the film industry and the public at large, and in part to his looks, about which he was bitterly self-deprecating. "I have a face that would stop a sundial and that frightens small children," he once remarked. As a result, he was often difficult to work with. Korda commented, "With him acting was an act of childbirth. What he needed was not so much a director as

a midwife," and Alfred Hitchcock would say, "You can't direct a Laughton picture. The best you can hope for is to referee." Despite many fine performances over the years, Laughton never won another Oscar (he was nominated twice more) before his death of cancer in 1962.

Continuing the English flavor, the Best Picture winner was **Cavalcade**. Noel Coward wrote his patriotic pageant for the stage in 1930 "to test my powers on a large scale." This seldom revived leviathan of a play, which had stretched the resources of London's vast Drury Lane Theatre to the limit, was expensively adapted by Fox to the screen with all its sentimentality, jingoism and patronizing attitudes intact, but also with a certain grand old Hollywood style. (William S. Darling was honored for his Interior Decoration.)

The episodic scenario told of the effects of world events on the upper-class upstairs Marryot family (mother Diana Wynyard and father Clive Brook) and the lower-class downstairs Bridges (mother Una O'Connor and father Herbert Mundin) during three decades between 1899 and 1932, including the Boer War, the death of Queen Victoria, the sinking of the *Titanic* and the First World War. The old order is challenged when the Marryots'

youngest son (Frank Lawton) falls in love with the Bridges' daughter (Ursula Jeans), a class conflict solved by the boy's death on the battlefield. A toast is offered in the end to "our sons who made part of the pattern and to our hearts who died with them."

Sean O'Casey compared the rather sketchy characters in **Cavalcade** to "a tiny monogram on a huge bedspread", but many agreed with the critic who wrote of its "sheer luminosity, restraint in handling tragic detail, and its romantic adventurousness." It was also one of the rare Hollywood movies set in England which had an all-British cast, although Clive Brook made his name in the USA. There is no doubt that at least five of the other nine nominees for the Best Picture prize, **42nd Street, A Farewell To Arms** (which gathered the cinematography Oscar for Charles Bryant Lang Jr and for Harold C. Lewis' sound recording), **Lady For A Day**, George Cukor's **Little Women** (starring Katharine Hepburn as Jo), and **State**

Fair (featuring the aforementioned Will Rogers), were better and more enduring films, but **Cavalcade** obviously appealed to the nostalgic taste of the day.

Few aspersions were cast on the taste of the Academy in giving Katharine Hepburn the Best Actress award for **Morning Glory**, only her third screen role. In it she played Eva Lovelace, a young actress who comes to New York determined to succeed on the stage and prove she is "the finest actress in the world." She took a little more time to convince characters in the movie of her abilities than she did movie audiences. When she says in her distinctive nasal voice, "There will always be a Shaw play in my repertoire as long as I remain in the theatre. And, of course, I shall die in the theatre. My star will never set," it was not difficult to believe! (Susan Strasberg did not convince in **Stage Struck**, the lame 1957 remake.) The sharp comedy-drama, directed by Lowell Sherman, had its share of plot and dialogue cliches. For one thing, Hepburn gets her chance on opening night when the temperamental star walks out, and theatrical manager Adolphe Menjou says to her after her triumph, "You don't belong to any man now . . . You belong to Broadway."

A year previously, the tall, slim girl with the high cheek bones burst onto the screen as John Barrymore's daughter in **A Bill Of Divorcement**. After **Morning Glory** and **Little Women**, Hepburn returned to the Broadway stage in a play called *The Lake*, a disaster which prompted Dorothy Parker's remark that the young actress "ran the gamut of emotions from A to B". Thankfully, the flop led to Hepburn's return to motion pictures, and further successes. It was over 30 years before she would win her next Oscar for **Guess Who's Coming To Dinner** (1967), and then two further Academy Awards for **The Lion In Winter** (1968), and **On Golden Pond** (1981), an achievement yet to be surpassed. She has kept her private life – especially her almost legendary relationship with Spencer Tracy – closed to gossip columnists, and avoids autograph hunters, interviews and receptions. She would later say, "I'm not as sure about things as I seem . . . but I'm sure about one thing—I'm a professional actress."

Walt Disney won an Oscar for the second year running for his Technicolor cartoon **Three Little Pigs**, featuring the hit song, 'Who's Afraid Of The Big Bad Wolf?', and the first of his films to bring large financial rewards. The awards, presented in March 1934 covered a 17-month period (August 1, 1932 to December 31, 1933) in order to allow the Academy Awards to be given each calendar year thenceforth.

WINNERS 1932/3

Nominations Announced: February 26, 1934
Awards Ceremony: March 16, 1934
Ambassador Hotel-Banquet

Best Picture
CAVALCADE, Fox

Actor
CHARLES LAUGHTON in *The Private Life Of Henry VIII*, London/UA (British)

Actress
KATHARINE HEPBURN in *Morning Glory*, RKO Radio

Directing
FRANK LLOYD for *Cavalcade*

Assistant Director
(New Category)
(Multiple Award given this year only.)
CHARLES BARTON, Paramount
SCOTT BEAL, Universal
CHARLES DORIAN, MGM
FRED FOX, UA
GORDON HOLLINGSHEAD, Warner Bros.
DEWEY STARKEY, RKO Radio
WILLIAM TUMMEL, Fox

Writing
(Adaptation)
LITTLE WOMEN, RKO Radio: VICTOR HEERMAN and SARAH Y. MASON
(Original Story)
ONE WAY PASSAGE, Warner Bros.: ROBERT LORD

Cinematography
A FAREWELL TO ARMS, Paramount: CHARLES BRYANT LANG Jr

Interior Decoration
CAVALCADE: WILLIAM S. DARLING

Sound Recording
A FAREWELL TO ARMS: HAROLD C. LEWIS

Short Subjects
(Cartoons)
THE THREE LITTLE PIGS, Disney/UA
(Comedy)
SO THIS IS HARRIS, RKO Radio. (Special)
(Novelty)
KRAKATOA, Educational. (Three-reel Special)

Special Award
(Not given this year.)

1934

WHEN THE LIST of nominees for the Best Actress Academy Award for 1934 was announced, there was an uproar. Indignant articles, telegrams, letters and phone calls attacked the Academy's oversight in not including Bette Davis, whose performance as the sluttish waitress Mildred in **Of Human Bondage** was considered by many to have been the best of the year. It was certainly a turning point for the actress who later said, "Everything in my career dates BB (Before Bondage) and AB (After Bondage)." Such was the furore, that the Academy proposed that voters on the final ballot would be allowed to add any name they pleased to the official list of nominees, which consisted of Norma Shearer as Elizabeth Barrett Browning in **The Barretts Of Wimpole Street**, opera singer Grace Moore in **One Night Of Love**, and Claudette Colbert in **It Happened One Night**.

An atmosphere of suspense hung over the Biltmore Bowl on February 27, 1935, as the 900 guests waited for the results. Even though some of the ballots had already been marked before the new 'write in' ruling, it was generally felt that Davis would carry off an exceptional victory. Colbert was so certain that she hadn't a hope of winning in such company, that she was boarding a train for New York when Academy officials found her and told her she had won. The train was held up while she dashed off to the Biltmore banquet, dressed in a tailored traveling suit and carrying a fur coat over her arm, to receive her prize before hurrying back to catch her train seven minutes later. (The unnominated Bette Davis came fourth, but would win the Oscar the following year.) The Academy announced that thereafter only officially named nominees could be given a vote.

The Best Actress award was not the only surprise verdict caused by **It Happened One Night**, the economically made comedy which had opened with little fuss in Hollywood some months before. William Powell was the favorite to win the Best Actor prize for his witty portrayal of suave, high-living detective Nick Charles in **The Thin Man**, the first of the popular film series, followed by Frank Morgan's huffing, henpecked Duke of Florence in **The Affairs Of Cellini**. But it was Clark Gable in **It Happened One Night** who scraped home.

The latter movie also carried off the Best Picture Oscar, beating **The Thin Man, The Barretts Of Wimpole Street, One Night Of Love, Viva Villa, The House Of Rothschild, The Gay Divorcee** (the first Fred Astaire-

ABOVE *Although considered by most critics (and by herself) to have given the best performance of the year in* Of Human Bondage, *Bette Davis (seen here tormenting Leslie Howard) was inexplicably not even officially nominated. The RKO-Somerset Maugham adaptation was also missing from all other categories*

Ginger Rogers starring vehicle), **Imitation Of Life**, and Cecil B. DeMille's **Cleopatra** (both also starring Claudette Colbert). Not only did **It Happened One Night** carry off the highest accolade for a film, but was the first in which both the male and female leads won the top acting awards. It also gained an Oscar for director Frank Capra and screenwriter Robert Riskin, a grand slam unequaled by any picture until **One Flew Over The Cuckoo's Nest**, 41 years later.

The original story from which the movie came was *Night Bus* by Samuel Hopkins Adams. It had been bought

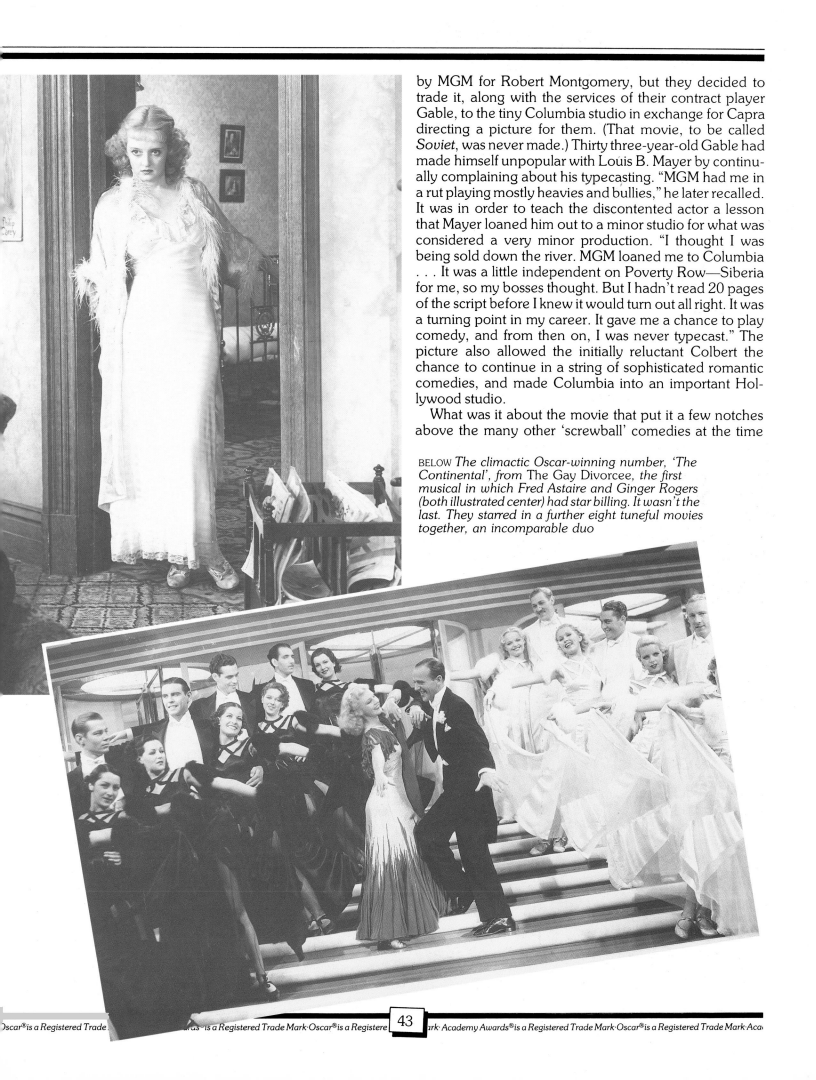

by MGM for Robert Montgomery, but they decided to trade it, along with the services of their contract player Gable, to the tiny Columbia studio in exchange for Capra directing a picture for them. (That movie, to be called *Soviet*, was never made.) Thirty three-year-old Gable had made himself unpopular with Louis B. Mayer by continually complaining about his typecasting. "MGM had me in a rut playing mostly heavies and bullies," he later recalled. It was in order to teach the discontented actor a lesson that Mayer loaned him out to a minor studio for what was considered a very minor production. "I thought I was being sold down the river. MGM loaned me to Columbia . . . It was a little independent on Poverty Row—Siberia for me, so my bosses thought. But I hadn't read 20 pages of the script before I knew it would turn out all right. It was a turning point in my career. It gave me a chance to play comedy, and from then on, I was never typecast." The picture also allowed the initially reluctant Colbert the chance to continue in a string of sophisticated romantic comedies, and made Columbia into an important Hollywood studio.

What was it about the movie that put it a few notches above the many other 'screwball' comedies at the time

BELOW *The climactic Oscar-winning number, 'The Continental', from* The Gay Divorcee, *the first musical in which Fred Astaire and Ginger Rogers (both illustrated center) had star billing. It wasn't the last. They starred in a further eight tuneful movies together, an incomparable duo*

about wacky heiresses and hard-boiled reporters? The simple plot told of how a wilful heiress (Colbert) runs away after her marriage to a fortune hunter has been annulled by her father. She loses her money on a bus trip to New York and meets an unemployed newspaperman (Gable) who agrees to help her in return for an exclusive story. During their journey, they are forced to hitchhike (Colbert lifts her skirt instead of a thumb), sleep in a haystack, and share a motel room while pretending to be man and wife. The latter 'Walls of Jericho' scene, in which they

BELOW *Miniature statuette winner, curly-headed moppet Shirley Temple, doing the 'Polly Wolly Doodle' stair dance routine with top toe-tapper Bill 'Bojangles' Robinson from* The Littlest Rebel, *one of four musicals they made together*
BOTTOM *The sumptuous Royal Bedroom set from Ernst Lubitsch's* The Merry Widow, *occupied by the King and Queen of Marshovia, and realized by Oscar-winning MGM art directors Cedric Gibbons and Frederic Hope – the apogee of 30s Hollywood kitsch*

undress and sleep behind blankets strung up between them to act as screens, has become a justly famous anthology piece. Such was the impact when Gable took off his shirt to reveal a bare chest, that sales of men's undershirts plummeted in the USA. The witty and refreshing script, Capra's rapid, hard-edged direction, and the light and engaging playing of the two leads, who built up their growing relationship convincingly, was just what the doctor ordered as a tonic for a depression-weary country. (There was a weak and irrelevant musical remake in 1956 called **You Can't Run Away From It**, starring June Allyson and Jack Lemmon.)

By the end of the decade, Clark Gable was dubbed 'The King Of Hollywood.' In typical self-deprecating fashion he said, "The 'King' stuff is pure bull. I'm just a slob from Ohio who happened to be in the right place at the right time." The right place was obviously in **It Happened One Night**, which crystallized his brash, rugged, cheerful, no-nonsense personality, although he had ably demonstrated its potential already in **Red Dust** (1932) opposite Jean Harlow, and **No Man Of Her Own** (1932), the only film he made with his future third wife Carole Lombard. The period of his greatest fame was launched with the Capra movie, reaching its peak in **Gone With The Wind** (1939). After **The Misfits** (1960), one of his most profound performances, Gable died suddenly of a

heart attack at the age of 59.

Claudette Colbert was at her best as a vivacious, sophisticated comedienne as she amply proved in her Oscar-winning role. She brought a Gallic frothiness to her performances, probably inherited from her family who emigrated from France when she was six. Colbert's career continued undiminished throughout the 1940s. An injured back forced her to give up the role of the ageing actress Margot Channing (taken by Bette Davis) in **All About Eve** (1950), which had originally been intended as a vehicle for her. She has made only nine films since 1950, the last being **Parrish** (1961), and lives in semi-retirement (she does stage work) in Barbados. Neither Gable nor Colbert ever won another Oscar, although both were nominated twice more.

Despite the overwhelming domination of **It Happened One Night** over the evening's proceedings, the highlight came when the writer Irvin S. Cobb, acting as M.C., presented a miniature statuette to seven-year-old Shirley Temple "in grateful recognition of her outstanding con-tribution to screen entertainment during the year of 1934." After only one year in the business, the bright-eyed, curly-topped, dimpled little Shirley had already become a national institution. Cobb continued by saying that "when Santa Claus brought you down creation's chimney, he brought the loveliest Christmas present he had ever given the world." Also in a childlike vein, Walt Disney won the cartoon award for the third year running for his animated version of the Aesop fable, **The Tortoise And The Hare**.

Three new Academy Awards were created that year in recognition of the importance of music and editing in the making of movies. Both the first two music awards were given for work on musicals: Con Conrad (lyrics) and Herb Magidson (music) for 'The Continental' in **The Gay Divorcee**, voted the Best Song, and Louis Silvers for **One Night Of Love**, the Best Score. The editor Conrad Nervig was honored for making the documentary footage of the impressive **Eskimo**, shot in the north of Alaska, into a coherent whole.

WINNERS 1934

Nominations Announced: February 5, 1935
Awards Ceremony: February 27, 1935
Biltmore Hotel – Banquet

Best Picture
IT HAPPENED ONE NIGHT, Columbia

Actor
CLARK GABLE in *It Happened One Night*

Actress
CLAUDETTE COLBERT in *It Happened One Night*

Directing
FRANK CAPRA for *It Happened One Night*

Assistant Director
JOHN WATERS for *Viva Villa*, MGM

Writing
(Adaptation)
IT HAPPENED ONE NIGHT: ROBERT RISKIN
(Original Story)
MANHATTAN MELODRAMA, MGM: ARTHUR CAESAR

Cinematography
CLEOPATRA, Paramount: VICTOR MILNER

Interior Decoration
THE MERRY WIDOW, MGM: CEDRIC GIBBONS and FREDERIC HOPE

Sound Recording
ONE NIGHT OF LOVE, Columbia: PAUL NEAL

Film Editing
(New Category)
ESKIMO, MGM: CONRAD NERVIG

Music
(New Category)
(From 1934 to 1937, this was a Music Department Achievement and the Award was presented to the departmental head instead of to the composer.)
(Best Score)
ONE NIGHT OF LOVE, Columbia Studio Music Department: LOUIS SILVERS, Head
Thematic Music: VICTOR SCHERTZINGER and GUS KAHN
(Best Song)
THE CONTINENTAL from *The Gay Divorcee*, RKO Radio
Music: CON CONRAD
Lyrics: HERB MAGIDSON

Short Subjects
(Cartoons)
THE TORTOISE AND THE HARE, Disney
(Comedy)
LA CUCARACHA, RKO Radio. (Special)
(Novelty)
CITY OF WAX, Educational. (Battle For Life)

Special Award
SHIRLEY TEMPLE in grateful recognition of her outstanding contribution to screen entertainment during the year 1934. (miniature statuette)

1935

NINETEEN THIRTY FIVE may have been the eighth year of Academy Award presentations, but it was the first year that the gold statuettes were actually called Oscars. Whether they were named after a music hall joke, 'Will you have a cigar, Oscar?', as claimed by Hollywood columnist Sidney Skolsky, or Academy executive and librarian Margaret Herrick's uncle Oscar Pierce, or Bette Davis' first husband Harmon Oscar Nelson Jr, the cognomen was rapidly taken up by the members of the Academy and the public at large.

Bette Davis herself was the recipient of the Best Actress Oscar, also called, in this case, the Holdover award. That is, in showbiz parlance, an award given implicitly for previous unrewarded work. After what many considered the scandalous oversight of 1934, when she was not officially nominated for **Of Human Bondage**, amends were made

by giving her an Oscar for **Dangerous**. Miss Davis considered it a consolation prize and generously remarked that "Katharine Hepburn gave by far the best performance of the year in **Alice Adams**." Certainly, Hepburn, in the role of the exasperating, snobbish, small-town girl with social ambitions, was better than the simpering, suffering Elisabeth Bergner in **Escape Me Never**, Claudette Colbert as 'the finest doctor in the country' in **Private Worlds**, the wooden Merle Oberon in **The Dark Angel**, or Miriam Hopkins' reading of **Becky Sharp** as "a cute little cookie with a yen for men", in critic David Shipman's phrase. However, Davis undeniably brought some conviction to the minor, cliché-ridden Warner Bros. melodrama in which she starred.

Dangerous concerned a self-centered ex-Broadway star who takes to the bottle because she feels she is jinxed in regard to men. She is rescued from complete degradation by the understanding and kindness of architect Franchot Tone. Typically, Davis insisted on looking as unglamorous as possible in the first half of the picture so as to lend her appearance the kind of authenticity the rest of the film lacked. Although her award was generally greeted favorably, she provoked negative comments

BELOW *(left to right) Irving Thalberg, producer of* Mutiny On The Bounty, *Bette Davis in her informal dress, Frank Capra, the President of the Academy, and Best Actor Victor McLaglen pose for the camera after the Oscar ceremony at the Biltmore Hotel*

ABOVE *Bette Davis rose above the so-so material of* Dangerous *as a Broadway star on the skids helped out of the gutter by architect Franchot Tone (both illustrated). Her Best Actress Oscar came as a consolation for losing out the previous year*

from the press the next day for appearing at the ceremony in a navy and white checkered dress, when the rest of the guests gathered at the Biltmore Hotel were all in formal attire. Davis had already made 21 films in her four years in the movies, but the award brought her due recognition and the ability to choose better roles in the future, although she was constantly at war with studio boss Jack Warner, even to legal battles.

Best Actor winner Victor McLaglen had far better material to work with in **The Informer** than Bette Davis did in **Dangerous**. In fact, **The Informer** reaped more awards than any other picture. John Ford was chosen as Best Director, Dudley Nichols received the Best Screenplay prize, and the Best Music Score went to Max Steiner (his first of three). Steiner remarked, "**The Informer** without the music would never have been what it was. Music did just the little bit needed to put it over, because in that movie Victor McLaglen was great. I put the harp in the music when McLaglen sold the guy down the river. And in the very end, I had him sing when his mother forgave him in church. It brought a few tears."

McLaglen's Gyppo Nolan was a drunken Irish braggart in Dublin during the Troubles of 1922, who sells his best friend, a wanted rebel, to the police for £20 to help him get to America. He spends the money on a drunken spree trying to drown his guilt, and is eventually 'executed' by the IRA. It all takes place during one gloomy night, atmospherically created by Ford with misty lighting and impressionistic sets. "It was the easiest film I ever directed," he said. "I had been dreaming of it for five years." In a memorable moment, the wind makes Gyppo's friend's 'Wanted' poster follow him like a ghost. The six foot-three, 225-pound character actor McLaglen, often billed as 'The Beloved Beast' in his early days, gave a dynamic performance in his greatest role. He made five further films with John Ford, generally typecast as a brawling, boozing, big-hearted bully. He died in 1959 aged 73 of a heart attack, never having equaled his performance in **The Informer**.

All of McLaglen's rivals for the Best Actor award, Clark Gable, Charles Laughton and Franchot Tone, appeared in **Mutiny On The Bounty**, making it the first and only time that three actors have been nominated in the same movie. The film itself, billed by MGM as "One of the great adventures of all times lives again in a screen epic it took two years and two million dollars to make . . . a cast of thousands, including exotic native girls of Tahiti!", won the Best Picture Oscar. Louis B. Mayer had initially vet-

RIGHT *Rugged Victor McLaglen (illustrated with Margot Grahame) winning his only Oscar in the best role of his life as Gyppo Nolan in* The Informer. *He was much helped by John Ford's Best Direction of the Liam O'Flaherty story of the Irish Troubles*

ABOVE *On board HMS Bounty, Clark Gable as Fletcher Christian, leader of the mutineers, invites the antagonism of Charles Laughton as ruthless Captain Bligh in Best Picture* Mutiny On The Bounty. *The personality clash of the characters reflected that of the two stars off the set*

oed the project, reckoning that there was no room in it for a traditional love story, and that a film that had a mutineer for a hero would have no appeal. But Irving Thalberg, head of production, convinced him that "People are fascinated by cruelty, and that's why *Mutiny* will have appeal." Thalberg was right as the film grossed $4½ million. Mind you, the blurb did not exaggerate its cost.

After the lean spending days of the Depression, million-dollar movies were coming back, and **Mutiny On The Bounty** was the most expensive. However, much of the cost was due to the fact that the entire footage of months of filming in the South Seas was found to be underexposed. Later, when many of the scenes were being re-shot on California's Catalina Island, a camera barge sank, one assistant was drowned and $50,000 worth of equipment destroyed. Tension also ran high on the set, as Thalberg and the director Frank Lloyd were constantly at each other's throats, and Gable and Laughton did not get on. On top of which, Laughton had to battle with recurrent bouts of seasickness.

Gable was reluctant to play the role of Fletcher Christian, the leader of the mutineers on *HMS Bounty* in 1789. He told Thalberg, "I'm a realistic kind of actor; I've never played in a costume picture in my life. Now you want me to wear a pigtail and velvet knee pants and shoes with silver buckles! The audience will laugh me off the screen. And I'll be damned if I'll shave off my moustache just because the British navy didn't allow them. This moustache has been damned lucky for me." But he did shave it off and, despite making no attempt at a British accent, was a successfully dashing hero. Laughton, giving one of his most famous performances in a role that has fed generations of impersonators, got the part of the sadistic Captain Bligh over Wallace Beery, who was considered too American. Much of the pleasure of the film comes from the vigorous clash of the personalities of the two main roles. There is little in Franchot Tone's workmanlike performance as the humane midshipman (a part first offered to Cary Grant) who details Bligh's score of injustices at the trial to suggest why he should have been Oscar-nominated. This popular yarn was remade in 1962 starring Marlon Brando and Trevor Howard, and in 1983 with Mel Gibson and Anthony Hopkins in the roles of Christian and Bligh. Neither was a success.

Among the other Best Picture nominees were two other adventure tales, **Captain Blood** and **Lives Of A Bengal Lancer**, three splendid musicals, **Top Hat, Naughty Marietta** and **Broadway Melody of 1936**, three adaptations of classics, **David Copperfield, A Midsummer Night's Dream** and **Les Miserables**, a brilliant Preston Sturges comedy, **Ruggles Of Red Gap**, and **The Informer**, any one of which could have won the award. A new category was introduced for Dance Direction and the award was given to Dave Gould for his numbers in the Maurice Chevalier musical **Folies Bergere** and **Broadway Melody of 1936**. Surprisingly, Busby Berkeley was passed over for his spectacular and original choreography in **Gold Diggers Of 1935**, and, even more surprisingly, never won an Academy Award. A special Oscar was presented to D. W. Griffith, genius of the silent cinema, most of whose films predated the awards, for "his distinguished creative achievements as director and producer and his invaluable initiative and lasting contributions to the progress of the motion picture arts."

WINNERS 1935

Nominations Announced: February 7, 1936
Awards Ceremony: March 5, 1936
Biltmore Hotel – Banquet

Best Picture
MUTINY ON THE BOUNTY, MGM

Actor
VICTOR McLAGLEN in *The Informer*, RKO Radio

Actress
BETTE DAVIS in *Dangerous*, Warner Bros.

Directing
JOHN FORD for *The Informer*

Assistant Director
CLEM BEAUCHAMP for *Lives Of A Bengal Lancer*, Paramount
PAUL WING for *Lives Of A Bengal Lancer*

Writing
(Original Story)
THE SCOUNDREL, Paramount: BEN HECHT and CHARLES MacARTHUR
(Screenplay)
THE INFORMER: DUDLEY NICHOLS

Cinematography
A MIDSUMMER NIGHT'S DREAM, Warner Bros.: HAL MOHR

Interior Decoration
THE DARK ANGEL, Goldwyn/UA: RICHARD DAY

Sound Recording
NAUGHTY MARIETTA, MGM: DOUGLAS SHEARER

Film Editing
A MIDSUMMER NIGHT'S DREAM: RALPH DAWSON

Music
(Best Score)
THE INFORMER, RKO Radio Studio Music Department: MAX STEINER, Head
Score: MAX STEINER
(Best Song)
LULLABY OF BROADWAY from *Gold Diggers Of 1935*, Warner Bros.
Music: HARRY WARREN
Lyrics: AL DUBIN

Dance Direction
(New Category)
DAVE GOULD for 'I've Got A Feeling You're Fooling' from *Broadway Melody Of 1936*, MGM; 'Straw Hat' from *Folies Bergere*, 20th Century/UA

Short Subjects
(Cartoons)
THREE ORPHAN KITTENS, Disney/UA
(Comedy)
HOW TO SLEEP, MGM. (Miniature)
(Novelty)
WINGS OVER MOUNT EVEREST, Educational. (Special)

Special Award
DAVID WARK GRIFFITH for his distinguished creative achievements as director and producer and his invaluable initiative and lasting contributions to the progress of the motion picture arts. (statuette)

1936

As far as the Academy was concerned, 1936 was the year of the film biography, affectionately known as the biopic. Four top awards—Best Picture, Actor, Actress and Screenplay—were shared by two biopics, each widely contrasted to the other in both subject and scale. They were **The Great Ziegfeld**, MGM's three-hour, extravagant million-dollar tribute to the spectacular Broadway showman, Florenz Ziegfeld, and Warner Bros.' 85-minute $330,000-costing **The Story Of Louis Pasteur**, both films succeeding brilliantly in their different ways. Incidentally, the previous year's Best Picture, **Mutiny On The Bounty**, was also based on historical fact, as would be the following year's winner, **The Life Of Emile Zola**. There was not to be another biopic so honored again until **Lawrence Of Arabia** in 1962.

"You will never see another musical film that exceeds it in opulence, in visual inventiveness, in Babylonian splendor," raved the *New York Evening Post* about **The Great Ziegfeld**, the Best Picture winner. MGM's costliest production since **Ben-Hur** (1925) took over two years to make, and contained seven lavish production numbers and 23 songs. Ziegfeld stage stars Ray Bolger, Fanny Brice, Gilda Gray, Harriet Hoctor and Leon Errol appeared as themselves, but two of the greatest attractions of the Ziegfeld Follies, Marilyn Miller and Eddie Cantor, asked for more in fees than even MGM was prepared to pay. The centerpiece of the picture was the mammoth 'A Pretty Girl Is Like A Melody' production number (staged by Seymour Felix, winner of the Dance Direction Oscar – a category soon to be dropped). Added after regular shooting was completed, and costing a record $222,000, it featured a gigantic revolving spiral wedding

RIGHT *Viennese beauty Luise Rainer was so impressive as Anna Held, the neglected first wife of Florenz Ziegfeld (William Powell, illustrated) in her few scenes in Best Picture* The Great Ziegfeld, *that she ran off with the first of her two successive Oscars*
BELOW *Gale Sondergaard (illustrated with Claude Rains) started her screen career by winning the Best Supporting Actress award in* Anthony Adverse. *She played a nasty piece of work, and continued in the same vein throughout her career*

cake structure around which 192 singers and dancers interpolated extracts from the popular classics. As Dennis Morgan (then known as Stanley Morner, and for some reason dubbed by tenor Allan Jones) in top hat and tails 'sings' the Irving Berlin melody, the camera works its way up towards Virginia Bruce perched on top of the edifice while billowing satin curtains descend in folds around it. For sheer spectacle, the number has never been equaled.

Less exciting was the plot which followed impresario Florenz Ziegfeld from his beginnings as a sideshow promoter in 1893, the launching of his Follies in 1907, his two marriages – the first to temperamental Continental actress Anna Held and the second to comedienne Billie Burke – his bankruptcy during the Wall Street Crash, and his death at 65, still dreaming of mounting another show. The cantankerous, consumptive, womanizing Ziegfeld was expertly played by handsome, suave William Powell, while Myrna Loy, Powell's perfect partner in so many movies, took the role of Billie Burke. (Miss Burke herself acted as 'technical adviser'.) In the relatively small role of Anna Held, Viennese beauty Luise Rainer, in only her

BELOW *Walter Brennan (left) was the first of a long line of distinguished Best Supporting Actor winners (sometimes more interesting than the stars) for his role of the best friend of a lumber tycoon and his wife (Edward Arnold and Frances Farmer, both illustrated) in* Come And Get It

Anna . . . Congratulations . . . I? . . . Oh wonderful . . . Never better in my whole life," she says through controlled tears. "It's all so wonderful and I'm so happy . . . I hope you are happy too . . ." It was enough to sway the voters of the Academy away from 36-year-old Norma Shearer's brave performance as the 14-year-old 'star-crossed lover' of 43-year-old Leslie Howard in Shakespeare's evocation of youthful(!) passion, **Romeo And Juliet**, directed by George Cukor. Rainer's other rivals were Irene Dunne letting her hair down for the first time in **Theodora Goes Wild**, the sublime Carole Lombard in **My Man Godfrey**, both of them fine examples of screwball comedy, and Gladys George in the weepie, **Valiant Is The Word For Carrie**.

Like Luise Rainer, the winner of the Best Actor award, Paul Muni, was born in Austria, but had emigrated to the USA with his parents when he was seven. Muni was trained in the Yiddish theatre, and only began acting in English at the age of 31. Although he was already known for his fine performances in **Scarface** (1932), Howard Hawks' thinly disguised and brutal portrait of Al Capone, and **I Am A Fugitive From A Chain Gang** (1932), for which he was Oscar-nominated, Muni's wider fame was gained through his portrayals – aided by heavy and expert make-up – of Great Men such as Louis Pasteur, Emile Zola, Benito Juarez, and Frederic Chopin's music teacher, Joseph Elsner. In the first of these, **The Story Of Louis Pasteur**, directed by William Dieterle, Muni gave a passionate and intelligent performance as the dedicated 19th-century country doctor who takes on the whole of the French medical establishment as he pursues his cures for anthrax and rabies, and fights for the sterilization of medical instruments.

Warner Bros. produced the film on a low budget, fearing such an unglamorous subject would fail at the box-office. In fact, many of the sets were leftovers from other pictures, doctored for the occasion. For example, the Academy of Science amphitheater was a re-dressed nightclub from a Busby Berkeley production number. After the film's success, Warners poured rather more money into its next biopic, **The Life Of Emile Zola**, also starring Muni, and directed by Dieterle. Muni was known for the intensive research and preparation he put into his roles. "My work is the theater. I work on it like a scientist who works on an invention," he explained. As a result, he made only 23 films in his entire career, but was Oscar-nominated no less than five times. In the mid-1940s, Muni terminated his contract with Warner Bros. when they shelved his plans for a picture on the life of Beethoven. His final film was **The Last Angry Man** (1959) after which, sadly, deteriorating health and advancing blindness kept him from working until his death in 1967, aged 72.

second Hollywood movie, surprised everyone by carrying off the Best Actress award.

When Miss Rainer received her prize from Master of Ceremonies George Jessel, she simply said, "I thank everyone who made me capable of getting it." Among those in her thoughts might have been Gottfried Reinhardt, son of the great German stage producer Max Reinhardt, who got MGM to persuade Rainer to leave his father's Berlin company to take the role of a Viennese girl in **Escapade** (1935) opposite William Powell, when Myrna Loy opted out. The latter movie was directed by Robert Z. Leonard, who also guided her through **The Great Ziegfeld**, notably in a short, poignant scene in which she telephones her ex-husband to congratulate him on his new marriage. "Hello, Flo? . . . Yes, this is

Muni's superb rivals for the Best Actor prize in 1936 were Walter Huston in **Dodsworth**, Gary Cooper in **Mr Deeds Goes To Town** (which gave Frank Capra his second Best Director Oscar), Spencer Tracy in **San Francisco**, and William Powell, not for **The Great Ziegfeld**, but for **My Man Godfrey**. And surprise, surprise! Walt Disney walked off with the cartoon trophy for the fifth successive year for his **Country Cousin**. But two new major Academy Awards were introduced, adding to the appeal of the ceremony. The Academy decided that the contribution to the success of movies by supporting performers should be honored with a special plaque. (It was only in 1943 that it was decided to give full-sized statuettes.) The first recipient of the Best Supporting Actor award

was Walter Brennan, veteran of over 40 films, for his role as Edward Arnold's faithful lumberjack friend in **Come And Get It**. (Brennan was to come and get the award twice more.) Gale Sondergaard, the Best Supporting Actress, had reluctantly agreed to make her film debut as the villainous Faith Paleologus in **Anthony Adverse**, the costly 136-minute version of Hervey Allen's rambling novel. The latter movie also won the Oscars for Cinematography (Tony Gaudio), Editing (Ralph Dawson) and Music Score (Leo Forbstein). Curiously, Forbstein was only the music director, so the statuette should really have gone by right to the composer, Erich Wolfgang Korngold. However, the latter would win it in 1938 for **The Adventures Of Robin Hood**.

WINNERS 1936

Nominations Announced: February 7, 1937
Awards Ceremony: March 4, 1937
Biltmore Hotel-Banquet

Best Picture
THE GREAT ZIEGFELD, MGM

Actor
PAUL MUNI in *The Story Of Louis Pasteur*, Warner Bros.

Actress
LUISE RAINER in *The Great Ziegfeld*

Supporting Actor
(New Category)
WALTER BRENNAN in *Come And Get It*, Goldwyn/UA

Supporting Actress
(New Category)
GALE SONDERGAARD in *Anthony Adverse*, Warner Bros.

Directing
FRANK CAPRA for *Mr Deeds Goes To Town*, Columbia

Assistant Director
JACK SULLIVAN for *The Charge Of The Light Brigade*, Warner Bros.

Writing
(Original Story)
THE STORY OF LOUIS PASTEUR: PIERRE COLLINGS and SHERIDAN GIBNEY
(Screenplay)
THE STORY OF LOUIS PASTEUR: PIERRE COLLINGS and SHERIDAN GIBNEY

Cinematography
ANTHONY ADVERSE: GAETANO GAUDIO

Interior Decoration
DODSWORTH, Goldwyn/UA: RICHARD DAY

Sound Recording
SAN FRANCISCO, MGM: DOUGLAS SHEARER

Film Editing
ANTHONY ADVERSE: RALPH DAWSON

Music
(Best Score)
ANTHONY ADVERSE, Warner Bros. Studio Music Department: LEO FORBSTEIN, Head
Score: ERICH WOLFGANG KORNGOLD
(Best Song)
THE WAY YOU LOOK TONIGHT from *Swing Time*, RKO Radio
Music: JEROME KERN
Lyrics: DOROTHY FIELDS

Dance Direction
SEYMOUR FELIX for 'A Pretty Girl Is Like A Melody' from *The Great Ziegfeld*

Short Subjects
(Cartoons)
COUNTRY COUSIN, Disney/UA
(One-reel)
BORED OF EDUCATION, Roach/MGM. (Our Gang)
(Two-reel)
THE PUBLIC PAYS, MGM. (Crime Doesn't Pay)
(Color)
GIVE ME LIBERTY, Warner Bros. (Broadway Brevities)

Special Awards
THE MARCH OF TIME for its significance to motion pictures and for having revolutionized one of the most important branches of the industry – the newsreel. (statuette)
W. HOWARD GREENE and HAROLD ROSSON for the color cinematography of the Selznick International Production, *The Garden Of Allah*. (plaques)

1937

LUISE RAINER WAS content to stay at home in her bedroom slippers on the evening of the tenth annual Academy Awards ceremony being held at the Biltmore Hotel in front of 1300 guests. After all, although she had been nominated for her role in **The Good Earth**, she had already won the Best Actress Oscar (controversially) the year before for **The Great Ziegfeld**. In addition, her rivals this time round were Greta Garbo for her properly acclaimed, tragically beautiful Marguerite Gautier in **Camille** (her third nomination), Barbara Stanwyck's memorable portrayal of the self-sacrificial but vulgar mother in **Stella Dallas** (the first of her four nominations), Irene Dunne's brilliantly witty and stylish divorcing wife in **The Awful Truth** (her third nomination), and Janet Gaynor, the first ever winner of

the award, playing Vickie Lester, an Oscar-winning actress in **A Star Is Born**.

Impressive as Rainer was as the long-suffering Chinese peasant O-Lan in MGM's expensive and effective adaptation of Pearl S. Buck's Pulitzer Prize novel, there seemed little chance that she would win the coveted trophy for the second year running in her third Hollywood film, particularly in the face of such strong and deserving competition. However, at 8.35 pm, the names of the winners were given to the press, and a member of the Academy telephoned Rainer at home to tell her she had won. She had to quickly change into evening dress and dash down town with her husband, playwright Clifford Odets, to receive her second statuette from hillbilly comedian Bob Burns, acting as M.C. This extraordinary triumph made the Viennese actress the first performer, male or female, to win two Oscars – and in succession at that.

"For my second and third (Hollywood) pictures I won Academy Awards. Nothing worse could have happened to me," said Rainer looking back some years later. By the

BELOW *Special Oscar winner Mack Sennett, the maker of rapid, irreverent, slapstick comedies in the silent era, and the creator of the Keystone Kops, whose name derived from Sennett's production company, is jokingly unable to get in to see one of his films due to lack of funds*

time the next Academy Award ceremony came round, her career was almost at an end. Somehow her fame flared up and then faded just as quickly. The five movies that followed **The Good Earth** were ill-chosen and failed to increase her reputation. Some time near the end of her MGM contract, Louis B. Mayer, who was paying the star $250 a week, told her, after she had been complaining about something, "We made you and we're going to kill you." She replied calmly. "God made me." Rainer made her last film in 1943 before retiring to London with her second husband.

Luise Rainer made an exceptional jump from playing Flo Ziegfeld's glamorous and sophisticated first wife Anna Held to the little Chinese woman who works in the fields with her husband (Paul Muni), bears his children, begs for food during the famine, and dies quietly years later when the family have achieved some prosperity. The overwhelming majority of the cast were Occidentals with a variety of accents, but both she and Muni gained authenticity from their months of observing the behavior and postures of the people of San Francisco's Chinatown,

ABOVE *After winning an Oscar in the previous year as the glamorous actress wife of impresario Flo Ziegfeld, Austrian Luise Rainer transformed herself into the Chinese peasant woman O-Lan in* The Good Earth, *and was named Best Actress again*

before shooting began on the enormous set built in the San Fernando Valley. Some of the exteriors were actually shot in China, and these were cleverly combined with the American footage. (Cinematographer Karl Freund gained an Oscar for his contribution to the movie.) The picture, a great hit, was initially vetoed by Louis B. Mayer. As he told MGM production chief Irving Thalberg, "Irving, the public won't buy pictures about American farmers. And you want to give them Chinese farmers?"

The Good Earth was the last film supervised by Irving Thalberg, who died of pneumonia aged 37 five months before it was released. The opening of the movie contains a dedication to him, and the Academy immediately set up the Irving G. Thalberg Memorial Award "for the most consistent high level of production achievement by an individual producer." Darryl F. Zanuck, the man at the helm

ABOVE *Best Actor Spencer Tracy (center) as Manuel, the simple Portuguese fisherman in* Captains Courageous, *teaches spoilt brat Freddie Bartholomew (left) the ways of the sea while a sceptical John Carradine (right) looks on*

of 20th Century-Fox, became its first recipient. At the same ceremony, Mack Sennett was given a special statuette "for his lasting contribution to the comedy technique of the screen", and ventriloquist Edgar Bergen (Candice's father) was presented with a special Oscar made of wood with a hinged mouth "for his outstanding comedy creation Charlie McCarthy." The dummy himself was there to receive it on behalf of Bergen. Two winners were absent, though: Alice Brady, named as Best Supporting Actress for her role as the mother of Tyrone Power and Don Ameche in **In Old Chicago**, was laid up with a broken ankle, and Best Actor winner Spencer Tracy was in hospital.

Tracy was so certain that his role of Manuel, the simple Portuguese fisherman in **Captains Courageous**, would be overlooked in favor of either Fredric March's actor on

the skids in **A Star Is Born**, Charles Boyer's wily Napoleon in **Conquest**, Robert Montgomery's psychopathic killer in **Night Must Fall**, or Paul Muni (going for his second award in a row) in the title role of **The Life Of Emile Zola**, that he arranged to undergo a necessary hernia operation at the same time as the award ceremony. "Can you imagine," Tracy recalled later, "what I felt like—lying there, in all those itchy bandages around my middle, and plenty of pain—when the word came through, I'd won it?" The second surprise came when Mrs Tracy, accepting the Oscar for her husband, discovered that it had mistakenly been engraved 'Dick Tracy'!

Tracy had not been happy during the filming of **Captains Courageous**, MGM's exciting and warm-hearted adaptation of the Rudyard Kipling sea story. The role of Manuel required him to speak with a Portuguese accent, sing several sea shanties, and wear a curly-headed wig. (One day, Joan Crawford passing him on the lot commented, "My God, it's Harpo Marx!") Tracy remembered that "I used to pray that something would halt production. I was positive I was doing the worst job of my life." But as

the *New York Herald Tribune* wrote, "You may find Spencer Tracy's Portuguese accent a trifle startling at first. But once he takes the little chap he fished out of the sea in hand, he gives an impersonation that can only be called perfect." 'The little chap' was 13-year-old Freddie Bartholomew as Harvey Cheyne (Kipling's 19-year-old made younger to suit the child star), the spoiled, rich boy who falls overboard a liner and is picked up by a fishing vessel. There, under the kindly tutelage of Manuel, he learns the value of work and comradeship. More salt water was shed by audiences at the demise of the Tracy character than was contained in the vast ocean depicted in the film.

Captains Courageous was among the movies up for the Best Picture prize, a list which included **The Good Earth, A Star Is Born, Lost Horizon** and **The Awful Truth** (for which Leo McCarey was named Best Director.) However, the stolid virtues of William Dieterle's **The Life Of Emile Zola** carried the day. Actually, the film's title was something of a misnomer. The life of the great 19th-century French novelist was covered only in a 30-minute prologue in Norman Reilly Raine, Heinz Herald and Geza

Herczeg's Oscar-winning screenplay. The remaining 86 minutes concentrated on Zola's crusade against the army, the law and the government to prove the innocence of Captain Alfred Dreyfus (Joseph Schildkraut, winner of the Best Supporting Actor award), wrongfully accused of treason and serving a life imprisonment on Devil's Island because of the anti-Semitism in the hierarchy of the French army. Strangely, the word 'Jew' is never pronounced in the film.

A heavily bewhiskered *Mr* Paul Muni, as Warners deferentially billed him (they had similarly billed George Arliss in the days when he too played Great Men of History), gave a passionate rendering of the celebrated 'I Accuse' speech. The German-born director William Dieterle seemed to have cornered the market in solemn biopics.

Besides those of Louis Pasteur, Zola and Juarez with Muni, Dieterle made two starring Edward G. Robinson, **Dr Ehrlich's Magic Bullet**, about the man who found a cure for VD, and **A Dispatch From Reuters** (both 1940), about the news-service man. He also tackled the lives of Madame Du Barry (1934), Florence Nightingale (**The White Angel**, 1936) and Richard Wagner (**Magic Fire**, 1956). But none was as prestigious as **The Life Of Emile Zola**, which gained Dieterle his only nomination and Warner Bros. their very first Best Picture award.

WINNERS 1937

Nominations Announced: February 6, 1938
Awards Ceremony: Postponed from March 3
to March 10, 1938 because of flooding.
Biltmore Hotel-Banquet

Best Picture
THE LIFE OF EMILE ZOLA, Warner Bros.

Actor
SPENCER TRACY in *Captains Courageous*, MGM

Actress
LUISE RAINER in *The Good Earth*, MGM

Supporting Actor
JOSEPH SCHILDKRAUT in *The Life Of Emile Zola*

Supporting Actress
ALICE BRADY in *In Old Chicago*, 20th Century-Fox

Directing
LEO McCAREY for *The Awful Truth*, Columbia

Assistant Director
(Not given after this year.)
ROBERT WEBB for *In Old Chicago*

Writing
(Original Story)
A STAR IS BORN, Selznick/UA: WILLIAM A. WELLMAN and ROBERT CARSON
(Screenplay)
THE LIFE OF EMILE ZOLA: HEINZ HERALD, GEZA HERCZEG and NORMAN REILLY RAINE

Cinematography
THE GOOD EARTH: KARL FREUND

Interior Decoration
LOST HORIZON, Columbia: STEPHEN GOOSSON

Sound Recording
THE HURRICANE, Goldwyn/UA: THOMAS MOULTON

Film Editing
LOST HORIZON: GENE HAVLICK and GENE MILFORD

Music
(Best Score)
ONE HUNDRED MEN AND A GIRL, Universal Studio
Music Department: CHARLES PREVIN, Head
Score: No composer credit

(Best Song)
SWEET LEILANI from *Waikiki Wedding*, Paramount
Music and Lyrics: HARRY OWENS

Dance Direction
(Not given after this year.)
HERMES PAN for 'Fun House' from *Damsel In Distress*, RKO Radio

Short Subjects
(Cartoons)
THE OLD MILL, Disney/RKO Radio
(One-reel)
PRIVATE LIFE OF THE GANNETS, Educational
(Two-reel)
TORTURE MONEY, MGM. (Crime Doesn't Pay)
(Color)
PENNY WISDOM, Smith/MGM. (Pete Smith Specialties)

Special Awards
MACK SENNETT – 'for his lasting contribution to the comedy technique of the screen, the basic principles of which are as important today as when they were first put into practice, the Academy presents a Special Award to that master of fun, discoverer of stars, sympathetic, kindly, understanding comedy genius – Mack Sennett.' (statuette)
EDGAR BERGEN for his outstanding comedy creation, Charlie McCarthy. (wooden statuette)
THE MUSEUM OF MODERN ART FILM LIBRARY for its significant work in collecting films dating from 1895 to the present and for the first time making available to the public the means of studying the historical and aesthetic development of the motion picture as one of the major arts. (scroll certificate)
W. HOWARD GREENE for the color photography of *A Star Is Born*. (This Award was recommended by a committee of leading cinematographers after viewing all the color pictures made during the year.) (plaque)

Irving G. Thalberg Memorial Award
(New Category)
DARRYL F. ZANUCK

for **Jezebel**, and Walter Brennan also made his second trip to the speaker's platform to receive the Best Supporting Actor plaque for his role as a horse-breeder in **Kentucky**. Walt Disney, the most frequent visitor to the rostrum, earned a seventh cartoon award for his **Ferdinand The Bull**, as well as receiving one large Oscar and seven miniatures from ten-year-old Shirley Temple for **Snow White And The Seven Dwarfs**, the first of Disney's full-length features and a breakthrough in the history of animation. Another familiar face was that of Frank Capra, named Best Director for the third time in five years for **You Can't Take It With You.**

You Can't Take It With You, the warm-hearted and comic tribute to 'the little folks of the planet' was preferred as Best Picture by the Academy to, among others, the

A SENSE OF *déjà vu* hovered around the eleventh annual Academy Award banquet held at the Biltmore Hotel on February 23, 1939. Many of the top honors went to those who had already received Oscars in the past. Spencer Tracy, the previous year's winner for **Captains Courageous**, gained his second in a row for **Boys Town**. Pressure from MGM executives made sure that he was there to receive it this time, and the Academy was careful to engrave it correctly after the 'Dick Tracy' embarrassment. This made Tracy the first and last actor ever to win in consecutive years.

Bette Davis, who had won the Best Actress prize for **Dangerous** (1935), was the recipient of a second Oscar

RIGHT *A scene from Walt Disney's first animated feature film,* Snow White And The Seven Dwarfs, *which won a Special award for being 'a significant screen innovation which has charmed millions and pioneered a great new entertainment field for the motion picture cartoon'*
BELOW *Bette Davis (right) may not have got the plum role of Scarlett O'Hara, but she did carry off her second Oscar as a spoiled Southern belle in William Wyler's* Jezebel. *Fay Bainter (left), seen comforting her, took the Best Supporting Actress award*

good-looking, colorful swashbuckler **The Adventures Of Robin Hood** (a triple Oscar-winner anyway for Art Direction, Music Score and Editing), the tune-laden musical **Alexander's Ragtime Band**, two distinguished British productions, **The Citadel** and **Pygmalion**, and Jean Renoir's anti-war masterpiece **La Grande Illusion**. (It was not until 1956 that the Academy instituted a separate Best Foreign Language film award.)

The Capra movie, based on George S. Kaufman and Moss Hart's stage play, told of a happy-go-lucky eccentric household consisting of grandpa Lionel Barrymore who refuses to pay taxes, mother Spring Byington, who took up writing when a typewriter was accidentally left at the house, Ann Miller, a student ballerina who needs no excuse to display her art, her temperamental ballet teacher Mischa Auer, and Donald Meek, a dubious inventor. The only seemingly normal member of the family is Jean Arthur who falls for James Stewart, the son of bloated capitalist Edward Arnold, who wishes to dispossess them. However, at the happy ending, the money man learns to have fun by playing the harmonica with Grandpa. It was a typical 'New Deal' fairy tale that caught the public's imagination, thanks in no small measure to the fine ensemble playing by the splendid cast.

If **You Can't Take It With You** preached that money doesn't bring happiness, **Boys Town** preached the philosophy that "there isn't any such thing in the world as a bad boy . . . but a boy left alone, frightened, bewildered . . . the wrong hand reaches for him . . . he needs a friend . . . that's all he needs", as spoken by Spencer Tracy in his role as Father Edward J. Flanagan. This well-made weepie with a message, directed by Norman Taurog (nominated), was based on the real Father Flanagan who established a 200-acre community for wayward boys near Omaha, Nebraska. Tracy spent some weeks prior to shooting at the actual Boys' Town studying the characteristics and mannerisms of the reformist priest. A

BELOW *Son of a Wall street businessman, James Stewart (standing) finds himself hopelessly involved with the zany Vanderhof household whose members include Donald Meek (left foreground), Spring Byington (center) and Halliwell Hobbes (right) in Frank Capra's Best Picture winner* You Can't Take It With You
BELOW LEFT *Spencer Tracy as the sympathetic Father Flanagan in* Boys Town *has his hands full with Mickey Rooney, a tough, poker-playing rebel (both illustrated). While Tracy gained his second Oscar in a row, Rooney was honored with a special award*

Catholic himself, Tracy stated, "I knew Father Flanagan personally, and felt that nobody could put over his warmth, inspiration, and humaneness of feeling in the picture. But I became so absorbed in the characterization that by the end of the first week I had stopped worrying." In fact, Tracy gave his Oscar to Father Flanagan with the added inscription, "To Father Edward J. Flanagan, whose great human qualities, kindly simplicity, and inspiring courage were strong enough to shine through my humble efforts."

Tracy certainly managed to exude all the qualities he described the priest as having. The plot mainly involved his efforts to gain financial support for his scheme to move his refuge for tough neighborhood kids from the shabby building in the city to the country, and the rehabilitation of a young hoodlum, played pugnaciously by Mickey Rooney. They both reprised their roles in the popular sequel, **Men Of Boys Town** (1941). Although Tracy never won another Oscar, he received a total of seven nominations in the course of his long career. The star's second Academy Award in a row left James Cagney's tough hoodlum in **Angels With Dirty Faces**, Robert Donat's idealistic doctor in **The Citadel**, Charles Boyer's romantic crook in **Algiers**, and Leslie Howard's impeccable Professor Higgins in **Pygmalion** emptyhanded. However, Donat only had to wait one year for his award, and Cagney four years. Neither Howard (killed in an aircrash in 1943) nor Boyer ever received an Oscar.

In contrast to the saintly father portrayed by Spencer Tracy, Bette Davis in **Jezebel** was "half-angel, half-siren, all woman!" according to the billboards. In this $1 million saga set in pre-Civil War New Orleans, Davis played a spoiled, headstrong and fickle Southern belle who flits from Henry Fonda to George Brent and back again when the former contracts yellow fever. On receiving her Oscar from Cedric Hardwicke, Davis, who was magnetic in a difficult and unsympathetic role, effusively thanked William Wyler (her director on two further excellent occasions for which she was nominated, **The Letter**, 1940, and **The Little Foxes**, 1941). In the most famous scene, Davis arrives at a ball, at which unmarried girls traditionally wear white, garbed in a scarlet gown in order to shock the assembled company. The impact of the color was brilliantly suggested by Ernest Haller's black and white photography.

Not only was the dress scarlet, but the role was slightly Scarlett. In 1936, Warner Bros. bought an option on the yet-to-be-published **Gone With The Wind** as a possible vehicle for Bette Davis and Errol Flynn. It was said that when Warners dropped the idea, she was so furious that they offered her **Jezebel** to placate her. Another side of the story tells how Davis, not realizing the potential of the project, and expressing a dislike for Flynn, rejected the offer. However, she later bid for the role of Scarlett O'Hara when MGM were to film it. She could offer her performance in **Jezebel** as proof of her suitability for the most sought after role in the industry. Of course, Vivien Leigh ended up as Scarlett, and gained an Oscar. Further Academy Awards have eluded the 78-year-old Bette Davis, although she has been nominated on a further eight occasions.

Among the old hands receiving the golden statuette were a number of first timers at the ceremony – during which blonde Polish coloratura soprano Miliza Korjus, nominated for her supporting role in her only Hollywood film, **The Great Waltz**, sang 'The Star-Spangled Banner.' Fay Bainter, as Davis' sympathetic Aunt Belle in **Jezebel** beat Korjus for the award. Bainter had also been nominated as Best Actress for her pedlar in **White Banners** along with Wendy Hiller's Eliza Doolittle in **Pygmalion** (Miss Hiller had to wait 20 years for an Oscar), Norma Shearer losing her head as **Marie Antoinette**, and the delicate Margaret Sullavan in **Three Comrades**.

Edgar Bergen and Charlie McCarthy presented miniature statuettes to Deanna Durbin and Mickey Rooney for their "significant contribution in bringing to the screen the spirit and personification of youth, and as juvenile players setting a high standard of ability and achievement." Another first time Oscar winner was 82-year-old playwright George Bernard Shaw, cited for the year's Best Screenplay, although it was W. P. Lipscomb, Cecil Lewis and Ian Dalrymple (also Oscar winners) who adapted

Pygmalion for the screen. In England, on hearing the news, Shaw reacted in a typically irascible and Shavian manner. "It's an insult," he said. "It's perfect nonsense. My position as a playwright is known throughout the world. To offer an award of this sort is an insult, as if they had not heard of me before—and it's very likely they never had." It would have been interesting to hear his comments on **My Fair Lady** (1964), the musical version of **Pygmalion**, and winner of eight Academy Awards, none of them given to Shaw posthumously.

WINNERS 1938

Nominations Announced: February 12, 1939
Awards Ceremony: February 23, 1939
Biltmore Hotel-Banquet

Best Picture
YOU CAN'T TAKE IT WITH YOU, Columbia

Actor
SPENCER TRACY in *Boys Town*, MGM

Actress
BETTE DAVIS in *Jezebel*, Warner Bros.

Supporting Actor
WALTER BRENNAN in *Kentucky*, 20th Century-Fox

Supporting Actress
FAY BAINTER in *Jezebel*

Directing
FRANK CAPRA for *You Can't Take It With You*

Writing
(Adaptation)
PYGMALION, MGM (British): IAN DALRYMPLE, CECIL LEWIS and W.P. LIPSCOMB
(Original Story)
BOYS TOWN: ELEANOR GRIFFIN and DORE SCHARY
(Screenplay)
PYGMALION: GEORGE BERNARD SHAW

Cinematography
THE GREAT WALTZ, MGM: JOSEPH RUTTENBERG

Interior Decoration
THE ADVENTURES OF ROBIN HOOD, Warner Bros.: CARL J. WEYL

Sound Recording
THE COWBOY AND THE LADY, Goldwyn/UA: THOMAS MOULTON

Film Editing
THE ADVENTURES OF ROBIN HOOD: RALPH DAWSON

Music
(Best Score)
ALEXANDER'S RAGTIME BAND, 20th Century-Fox: ALFRED NEWMAN
(Original Score)
THE ADVENTURES OF ROBIN HOOD: ERICH WOLFGANG KORNGOLD

(Best Song)
THANKS FOR THE MEMORY from *Big Broadcast Of 1938*, Paramount
Music: RALPH RAINGER
Lyrics: LEO ROBIN

Short Subjects
(Cartoons)
FERDINAND THE BULL, Disney/RKO Radio
(One-reel)
THAT MOTHERS MIGHT LIVE, MGM. (Miniature)
(Two-reel)
DECLARATION OF INDEPENDENCE, Warner Bros. (Historical Featurette)

Special Awards
DEANNA DURBIN and MICKEY ROONEY for their significant contribution in bringing to the screen the spirit and personification of youth, and as juvenile players setting a high standard of ability and achievement. (miniature statuettes)
HARRY M. WARNER in recognition of patriotic service in the production of historical short subjects presenting significant episodes in the early struggle of the American people for liberty. (scroll)
WALT DISNEY for *Snow White And The Seven Dwarfs*, recognized as a significant screen innovation which has charmed millions and pioneered a great new entertainment field for the motion picture cartoon. (one statuette – seven miniature statuettes)
OLIVER MARSH and ALLEN DAVEY for the color cinematography of the MGM production, *Sweethearts*. (plaques)
For outstanding achievement in creating Special Photographic and Sound Effects in the Paramount production, *Spawn Of The North*. Special Effects: GORDON JENNINGS, assisted by JAN DOMELA, DEV JENNINGS, IRMIN ROBERTS and ART SMITH; Transparencies: FARCIOT EDOUART, assisted by LOYAL GRIGGS; Sounds Effects: LOREN RYDER, assisted by HARRY MILLS, LOUIS H. MESENKOP and WALTER OBERST. (plaques)
J. ARTHUR BALL for his outstanding contributions to the advancement of color in motion picture photography. (scroll)

Irving G. Thalberg Memorial Award
HAL B. WALLIS

1939

"**D**ON'T BE A damn fool, David. This picture is going to be one of the biggest white elephants of all time," director Victor Fleming told producer David O. Selznick. "It's going to be the biggest bust of all time," commented Jack L. Warner, and the usually acute Irving Thalberg advised Louis B. Mayer in 1936, "Forget it, Louis. No Civil War picture ever made a nickel." The picture was, of course, **Gone With The Wind**, which blew into the Academy Award ceremony on February 29, 1940 at the Ambassador Hotel, and blew out again with a then record number of nine Oscars.

Selznick received the Best Picture prize, and Victor Fleming was named Best Director. Vivien Leigh, who attended with her fiance Laurence Olivier (nominated for his fiery Heathcliff in **Wuthering Heights**), looked ravishing as she received her Best Actress Oscar from Spencer Tracy. (The tradition was begun of the previous year's male and female winners presenting the awards to their current opposites.) The warmest reception of the evening was given to Hattie McDaniel, the first black performer to win an Oscar (the next would be Sidney Poitier 24 years later) for her performance as Mammy, Scarlett O'Hara's lovable and faithful nurse. Wearing six gardenias in her hair and a green velvet sash around her middle, Miss McDaniel burst into tears as she received her Best Supporting Actress plaque.

Nobel Prize-winning novelist Sinclair Lewis accepted the Best Screenplay Oscar on behalf of Sidney Howard, who had died, aged 48, the previous year. Others honored for what members of the American Film Institute in 1977 named "The Greatest Film Ever Made", were Ernest Haller and Ray Rennahan for their Color Cinematography, art director Lyle Wheeler, and editors Hal C. Kern

BELOW *'I like to apologize, Mr Rhett, for it not being a boy,' says Best Supporting Actress Hattie McDaniel to Clark Gable in* Gone With The Wind *as they get drunk together to celebrate the birth of his daughter, later killed in a riding accident*

and James E. Newcom, with a special award going to the distinguished production designer, William Cameron Menzies, "for outstanding achievement in the use of color for the enhancement of dramatic mood in the production." In addition, the Irving Thalberg Memorial award was handed to Selznick, which prompted Bob Hope, as M.C. for the first of many times, to quip, "Isn't it wonderful, this benefit for David Selznick!"

Selznick had bought the rights of Margaret Mitchell's novel for $50,000, only a month after its publication in 1936. After it became a bestseller and a film was in the offing, the public demanded that Clark Gable should play the roguish and virile Captain Rhett Butler. In order to get Gable, Selznick was forced to give MGM exclusive distribution rights and 50% of the profits. Gable refused the role at first. "I don't want the part for money, chalk or marbles," he said. Happily, a $2,500-a-week salary and a $100,000 bonus helped him change his mind. (The money enabled him to divorce his second wife and marry his lover Carole Lombard). The author herself seemed uninterested by the film. When asked who she thought should play Rhett, she replied, "Groucho Marx!"

The search for the right actress to play the wilful Southern minx, Scarlett O'Hara, took over two years, during which 1,400 women were interviewed and 90 tested — among them Tallulah Bankhead, Katharine Hepburn, Jean Arthur, Bette Davis, Lucille Ball, Susan Hayward, Lana Turner, Frances Dee, Loretta Young and Joan Bennett. Paulette Goddard was about to sign when Selznick asked her to inform the press that she was genuinely married to Charles Chaplin. (They had been married secretly at sea.) Goddard blew her contract when she replied, "It's none of their goddam business."

Vivien Leigh was a virtually unknown English actress who had come to Hollywood to be near Laurence Olivier while he was filming **Wuthering Heights**, in which she had rejected a supporting role. The story goes that agent Myron Selznick, David's brother, brought Leigh onto the MGM lot where they were burning old scenery for the destruction of Atlanta scene. Myron introduced her to David saying, "David, I want you to meet Scarlett O'Hara." The exquisite green-eyed 25-year-old brunette was illuminated by the glow of the burning sets, and the quest was over. Although she was not enamored with the character of Scarlett – "This woman is a terrible bitch", she remarked – and had to overcome changes of director and script, and a dislike (mutual) of Clark Gable (unromantically, she complained of his bad breath), she triumphed in the role. From her very first words, "If either of you says 'war' once more, I'll go in the house and shut the door," she seduced the initially resistant public. "Perhaps if I'd struggled, wished and worried about getting the role, I

RIGHT *Scarlett O'Hara and Rhett Butler, perfectly embodied by Vivien Leigh and Clark Gable, seen in a happy moment of their tempestuous marriage in the nine-Oscar winning* Gone With The Wind. *Leigh became the first British female star to receive a Best Actress award*

might have been fearful. As it was, I had no time to let worry get the upper hand."

Apart from the memorably spectacular moments of the movie, such as the burning of Atlanta, the huge party at Twelve Oaks, the ball, and the superb visual evocation of the Old South represented by Tara, the O'Hara's immense white mansion, the central relationship between Rhett and Scarlett – a monument to devouring passion brilliantly embodied by Gable and Leigh – lifted the film into the highest category. Both characters are spirited, arrogant, self-centered and amoral, and therefore their marriage is doomed. In the end, when Rhett decides to leave her, she sobs, "What's to become of me?" Turning in the doorway, the handsome Rhett replies in one of the cinema's most notorious lines, "Frankly, my dear, I don't give a damn." However, audiences for over four-and-a-half decades have given more than a damn for what probably remains the most popular and successful motion picture of all time.

Many people still think that Gable won his second Oscar that evening. It seems logical that the actor, an essential element in the success of **Gone With The Wind**, in one of his most celebrated roles, should have been among the winners. But he lost out to Robert Donat's poignant portrayal of the chalky, English public schoolmaster Mr Chipping in **Goodbye Mr Chips**, from James Hilton's bestselling novel. There could be no greater contrast than that between the King of Hollywood and the slim, gentle, sickly actor with the melodious voice. Due to Donat's life-long struggle against chronic asthma, his perfectionism and his dislike of Hollywood (he only filmed **The Count Of Monte Cristo**, 1934, there), he made only 19 films in his career, turning down about ten times as many, including **Romeo And Juliet, Dr Jekyll And Mr Hyde** and **Robin Hood**. In order to pay his mounting medical bills, he accepted the role of the Chinese manda-

rin in **The Inn Of The Sixth Happiness** (1958), but died a week after its completion, aged 53.

As Mr Chipping, nicknamed Mr Chips by over four generations of boys at Brookfield School, Donat aged convincingly from 24 to 80. On his deathbed, in reply to a remark that it was a pity he never had any children, he says, "You're wrong. I have . . . thousands of them, thousands of them . . . and all boys." It is a measure of Donat's acting skill that he makes the over-sentimental scene work. One of the child actors in the film commented years later that "Donat made a deep impression on me by always remaining in character as the old Mr Chips, even when he was off-camera. Many people thought this was rather affected of him, but it was a deep dedication he felt toward the role and I thought it was splendid." Donat's affectionate portrayal not only edged out Gable, but Laurence Olivier's passionate Heathcliffe in William Wyler's **Wuthering Heights**, Mickey Rooney's ebullient showbiz kid in **Babes In Arms**, and James Stewart's *tour de force* performance in Frank Capra's **Mr. Smith Goes To Washington**. (Stewart was to be compensated by winning the Oscar the following year.)

Producer Victor Saville accepted the Best Actor award for Donat, who was in England. Walter Wanger presented Douglas Fairbanks Jr with a commemorative Oscar honoring his father who had died two months earlier, and

Mickey Rooney gave a miniature statuette to his regular screen partner, 17-year-old Judy Garland "for her outstanding performance as a screen juvenile during the past year." Judy then sang 'Over The Rainbow' (Harold Arlen and E. Y. Harburg's Best Song winner) from **The Wizard Of Oz**. Thomas Mitchell gained his Best Supporting Actor award for his role as the drunken Doc Boone in John Ford's greatest Western **Stagecoach**, but he had also played Scarlett O'Hara's father in **Gone With The Wind**, the film that dominated the evening. Ironically, the name of Margaret Mitchell, *GWTW*'s creator, was not mentioned once during the ceremonies.

WINNERS 1939

Nominations Announced: February 12, 1940
Awards Ceremony: February 29, 1940
Ambassador Hotel-Banquet

Best Picture
GONE WITH THE WIND, Selznick/MGM

Actor
ROBERT DONAT in *Goodbye, Mr Chips*, MGM (British)

Actress
VIVIEN LEIGH in *Gone With The Wind*

Supporting Actor
THOMAS MITCHELL in *Stagecoach*, Wanger/UA

Supporting Actress
HATTIE McDANIEL in *Gone With The Wind*

Directing
VICTOR FLEMING for *Gone With The Wind*

Writing
(Original Story)
MR SMITH GOES TO WASHINGTON, Columbia: LEWIS R. FOSTER
(Screenplay)
GONE WITH THE WIND: SIDNEY HOWARD

Cinematography
(Black-and-White)
WUTHERING HEIGHTS, Goldwyn/UA: GREGG TOLAND
(Color)
GONE WITH THE WIND: ERNEST HALLER and RAY RENNAHAN

Interior Decoration
GONE WITH THE WIND: LYLE WHEELER

Sound Recording
WHEN TOMORROW COMES, Universal: BERNARD B. BROWN

Film Editing
GONE WITH THE WIND: HAL C. KERN and JAMES E. NEWCOM

Music
(Best Score)
STAGECOACH: RICHARD HAGEMAN, FRANK HARLING, JOHN LIEPOLD and LEO SHUKEN

(Original Score)
THE WIZARD OF OZ, MGM: HERBERT STOTHART
(Best Song)
OVER THE RAINBOW from *The Wizard Of Oz*
Music: HAROLD ARLEN
Lyrics: E.Y. HARBURG

Short Subjects
(Cartoons)
THE UGLY DUCKLING, Disney/RKO Radio
(One-reel)
BUSY LITTLE BEARS, Paramount. (Paragraphics)
(Two-reel)
SONS OF LIBERTY, Warner Bros. (Historical Featurette)

Special Effects
(New Category)
THE RAINS CAME, 20th Century-Fox: E.H. HANSEN and FRED SERSEN

Special Awards
DOUGLAS FAIRBANKS (Commemorative Award) – recognizing the unique and outstanding contribution of Douglas Fairbanks, first President of the Academy, to the international development of the motion picture. (statuette)
MOTION PICTURE RELIEF FUND – acknowledging the outstanding services to the industry during the past year of the Motion Picture Relief Fund and its progressive leadership. Presented to JEAN HERSHOLT, President; RALPH MORGAN, Chairman of the Executive Committee; RALPH BLOCK, First Vice-President; CONRAD NAGEL. (plaques)
JUDY GARLAND for her outstanding performance as a screen juvenile during the past year. (miniature statuette)
WILLIAM CAMERON MENZIES for outstanding achievement in the use of color for the enhancement of dramatic mood in the production of *Gone With The Wind*. (plaque)
TECHNICOLOR COMPANY for its contributions in successfully bringing three-color feature production to the screen. (statuette)

Irving G. Thalberg Memorial Award
DAVID O. SELZNICK

A NEW ELEMENT WAS added to the Academy Awards ceremony held before 1400 guests at the Biltmore Hotel on February 27, 1941. It was the institution of sealed envelopes to conceal the names of the final winners until the very last moment. (They were sent from the impeccable Price Waterhouse accounting firm to the banquet hall on the evening.) For the first time, the results were kept absolutely secret from the press, public and nominees alike. Thus, suspense now co-existed with glamor at the annual event.

There was also suspense a-plenty in the year's Best Picture winner **Rebecca**. Producer David O. Selznick had the foresight to bring Alfred Hitchcock, the British master of suspense, to Hollywood for the first time. From the opening line, "Last night I dreamt I went to Manderley again," Hitchcock established the atmosphere of Daphne Du Maurier's mock Gothic novel with the mobility and stylishness of his camera. The result was a superb blend of romance, comedy, melodrama and psychological mystery story. He also managed to draw strong characterizations from his splendid cast, headed by Laurence Olivier (nominated) as the haunted, moody Max de Winter.

It was thought that a well-known actress would be given the coveted role of the second Mrs de Winter (her forename is never mentioned). Olivier's new wife Vivien Leigh, 16-year-old Anne Baxter, and Margaret Sullavan were all considered for the part. But Selznick, with director George Cukor's encouragement, went for Joan Fontaine, a seemingly rather colorless ingenue at RKO, known principally as Olivia de Havilland's younger sister, and Brian Aherne's wife. However, under Hitchcock's direction, she gave a sensitive and moving performance to gain an Oscar nomination. "In the early stages of filming, Joan was a little self-conscious," recalled Hitch, "but I could see her potential for restrained acting, and I felt she would play the character in a quiet, shy manner." Fontaine's promise was fulfilled the following year when she won the Oscar in Hitchcock's **Suspicion**. But it was the image of Judith Anderson (nominated for Best Support-

RIGHT *Sinister housekeeper Mrs Danvers (Judith Anderson, right) catches the timid, newly-wed Mrs de Winter (Joan Fontaine) unawares in a room in the brooding mansion, Manderley, in Alfred Hitchcock's first American film, Rebecca. Although the movie was a Best Picture winner, Hitch, himself, nominated for this one and four others, never won the Oscar*

ing Actress) as Mrs Danvers, the sinister housekeeper of Manderley, the somber Cornish mansion, with her maniacal loyalty to the first Mrs de Winter, the 'Rebecca' of the title, that made the most lasting impression.

Hitchcock's second Hollywood film, **Foreign Correspondent**, was also nominated, as were Charles Chaplin's belated first talkie **The Great Dictator**, William Wyler's **The Letter**, George Cukor's **The Philadelphia Story**, and two John Ford pictures, **The Long Voyage Home** and **The Grapes Of Wrath**. Ford received the second of his four Best Director Oscars for the latter humanistic, poetic masterpiece. Of the acting awards, the most popular was Jane Darwell's Best Supporting Actress Oscar for her memorable Ma Joad ("We're the people") in the same film. Walter Brennan as Judge Roy Bean, "the sole law west of the Pecos", in **The Westerner**, earned his third Best Supporting Actor prize in five years, a record that still stands. The Best Actor and Actress awards were more surprising and controversial.

Nobody was more astonished than James Stewart when it was announced that he had won for his performance in **The Philadelphia Story**. He later admitted that he had voted for his friend Henry Fonda whose heart-rending Tom Joad in **The Grapes Of Wrath** made him the favorite in a field which also included Chaplin, Olivier and Raymond Massey as **Abe Lincoln In Illinois**. Stewart felt

BELOW *Henry Fonda (nominated), Jane Darwell (Best Supporting Actress, center), and Dorris Bowden finally arrive at the promised land of California in their battered old Ford in* The Grapes Of Wrath. *Not so old or battered was John Ford, the Best Director winner*

he was the recipient of the Holdover award for having lost out the previous year. There is no doubt that in Frank Capra's **Mr Smith Goes To Washington** (1939), he had a more demanding and memorable assignment than his role as Mike Connor, reporter on the insalubrious 'Spy Magazine' sent to cover the marriage of spoiled socialite Tracy Lord (Katharine Hepburn). But his elegant playing of the cynical journalist who is smitten with the would-be bride, proved he was a light comedian of the highest caliber. In this sparkling and sophisticated comedy of manners, he more than holds his own with Hepburn and Cary Grant. He is particularly good in a drunk scene with Grant, and his marriage proposal to Hepburn.

On the night he received his award, Stewart's father, a hardware store owner, called him from Pennsylvania. "You'd better send the trophy back to the store," he advised his son. The statuette remains in a glass case there to this day. Unfortunately, Stewart has not yet (he is 78) added to it. His next appearance at the Academy Award ceremony the following year found him in uniform. He joined the Army Air Corps as a private, returning from the war four years later a Lieutenant Colonel. Stewart later became Brigadier-General in the peace-time Air Force Reserve, making him the highest ranking entertainer in the US military.

Also flying high was Ginger Rogers who beat off strong

LEFT *In the wedding finale from George Cukor's sophisticated comedy* The Philadephia Story, *Katharine Hepburn (second right) rejects her fiance at the last minute to remarry her ex-husband Cary Grant (center). Another surprise was that the Best Actor Oscar went to James Stewart (left)*
BELOW *Proving she was more than just Fred Astaire's dancing partner, Ginger Rogers, (sitting between Gladys Cooper and Dennis Morgan), won her only Best Actress Oscar for* Kitty Foyle, *the girl from the wrong side of the tracks*

Just as she had in all three of her previous movies, Rogers played a girl from the wrong side of the tracks who moves into higher circles. Here she has to choose between rich married socialite Dennis Morgan and struggling young doctor James Craig. Of course, she finds true happiness with the man more her social equal. Rogers gave a gutsy performance, having to age from 15 to 26 through four separate phases of her life, using the device of a reflection in the mirror acting as her *alter* ego. The role was proof that the 29-year-old star, her blonde hair darkened, was able to make audiences weep as well as smile.

competition to win the Best Actress Oscar for her dramatic performance in **Kitty Foyle**. Perhaps her role as a working girl was more in keeping with the democratic spirit of the times than Katharine Hepburn's uppercrust snob in **The Philadelphia Story**, Bette Davis' British colonial wife in **The Letter**, Joan Fontaine's mousy lady of the manor in **Rebecca**, or newcomer Martha Scott's idealized young wife in the screen version of **Our Town** – all rather remote from everyday life. As Kitty says, "I read about the guts of the pioneer woman and the woman of the dust bowl and the gingham goddess of the covered wagon. What about the woman of the covered typewriter? What has she got when she leaves the office?"

In 1939, after nine musicals with Fred Astaire, she announced that she was giving up dancing to concentrate on straight roles. This is gently satirized in the plot of **The Barkleys Of Broadway** (1949), her Technicolor reunion with Astaire. (Her only other musical after 1939 was **Lady In The Dark**, 1944.) Rogers' sole Oscar was ample reward for her overwhelming desire to be taken seriously as a dramatic actress.

The dark events then taking place in Europe lent a slight air of solemnity to the year's proceedings at which President Franklin D. Roosevelt gave a six-minute direct line radio address from Washington. In it, he paid fulsome tribute to the part the motion picture industry was playing in national defence, and the sense of solidarity their members showed with the beleaguered nations of Europe, after which Judy Garland gave a moving rendition of 'America'. It was, in fact, the last Oscar night held before the United States would be plunged into war. As far as the content of the majority of films was concerned, war was still literally far away. The only picture honored with an Academy Award that referred to it was **Arise, My Love** for Benjamin Glazer and John S. Toldy's original story.

The tone was lightened by Bob Hope, acting as M.C. again. Hope, who received a special award "in recognition of his unselfish service to the motion picture industry", cracked, "I see that Paramount has a table, Warners has a table, MGM has a table, and RKO has a table. Monogram has a stool." Donald Ogden Stewart also added some gaiety to the ceremony in his acceptance speech after receiving the Best Screenplay Oscar. "There has been so much niceness here tonight that I am happy to say that I am entirely and solely responsible for the success of **The Philadelphia Story**", he pronounced.

WINNERS 1940

Nominations Announced: February 10, 1941
Awards Ceremony: February 27, 1941
Biltmore Hotel-Banquet

Best Picture
REBECCA, Selznick/UA

Actor
JAMES STEWART in *The Philadelphia Story*, MGM

Actress
GINGER ROGERS in *Kitty Foyle*, RKO Radio

Supporting Actor
WALTER BRENNAN in *The Westerner*, Goldwyn/UA

Supporting Actress
JANE DARWELL in *The Grapes Of Wrath*, 20th Century-Fox

Directing
JOHN FORD for *The Grapes Of Wrath*

Writing
(Original Story)
ARISE, MY LOVE, Paramount: BENJAMIN GLAZER and JOHN S. TOLDY
(Original Screenplay)
THE GREAT McGINTY, Paramount: PRESTON STURGES
(Screenplay)
THE PHILADELPHIA STORY: DONALD OGDEN STEWART

Cinematography
(Black-and-White)
REBECCA: GEORGE BARNES
(Color)
THE THIEF OF BAGDAD, Korda/UA (British): GEORGE PERINAL

Interior Decoration
(Black-and-White)
PRIDE AND PREJUDICE, MGM: CEDRIC GIBBONS and PAUL GROESSE
(Color)
THE THIEF OF BAGDAD: VINCENT KORDA

Sound Recording
STRIKE UP THE BAND, MGM: DOUGLAS SHEARER

Film Editing
NORTH WEST MOUNTED POLICE, Paramount: ANNE BAUCHENS

Music
(Best Score)
TIN PAN ALLEY, 20th Century-Fox: ALFRED NEWMAN
(Original Score)
PINOCCHIO, Disney/RKO Radio: LEIGH HARLINE, PAUL J. SMITH and NED WASHINGTON
(Best Song)
WHEN YOU WISH UPON A STAR from *Pinocchio*
Music: LEIGH HARLINE
Lyrics: NED WASHINGTON

Short Subjects
(Cartoons)
MILKY WAY, MGM. (Rudolph Ising Series)
(One-reel)
QUICKER 'N A WINK, Smith/MGM
(Two-reel)
TEDDY, THE ROUGH RIDER, Warner Bros. (Historical Featurette)

Special Effects
THE THIEF OF BAGDAD
Photographic: LAWRENCE BUTLER
Sound: JACK WHITNEY

Special Awards
BOB HOPE in recognition of his unselfish services to the motion picture industry. (special silver plaque)
COLONEL NATHAN LEVINSON for his outstanding service to the industry and the Army during the past nine years, which has made possible the present efficient mobilization of the motion picture industry facilities for the production of Army Training Films. (statuette)

Irving G. Thalberg Memorial Award
None

1941

THE 14TH ANNUAL Academy Award presentation ceremony was held at the Biltmore Hotel on February 26, 1942, two months after the bombing of Pearl Harbor and America's entry into the war. Academy President Bette Davis asked that the event be held in a large auditorium, open to the public for the price of a ticket, the proceeds of which would go to the Red Cross. When the Academy refused her request, preferring to keep it a private affair, Davis resigned. However, in keeping with the somber spirit of the times, formal attire was banned, there were no searchlights playing outside the venue to catch the celebrities as they arrived, and the banquet was

downgraded to a dinner. Sixty-one year old character actor Donald Crisp, Best Supporting Actor winner for **How Green Was My Valley**, a veteran of the Boer War and World War I, presented himself in uniform. James Stewart, the previous year's Best Actor, was in his Air Corps Lieutenant's uniform as he handed over the statuette to Gary Cooper, the star of **Sergeant York**.

"This uniform ain't for sale," said World War I hero Sergeant Alvin York in 1919 when producer Jesse Lasky approached him with an offer to make a film of his life. When Lasky went to him again in 1940, York agreed after being convinced that his story would inspire a new generation of soldiers. However, he stipulated that he would oversee the production to eradicate any inaccuracies, that no Hollywood sex goddess must play his wife (Joan Leslie did), and that Gary Cooper should play him. (Coop never saw any action beyond film sets.) With the money earned from the picture, York founded a Bible institute.

Sergeant York, directed by Howard Hawks, ex-pilot

BELOW *Best Supporting Actress Mary Astor (left) in a confrontation with Bette Davis (right) in Warner Bros.'* The Great Lie. *Miss Davis was nominated in the same year for her viperish performance, one of her best, as Regina in* The Little Foxes

with the Army Air Corps in World War I, was an affecting tale told in two parts. The first showed Cooper as a simple, irresponsible Tennessee mountain farmer trying to scratch a living out of the rocky earth. He finds a girl and religion, the latter forcing him to take a pacifist stance at the beginning of the war. However, he gradually adapts his Christian beliefs to the circumstances, plainly a hint to American audiences emerging from isolationism. In one of the most heroic actions of the war the soldier, with born-again belligerence and armed with a Springfield rifle, wipes out 35 German machine gunners and captures 132 prisoners almost single-handed. Despite certain artificialities, especially the studio back-lot doubling for a rather idealized Tennessee, the film offered a perfect framework for Cooper's sincerity and underplaying which exuded the goodness and piety of the character. Cooper's York was, as the poet Carl Sandburg wrote, "one of the most beloved illiterates this country has ever known." Cooper's first Oscar (he won a second as another loner in **High Noon**, 1952) for playing a war hero was appropriate to the tone of the ceremony.

However, a far more remarkable epic performance was given by Orson Welles, nominated for his Hearst-inspired tycoon in **Citizen Kane**, while also in the running were Cary Grant in the tear-jerking **Penny Serenade**, Walter Huston as the Devil in **All That Money Can Buy**, and Robert Montgomery as a dead man sent back from Heaven to earth in **Here Comes Mr Jordan**.

An extra piquancy was added to the Best Actress race by the fact that two sisters were up for the same award. Olivia de Havilland, nominated for the classy soap opera **Hold Back The Dawn**, had become a star some years before her year-younger sister Joan Fontaine emerged in **Rebecca** (1940). Now Fontaine was nominated for the second year running, and again in a Hitchcock movie, **Suspicion**. What got people's tongues wagging was the rumor that they were not on the best of terms. "I adore, respect and like my sister," insisted Fontaine, "but we don't seek out each other's company. We're such complete opposites." In order not to trade on her elder sibling's fame, Joan de Beauvoir de Havilland started in films as Joan Burfield, then became Joan Fontaine. In the event, it was the younger sister who won the Oscar first. (De Havilland was to surpass this by winning two Oscars for **To Each His Own** and **The Heiress** in 1946 and 1949.) Besides the rival sisters, the nominees were Bette Davis' brilliant venomous vixen in **The Little Foxes**, Barbara Stanwyck's burlesque stripper vamping professor Gary Cooper in **Ball Of Fire**, and Greer Garson nobly running an orphanage in **Blossoms In The Dust**.

As in **Rebecca**, Fontaine played another insecure wife in **Suspicion**, the title of which pervades the whole film. She suspects her playboy husband (Cary Grant) of being a liar, a thief, a fortune hunter and a potential wife killer. Again, under Hitchcock's brilliant direction, she gave a sensitive and believable portrayal of a woman living in fear, even though the filmed-in-Hollywood England was less convincing. In one scene, when she suspects a glass

of milk her husband brings her might be poisoned, Hitchcock lit the glass from within to give it an eerie glow. In the original ending Grant turns out to be a murderer, but RKO, fearing for the star's image, imposed a different conclusion on it in which he is exonerated and everything sinister is explained away. Surprisingly, Fontaine's performance was the only one in a Hitchcock picture ever to win an Oscar.

Among the nominees for Best Picture were two

extraordinary first films, Orson Welles' **Citizen Kane** and John Huston's **The Maltese Falcon**. But it was John Ford's **How Green Was My Valley** that the Academy electorate considered superior, an opinion not accepted by posterity. But then optimism was the order of the day. There was much to admire in this episodic drama, set in a small Welsh mining village at the turn of the century, and seen through the eyes of young Huw Morgan (13-year-old Roddy McDowall evacuated to the USA during the London Blitz in 1940). The scenario concentrated on the Morgan family and how they are affected by conflict with the mine owners, strikes and mine disasters. There is also an abortive romance between Huw's sister (20-year-old Maureen O'Hara) and the local pipe-smoking preacher (Walter Pidgeon) who won't marry her because he doesn't want her to live a life of genteel poverty.

Twentieth Century-Fox studios converted 200 acres of California Valley into a South Wales landscape at a cost of $110,000. Art directors Richard Day and Nathan Juran's

ABOVE *One hundred and thirty two German soldiers were captured during World War I due to the bravery of* Sergeant York, *alias Gary Cooper (left) seen here conferring with George Tobias. The Howard Hawks movie was nominated in seven categories, and won Cooper his first Oscar*
RIGHT *Could handsome playboy Cary Grant want to murder his wealthy young wife Joan Fontaine (both illustrated) in Alfred Hitchcock's* Suspicion? *Fontaine survived to collect the Best Actress award*

ABOVE *Disaster strikes at a Welsh mine in John Ford's five-Oscar winning* How Green Was My Valley. *Anna Lee (seated far right), whose husband lies dead on the stretcher, is being consoled by, left to right, Walter Pidgeon, John Loder and Donald Crisp (Best Supporting Actor)*

vast set of the village with its cobbled streets, stone houses and colliery earned them an Academy Award, one of the five the film won. Although only Rhys Williams, who narrated, played the role of the ex-pugilist and acted as technical adviser, was Welsh, the mine shafts and a Welsh choir lent authenticity to the sentimental tale. Best of all the cast were Donald Crisp as the stern but just father of the brood (winning his only Oscar in his 55-year-long screen career), and 58-year-old Irish character actress Sara Allgood as the loving mother who almost dies defending her husband against a mob. Allgood, nominated as Best Supporting Actress, lost out to Mary Astor

whose selfish concert pianist in **The Great Lie** even put her co-star Bette Davis in the shade.

Despite the nomination of Orson Welles as Best Director for **Citizen Kane**, John Ford walked off with his third award, and second in a row, for **How Green Was My Valley**. In fact, the Welles movie, constantly judged throughout the years as the greatest American film ever made and nominated in nine categories, only managed one Oscar – Best Original Screenplay by Welles and Herman J. Mankiewicz. Walt Disney won his customary award for a cartoon, **Lend A Paw**, as well as being the recipient of the Irving Thalberg Memorial Award. However, the war was never far from the guests' thoughts. The beautiful and talented Carole Lombard, Clark Gable's wife since 1939, was killed in a plane crash while returning to California from a US war bond selling tour of the Midwest only a month previously. The sadly missed star was the movie industry's first casualty of the war.

WINNERS 1941

Nominations Announced: February 9, 1942
Awards Ceremony: February 26, 1942
Biltmore Hotel-Banquet

Best Picture
HOW GREEN WAS MY VALLEY, 20th Century-Fox

Actor
GARY COOPER in *Sergeant York*, Warner Bros.

Actress
JOAN FONTAINE in *Suspicion*, RKO Radio

Supporting Actor
DONALD CRISP in *How Green Was My Valley*

Supporting Actress
MARY ASTOR in *The Great Lie*, Warner Bros.

Directing
JOHN FORD for *How Green Was My Valley*

Writing
(Original Story)
HERE COMES MR JORDAN, Columbia: HARRY SEGALL
(Original Screenplay)
CITIZEN KANE, Mercury/RKO Radio: HERMAN J.
MANKIEWICZ and ORSON WELLES
(Screenplay)
HERE COMES MR JORDAN: SIDNEY BUCHMAN and
SETON I. MILLER

Cinematography
(Black-and-White)
HOW GREEN WAS MY VALLEY: ARTHUR MILLER
(Color)
BLOOD AND SAND, 20th Century-Fox: ERNEST
PALMER and RAY RENNAHAN

Interior Decoration
(Black-and-White)
HOW GREEN WAS MY VALLEY: RICHARD DAY and
NATHAN JURAN
Interior Decoration: THOMAS LITTLE
(Color)
BLOSSOMS IN THE DUST, MGM: CEDRIC GIBBONS
and URIE McCLEARY
Interior Decoration: EDWIN B. WILLIS

Sound Recording
THAT HAMILTON WOMAN, Korda/UA: JACK WHITNEY,
GENERAL SERVICE

Film Editing
SERGEANT YORK: WILLIAM HOLMES

Music
(Scoring of a Dramatic Picture)
ALL THAT MONEY CAN BUY, RKO Radio: BERNARD
HERRMANN
(Scoring of a Musical Picture)
DUMBO, Disney/RKO Radio: FRANK CHURCHILL and
OLIVER WALLACE
(Best Song)
THE LAST TIME I SAW PARIS from *Lady Be Good*, MGM
Music: JEROME KERN
Lyrics: OSCAR HAMMERSTEIN II

Short Subjects
(Cartoons)
LEND A PAW, Disney/RKO Radio
(One-reel)
OF PUPS AND PUZZLES, MGM. (Passing Parade Series)
(Two-reel)
MAIN STREET ON THE MARCH, MGM. (Special)

Documentary
(New Category)
CHURCHILL'S ISLAND, National Film Board of Canada/UA

Special Effects
I WANTED WINGS, Paramount
Photographic: FARCIOT EDOUART and GORDON
JENNINGS
Sound: LOUIS MESENKOP

Special Awards
REY SCOTT for his extraordinary achievement in
producing *Kukan*, the film record of China's struggle,
including its photography with a 16mm camera under the
most difficult and dangerous conditions. (certificate)
THE BRITISH MINISTRY OF INFORMATION for its vivid
and dramatic presentation of the heroism of the RAF in the
documentary film, *Target For Tonight*. (certificate)
LEOPOLD STOKOWSKI and his associates for their unique
achievement in the creation of a new form of visualized
music in Walt Disney's production *Fantasia*, thereby
widening the scope of the motion picture as entertainment
and as an art form. (certificate)
WALT DISNEY, WILLIAM GARITY, JOHN N.A.
HAWKINS and the RCA MANUFACTURING COMPANY
for their outstanding contribution to the advancement of the
use of sound in motion pictures through the production of
Fantasia. (certificates)

Irving G. Thalberg Memorial Award
WALT DISNEY

1942

THE WAR WAS reflected in almost every aspect of the Academy Award ceremony held at the Ambassador Hotel on March 4, 1943, the last of the private banquets. Most of the awards honored films that had some connection with the world conflict. Even Walt Disney's Oscar-winning Donald Duck cartoon **Der Fuehrer's Face** was preoccupied with the situation. M.C. Bob Hope read messages from President Roosevelt and Madame Chiang Kai-Shek to the assembled company flecked with uniforms. Jeanette MacDonald sang the National Anthem, and Marine and Air Force privates Tyrone Power and Alan Ladd unfurled a flag disclosing the names of 27,677 members of the film industry who were in the armed forces. (The first Hollywood actor to be killed in action was 33-year-old Phillips Holmes, best known as the star of **An American Tragedy**, 1931.) Lieutenant Van Heflin accepted the Best Supporting Actor plaque for his drunken, intellectual sidekick to Robert Taylor's hoodlum in **Johnny Eager**, and Mrs William Wyler was there to receive her distinguished husband's Best Director trophy for **Mrs Miniver**, one of six – including Best Film – that it carried off, because Major Wyler was on a bombing raid over Germany that very night.

Time Magazine thought **Mrs Miniver** had achieved "an almost impossible feat. A great war picture that photographs the inner meaning instead of the outward realism of World War II." Dr Goebbels cited the film as "an exemplary propaganda film for the German industry to copy", and Winston Churchill ordered leaflets of the film's closing speech to be dropped over enemy lines. Spoken by the vicar (Henry Wilcoxon) standing in a semi-destroyed church, the words were, "This is the people's war! It is our war! We are the fighters. Fight it then. Fight it with all that is in us. And may God defend the right!" All of this was an illustration of the impact the Best Picture winner had at the time – an impact now somewhat diminished with the passage of years.

Without showing any battle scenes, Wyler revealed the effect of the war on the British people, slouching home wearily after helping at Dunkirk, and keeping their spirits up in the bomb shelters as the Blitz raged above them in the London streets (re-created in the MGM studios). The Oscar-winning script, by Arthur Wimperis, George Froeschel, James Hilton and Claudine West, concentrated on how a particularly idealized upper middle-class English family bore up bravely during the war.

The Miniver family consisted of the architect father (Walter Pidgeon), indomitable and indefatigable mother (Greer Garson), their soldier son (Richard Ney) married to an aristocratic but democratic girl (Best Supporting Actress Teresa Wright), and two young children. Garson and Pidgeon, who had already appeared together successfully in the nominated **Blossoms In The Dust**, formed one of the screen's most popular romantic duos, appearing in nine films as a team, including the disastrous sequel

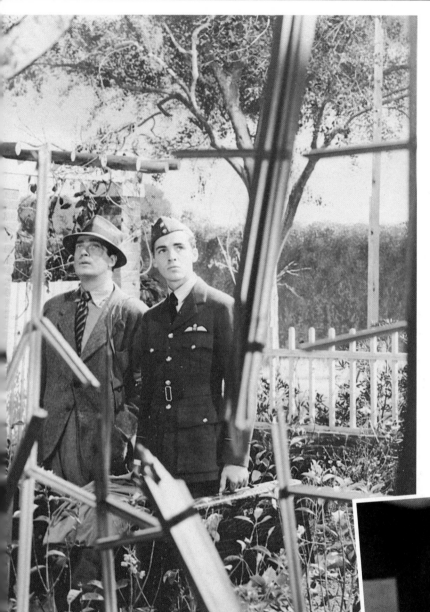

The Miniver Story (1950). At first, Pidgeon (Oscar-nominated) refused to make **Mrs Miniver** because of director Wyler's reputation as a hard taskmaster. "I shudder when I think of the fight I put up to get out of doing the picture," he later recalled.

In contrast, the 34-year-old Irish-born redhead Greer Garson put up a fight to get the choice part. MGM had originally bought the script as a vehicle for Norma Shearer, but the 41-year-old star's ego prevented her from playing the mother of a grown-up son. The role went to Louis B. Mayer's current pet Garson, who then proceeded, much to his displeasure, to have a love affair with her screen son Richard Ney, ten years her junior. They announced their engagement during shooting, but Mayer begged them not to tell the press, and to delay their marriage until after the film's first major release. The couple complied, and their marriage was further delayed when Ney was called into the navy after the filming.

Despite the romance, or because of it, Garson gave a gracious, warmhearted performance as a woman who helps the war effort, judges a flower show, reads stories to her children during a bomb raid, and captures a German soldier single-handed. Her Best Actress award came despite formidable competition from Bette Davis in **Now, Voyager** (one of her greatest roles), Katharine Hepburn in **Woman Of The Year**, Rosalind Russell in **My Sister Eileen** and Teresa Wright (unusually competing in two categories) in **Pride Of The Yankees**.

ABOVE *The Minivers (Walter Pidgeon, second right and Greer Garson, left), and their son (Richard Ney, right) and daughter-in-law (Teresa Wright, center) contemplate the ruins of the bombed house in Mrs Miniver*
RIGHT *Van Heflin, Best Supporting Actor, resists Robert Taylor's remedy to sober him up in Johnny Eager, MGM's gangster drama which also starred a young Lana Turner. Although the picture was advertised as TNT (Taylor 'n Turner), it was Heflin who made the most impression*

83

*Oscar®is a Registered Trade Mark·Academy Awards®is a Registered Trade Mark·Oscar®is a Registere... ...ark·Academy Awards®is a Registered Trade Mark·Oscar®is a Registered Trade Mark·Aca...

Miss Garson then gave the longest acceptance speech in the Academy's history. For almost an hour she thanked everyone under the sun for her success. As she plowed on, poor Joan Fontaine, who had presented her with the Oscar, gradually backed away from her side to find a chair. After the speech, one wag commented that it was longer than her entire role in **Mrs Miniver**. Garson's long-winded address caused the Academy to ask future winners to limit their acceptance speeches to three minutes. When, in 1951, Garson was asked to say 'a few words' at the award ceremony, she remarked good-naturedly, "If I have time, I have a few things left over to say . . ." Although she never won another Oscar, Garson's five

nominations in five successive years – 1941, 1942, 1943, 1944, 1945 – remain an equal record with Bette Davis. In 1942, she also starred, with Ronald Colman, in **Random Harvest**, another of the year's Best Picture nominees, in which she demonstrated that the attributes she brought to Mrs Miniver were no accident. "Metro's Glorified Mama", as she called herself, saw her career wane in the 1950s, but she gained her seventh nomination for her Eleanor Roosevelt in **Sunrise At Campobello** (1960).

Yankee Doodle Dandy begins in 1937 with James Cagney in the role of composer-singer-playwright-actor-dancer-producer George M. Cohan recounting his life story to President Franklin D. Roosevelt. Afterwards, the

LEFT *Dynamic James Cagney as composer-entertainer George M. Cohan saluting the 'Grand Old Flag' in a patriotic number from Warner Bros.' Yankee Doodle Dandy, in which Cagney danced himself towards a Best Actor Oscar*
BELOW *Ship's captain Noel Coward comforts a dying member of his crew in* In Which We Serve, *Coward's tribute to the British navy in World War II. Although the movie was nominated for Best Picture of 1943, the English actor-director-playwright actually won a special Award the previous year for this film*

the 'Cohan Strut', even outdid its originator, so that future generations of Cohan mimics found themselves imitating Cagney rather than the real thing. Cagney's exuberant singing and dancing was best exhibited in a lengthy extract from Cohan's hit show *Little Johnny Jones*, containing two of its most successful ditties, the title song and 'Give My Regards To Broadway'. Alas, there are too few examples of Cagney's elastically alert hoofing on film, but enough to prove that the gangster movie's gain was the musical's loss. On receiving his award, he said merely, "An actor is only as good as people think he is and as bad as people think he is. I'm so glad so many people thought I was good."

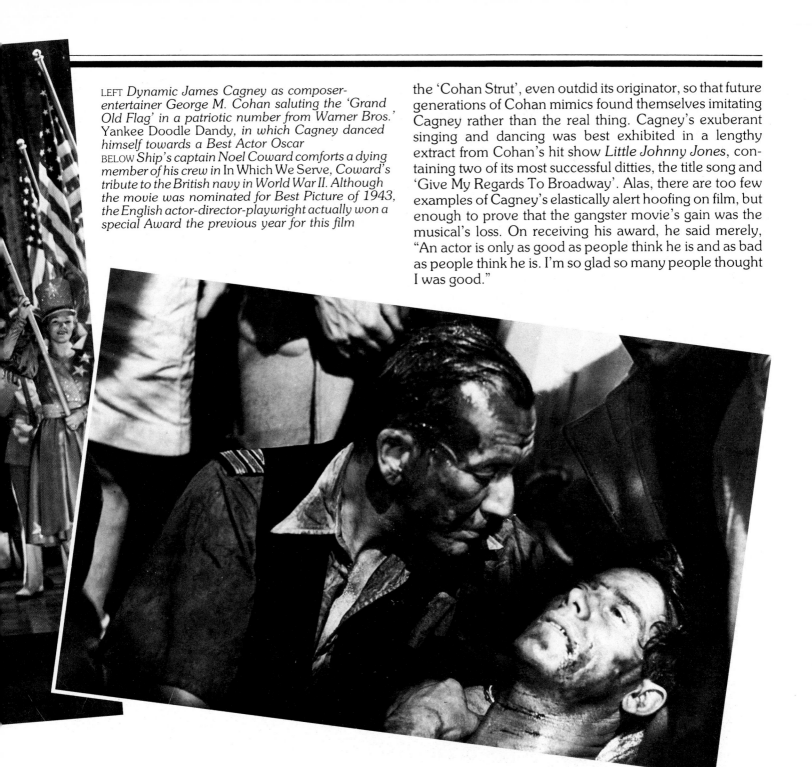

President decorates him for his services to the American Musical Theater, a medal that the multi-talented Cagney has convinced us was merited. So was his Best Actor Oscar, making him the first male performer to win one in a musical role. Cagney emoted, sang and hoofed his way into the hearts of millions with his portrayal of the pint-sized showman. The biopic also went down a treat with World War II audiences, as it was not only a nostalgic extravaganza but a patriotic pageant featuring songs like 'You're A Grand Old Flag.'

When Cohan sold Warner Bros. the rights to his life story, he insisted that James Cagney play him. In fact, Cagney, with his head forward and bottom sticking up in

James Cagney had swept aside the challenge from Ronald Colman as the amnesiac in **Random Harvest**, the previous year's winner Gary Cooper as baseball star Lou Gehrig in **Pride Of The Yankees**, irascible child-hating Monty Woolley leading children out of occupied France in **The Pied Piper**, and Walter Pidgeon as Mr Miniver. **Yankee Doodle Dandy** also picked up two more Oscars—Best Sound Recording (Nathan Levinson) and Best Scoring of a Musical (Ray Heindorf and Heinz Roemheld). But the Best Song award was carried off by 'White Christmas', the Irving Berlin number from **Holiday Inn**, which became – and remains – one of the all-time greatest hits.

WINNERS 1942

Nominations Announced: February 8, 1943
Awards Ceremony: March 4, 1943
Ambassador Hotel-Banquet

Best Picture
MRS MINIVER, MGM

Actor
JAMES CAGNEY in *Yankee Doodle Dandy*, Warner Bros.

Actress
GREER GARSON in *Mrs Miniver*

Supporting Actor
VAN HEFLIN in *Johnny Eager*, MGM

Supporting Actress
TERESA WRIGHT in *Mrs Miniver*

Directing
WILLIAM WYLER for *Mrs Miniver*

Writing
(Original Story)
THE INVADERS, Ortus/Columbia (British): EMERIC
PRESSBURGER
(Original Screenplay)
WOMAN OF THE YEAR, MGM: MICHAEL KANIN and
RING LARDNER Jr
(Screenplay)
MRS MINIVER: GEORGE FROESCHEL, JAMES HILTON,
CLAUDINE WEST and ARTHUR WIMPERIS

Cinematography
(Black-and-White)
MRS MINIVER: JOSEPH RUTTENBERG
(Color)
THE BLACK SWAN, 20th Century-Fox: LEON SHAMROY

Interior Decoration
(Black-and-White)
THIS ABOVE ALL, 20th Century-Fox: RICHARD DAY and
JOSEPH WRIGHT
Interior Decoration: THOMAS LITTLE
(Color)
MY GAL SAL, 20th Century-Fox: RICHARD DAY and
JOSEPH WRIGHT
Interior Decoration: THOMAS LITTLE

Sound Recording
YANKEE DOODLE DANDY: NATHAN LEVINSON

Film Editing
THE PRIDE OF THE YANKEES, Goldwyn/RKO Radio:
DANIEL MANDELL

Music
(Scoring of a Dramatic or Comedy Picture)
NOW, VOYAGER, Warner Bros.: MAX STEINER
(Scoring of a Musical Picture)
YANKEE DOODLE DANDY: RAY HEINDORF and HEINZ
ROEMHELD
(Best Song)
WHITE CHRISTMAS from *Holiday Inn*, Paramount
Music and Lyrics: IRVING BERLIN

Short Subjects
(Cartoons)
DER FUEHRER'S FACE, Disney/RKO Radio
(One-reel)
SPEAKING OF ANIMALS AND THEIR FAMILIES,
Paramount. (Speaking Of Animals)
(Two-reel)
BEYOND THE LINE OF DUTY, Warner Bros. (Broadway
Brevities)

Documentary
BATTLE OF MIDWAY, US Navy/20th Century-Fox
KOKODA FRONT LINE, Australian News Information
Bureau
MOSCOW STRIKES BACK, Artkino (Russian)
PRELUDE TO WAR, US Navy Special Services

Special Effects
REAP THE WILD WIND, Paramount
Photographic: FARCIOT EDOUART, GORDON
JENNINGS and WILLIAM L. PEREIRA
Sound: LOUIS MESENKOP

Special Awards
CHARLES BOYER for his progressive cultural achievement
in establishing the French Research Foundation in Los
Angeles as a source of reference for the Hollywood motion
picture industry. (certificate)
NOEL COWARD for his outstanding production
achievement in *In Which We Serve*. (certificate)
MGM STUDIO for its achievement in representing the
American Way of Life in the production of the *Andy Hardy*
series of films. (certificate)

Irving G. Thalberg Memorial Award
SIDNEY FRANKLIN

1943

THE ERA OF banquets closed to all but Academy members and their guests was over on March 2, 1944, when the Academy Award ceremony was moved to Grauman's Chinese Theatre. The large audience, which included many servicemen and women, saw Jack Benny as M.C., dwarfed by a huge replica of the Oscar statuette on stage, introduce the stars on a show that was broadcast to the Armed Forces overseas.

Among those who came up to receive awards was executive producer at Warner Bros., Hal B. Wallis, who was not only presented with the Irving Thalberg Memorial Award, but also with an Oscar for **Casablanca**, the unani-

mous Best Picture winner. Three of its nearest rivals for the top prize also had war as their theme: **For Whom The Bell Tolls**, a turgid adaptation of Ernest Hemingway's Spanish Civil War novel, **Watch On The Rhine**, a somewhat belated cautionary tale on Nazism, and Noel Coward's stirring sea drama, **In Which We Serve**. Coward, in fact, had received a special award from the Academy the previous year for his achievement.

To Warners' great joy (and that of millions of other people), American forces liberated French North Africa in the same year that **Casablanca** was released. Soon after, President Roosevelt, Winston Churchill and other Allied officials met in the Moroccan city, thus giving the movie a topical title. But as Hungarian-born director Michael Curtiz told Jack Warner, "Well, Jock. The scenario isn't the exact truth, but ve haff the facts to prove it." Truth or not, the strong plot, piquant dialogue (by Oscar-winning Julius J. Epstein, Philip G. Epstein and Howard Koch), cherishable performances from a magnificent cast

BELOW *Sam (Dooley Wilson) at the piano, plays 'As Time Goes By' to bring back poignant memories of the past love affair between Humphrey Bogart and Ingrid Bergman (both illustrated) in Best Director Michael Curtiz's Best Picture,* Casablanca

headed by Humphrey Bogart (nominated), Ingrid Bergman, Claude Rains (nominated), Paul Henreid, Conrad Veidt, Sidney Greenstreet, Peter Lorre and S. Z. Sakall, and the emotional Max Steiner score – not forgetting Dooley Wilson as Sam playing 'As Time Goes By' – and atmospheric photography by Arthur Edeson (nominated), made the picture the epitome of 1940s Hollywood romance. And as time goes by it looks better and better and acquires still more fans.

Most of the movie takes place in and around the Café-Américain run by Rick (Bogart), a hardboiled isolationist who gets involved in the Free French cause in order to help Victor Laszlo (Henreid), a resistance leader and husband of his former love (Bergman) escape to the USA. The poignant and passionate Bergman-Bogart teaming, with flashbacks of their love affair in prewar Paris, is one of the most celebrated in cinema history. And to think the film was originally planned as a vehicle for Ann Sheridan and Ronald Reagan! Strangely, this most structured and beloved of films was made in a manner that left everyone on set confused about what was happening. Everyone, it seems, except Curtiz who brought it all together with his expert hand. A veteran of hundreds of Warner Bros. movies of every conceivable genre, he walked off with a deserved Best Director award.

Ingrid Bergman who was nominated, not for **Casablanca**, but for her Spanish peasant in **For Whom The Bell Tolls**, remarked after seeing her close friend Jennifer Jones as a French peasant in **The Song Of Bernadette**, "I cried all the way through, because Jennifer was so moving and because I realized then I had lost the award." The others up for the Best Actress Oscar—Jean Arthur in **The More The Merrier**, Joan Fontaine (nominated for the third time in four years) in **The Constant Nymph**, and Greer Garson in **Madame Curie**, might have felt the same way on seeing the 24-year-old, fresh-faced Jones in what was virtually her debut film. (She had appeared four years earlier under her real name, Phyllis Isley, in a *Dick Tracy* serial and a B Western.)

In 1941, the starlet, married to the then unknown actor Robert Walker, signed a contract with David O. Selznick who changed her name and groomed her for stardom. He gave her two years of extensive training in drama and kept her in New York until she was ready. "I refused to launch her until exactly the right role came along," Selznick said. After a six-months' search, 20th Century-Fox had narrowed the list of girls to play Bernadette down to six. They were each asked by director Henry King to imagine that the stick he was holding was a vision. "Only Jennifer saw a vision," he later remarked. Because of the nature of the role, Miss Jones was given no publicity buildup, was kept from granting interviews, and also kept out of the gossip columns. As a result her presence on screen came as a refreshing surprise to the public.

Wearing only a simple peasant's dress and a minimum of make-up, Jones gave a pleasantly natural performance as the French girl who, in 1858, saw a vision of the Virgin Mary and discovered a healing spring at Lourdes. She also matured credibly from the age of 14 to the nun and eventual saint. The 158-minute movie, a skilful Hollywood blend of pious storytelling and 'woman's picture' (but without the usual central love story), was a great success and won most of the awards of the evening. Besides Best Actress, it took Oscars for Black and White Cinematography (Arthur Miller), Art Direction (James Basevi, William Darling), Black and White Interior Decoration (Thomas Little) and Music Score (Alfred Newman).

RIGHT *Young French peasant girl Jennifer Jones tells her tale of her vision of the Virgin Mary to John Maxwell Hayes (left) and Charles Bickford (center) in* The Song of Bernadette. *The picture gained four Oscars including Best Actress for Miss Jones*

ABOVE *Best Actor Paul Lukas (left), the anti-Nazi, and his wife Bette Davis (center) confront Nazi agent George Coulouris (right) in* Watch On The Rhine, *Warner Bros.' version of Lillian Hellman's cautionary World War II play. Dashiell Hammett, Hellman's lover, was nominated for his screenplay*

Jennifer Jones' career continued to be carefully planned by Selznick whom she married in 1949. (Robert Walker, a gifted actor, died prematurely in 1951, a victim of depression, breakdowns, drink and sedatives.) She went on to play many more pure women, interspersed with a number of tempestuous *femmes fatales* as in **Duel In The Sun** (1946), **Madame Bovary** (1949, in which she was particularly striking) and **Ruby Gentry** (1953), worlds away from Bernadette. Miss Jones never won another Oscar, but she was nominated a further four times.

Unlike Jennifer Jones, the Best Actor winner 49-year-old Paul Lukas (born Pál Lukács in Hungary) had been in pictures since the silent era. He came to Hollywood in 1927 where he embarked on a long career generally playing smooth Continental lovers until, with the outbreak of war, he found himself in demand in Nazi roles. But it was in a powerful anti-Nazi role that he won his only Oscar. As the gentle engineer who becomes a member of the German resistance movement and escapes with his

ABOVE *Russian-born Akim Tamiroff (Best Supporting Actor nominee) and Greek actress Katina Paxinou (Best Supporting Actress winner) as loyalist Spanish fighters in* For Whom The Bell Tolls. *Other 'Spaniards' in the picture were Ingrid Bergman (nominated) and Vladimir Sokoloff*

ABOVE *Best Supporting Actor Charles Coburn caught in an embarrassing position by his landlady Jean Arthur in the ironically titled George Stevens housing shortage comedy,* The More The Merrier. *Arthur, whom Stevens called 'one of the greatest comediennes the screen has ever seen', gained her only ever nomination for this role*

family to Washington in **Watch On The Rhine**, Lukas stood out from an excellent cast which included Bette Davis, self-effacing as his brave wife, George Coulouris as a slimy Nazi agent, Lucile Watson, a selfish bystander, Geraldine Fitzgerald and Beulah Bondi.

Warner Bros. proved that their casting of Lukas, who had appeared in the same role on Broadway in Lillian Hellman's effective agitprop play, was justified after both Errol Flynn and Robert Hutton had been considered. The play, which shocked audiences with its warnings about the dangers of Fascism, was transposed almost intact to the screen where it retained its original impact. Lukas' award was greeted symphathetically, although the audience might have preferred to have seen Bogart, Gary Cooper in **For Whom The Bell Tolls** (his third nomination in a row), Walter Pidgeon in **Madame Curie** or Mickey Rooney in **The Human Comedy** go up on stage to receive a statuette. It was the highest point in Lukas' career. He gave up acting 18 films and 25 years later, and died of a heart attack in 1971 aged 77 in Tangier while looking for a retirement home.

Supporting players, who had hitherto received only a

plaque, were now to be rewarded with a full-sized statuette. The first beneficiaries were 67-year-old Charles Coburn for his irresistible, matchmaking Mr Dingle in George Stevens' housing shortage comedy **The More The Merrier**, and Greek actress Katina Paxinou as the fiery anti-Fascist Spanish peasant leader, Pilar, in **For Whom The Bell Tolls**, her first American film. The air of patriotism that hung over the occasion extended to the cartoon award for **Yankee Doodle Mouse** in which Tom and Jerry did their bit for the war effort.

WINNERS 1943

Nominations Announced: February 7, 1944
Awards Ceremony: March 2, 1944
Grauman's Chinese Theatre

Best Picture
CASABLANCA, Warner Bros.

Actor
PAUL LUKAS in *Watch On The Rhine*, Warner Bros.

Actress
JENNIFER JONES in *The Song Of Bernadette*, 20th Century-Fox

Supporting Actor
CHARLES COBURN in *The More The Merrier*, Columbia

Supporting Actress
KATINA PAXINOU in *For Whom The Bell Tolls*, Paramount

Directing
MICHAEL CURTIZ for *Casablanca*

Writing
(Original Story)
THE HUMAN COMEDY, MGM: WILLIAM SAROYAN
(Original Screenplay)
PRINCESS O'ROURKE, Warner Bros.: NORMAN KRASNA
(Screenplay)
CASABLANCA: JULIUS J. EPSTEIN, PHILIP G. EPSTEIN and HOWARD KOCH

Cinematography
(Black-and-White)
THE SONG OF BERNADETTE: ARTHUR MILLER
(Color)
PHANTOM OF THE OPERA, Universal: HAL MOHR and W. HOWARD GREENE

Interior Decoration
(Black-and-White)
THE SONG OF BERNADETTE: JAMES BASEVI and WILLIAM DARLING
Interior Decoration: THOMAS LITTLE
(Color)
PHANTOM OF THE OPERA: ALEXANDER GOLITZEN and JOHN B. GOODMAN
Interior Decoration: RUSSELL A. GAUSMAN and IRA S. WEBB

Sound Recording
THIS LAND IS MINE, RKO Radio: STEPHEN DUNN

Film Editing
AIR FORCE, Warner Bros.: GEORGE AMY

Music
(Scoring of a Dramatic or Comedy Picture)
THE SONG OF BERNADETTE: ALFRED NEWMAN
(Scoring of a Musical Picture)
THIS IS THE ARMY, Warner Bros.: RAY HEINDORF
(Best Song)
YOU'LL NEVER KNOW from *Hello, Frisco, Hello*, 20th Century-Fox
Music: HARRY WARREN
Lyrics: MACK GORDON

Short Subjects
(Cartoons)
YANKEE DOODLE MOUSE, MGM: FREDERICK QUIMBY, Producer
(One-reel)
AMPHIBIOUS FIGHTERS, Paramount: GRANTLAND RICE, Producer
(Two-reel)
HEAVENLY MUSIC, MGM: JERRY BRESLER and SAM COSLOW, Producers

Documentary
(Short Subjects)
DECEMBER 7TH, US Navy Field Photographic Branch/Office of Strategic Services
(Features)
DESERT VICTORY, British Ministry of Information

Special Effects
CRASH DIVE, 20th Century-Fox
Photographic: FRED SERSEN
Sound: ROGER HEMAN

Special Awards
GEORGE PAL for the development of novel methods and techniques in the production of short subjects known as Puppetoons. (plaque)

Irving G. Thalberg Memorial Award
HAL B. WALLIS

"**I**'M SO HAPPY to have won," said Ingrid Bergman on receiving her Academy Award for **Gaslight**. "I'm afraid if I came on the set tomorrow morning without an Oscar, Bing and Leo wouldn't have anything to do with me." Coincidentally, Bergman was working at the time on **The Bells Of St Mary's**, the sequel to this year's Best Picture **Going My Way**, with the Best Actor and Best Director winners, Bing Crosby and Leo McCarey. Bergman accepted the award from her 1943 rival Jennifer Jones who said, "I don't know what I would have done if Ingrid hadn't won. My whole speech was planned with her in mind."

Bergman's role as the wife being subtly driven mad by her fortune-hunting husband (Charles Boyer) defeated hefty competition from three previous winners – Bette Davis (**Mr Skeffington**), Claudette Colbert (**Since You Went Away**) and Greer Garson (**Mrs Parkington**), plus the strongest contender of all, blonde-wigged Barbara Stanwyck (**Double Indemnity**). As the *New York Post* critic wrote of Bergman, "her mingling of love, terror and the growing sense of her own mind's failure, represents one of the better achievements of the season." For this psychological Victorian thriller, based on Patrick Hamilton's play originally titled *Angel Street*, and directed by George Cukor, she had to age from an impressionable teenager to a mature married woman. The husband, who had murdered her aunt, now tries to gain the inheritance by having her committed. In the end, when he is arrested, he begs her to help him, but she turns on him saying, "I hate you! Without a shred of pity . . . without a shred of regret . . . I watch you go with glory in my heart!"

In preparation for the role, Bergman spent some time visiting a mental institution to observe the patients' behavior. "One young woman there interested me and much of her strange qualities went into my characterization," she recalled. Cukor later remarked that Bergman "had no difficulty in grasping the character of Paula Alquist's essential frailty, but she would complain, 'Oh, I look so healthy.' However, I think healthy people can be frightened. In fact, very often it's perhaps more moving."

RIGHT *Newly-wed Ingrid Bergman (Best Actress) is unaware that her husband Charles Boyer (nominated) is planning to gain her inheritance by driving her slowly insane in* Gaslight. *Angela Lansbury, as the cocky cockney maid, gained a supporting actress nomination in this, her first picture*

It was precisely Bergman's healthy, unspoiled, natural looks and personality that made her such a popular star in the 1940s. Her private life also seemed beyond reproach, married as she was to Swedish dentist Peter Lindstrom with a daughter Pia. But in 1949, after she had played a nun in **The Bells Of St Mary's** (1945) and the saint **Joan Of Arc** (1948), Hollywood was shocked when she deserted her family for Italian director Roberto Rossellini. It was seven years before she made another American movie, winning her second Academy award for **Anastasia** (1956), a triumphant comeback.

Until **Going My Way**, Bing Crosby's immense popularity derived from his crooning and his easygoing personality in over 30 routine musicals for Paramount Studios. (Bing headed the 1944 list of the ten biggest box-office stars.) When Leo McCarey at RKO conceived the idea of the happy-go-lucky priest who is sent to St Dominic's to "get the parish in shape", he naturally thought of Spencer Tracy, who had been splendid in dog collar in **San Francisco** (1936) and **Boys Town** (1939). When Tracy proved unavailable, James Cagney was approached. After that fell through, McCarey hit on the idea of Crosby to essay his first semi-dramatic role. Granted, the part of Father Chuck O'Malley was trimmed to suit Bing's relaxed style, even allowing for a number of songs including the Oscar-winning Johnny Burke-Jimmy Van Heusen tune, 'Swinging On A Star'.

Crosby was perfect as the young priest who takes over the day-to-day running of St Dominic's from the ageing and crotchety Father Fitzgibbon (Barry Fitzgerald). At first the new priest, who croons, and who likes a tot of whisky and a round of golf, meets with resistance from the old man, but gradually wins him over with his charm. He helps a young couple marry, and organizes the neighborhood toughs into a choir that tours the country, earning enough money to pay off the church mortgage. About the role of the pipe-smoking priest Crosby commented that he was "a sort of better version of myself—the guy I'd like to be". Incidentally, Crosby's only statuette, the wartime plaster version, was decapitated when Bing was practising a golf swing in his living room.

Competing with Crosby for the award were Charles Boyer, cast against his romantic French matinee idol image as the scheming murderer in **Gaslight**, Cary Grant, also playing against type, as the cockney drifter in **None But The Lonely Heart**, Alexander Knox in the title role of the US President **Wilson**, and none other than Bing's co-star Barry Fitzgerald, unusually nominated for the same role in **Going My Way** in both the Best Actor and Best

BELOW *Laid-back, crooning priest – and Best Actor – Bing Crosby (right) finds his modern ways challenged by stubborn old priest and Best Supporting Actor Barry Fitzgerald in Leo McCarey's Best Picture winner,* Going My Way

ABOVE *Insurance man Walter Neff (Fred MacMurray, right) and Phyllis Dietrichson (Barbara Stanwyck, left) plan to do away with her husband (Tom Powers, second right) so they can live together on his life insurance in Billy Wilder's superb film noir,* Double Indemnity. *The picture, nominated in four categories, came away empty-handed. Stanwyck received the third of her four nominations for one of her most striking roles. She never won an Oscar*

ABOVE *Ethel Barrymore won the Best Supporting Actress award for her role of the poverty-stricken mother of Cary Grant (both illustrated) in* None But The Lonely Heart. *Grant, in one of his rare dramatic parts, received an Oscar nomination*

Supporting Actor categories. (He won the latter.) The line between the two awards was still rather blurred. For example, Paulette Goddard had been nominated in 1943 as a supporting player in **So Proudly We Hail** in which she had received top billing with Claudette Colbert. Anyway, Fitzgerald deserved his Oscar for bringing both spice and pathos into his old priest, thus making a major contribution to the success of the film.

Part of the achievement of **Going My Way** was that, although the story took place in and around a Roman Catholic church, it managed to avoid any sermonizing and over-sentimentality (although it came close to it a number of times). But it was played and directed with such a sure touch that even an atheist was hard put to it to resist. All in all, the film garnered seven Academy Awards. Besides Best Picture, Actor, Supporting Actor, Director and Song, it won Best Screenplay (Frank Butler and Frank Cavett) and Best Original Story (McCarey).

Only one person seemed disgruntled at the runaway success of **Going My Way**, and that was producer Darryl F. Zanuck. He complained that **Wilson**, his long, expensive, prestige production was overlooked because it

didn't do well at the box-office. So piqued was he, that he referred to his disappointment three years later when accepting the Best Picture award for **Gentleman's Agreement**. Mind you, Zanuck's rather stodgy biopic did win five Oscars (Original Screenplay, Color Cinematography, Color Art Direction and Interior Decoration, Sound Recording and Editing). In addition, Zanuck, the top dog at 20th Century-Fox, was the recipient of the Irving Thalberg Award, presented to him by Norma Shearer, Thalberg's widow, an honor that had not been previously accorded to other winners.

Ethel Barrymore won the Best Supporting Actress award for her role as Cary Grant's mother in **None But The Lonely Heart**, her first film for 11 years after a long sojourn on Broadway. Her older brother Lionel had won an Oscar in 1931, thus making them the first brother and sister to win the award. (Younger brother John Barrymore was never even nominated for one.) Other sibling winners have been rival sisters Joan Fontaine and Olivia de Havilland, and Shirley MacLaine and Warren Beatty, the latter, however, gaining his as the director of **Reds** (1981). Margaret O'Brien took the prize for the most outstanding child actress of 1944. She had appeared in five films that year, making her biggest impression in Vincente Minnelli's beautifully made and scandalously overlooked musical, **Meet Me In St Louis**. The M.C.s at the ceremony, the first to be broadcast in its entirety over a national radio network, were director John Cromwell and comedian Bob Hope, the latter receiving a special award "for his many services to the Academy" and a life membership of the august institution. Danny Kaye and the Andrews Sisters entertained the audience at what, in the event, was the last of the wartime Oscar nights.

WINNERS 1944

Nominations Announced: February 5, 1945
Awards Ceremony: March 15, 1945
Grauman's Chinese Theatre

Best Picture
GOING MY WAY, Paramount

Actor
BING CROSBY in *Going My Way*

Actress
INGRID BERGMAN in *Gaslight*, MGM

Supporting Actor
BARRY FITZGERALD in *Going My Way*

Supporting Actress
ETHEL BARRYMORE in *None But The Lonely Heart*, RKO Radio

Directing
LEO McCAREY for *Going My Way*

Writing
(Original Story)
GOING MY WAY: LEO McCAREY
(Original Screenplay)
WILSON, 20th Century-Fox: LAMAR TROTTI
(Screenplay)
GOING MY WAY: FRANK BUTLER and FRANK CAVETT

Cinematography
(Black-and-White)
LAURA, 20th Century-Fox: JOSEPH LaSHELLE
(Color)
WILSON: LEON SHAMROY

Interior Decoration
(Black-and-White)
GASLIGHT: CEDRIC GIBBONS and WILLIAM FERRARI
Interior Decoration: EDWIN B. WILLIS and PAUL HULDSCHINSKY
(Color)
WILSON, 20th Century-Fox: WIARD IHNEN
Interior Decoration: THOMAS LITTLE

Sound Recording
WILSON: E.H. HANSEN

Film Editing
WILSON: BARBARA McLEAN

Music
(Scoring of a Dramatic or Comedy Picture)
SINCE YOU WENT AWAY, Selznick/UA: MAX STEINER
(Scoring of a Musical Picture)
COVER GIRL, Columbia: CARMEN DRAGON and MORRIS STOLOFF
(Best Song)
SWINGING ON A STAR from *Going My Way*
Music: JAMES VAN HEUSEN
Lyrics: JOHNNY BURKE

Short Subjects
(Cartoons)
MOUSE TROUBLE, MGM: FREDERICK C. QUIMBY, Producer
(One-reel)
WHO'S WHO IN ANIMAL LAND, Paramount. (Speaking of Animals): JERRY FAIRBANKS, Producer
(Two-reel)
I WON'T PLAY, Warner Bros. (Featurette): GORDON HOLLINGSHEAD, Producer

Documentary
(Short Subjects)
WITH THE MARINES AT TARAWA, US Marine Corps
(Features)
THE FIGHTING LADY, 20th Century-Fox/US Navy

Special Effects
THIRTY SECONDS OVER TOKYO, MGM
Photographic: A. ARNOLD GILLESPIE, DONALD JAHRAUS and WARREN NEWCOMBE
Sound: DOUGLAS SHEARER

Special Awards
BOB HOPE for his many services to the Academy, a Life Membership in the Academy of Motion Picture Arts and Sciences.

Irving G. Thalberg Memorial Award
DARRYL F. ZANUCK

1945

THE WAR WAS over. On the night of March 4, 1946, searchlights played once again outside Grauman's Chinese Theater as fans fought to catch a glimpse of their favorite stars emerging in glittering evening dress from their limousines. Glamor had returned to the Oscar ceremony after the grim war years. Absent from the star-studded occasion was Joan Crawford, nominated for **Mildred Pierce**, who was confined to her bed with influenza and a fever. Her bevy of beautiful rivals, however, were all there, dressed to the nines: Ingrid Bergman (**The Bells of St Mary's**), Greer Garson (**The Valley Of Decision**), Jennifer Jones (**Love Letters**) and Gene Tierney (**Leave Her To Heaven**).

Crawford repined at home listening to the presentations on the radio. No sooner had Charles Boyer announced her the winner than cars had begun racing to her Brentwood mansion. Champagne was uncorked, and Michael Curtiz, the director of the picture, handed her the statuette. It seemed to act as an instant cure, for she sat up in bed smiling for photographers while clutching her trophy. "It was the greatest moment of my life," she later recalled.

For the 41-year-old actress, it couldn't have come at a better time. Joan Crawford had been a major star for over 20 years, had influenced women's fashions, and monopolized the fan magazines. But her vehicles during the war years were failures and she had come to be regarded in the industry as 'box-office poison'. After 17

BELOW *After a lull in her career, Joan Crawford (left), star of the 20s and 30s, clawed her way back up to the top with her Best Actress-winning portrayal of* Mildred Pierce, *a woman who sacrifices happiness to give her spoiled-brat daughter Ann Blyth (right) the luxuries she herself never had*

years with MGM, she asked them to release her from her contract (which they did gladly) and went home to wait for the right script to be offered to her. **Mildred Pierce**, the James M. Cain story of a self-sacrificing mother was a Warner Bros. property, and the studio first offered it to Bette Davis. When Davis turned it down, Warners wanted Ann Sheridan and Curtiz opted for Barbara Stanwyck, who had made a splash the previous year in **Double Indemnity**, another Cain opus. But producer Jerry Wald decided to gamble on the 'poisonous' Crawford.

On hearing of Wald's decision, Curtiz was said to have shouted, "Her and her shoulder pads!" Conventional clothes had never suited the star's figure with its wide shoulders, long waist and short legs, so MGM designer Adrian had come up with the idea of making her shoulders even broader. The rest of her appearance was also overstated, with enormous eyes and a large mouth wide-

ned into 'The Crawford Smear'. Curtiz got rid of all this for **Mildred Pierce**. Her make-up was more natural and she wore off-the-peg dresses for her role of the middle-class housewife who indulges her selfish monster of a daughter (Ann Blyth receiving a well-earned Supporting Actress nomination). Even Crawford's usual all-stops-out acting was toned down, giving a conviction to the rather far-fetched melodrama which contained murder, adultery, blackmail, mother love, tragedy and some comedy. The latter was provided by Eve Arden (also nominated) whose wisecracks included the line, "I'm awfully tired of men talking to me man to man."

The publicity line for the movie was "Don't tell what Mildred Pierce did!" What she did was leave her first husband (Bruce Bennett), become a waitress, work her way up to being a wealthy restaurant owner with the help of a millionaire (Zachary Scott), and use another man (Jack

LEFT *Driven by desperation for a drink Ray Milland (left), as alcoholic Don Birnam in Billy Wilder's four-Oscar winning* The Lost Weekend, *tries unsuccessfully to steal from two strangers in a New York bar. The location shooting, rare in those days, added to the picture's realistic impact*
BELOW *An unshaven Ray Milland, Best Actor winner, sees a bat in his bedroom while suffering delirium tremens in* The Lost Weekend. *Playing an alcoholic always seemed to guarantee at least an Oscar nomination – witness James Mason in* A Star Is Born *(1954), Bing Crosby in* The Country Girl *(1954), Susan Hayward in* I'll Cry Tomorrow *(1955) and Jack Lemmon in* Days Of Wine And Roses *(1963)*

Jackson's powerful novel, "I had to pour myself a double Scotch. It was a fine book and a great part."

Forty-year-old Ray Milland had been a handsome, likeable leading man in scores of pictures, mainly at Paramount, since the 1930s, but never revealed much depth. "I knew that I had the best part I would ever get. I gave it everything I had." He was right. It was the finest moment of his career, well rewarded by a Best Actor Oscar. Nothing quite like it ever came his way again, although he continued to work until his death in March 1986 and was known to a younger generation

Carson). What Joan Crawford did was get back to the top of the heap, where she remained, more or less, until her death in 1977.

When the commitment of Broadway actor José Ferrer prevented him from making his screen debut as the alcoholic in **The Lost Weekend**, producer-director Billy Wilder asked Ray Milland if he would be willing to risk damaging his career by taking on the downbeat role. "After I read it," Milland said, commenting on Charles R.

as Ryan O'Neal's father in both **Love Story** (1970) and **Oliver's Story** (1978).

In order to research the role in **The Lost Weekend**, Milland spent weeks studying drunks in bars and on the Bowery. "It got so I could tell an alcoholic from a drunk, a dipso from a sot. I watched the way alcoholics walked and talked, the way they screwed up their faces, hunched their shoulders, bent their heads." The research paid off in the reality brought by Milland to his portrayal of a writer who

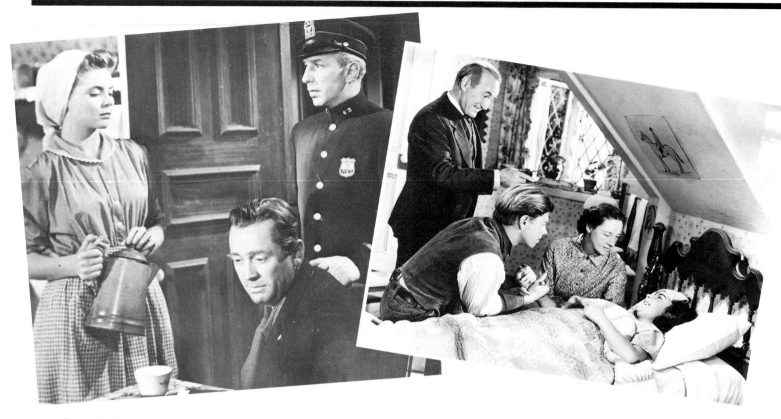

ABOVE *Dorothy McGuire (left) attempts to sober up husband James Dunn (seated), Best Supporting Actor, who has been brought home drunk by kindly cop Lloyd Nolan (right) in Elia Kazan's debut movie,* A Tree Grows In Brooklyn

ABOVE RIGHT *Father Donald Crisp (standing left), mother Anne Revere (Best Supporting Actress, second right), horse-mad daughter, twelve-year-old Elizabeth Taylor (in bed) and stable lad Mickey Rooney (seated left) in MGM's hit children's classic* National Velvet

hocks his typewriter, begs, borrows and steals to get a drink. The actor became so associated with the role that for many years he could never order a drink in public without being kidded.

The Lost Weekend also walked off with the Best Picture, Best Director (Wilder), and Best Screenplay (Wilder and Charles Brackett) awards. In its unflinching view of five days in the life of an alcoholic, it became the first film to treat the subject with any seriousness, and also proved that audiences were prepared to see movies that dealt with everyday social problems. Its success opened up the way for other films on drink problems, drug addiction and racial hatred. The Academy recognized this by honoring the picture whose rivals, though expert, were all at one remove from reality – the MGM musical **Anchors Aweigh** (for which dancer Gene Kelly received an acting nomination), **The Bells Of St Mary's** (Bing Crosby nominated), **Mildred Pierce**, and Alfred Hitchcock's psychodramatic thriller **Spellbound**. In the following few years, the top prize would go to films that dealt with social issues.

Ironically, **The Lost Weekend** was very nearly a lost film. When it was first shown at previews, audiences reacted negatively. Perhaps they were not expecting such strong stuff from Paramount, a studio not noted at the time for dramatic pictures, nor from such hitherto lightweight performers as Ray Milland or Jane Wyman, who played the man's long-suffering girlfriend. After the initial reactions, studio executive Henry Ginsberg said, "We all make a bad one now and then," and postponed the film's release. However, after some private screenings, its reputation grew by word of mouth, and it was released, becoming one of the season's top money-spinners amongst a plethora of musicals.

Billy Wilder chose to approach the story as realistically as possible, filming it on location mainly around New York's Third Avenue and Bellevue Hospital. He also attempted to reproduce the terror felt by drinkers suffering from delirium tremens. In one scene, the haggard, unshaven Milland sees a bat swooping down on a mouse in his bedroom, and there is an extraordinary close-up of his right eyeball. The one thing that didn't ring true was the rather tacked-on happy ending, a betrayal of what had gone before.

Future double Oscar-winning director Elia Kazan's first film, **A Tree Grows In Brooklyn**, a sensitive study of urban poverty, gained a Best Supporting Actor award for James Dunn (although he was one of the leads) as the goodhearted but drunken father of Peggy Ann Garner, herself given a Special Award as the outstanding child actress of 1945. Anne Revere won her Best Supporting Oscar as Elizabeth Taylor's understanding mother in **National Velvet**. Bob Hope and James Stewart were the cheerful M.C.s on the night the Academy Award ceremony put the war years behind it. The appropriate Oscar-winning song was 'It Might As Well Be Spring' by Richard Rodgers and Oscar Hammerstein II from **State Fair**.

WINNERS 1945

Nominations Announced: January 28, 1946
Awards Ceremony: March 7, 1946
Grauman's Chinese Theatre

Best Picture
THE LOST WEEKEND, Paramount

Actor
RAY MILLAND in *The Lost Weekend*

Actress
JOAN CRAWFORD in *Mildred Pierce*, Warner Bros.

Supporting Actor
JAMES DUNN in *A Tree Grows In Brooklyn*, 20th Century-Fox

Supporting Actress
ANNE REVERE in *National Velvet*, MGM

Directing
BILLY WILDER for *The Lost Weekend*

Writing
(Original Story)
THE HOUSE ON 92ND STREET, 20th Century-Fox:
CHARLES G. BOOTH
(Original Screenplay)
MARIE-LOUISE, Praesens (Swiss): RICHARD
SCHWEIZER
(Screenplay)
THE LOST WEEKEND: CHARLES BRACKETT and BILLY
WILDER

Cinematography
(Black-and-White)
THE PICTURE OF DORIAN GRAY, MGM: HARRY
STRADLING
(Color)
LEAVE HER TO HEAVEN, 20th Century-Fox: LEON
SHAMROY

Interior Decoration
(Black-and-White)
BLOOD ON THE SUN, Cagney/UA: WIARD IHNEN
Interior Decoration: A. ROLAND FIELDS
(Color)
FRENCHMAN'S CREEK, Paramount: HANS DREIER and
ERNST FEGTE
Interior Decoration: SAM COMER

Sound Recording
THE BELLS OF ST MARY'S, Rainbow/RKO Radio:
STEPHEN DUNN

Film Editing
NATIONAL VELVET: ROBERT J. KERN

Music
(Scoring of a Dramatic or Comedy Picture)
SPELLBOUND, Selznick/UA: MIKLOS ROZSA
(Scoring of a Musical Picture)
ANCHORS AWEIGH, MGM: GEORGE STOLL
(Best Song)
IT MIGHT AS WELL BE SPRING from *State Fair*, 20th
Century-Fox
Music: RICHARD RODGERS
Lyrics: OSCAR HAMMERSTEIN II

Short Subjects
(Cartoons)
QUIET PLEASE, MGM. (Tom & Jerry): FREDERICK
QUIMBY, Producer
(One-reel)
STAIRWAY TO LIGHT, MGM. (John Nesbitt Passing
Parade): HERBERT MOULTON, Producer
(Two-reel)
STAR IN THE NIGHT, Warner Bros. (Broadway Brevities):
GORDON HOLLINGSHEAD, Producer

Documentary
(Short Subjects)
HITLER LIVES?, Warner Bros./Library of
Congress/Overseas Motion Picture Bureau/Office of War
Information
(Features)
THE TRUE GLORY, Government of Great Britain and USA

Special Effects
WONDER MAN, Goldwyn/RKO Radio
Photographic: JOHN FULTON
Sound: A.W. JOHNS

Special Awards
WALTER WANGER for his six year service as President of
the Academy of Motion Picture Arts and Sciences. (special
plaque)
PEGGY ANN GARNER, outstanding child actress of 1945.
(miniature statuette)
THE HOUSE I LIVE IN, tolerance short subject, RKO Radio.
Producers: FRANK ROSS and MERVYN LeROY; Director:
MERVYN LeROY; Screenplay: ALBERT MALTZ; Song:
'The House I Live In' – Music: EARL ROBINSON; Lyrics:
LEWIS ALLEN; starring FRANK SINATRA. (statuette)
REPUBLIC STUDIO, DANIEL J. BLOOMBERG and the
REPUBLIC SOUND DEPARTMENT for the building of an
outstanding musical scoring auditorium which provides
optimum conditions and combines all elements of acoustic
and engineering design. (certificates)

Irving G. Thalberg Memorial Award
None

1946

ALTHOUGH IT WAS thought that audiences of 1946 wouldn't want to be reminded of the war, the biggest hit of the year (earning over $11 million on US rentals alone), and the film that swept the board at the nineteenth Oscar night, did just that. **The Best Years Of Our Lives** concentrated on the difficulties faced by thousands of soldiers returning from the war in adjusting to civilian life. Specifically, it followed the lives of three ex-servicemen, each representing a different armed service and social class. The result was a brilliant, moving, revealing portrait of postwar America which was the deserved winner of no less than seven Academy Awards. It became *the* returning

vet movie and an influence on a much later Oscar winner, **The Deer Hunter** (1978), which dealt with the aftermath of the Vietnam war and its similar attendant problems.

During the war, producer Samuel Goldwyn made mainly escapist pictures, but a *Time* Magazine story of returning soldiers gave him an idea for a film, which Robert E. Sherwood turned into a screenplay. The film's director, William Wyler, whose 1942 award-winning **Mrs Miniver** told of British courage on the home front during the war, had himself just returned to civilian life with the rank of lieutenant colonel and an Air Medal. He had also lost the hearing in one ear during combat. Wyler, with a splendid use of deep-focus photography (**Citizen Kane**'s Gregg Toland was the cinematographer), and intricate shots, expertly linked the three lives to their environment.

The film followed Fredric March, a bank manager returning to his loving wife (top-billed Myrna Loy) only to find his children (Teresa Wright and Michael Hall) have

BELOW *Harold Russell (foreground), Dana Andrews (center), and Fredric March (right) as three war-weary servicemen winging their way home after World War II in Samuel Goldwyn's seven-Oscar winner,* The Best Years Of Our Lives. *It won in all major categories in which it was nominated*

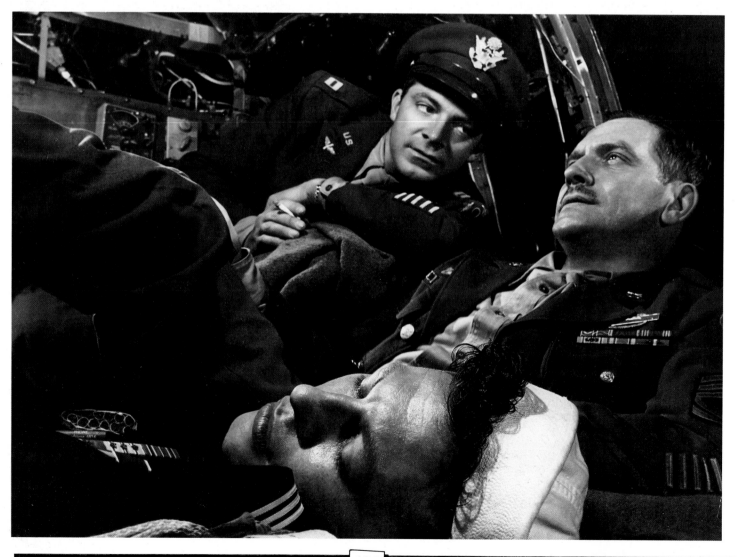

Harold Russell (foreground), Dana Andrews (center), and Fredric March (right) as three war-weary servicemen winging their way home after World War II in Samuel Goldwyn's seven-Oscar winner, The Best Years Of Our Lives. *It won in all major categories in which it was nominated*

grown up in his absence, and his job lacks the appeal it once had. Dana Andrews, an airforce captain, arrives back to a shabby home to find that his wife (Virginia Mayo) has been unfaithful. Sailor Harold Russell has to face the reactions of his family and fiancée (Cathy O'Donnell) when they see he has lost both his hands and has hooks in their place. In a classic sequence, the three men fly back into their home town pointing out familiar landmarks, while Hugo Friedhofer's effective score underlines their emotions. Always poignant, never maudlin, the picture gained from the magnificent performances of the cast. Particularly memorable was Russell, who had actually lost his hands in war and used his hooks with great dexterity. The scene where embarrassment causes him to drop a glass is painfully observed.

"To me characterization is the whole fun of acting," wrote Fredric March. "Every part is a character part." March was 49 years old and no longer a handsome leading man when he took on the role of the oldest and weal-thiest of the three servicemen, a true character part. In **The Best Years Of Our Lives**, his performance ranges from confused veteran to beloved father and husband, sturdy when defending the ideals he fought in the war to preserve, and wonderfully liberated on a drunken binge. It was truly one of his most distinguished portrayals in a long and distinguished career.

Twenty-one-year-old Cathy O'Donnell, who made her screen debut in the role of the amputee's sympathetic sweetheart, accepted the Best Actor award for March who was appearing on Broadway at the time. He had won the same recognition for **Dr Jekyll And Mr Hyde** 14 years previously. Non-professional Harold Russell went up to the stage to receive two Oscars for the same role. One as Best Supporting Actor, and the other "for bringing hope and courage to his fellow veterans through his appearance in **The Best Years Of Our Lives**." He handled the statuette with the same manipulative skill he had displayed in the movie. A student at Boston University before the war, Russell returned to his studies, but in 1949 he wrote his autobiography, **Victory In My Hands**. His only other film has been **Inside Moves** (1981).

Samuel Goldwyn was there to receive the Best Picture Oscar for the film, remarkably – in view of his wonderful record – the only production of his ever to receive the top award. In his acceptance speech in which he mentioned the entire cast of the picture, he mistakenly referred to Hoagy Carmichael, who played Russell's piano-playing uncle, as Hugo Carmichael. Goldwyn also received the Irving Thalberg Memorial Award. Making up the tally of Academy Awards **The Best Years Of Our Lives** gained, were those for Best Director, Screenplay, Music Score and Editing (Daniel Mandell).

Hoagy Carmichael joined Dinah Shore and Dick Haymes in singing the nominated songs including the

RIGHT Olivia de Havilland (illustrated with Griff Barnett) in an early scene from Paramount's successful soap opera, To Each His Own. *It was the first of the star's two Best Actress Oscars out of five nominations, in contrast to her sister Joan Fontaine's one Oscar and two nominations*
BELOW John Payne and two nurses try to restrain dipsomaniac Anne Baxter, Best Supporting Actress, in a dramatic moment from The Razor's Edge, 20th Century-Fox's *version of Somerset Maugham's novel. Clifton Webb as the snobbish Elliott Templeton was nominated for Best Supporting Actor*

winner, 'On The Atchison, Topeka And The Santa Fe' by Johnny Mercer and Harry Warren from the Judy Garland musical **The Harvey Girls**. The ticket-paying public at the huge Shrine Auditorium were also able to see Anne Baxter accept her Best Supporting Actress trophy for her role as the tragic young wife who takes to drink after the death of her husband and child in the starry **The Razor's Edge**, and the ageing (18-year-old) Shirley Temple present 12-year-old Claude Jarman Jr of **The Yearling** with a miniature Oscar as the finest child actor of the year. Laurence Olivier was also honored "for his outstanding achievement as actor, producer and director in bringing **Henry V** to the screen." But what the audience relished above all was the dramatic incident in connection with the Best Actress award.

Olivia de Havilland received the Oscar from Ray Milland for her tear-stained performance in **To Each His Own**. As she came down from the stage, her sister Joan Fontaine, who had beaten her for the award in 1941, held out her hand to congratulate the winner this time, but De Havilland merely hurried away muttering, "I don't know why she does that when she knows how I feel." Fontaine stood for a moment in embarrassed confusion, and then walked out. The celebrated sisterly feud had gone public and the newspapers had a field day. Fontaine was absent from the ceremony when her sister won her second Oscar in 1949 for **The Heiress**.

Generally sweet-seeming on screen, Olivia de Havil-

land was much tougher than she looked. In 1942, she vociferously complained about her roles at Warners, and was given a six-month suspension. At the end of her seven-year contract with them, they demanded an extra six months work from her in place of the time of suspension. She sued the studio, an action which cost her $13,000 and three years without work, but she won her case. During her court battles, producer and screenwriter Charles Brackett asked her to star in **To Each His Own** at Paramount when she was legally free to do so. Despite strong competition from English actress Celia Johnson (**Brief Encounter**), Jane Wyman (**The Yearling**), Jennifer Jones (**Duel In The Sun**), and Rosalind Russell (**Sister Kenny**), the favorite to win, De Havilland celebrated her comeback with the coveted statuette.

The picture was in the ancient Hollywood tradition of mother-love weepies with a lengthy, meaty role for Olivia

de Havilland at its center, ageing 27 years through two world wars. She played a lively young girl who has a baby before she can wed her air ace fiance who is killed in World War I. In order to cover up the scandal, she has the child adopted. Years later in a blitzed London, she meets her son, a pilot like his father. He doesn't know who she is, but she recognizes him. So she should, as the same actor, John Lund, played both father and son. It was the star's expertly deployed emoting that gave the movie its modicum of credibility.

American movies didn't have the field all to themselves; six English films, **Henry V, Brief Encounter, Perfect Strangers** (US title: **Vacation From Marriage**), **The Seventh Veil, Caesar And Cleopatra** and **Blithe Spirit**, won eleven nominations among them, and won three Oscars, an indication that Hollywood's almost total monopoly was slowly being broken.

WINNERS 1946

Nominations Announced: February 10, 1947
Awards Ceremony: March 13, 1947
Shrine Auditorium

Best Picture
THE BEST YEARS OF OUR LIVES, Goldwyn/RKO Radio

Actor
FREDRIC MARCH in *The Best Years Of Our Lives*

Actress
OLIVIA DE HAVILLAND in *To Each His Own*, Paramount

Supporting Actor
HAROLD RUSSELL in *The Best Years Of Our Lives*

Supporting Actress
ANNE BAXTER in *The Razor's Edge*, 20th Century-Fox

Directing
WILLIAM WYLER for *The Best Years Of Our Lives*

Writing
(Original Story)
VACATION FROM MARRIAGE, London/MGM (British):
CLEMENCE DANE
(Original Screenplay)
THE SEVENTH VEIL, Rank/Universal (British): MURIEL
BOX and SYDNEY BOX
(Screenplay)
THE BEST YEARS OF OUR LIVES: ROBERT E.
SHERWOOD

Cinematography
(Black-and-White)
ANNA AND THE KING OF SIAM, 20th Century-Fox:
ARTHUR MILLER
(Color)
THE YEARLING, MGM: CHARLES ROSHER, LEONARD
SMITH and ARTHUR ARLING

Interior Decoration
ANNA AND THE KING OF SIAM: LYLE WHEELER and
WILLIAM DARLING
Interior Decoration: THOMAS LITTLE and FRANK E.
HUGHES
(Color)
THE YEARLING: CEDRIC GIBBONS and PAUL
GROESSE
Interior Decoration: EDWIN B. WILLIS

Sound Recording
THE JOLSON STORY, Columbia: JOHN LIVADARY

Film Editing
THE BEST YEAR OF OUR LIVES: DANIEL MANDELL

Music
(Scoring of a Dramatic or Comedy Picture)
THE BEST YEARS OF OUR LIVES: HUGO FRIEDHOFER
(Scoring of a Musical Picture)
THE JOLSON STORY: MORRIS STOLOFF
(Best Song)
ON THE ATCHISON, TOPEKA AND THE SANTA FE from
The Harvey Girls, MGM
Music: HARRY WARREN
Lyrics: JOHNNY MERCER

Short Subjects
(Cartoons)
THE CAT CONCERTO, MGM. (Tom & Jerry): FREDERICK
QUIMBY, Producer
(One-reel)
FACING YOUR DANGER, Warner Bros. (Sports Parade):
GORDON HOLLINGSHEAD, Producer
(Two-reel)
A BOY AND HIS DOG, Warner Bros. (Featurettes):
GORDON HOLLINGSHEAD, Producer

Documentary
(Short Subjects)
SEEDS OF DESTINY, US War Department
(Features)
None

Special Effects
BLITHE SPIRIT, Rank/UA (British)
Visual: THOMAS HOWARD
Audible: No credit

Special Awards
LAURENCE OLIVIER for his outstanding achievement as
actor, producer and director in bringing *Henry V* to the
screen. (statuette)
HAROLD RUSSELL for bringing hope and courage to his
fellow veterans through his appearance in *The Best Years Of
Our Lives*. (statuette)
ERNST LUBITSCH for his distinguished contributions to
the art of the motion picture. (scroll)
CLAUDE JARMAN Jr, outstanding child actor of 1946.
(miniature statuette)

Irving G. Thalberg Memorial Award
SAMUEL GOLDWYN

1947

IT WAS GENERALLY considered that Rosalind Russell should have been the 1946 winner of the Best Actress award for her brave and moving portrayal of **Sister Kenny** whose fight to help polio victims inspired the film. Russell was nominated again in 1947 for her long, dramatic portrayal of the matricidally-minded Lavinia in the 173-minute film adaptation of Eugene O'Neill's play **Mourning Becomes Electra**. All the commentators and those in the know seemed to feel that her victory was a foregone conclusion, and that a celebration party had been prepared in her honor.

Miss Russell's nearest rival was Dorothy McGuire as a woman finding a streak of anti-Semitism in herself she never realized existed, in **Gentleman's Agreement**. Trailing in the betting were Joan Crawford in another gutsy role, that of a factory girl in search of riches in **Possessed**, and Susan Hayward, receiving the first of five nomina-

tions, in **Smash-Up—The Story Of A Woman** in which she was a nightclub singer who hits the bottle. The rank outsider was Loretta Young in **The Farmer's Daughter**. Each of the roles, but for the last named, offered the stars plenty of scope to display their histrionic talents, but it was Russell, nominated for a third time and a star since the 1930s, who seemed destined to gratefully clutch the statuette. But when Fredric March opened the envelope and read out the name of Loretta Young, an audible gasp went up from the huge audience that packed the Shrine Auditorium that evening on March 20, 1948.

Nobody was more surprised than Miss Young herself as she made her way up to the stage in her long, cumbersome emerald-green taffeta evening gown. Young, who happened to have been one of Russell's closest friends, whispered to her husband during a photo-call afterwards, "What about Roz? What'll I say to Roz?" In fact, when the two women met later at the Mocambo nightclub, they hugged each other warmly, in contrast to the previous year's chilly confrontation between sisters Olivia de Havilland and Joan Fontaine. All Young could say on receiving the Oscar was, "At long last."

It was an understandable comment from an actress

BELOW *Surprise Oscar winner Loretta Young (standing) asks penetrating questions of a politician in* The Farmer's Daughter. *Charles Bickford (seated on her right) received the second of his three nominations for Best Supporting Actor*

ABOVE *A Shakespearean actor (Best Actor winner Ronald Colman) begins to forget he is not on stage playing Othello, while a girl he has picked up (a slimline Shelley Winters in her first decent role) eyes him suspiciously in George Cukor's* A Double Life

who had been in the business for as long as she had. Actually, Loretta Young made her first screen appearance at the age of four, and had 84 films behind her by 1947. Her dependability in whatever role she undertook over the years earned her the label of 'Hollywood's beautiful hack'. She had impressed in a number of good films such as Frank Capra's **Platinum Blonde** (1931), in which she acted Jean Harlow off the screen; as the orphan girl in the curious **Zoo In Budapest** (1933); playing Spencer Tracy's shantytown sweetheart in Frank Borzage's **Man's Castle** (1933); and as the wife of Nazi Orson Welles in **The Stranger** (1946), but none of those performances came near to being considered for an Academy Award.

The Farmer's Daughter had originally been taken up by David O. Selznick for his contract star Ingrid Bergman. It seemed a natural role for her, but she felt that playing a Swedish-speaking farm girl wouldn't be enough of a challenge. (She rarely played a Swede in her whole career.) When Dore Schary left Selznick to become executive vice-president in charge of product at RKO, he took the property with him and offered it to Loretta Young. Ably directed by H. C. Potter, it told of how a headstrong Minnesota farm girl becomes maid to a political matriarch (Ethel Barrymore); the girl's homespun ideas earn her a seat in Congress in a contest against the man she loves (Joseph Cotten). In this implausible but amusing picture Young, in a blonde wig and Swedish accent, was charming and lovely. Strangely enough, the Oscar did very little

for her career which petered out in the early 1950s, only to be revived on television.

Ronald Colman was also at the tail end of his film career when he won his only Oscar for **A Double Life**. He was to appear in only three further films (the last two in cameos) before dying of a lung infection in 1958 at the age of 67. Once asked by a reporter if it was true that he had received a Cadillac limousine for his day's work in **Around The World In 80 Days** (1956), he replied, "No, for a lifetime's work." This might very well have applied also to the attractive English-born star's belated Academy Award.

Colman, one of Hollywood's most popular romantic stars, had been in films since 1918. His mellifluous voice carried him easily from the silent era into the talkies. He had already chosen his roles with great care, never allowing himself to become over-exposed. Before taking on the challenge of Ruth Gordon and Garson Kanin's script for **A Double Life**, Colman had made only two films in the preceding five years. The picture offered him his best dramatic role for some time as a Shakespearean actor who begins to identify too closely with the character of Othello which he has been playing for over two years. He

strangles a waitress (Shelley Winters) who arouses his jealousy, and almost kills his wife (Signe Hasso), playing opposite him as Desdemona, because he suspects she is having an affair with his press-agent (Edmond O'Brien).

Colman had made something of a reputation in playing double roles over the years, a few examples being **The Masquerader** (1933), **A Tale Of Two Cities** (1935), and **The Prisoner Of Zenda**. In more of a dual personality than a dual role in **A Double Life**, he gave a mesmeric study of a man possessed. Seldom off the screen, he also had the opportunity to deliver – rather well – several chunks from the Shakespeare play, filmed largely at New York's old Empire Theater.

Colman's rivals for the Best Actor prize were William Powell in **Life With Father**, Michael Redgrave in **Mourning Becomes Electra**, John Garfield giving an expressive bullish performance as the boxer in **Body And Soul**, and Gregory Peck (his third nomination) in **Gentleman's Agreement**. It was no surprise to anyone that the latter movie, nominated in six of the top categories, should have won the Best Picture and Best Director (Elia Kazan) awards. Among the cast, although Peck lost out to Colman, and Dorothy McGuire to Loretta Young, Celeste Holm (in her third film after smallish parts in two Fox musicals) was named Best Supporting Actress in the role of the chic but lonely fashion writer, beating Anne Revere, nominated for the same movie.

Based on Laura Z. Hobson's bestseller, it told of how

TOP *John Garfield (left), Gregory Peck (center), Dorothy McGuire (standing) and Best Supporting Actress Celeste Holm (right) in one of the few carefree moments from Best Picture* Gentleman's Agreement, *Best Director Elia Kazan's exposé of anti-Semitism in America*
ABOVE *Best Supporting Actor Edmund Gwenn (right) attempts to prove to a sceptical nine-year-old Natalie Wood (center) and her father John Payne (left) that he really is Father Christmas in 20th Century-Fox's whimsical* Miracle On 34th Street. *George Seaton and Valentine Davies each gathered an Oscar for their screenplay and story respectively*

ABOVE *Oscar winners Alfred Junge (art director) and Jack Cardiff (cinematographer) breathtakingly created the atmosphere of a convent high up in the Himalayas (actually shot in a studio) where a group of British nuns struggle against the desire for worldly things in Michael Powell's* Black Narcissus

journalist Peck, commissioned to write a series of articles on anti-Semitism, passes himself off as a Jew for six weeks to feel what it is like from the inside. He finds both covert and overt prejudice everywhere, even from his fiancée (McGuire) who is unhappy about not being able to tell her friends and family that he isn't really Jewish. He sees his Jewish best friend (John Garfield) abused, he is unwelcome at a country club, and his small son (Dean Stockwell) suffers at school. Although the picture was often stiffly didactic and well-meaning (it's a film Kazan himself dislikes), it was one of the first important social message films of the postwar period, had a tremendous impact at the time, and made Americans look into themselves. Curiously enough, the rarely treated subject of

anti-Semitism in the USA was also the theme of Edward Dmytryk's **Crossfire**, another of the year's Best Picture nominees.

Great Expectations, a British production, was also up for the top prize. In fact, 18-year-old English actress Jean Simmons made her way up to the stage four times to collect Oscars for two British films she had appeared in – the above mentioned David Lean version of the Charles Dickens classic, and **Black Narcissus**, each picture receiving awards for Cinematography and Art Direction (black-and-white and color respectively). It was also the first year in which foreign language movies were given an uncontested special award. (It was not until 1956 that they were considered in an Oscar category.) Vittorio De Sica's Italian neo-realist film **Shoeshine** was the first to be so honored for its powerful and touching semi-documentary treatment of poverty in postwar Italy using non-actors and real locations. The Oscar night, at which Dick Powell and Agnes Moorehead presided, showed a healthily widening interest in world cinema.

WINNERS 1947

Nominations Announced: February 15, 1948
Awards Ceremony: March 20, 1948
Shrine Auditorium

Best Picture
GENTLEMAN'S AGREEMENT, 20th Century-Fox

Actor
RONALD COLMAN in *A Double Life*, Kanin/U-I

Actress
LORETTA YOUNG in *The Farmer's Daughter*, RKO Radio

Supporting Actor
EDMUND GWENN in *Miracle On 34th Street*, 20th Century-Fox

Supporting Actress
CELESTE HOLM in *Gentleman's Agreement*

Directing
ELIA KAZAN for *Gentleman's Agreement*

Writing
(Original Story)
MIRACLE ON 34TH STREET: VALENTINE DAVIES
(Original Screenplay)
THE BACHELOR AND THE BOBBY-SOXER, RKO Radio:
SIDNEY SHELDON
(Screenplay)
MIRACLE ON 34TH STREET: GEORGE SEATON

Cinematography
(Black-and-White)
GREAT EXPECTATIONS, Rank-Cineguild/UI (British):
GUY GREEN
(Color)
BLACK NARCISSUS, Rank-Archers/U-I (British): JACK
CARDIFF

Art Direction-Set Decoration
(Prior to 1947 known as Interior Decoration.)
(Black-and-White)
GREAT EXPECTATIONS: JOHN BRYAN
Set Decoration: WILFRED SHINGLETON
(Color)
BLACK NARCISSUS: ALFRED JUNGE
Set Decoration: ALFRED JUNGE

Sound Recording
THE BISHOP'S WIFE, Goldwyn/RKO Radio: GOLDWYN
SOUND DEPARTMENT

Film Editing
BODY AND SOUL, Enterprise/UA: FRANCIS LYON and
ROBERT PARRISH

Music
(Scoring of a Dramatic or Comedy Picture)
A DOUBLE LIFE, Kanin/U-I: MIKLOS ROZSA

(Scoring of a Musical Picture)
MOTHER WORE TIGHTS, 20th Century-Fox: ALFRED
NEWMAN
(Best Song)
ZIP-A-DEE-DOO-DAH from *Song Of The South*,
Disney/RKO Radio
Music: ALLIE WRUBEL
Lyrics: RAY GILBERT

Short Subjects
(Cartoons)
TWEETIE PIE, Warner Bros. (Merrie Melodies): EDWARD
SELZER, Producer
(One-reel)
GOODBYE MISS TURLOCK, MGM. (John Nesbitt Passing
Parade): HERBERT MOULTON, Producer
(Two-reel)
CLIMBING THE MATTERHORN, Monogram. (Color):
IRVING ALLEN, Producer

Documentary
(Short Subjects)
FIRST STEPS, United Nations Division of Films and Visual
Education
(Features)
DESIGN FOR DEATH, RKO Radio: SID ROGELL,
Executive Producer; THERON WARTH and RICHARD O.
FLEISCHER, Producers

Special Effects
GREEN DOLPHIN STREET, MGM
Visual: A. ARNOLD GILLESPIE and WARREN
NEWCOMBE
Audible: DOUGLAS SHEARER and MICHAEL STEINORE

Special Awards
JAMES BASKETTE for his able and heart-warming
characterization of Uncle Remus, friend and storyteller to
the children of the world. (statuette)
BILL AND COO, in which artistry and patience blended in a
novel and entertaining use of the medium of motion
pictures. (plaque)
SHOESHINE – the high quality of this motion picture,
brought to eloquent life in a country scarred by war, is proof
to the world that the creative spirit can triumph over
adversity. (statuette)
COLONEL WILLIAM N. SELIG, ALBERT E. SMITH,
THOMAS ARMAT and GEORGE K. SPOOR – (one of) the
small group of pioneers whose belief in a new medium, and
whose contributions to its development, blazed the trail
along which the motion picture has progressed, in their
lifetime, from obscurity to world-wide acclaim. (statuettes)

Irving G. Thalberg Memorial Award
None

1948

I T WAS IN 1981 that Colin Welland, the screenwriter of **Chariots Of Fire**, brandished his Oscar statuette in the air and cried, "The British are coming!" Yet the British had come to Hollywood before and in force. In 1948 two British productions, Laurence Olivier's splendid version of **Hamlet** and Michael Powell's flamboyant ballet extravaganza **The Red Shoes**, secured a half-dozen Oscars between them. **Hamlet** was not merely the first British but also the first non-American film to receive the industry's Best Picture award.

Another of the year's 'firsts' involved the Huston family, son John and father Walter. The director John Huston carried off the Best Director and Best Screenplay awards for his gripping account of three men destroyed by gold fever, **The Treasure Of The Sierra Madre**, and the veteran Walter Huston was named Best Supporting Actor for his performance as a grizzled old prospector in the same film. As one observer enviously commented, "The Hustons are going home in a truck tonight." It was also the first time in the ceremony's history that the field of Costume Design was included (for color design, **Joan Of Arc**; for black-and-white, **Hamlet**); and, as in the past, charmingly, a special miniaturized Oscar – or Oscarette – was presented to nine-year-old Ivan Jandl, a non-English-speaking boy from Czechoslovakia who had learned his dialogue for Fred Zinnemann's **The Search** entirely by rote.

The evening's principal upset, however, concerned a couple of films for which the highest tally of Oscars had been forecast by the trade press. **The Snake Pit**, a socially conscious if somewhat dated drama on the theme of insanity (making a heartfelt plea for a kind of shock treatment which today would be regarded as barbaric), and **Johnny Belinda**, a tasteful melodrama centered on the plight of a young deaf-mute, had been nominated for a total of 16 awards – including, in both cases, that of Best Picture. In the event, they managed to win only one apiece, Sound Recording for the former and Best Actress (Jane Wyman) for the latter. It was a situation which would recur frequently in the years to come.

The ceremony itself, though lively enough as a spectacle – with musical interludes by Doris Day, Gordon Macrae, Jane Russell and Jo Stafford among others – proved to be a chaotically cramped affair. The decision to switch its locale to the 950-seat Academy Theater was admirably motivated – the major Hollywood studios, sensitive to charges of having previously brought their influence to bear on the voters, had withdrawn all direct financial support from the event – but it resulted in an undignified scramble for places and sulky resignation of the Academy's President, actor Jean Hersholt.

Said writer Alan Dent of his **Hamlet** adaptation, "One has to choose between making the meaning clear to 20,000,000 cinemagoers and causing 2,000 Shakespearean experts to wince." Perhaps the best measure of Olivier's shadowy, brooding film (it was shot in black-and-white as the director envisaged its visual quality as closer to that of an engraving than a painting) was that, while it may have attracted slightly fewer than twenty million paying customers, it certainly offended far fewer than two thousand experts. Obviously, by condensing a play whose running time is more than four hours to a 2-hour-35-minute film, Olivier was forced to gut the drama of those subtleties and ambiguities which have assured its enduring fascination. It was not, however, 'Hamlet without the Prince'.

The essentials were miraculously preserved, and no less miraculously made cinematic. A major problem of adapting the Bard to film – that it would be unthinkable to cut the best-known soliloquies – was deftly handled by allowing the camera to explore the sinuous, mazelike corridors and battlements of Elsinore while the actors themselves remained motionless. Olivier also emphasized the play's more extrovert features: **Hamlet**, we tend to forget,

BELOW *Dark-haired British classical actor Laurence Olivier, blonded for the role of* Hamlet. *He prefaced the film with a title declaring it 'the tragedy of a man who couldn't make up his mind'. The Academy made up its mind that it was the Best Picture and Olivier was the Best Actor*

ABOVE *Sixty-four-year-old Walter Huston (right) finally won an Oscar (albeit a supporting one), after nearly twenty sterling years in films, in his son John's gold-lust adventure* The Treasure Of The Sierra Madre. *Humphrey Bogart (left), a favorite of the director, was the star*

contains duels and swordfights, a ghost and a poisoned cup, and almost as many corpses cluttering the foreground as in a thick-ear thriller starring Charles Bronson. It is impossible, of course, to make an omelette without breaking a few eggs, or a **Hamlet** without cracking a few eggheads, but the challenge set himself by Olivier was triumphantly realized: to film Shakespeare in a manner both faithful and popular, as popular as the dramatist himself was in his own lifetime.

Much of the film's commercial success, nevertheless, can be attributed to Best Actor Olivier's own performance in the title role. Though no longer in his first youth (he was just 40 when he played the part and therefore virtually twice the age of the character as written by Shakespeare), he was still stunningly handsome; and his blond, charismatic presence was set to advantage by the film's predominantly sombre sets and photography. For American spectators in particular, whose experience of the Bard on

screen had mostly been confined to such homegrown performers as Norma Shearer, Mary Pickford and even James Cagney, he was a revelation. It's worth noting, too, as yet another unusual 'first' of 1948, that no film-maker prior to Olivier had ever directed himself into an Oscar-winning performance.

Olivier was more than ably supported by the youthful Jean Simmons as Ophelia (nominated as Best Supporting Actress), Eileen Herlie, Basil Sydney, and Stanley Holloway as a jocular Gravedigger. William Walton wrote the film's sumptuous musical score.

In the early years of her career, as a pert and brassy chorine, Jane Wyman would often complain that her dialogue amounted to little more than a series of impudent "Oh, yeahs!" directed at her better-known co-performers. Paradoxically, then, it was in a role which called for no spoken dialogue at all that she won her greatest acclaim. Though Oscars had, of course, been awarded to performers in the silent period, no one had ever received one for a silent role in a talking film. In **Johnny Belinda** Wyman played a deaf-mute farm girl who is raped and almost loses custody of her child because of her disability; and even if it represented the kind of bravura role which tends, unfairly, to monopolize the Oscar stakes, only a

cold-hearted spectator could remain unmoved by her affecting portrayal of a forlorn, unloved creature coming to terms with the world for the first time in her existence.

The patent sincerity of Wyman's performance was the result of long, dedicated study. She read extensively on the condition of deafness, worked with deaf-mutes and, on the set, wore plastic ear-plugs in order that her playing remain unaffected by the voices of her co-stars. It's also possible that the performance was lent a poignant edge by the fact that the baby she had been expecting when assigned the part (she was married to a future American President, Ronald Reagan) was born prematurely and lived only a few hours. Refusing to be swayed by the trauma of her loss, and perhaps even influenced by it, Wyman identified with her character to a degree rare in the cinema. It was actually claimed by gossip columnists that her singlemindedness was responsible for the break-up of her marriage to Reagan. "If it comes to a divorce," he was quoted as saying, "I think I'll name 'Johnny Belinda' as co-respondent." Alas, it came to a divorce

soon after, and Reagan married the present First Lady, actress Nancy Davis.

Wyman had already been mentioned before (for **The Yearling**, 1946) and was to be nominated on two further occasions (for **The Blue Veil**, 1951, and **Magnificent Obsession**, 1954), but **Johnny Belinda** was undoubtedly the high-water mark of her career. The film, directed by Jean Negulesco and co-starring Lew Ayres, Charles Bickford and Agnes Moorehead (all of them nominees), was a triumph at the box-office.

Claire Trevor received the Best Supporting Actress award for **Key Largo** and, finally, there was in 1948 a rare instance of an Oscar refused. The producer Walter Wanger was awarded a special Academy Award "for distinguished service to the industry in adding to its moral stature in the world community by his production of the picture **Joan Of Arc**". Incensed by the fact that **Joan Of Arc** had not been nominated through the customary channels, however, Wanger took the unusual step of declining the award altogether.

BELOW *Best Actress winner Jane Wyman (center), as deaf-mute* Johnny Belinda, *intently studies the lips of Charles Bickford speaking to Agnes Moorehead. Both Bickford and Moorehead were nominated for supporting Oscars*

WINNERS 1948

Nominations Announced: February 10, 1949
Awards Ceremony: March 24, 1949
Academy Award Theatre

Best Picture
HAMLET, Rank-Two Cities, U-I (British)

Actor
LAURENCE OLIVIER in *Hamlet*

Actress
JANE WYMAN in *Johnny Belinda*, Warner Bros.

Supporting Actor
WALTER HUSTON in the *Treasure Of The Sierra Madre*,
Warner Bros.

Supporting Actress
CLAIRE TREVOR in *Key Largo*, Warner Bros.

Directing
JOHN HUSTON for the *Treasure Of The Sierra Madre*

Writing
(Motion Picture Story)
THE SEARCH, Praesens Films, MGM (Swiss): RICHARD
SCHWEIZER and DAVID WECHSLER
(Screenplay)
THE TREASURE OF THE SIERRA MADRE: JOHN HUSTON

Cinematography
(Black-and-White)
THE NAKED CITY, Hellinger, U-I: WILLIAM DANIELS
(Color)
JOAN OF ARC, Sierra Pictures, RKO Radio: JOSEPH
VALENTINE, WILLIAM V. SKALL and WINTON HOCH

Art Direction-Set Decoration
(Black-and-White)
HAMLET: ROGER K. FURSE
Set Decoration: CARMEN DILLON
(Color)
THE RED SHOES, Rank-Archers-Eagle-Lion (British):
HEIN HECKROTH
Set Decoration: ARTHUR LAWSON

Sound Recording
THE SNAKE PIT, 20th Century-Fox: 20TH
CENTURY-FOX SOUND DEPARTMENT

Film Editing
THE NAKED CITY: PAUL WEATHERWAX

Music
(Scoring of a Dramatic or Comedy Picture)
THE RED SHOES: BRIAN EASDALE
(Scoring of a Musical Picture)
EASTER PARADE, Metro-Goldwyn-Mayer: JOHNNY
GREEN and ROGER EDENS

(Best Song)
BUTTONS AND BOWS from *The Paleface*, Paramount
Music and Lyrics by JAY LIVINGSTONE and RAY EVANS

Costume Design
(New Category)
(Black-and-White)
HAMLET: ROGER K. FURSE
(Color)
JOAN OF ARC: DOROTHY JEAKINS and KARINSKA

Short Subjects
(Cartoons)
THE LITTLE ORPHAN, Metro-Goldwyn-Mayer. (Tom &
Jerry): FRED QUIMBY, Producer
(One-reel)
SYMPHONY OF A CITY, 20th Century-Fox. (Movietone
Specialty): EDMUND H. REEK, Producer
(Two-reel)
SEAL ISLAND, Walt Disney, RKO Radio. (True Life
Adventure Series): WALT DISNEY, Producer

Documentary
(Short Subjects)
TOWARD INDEPENDENCE, U.S. Army
(Features)
THE SECRET LAND, U.S. Navy, MGM: O.O. DULL,
Producer

Special Effects
PORTRAIT OF JENNIE, The Selznick Studio
Visual: PAUL EAGLER, J. McMILLAN JOHNSON,
RUSSELL SHEARMAN and CLARENCE SLIFER
Audible: CHARLES FREEMAN and JAMES G. STEWART

Special Awards
MONSIEUR VINCENT (French) — the most outstanding
foreign language film released in the United States during
1948. (statuette)
IVAN JANDL for the outstanding juvenile performance of
1948 in *The Search*. (miniature statuette)
SID GRAUMAN, master showman, who raised the standard
of exhibition of motion pictures. (statuette)
ADOLPH ZUKOR, a man who has been called the father of
the feature film in America, for his services to the industry
over a period of forty years. (statuette)
WALTER WANGER for distinguished service to the industry
in adding to its moral stature in the world community by his
production of the picture *Joan Of Arc*. (statuette)

Irving G. Thalberg Memorial Award
JERRY WALD

1949

BY CONTRAST WITH the various excitements of the previous year, the 1949 ceremony (actually held on March 23, 1950) turned out to be a somewhat low-key affair. On the credit side, to be sure, the Oscar at last found a wholly suitable venue in Hollywood's 2812-seat Pantages cinema, as a result of which there was no reprise of the confusion at the Academy Theater. The show itself, however, struck its audience as sluggish and undercharged, doubtless because the year had not been a vintage one for the industry and the competition, in consequence, was less than fierce.

Though often given to expressions of public outrage at the Academy's more 'controversial' decisions, the Hollywood community thrives on surprises and reversals, of which 1949 had fewer than its share. What made this situation more serious than in other years was the fact that, after the boom of the immediate postward period, the major studios were beginning to sense the impact of television, and a shot of the old glamor and pizzazz was just what was required. Yet even the Master of Ceremonies, actor Paul Douglas, could not have been described as a top-flight star.

One of the slightly more unusual awards was the tiny statuette presented to Bobby Driscoll, the 12-year-old star of **The Window**, as "the outstanding juvenile actor of 1949". Poor Bobby's subsequent history was a wretched cautionary tale: a has-been at 20, he became a drug addict, was arrested more than once on vagrancy charges and was buried, at the age of 31, in a pauper's grave. More happily, two pillars of Hollywood society, Fred Astaire and the director Cecil B. DeMille (whose Biblical spectacular **Samson And Delilah** had been one of the year's few blockbusting hits), received special Oscars for their respective contributions to the art of the cinema. Finally, it is gratifying to note that the Oscar for Best Foreign Film released in the United States during 1949 was awarded, as is too rarely the case, to one of the medium's *bona fide* classics, Vittorio de Sica's **The Bicycle Thief** (GB: **Bicycle Thieves**), an eloquently affecting account of the desperate search by an unemployed Italian laborer for the bicycle which will guarantee him a job. While paying tribute to de Sica, however, Hollywood

BELOW *Lamberto Maggiorani (right) and Enzo Staiola (left), father and son in Vittorio De Sica's neo-realist classic* The Bicycle Thieves *confront one of the many people they suspect of stealing their bike. The two amateur leads never made another picture*

LEFT *Young Bobby Driscoll, the recipient of a special miniature statuette, was the slum boy who witnesses a murder, but nobody believes him in the tense little thriller* The Window. *Here, he is in mortal danger from Ruth Roman*

©A.M.P.A.S. ®

ABOVE *Here, happily clutching their Oscars, are (left to right): Broderick Crawford, Mercedes McCambridge, Olivia de Havilland, and Dean Jagger. McCambridge won the supporting award for her very first screen role in* All The King's Men *with Crawford, and Jagger was the other supporting winner for his air force officer in* Twelve O'Clock High

pointedly ignored his neo-realist colleague Roberto Rossellini, nominated as one of the scenarists of **Paisan** (which he also directed). In Hollywood's eyes Rossellini had blotted his copybook by conducting an adulterous, and much-publicized, romance with Ingrid Bergman.

The Best Picture Oscar went, as almost universally predicted, to **All The King's Men**, only the third film to have been directed by Robert Rossen. Based on a Pulitzer-Prizewinning novel by the poet Robert Penn Warren, it focused on a populist demagogue in the Deep South, a lawyer named Willie Stark whose initially honest and uncompromising intentions are insidiously corrupted by his election to the Governor's mansion: it takes an assassin's bullet to prevent his ascension to the White House itself. If that plot sounds a trifle familiar, such was the novelist's (and film-maker's) aim. As Welles had done in **Citizen Kane**, Rossen overtly modeled his protagonist on a notorious figure from American public life: the Louisiana politician Huey Long. **All The King's Men** was therefore a delicate project to be tackled by a Hollywood studio in that, though posthumously exposed as unscrupulous and Fascistic, the then recently deceased Long was still revered in many areas of the South.

It was to the credit of Rossen, one of Hollywood's most vocal liberals, that the distinct possibility of a negative backlash in no way influenced his indictment of political chicanery. And this sincerity was matched in the casting department. If Stark and his entourage had been portrayed by familiar Hollywood faces, not only the film's credibility but its authenticity would have been compromised: stars have a chronic tendency to render palatable whatever actions they are called upon to perform on the screen, however dubious. Rossen's decision to cast a relative unknown (Broderick Crawford) in the leading role was fully vindicated: for his performance, Crawford was nominated for Best Actor and won the sole Oscar of his career. The nominated Rossen, however, lost out to Joseph L. Mankiewicz, who was voted Best Director for **A Letter To Three Wives**.

Curiously, as with Bobby Driscoll, Hollywood was later to turn its back on Rossen. Though, when subpoenaed by the House UnAmerican Activities Committee in 1951, the director denied present membership in the Communist Party, he steadfastly refused to testify about past membership and was blacklisted for two years. Then, in 1953, having requested a new hearing, he admitted his past association with the Party and identified by name more

RIGHT *Best Actor winner Broderick Crawford as corrupt Willie Stark lies fatally shot at the end of* All The King's Men, *surrounded by (clockwise) Ralph Dumke, Will Wright, John Ireland, Mercedes McCambridge and Walter Burke*

ABOVE *All seems amiable as Ralph Richardson (head of table) plays host to Aunt Miriam Hopkins and Montgomery Clift, come to court his spinster daughter, Best Actress winner Olivia de Havilland (right) as The Heiress of the title. But Clift is a fortune hunter and heavy father Richardson knows it*

than 50 fellow members. In spite of his reintegration into the industry, however, he chose never to make another film in Hollywood and died in 1966 a bitter, tormented man.

Broderick Crawford's career was not a notably distinguished one as, with only a handful of exceptions, he was invariably cast in dumb-ox roles. As he put it sardonically, "I may not be the world's leading wit, but I don't want to spend the rest of my life playing half a one." That certainly appeared to be his fate: from his debut in 1937 to his portrayal of Willie Stark in **All The King's Men**, he had been routinely cast as thugs or bruisers in scores of indistinguishably forgettable B movies. Yet Rossen – perhaps feeling that more depth of character might be achieved with an actor eager to escape his run-of-the-treadmill past than with a star narcissistically conscious of his image – decided to offer the 6-foot, 210-pound, bulldog-faced Crawford the chance of his lifetime. But even he could not have foreseen that, while admirably conveying Willie Stark's glib, spellbinding mendacity, Crawford would also invest the character with a vulnerability that made him strangely poignant.

It was the actor's finest hour; for though he was gloriously droll as a mobster with unjustified pretensions to social mobility in George Cukor's **Born Yesterday** (1950) and as a down-at-heel confidence man in Federico Fellini's **Il Bidone** (1955), the second post-Oscar half of his career proved to be virtually a mirror image of the first, with such titles as **The Last Posse, New York Confidential, The Fastest Gun Alive** and **Terror In The Wax Museum** jostling for space in his uninspiring filmography. "I expect to wake up and find this is all a dream," he mused after being chosen to play Willie Stark. Perhaps it was.

The Best Actress Oscar was awarded to a very different personality, a self-consciously gracious star who might have been born with an Academy Award, like a silver spoon, in her mouth: Olivia de Havilland. De Havilland, the sister (and rival) of Joan Fontaine, could fairly be described as the Meryl Streep of the 1940s. Having already won an Oscar in 1946 for **To Each His Own**, and been nominated two years later for **The Snake Pit**, she finally bested her sister by carrying off a second statuette for her spine-chilling portrayal of a plain-Jane spinster who comes to the painful realization that her suitor's intentions are more mercenary than romantic in William Wyler's **The Heiress**, a soberly dramatic adaptation of the Henry James novel *Washington Square*. Though a beautiful woman, de Havilland possessed features that were slightly ageless and matronly, enabling her to carry off the masquerade of uncomeliness more plausibly than many actresses; and, like her co-stars Montgomery Clift and Ralph Richardson (nominated as Best Supporting Actor), she was sensitively coached by Wyler, very much an actor's director.

By one of those odd coincidences in which Hollywood's history is so rich, it was also by playing a mousy, unalluring creature, the nameless Mrs de Winter in Hitchcock's **Rebecca**, that Joan Fontaine, physically even more attractive than her sister, achieved one of her greatest screen triumphs.

WINNERS 1949

Nominations Announced: February 14, 1950
Awards Ceremony: March 23, 1950
RKO Pantages Theatre

Best Picture
ALL THE KING'S MEN, Rossen/Columbia

Actor
BRODERICK CRAWFORD in *All The King's Men*

Actress
OLIVIA DE HAVILLAND in *The Heiress*, Paramount

Supporting Actor
DEAN JAGGER in *Twelve O'Clock High*, 20th Century-Fox

Supporting Actress
MERCEDES McCAMBRIDGE in *All The King's Men*

Directing
JOSEPH L. MANKIEWICZ for *A Letter To Three Wives*,
20th Century-Fox

Writing
(Motion Picture Story)
THE STRATTON STORY, MGM: DOUGLAS MORROW
(Screenplay)
A LETTER TO THREE WIVES: JOSEPH L. MANKIEWICZ
(Story and Screenplay)
BATTLEGROUND, MGM: ROBERT PIROSH

Cinematography
(Black-and-White)
BATTLEGROUND: PAUL C. VOGEL
(Color)
SHE WORE A YELLOW RIBBON, Argosy/RKO Radio:
WINTON HOCH

Art Direction-Set Decoration
(Black-and-White)
THE HEIRESS: JOHN MEEHAN and HARRY HORNER
Set Decoration: EMILE KURI
(Color)
LITTLE WOMEN, MGM: CEDRIC GIBBONS and PAUL
GROESSE
Set Direction: EDWIN B. WILLIS and JACK D. MOORE

Sound Recording
TWELVE O'CLOCK HIGH: 20TH CENTURY-FOX
SOUND DEPARTMENT

Film Editing
CHAMPION, Screen Plays/UA: HARRY GERSTAD

Music
(Scoring of a Dramatic or Comedy Picture)
THE HEIRESS: AARON COPLAND

(Scoring of a Musical Picture)
ON THE TOWN, MGM: ROGER EDENS and LENNIE
HAYTON
(Best Song)
BABY, IT'S COLD OUTSIDE from *Neptune's Daughter*,
MGM
Music and Lyrics: FRANK LOESSER

Costume Design
(Black-and-White)
THE HEIRESS: EDITH HEAD and GILE STEELE
(Color)
ADVENTURES OF DON JUAN, Warner Bros.: LEAH
RHODES, TRAVILLA and MARJORIE BEST

Short Subjects
(Cartoons)
FOR SCENT-IMENTAL REASONS, Warner Bros. (Looney
Tunes): EDWARD SELZER, Producer
(One-reel)
AQUATIC HOUSE-PARTY, Paramount.
(Grantland Rice Sportlights): JACK EATON, Producer
(Two-reel)
VAN GOGH, Canton-Weiner: GASTON DIEHL and
ROBERT HAESSENS, Producers

Documentary
(Short Subjects, Two winners)
A CHANCE TO LIVE, March of Time/20th Century-Fox:
RICHARD DE ROCHEMONT, Producer
SO MUCH FOR SO LITTLE, Warner Bros.: EDWARD
SELZER, Producer
(Features)
DAYBREAK IN UDI, British Information Services: CROWN
FILM UNIT, Producer

Special Effects
MIGHTY JOE YOUNG, ARKO/RKO Radio

Special Awards
BICYCLE THIEVES (Italian) — the most outstanding foreign
language film released in the United States during 1949.
(statuette)
FRED ASTAIRE for his unique artistry and his contributions
to the technique of musical pictues. (statuette)
CECIL B. DeMILLE, distinguished motion picture pioneer,
for 37 years of brilliant showmanship. (statuette)
BOBBY DRISCOLL as the outstanding juvenile actor of
1949. (miniature statuette)
JEAN HERSHOLT for distinguished service to the motion
picture industry. (statuette)

Irving G. Thalberg Memorial Award
None

1950

I T WAS HARD to say whether the art form being honored by the 1950 Academy Awards ceremony was the cinema or the theater, whether the night belonged to Hollywood or Broadway. The Best Film (and the recipient of a record-breaking 14 nominations) was Joseph L. Mankiewicz's brittle, Martini-dry comedy of backstage life, **All About Eve**, no fewer than *five* of whose cast members were nominated – the actresses Bette Davis, Anne Baxter, Celeste Holm and Thelma Ritter (none of whom, however, gained an award) and the actor George Sanders (named Best Supporting Actor for his unforgettable performance as the sleek, acid-tongued critic Addison de Witt). Another film in the Best Picture stakes was George Cukor's **Born Yesterday**, adapted from a long-running stage farce which had made the effervescent comedienne Judy Holliday the toast of Broadway. By defeating Davis, Baxter *and* the indestructibly glamorous Gloria Swanson (enjoying her own glorious swansong as a half-demented silent screen star in Billy Wilder's brilliant **Sunset Boulevard**), Miss Holliday won the distinction of receiving an Oscar for her first starring role in the cinema.

On the male side, the victor was José Ferrer (best-known as a stage actor) for his memorable characterization as Cyrano de Bergerac in a film version of Edmond Rostand's classic verse drama. By an agreeable coincidence, a number of 1950's nominees happened to be based in New York when the ceremony was held in March 1950 (Swanson and Ferrer, who were appearing together in a Broadway revival of **Twentieth Century**, Holm, Ritter, Cukor and Sam Jaffe); and Ferrer hosted a reception for all of them in a fashionable Manhattan bistro, the evening being enlivened by regular broadcasts from the Pantages Theater over the restaurant's public address system. When the 53-year-old Swanson, who must have realized that **Sunset Boulevard** represented her last chance in the medium, heard of her defeat, she proved to be a gallant loser. To the assembled newsmen she gamely announced, "Well, this just means the old warhorse has got to go back to work."

But even if many of the evening's repercussions could be felt three thousand miles away across the continent, Hollywood cannily retained one ace up its sleeve – an ace calculated to trump all its rivals. The Best Foreign Film Oscar – won by a now obscure melodrama titled **The Walls Of Malapaga** – was presented to the Italian Consul by Marlene Dietrich in a slinky, form-fitting gown slit in

ABOVE *Bette Davis (left) as the caustic, ageing theater idol Margo Channing, Thelma Ritter (center) as her faithful dresser, and Celeste Holm (right) as her best friend, all three nominated for Oscars, in a not-so-cosy dressing room scene from* All About Eve, *Joseph Mankiewicz's poison pen letter to the New York theatrical world*

profile from her feet to her thighs. Dietrich's legs carried all before them.

No doubt because our attention is distracted by the stars who play them, it is rare in film history for characters' names to remain lodged in the collective memory (which is not at all the case in literature). Unusually, then, **All About Eve** can boast three such naggingly memorable protagonists: the ageing but still feisty actress Margo Channing (Davis), the ruthless, butter-wouldn't-melt-in-her-mouth aspirant star Eve Harrington (Baxter) and the Oscar Wilde of Times Square, Addison de Witt (Sanders). It was one of the delights of this, perhaps the most consistently witty of all film comedies, that performers and characters so seamlessly merged in our perception of them that it has become impossible to imagine the

slightest change in its cast. Which makes one all the more startled to learn that Davis, whose career was on the wane, had not been Mankiewicz's initial choice. Claudette Colbert had originally been scheduled to play the role of Margo Channing – who finds both her professional and private life subtly undermined by the presence of the falsely innocent young Eve – and was replaced by Davis when she cracked one of her spinal vertebrae. Said a grateful Miss Davis to Mankiewicz, "You resurrected me from the dead."

Intriguingly, the film itself was hardly richer in incident than its filming: during the shoot, Davis and her leading man, Gary Merrill, fell in love and were subsequently married; when the Oscar nominations were announced, Anne Baxter, peeved to find herself relegated to the Best Supporting Actress category, insisted that her name be

BELOW *"Fasten your seatbelts. It's going to be a bumpy night,"* says Bette Davis in All About Eve, *bracing herself for a rocky party. Among the guests seen here are Gregory Ratoff (standing), Anne Baxter (foreground left), Marilyn Monroe (foreground right), Gary Merrill (center left), George Sanders (center right), and Celeste Holm (top). Sanders as the acid critic Addison de Witt won the Best Supporting award*

ABOVE *Christian (William Prince, left) seems hypnotized by the long nose of* Cyrano de Bergerac *(Jose Ferrer), the poet-duellist. Audiences were hypnotized by Ferrer's dynamic, sonorous, comic and moving Oscar-winning performance. He repeated the role fourteen years later in Abel Gance's* Cyrano And D'Artagnan

switched to the more prestigious Best Actress prize (thereby splitting the number of potential votes for either Davis or herself); and, on the film's release, columnists made much of the striking resemblance between the cynical, chain-smoking Margo and the celebrated – indeed, infamous – theatrical prima donna Tallulah Bankhead, and proceeded to concoct a wholly imaginary feud between the two actresses.

Finally, it would be unthinkable not to mention yet another actress in the cast of **All About Eve**. Though onscreen for barely sixty seconds, playing a certain Miss Caswell, "a graduate", according to Addison de Witt, "of the Copacabana school of dramatic arts", she displayed, among other nice attributes, a certain *je ne sais quoi*. Her name was, of course, Marilyn Monroe.

That, in the theatrical repertory, there exist few characters as colorful and spectacular as Cyrano de Bergerac is not at all to diminish José Ferrer's achievement in portraying him, or to imply that he won his Oscar, as some wag of the period must have suggested, "by a nose". The secret of the role is to appear both extroverted and introverted, both flamboyant and retiring, both funny and

ABOVE *Gloria Swanson in an anguished moment from her splendid Oscar-nominated performance as silent-screen actress Norma Desmond in* Sunset Boulevard. *The star lost out, but the ten-award nominated picture won for Best Screenplay, Best Art Direction-Set Decoration, and Best Score*

moving, both a monster and a man. As the poetic 17th-century swordsman with a schnozzle-sized proboscis, forced to woo the object of his own love as the proxy of a handsome but tongue-tied young friend, Ferrer captured both the ebullient humor and latent tenderness of the character with equal skill; and, as a product of theatrical training, he never seemed ill-at-ease with Rostand's verbal pyrotechnics. Unfortunately, the film itself, a Stanley Kramer production directed by Michael Gordon, was academic and impersonal, an inadequate framework for Ferrer's virtuoso performance.

Ferrer was a versatile artist – actor, director (of plays and films), musician, singer, dancer, composer and designer – but the only other cinematic role in which he achieved a comparable celebrity also called for him to assume a humiliating physical deformity: the dwarfish painter Henri de Toulouse-Lautrec in John Huston's biopic **Moulin Rouge** (1952), played on his knees throughout, for which he again found himself among the Academy Award contenders.

Despite the stiff competition mentioned above, the Best Actress announcement was one of the most warmly received in the award's history. Judy Holliday, an unlikely

BELOW Best Actress Judy Holliday, who is transformed from dumb blonde to smart cookie in Born Yesterday, *watches as her egghead tutor William Holden (center) stands up to her boorish protector Broderick Crawford*

Cinderella, had nevertheless played the lead in a genuine showbiz fairy tale. When, through illness, Jean Arthur withdrew from Garson Kanin's stage comedy **Born Yesterday** only days before its premiere in Philadelphia, the unknown Holliday was offered her part, frantically memorizing her lines and eventually taking Broadway by storm. It was only when the film rights were purchased that the fairy tale threatened to turn sour. The property had been acquired by Columbia's boss Harry Cohn as a vehicle for the studio's biggest star, Rita Hayworth. Yet Hayworth (totally improbable casting in any case) chose just that moment to retire (temporarily) from the screen and marry Prince Aly Kahn. Literally dozens of stars were tested for the role, from Lucille Ball to Gloria Grahame, until Cohn was reluctantly obliged to settle for the actress who had turned the play into a smash hit.

In its film version, **Born Yesterday** proved no less triumphant for Judy Holliday than the play had done; and, until her untimely death from cancer in 1965, she enchanted audiences with her uniquely rasping voice and bubbly personality in such comedies as **The Marrying Kind**, the bizarrely titled **Phffft!** and **The Solid Gold Cadillac**. On Broadway she had regularly 'stopped the show' with her deadpan delivery of the play's most celebrated line of dialogue: "Do me a favor, will ya, Harry? Drop dead!" If the cinema allowed of such a possibility, then Judy would even now be 'stopping' **Born Yesterday** wherever it is screened.

WINNERS 1950

Nominations Announced: February 12, 1951
Awards Ceremony: March 29, 1951
RKO Pantages Theatre

Best Picture
ALL ABOUT EVE, 20th Century-Fox

Actor
JOSE FERRER in *Cyrano De Bergerac*, Kramer/UA

Actress
JUDY HOLLIDAY in *Born Yesterday*, Columbia

Supporting Actor
GEORGE SANDERS in *All About Eve*

Supporting Actress
JOSEPHINE HULL in *Harvey*, U-I

Directing
JOSEPH L. MANKIEWICZ for *All About Eve*

Writing
(Motion Picture Story)
PANIC IN THE STREETS, 20th Century-Fox: EDNA ANHALT and EDWARD ANHALT
(Screenplay)
ALL ABOUT EVE: JOSEPH L. MANKIEWICZ
(Story and Screenplay)
SUNSET BOULEVARD, Paramount: CHARLES BRACKETT, BILLY WILDER and D.M. MARSHMAN Jr

Cinematography
(Black-and-White)
THE THIRD MAN, Selznick-London/SRO (British): ROBERT KRASKER
(Color)
KING SOLOMON'S MINES, MGM: ROBERT SURTEES

Art Direction-Set Decoration
(Black-and-White)
SUNSET BOULEVARD: HANS DREIER and JOHN MEEHAN
Set Decoration: SAM COMER and RAY MOYER
(Color)
SAMSON AND DELILAH, DeMille/Paramount: HANS DREIER and WALTER TYLER
Set Decoration: SAM COMER and RAY MOYER

Sound Recording
ALL ABOUT EVE: 20TH CENTURY-FOX SOUND DEPARTMENT

Film Editing
KING SOLOMON'S MINES, MGM: RALPH E. WINTERS and CONRAD A. NERVIG

Music
(Scoring of a Dramatic or Comedy Picture)
SUNSET BOULEVARD: FRANZ WAXMAN
(Scoring of a Musical Picture)
ANNIE GET YOUR GUN, MGM: ADOLPH DEUTSCH and ROGER EDENS
(Best Song)
MONA LISA from *Captain Carey, USA*, Paramount
Music and Lyrics: RAY EVANS and JAY LIVINGSTON

Costume Design
(Black-and-White)
ALL ABOUT EVE: EDITH HEAD and CHARLES LeMAIRE
(Color)
SAMSON AND DELILAH, DeMille/Paramount: EDITH HEAD, DOROTHY JEAKINS, ELOIS JENSSEN, GILE STEELE and GWEN WAKELING

Short Subjects
(Cartoons)
GERALD McBOING-BOING, United Productions Of America/Columbia. (Jolly Frolics Series): STEPHEN BOSUSTOW, Executive Producer
(One-reel)
GRANDAD OF RACES, Warner Bros. (Sports Parade): GORDON HOLINGSHEAD, Producer
(Two-reel)
IN BEAVER VALLEY, Disney/RKO Radio. (True-Life Adventure): WALT DISNEY, Producer

Documentary
(Short Subjects)
WHY KOREA? 20th Century-Fox Movietone: EDMUND REEK, Producer
(Features)
THE TITAN: STORY OF MICHELANGELO, Michelangelo/Classics: ROBERT SNYDER, Producer

Special Effects
DESTINATION MOON, Pal/Eagle-Lion

Honorary Awards
(From 1927/8 to 1949 known as Special Awards)
THE WALLS OF MALAPAGA (Franco-Italian) — the most outstanding foreign language film released in the United States in 1950. (statuette)
GEORGE MURPHY for his services in interpreting the film industry to the country at large. (statuette)
LOUIS B. MAYER for distinguished service to the motion picture industry. (statuette)

Irving G. Thalberg Memorial Award
DARRYL F. ZANUCK

1951

THE TRADE MAGAZINES were unanimous – for the Best Picture Oscar of 1951 the only serious contenders were two heavyweight black-and-white melodramas, both of them adapted from contemporary American classics: in the left corner, Elia Kazan's **A Streetcar Named Desire**, from the play by Tennessee Williams; in the right, George Stevens' **A Place In The Sun**, from Theodore Dreiser's influential novel *An American Tragedy*. As is usually the case with surefire winners, both films brought in their wake several other nominations, totaling 19 between them.

The Academy voters have always shown a preference – unfairly, it is sometimes felt – for films belonging to a strictly dramatic category over the comedies, Westerns, thrillers and musicals which make up the medium's standard fare. It took the movie community completely by surprise, then, when Ronald Colman unsealed the fateful envelope to announce that the Best Picture Award had been scooped by an outsider: Vincente Minnelli's Gershwin-scored musical **An American In Paris**. Not only did **An American In Paris** capture the principal award of the evening, it won five further Oscars (for Story and Screenplay, Color Cinematography, Color Art Direction,

Color Costume Design and Best Score for a Musical Picture), not to mention the 1951 Irving G. Thalberg Memorial Award for its producer, the Diaghilev of the MGM backlot, Arthur Freed, and an honorary Oscar for Gene Kelly "in appreciation of his versatility as actor, singer, director and dancer".

Apparently no less astonished than the trade-paper pundits was MGM itself (which might have preferred a victory for another nominated film, **Quo Vadis**, one of the year's late releases and therefore in greater need of the publicity and prestige accruing to an Oscar-garlanded winner). In the following day's edition of *Daily Variety*, the studio adopted normal practice by running a full-page self-congratulatory advertisement – except that, on this occasion, its celebrated trademark, Leo the Lion, was seen to be sheepishly contemplating the Oscar statuette and protesting, "Honestly, I was just standing In the Sun waiting for A Streetcar."

That Oscar was in a skittish humor this year, opting for color, wit, myth and fantasy instead of downbeat dramatic gloom, had been demonstrated earlier in the evening by another unexpected victory: that of Humphrey Bogart as Best Actor over Marlon Brando, *Streetcar*'s electrifying

BELOW, LEFT *The title role in* The African Queen *was taken by a rusty old steamboat. Equally weather-beaten were Humphrey Bogart, winning his only ever Oscar as the gin-swigging captain, and Katharine Hepburn as a prim missionary, an unforgettable duo* BELOW *The Best Foreign Picture* Rashomon *created a stir as it was the first Japanese film to be shown widely in the West. The movie made its director Akira Kurosawa, and his favorite actor, the powerful Toshiro Mifune (right), world famous. It was feebly remade as* The Outrage *by Hollywood in 1964 with Paul Newman in the Mifune role*

Stanley Kowalski. Universally admired as he was, Bogart had never won an Oscar before (though he had already been nominated for **Casablanca** and would be again for his brilliantly intense performance as the paranoid Captain Queeg in **The Caine Mutiny**); and he was quite prepared to admit that he, too, had been taken aback by the result. "It's a long way from the Belgian Congo to the Pantages Theater," he muttered in his inimitable if much-imitated lisp, "but I'd rather be here than there." He was, of course, referring to the location of **The African Queen**. Brando's comments went unreported.

Finally, the Oscar for the most oustanding foreign film was awarded to Akira Kurosawa's **Rashomon**, the work which introduced Japanese cinema to the western world, a complex, multilayered fable of theft and deceit narrated from four different points of view.

But it was unquestionably Gene Kelly's night. Though **An American In Paris** proved that a musical whose only pretension was that of providing audiences with stylish, top-flight entertainment could be considered worthy of the industry's highest accolade, it was an awkward matter honoring those who appear in such films, where the notion of 'performance' becomes slightly smudged. The special Oscar presented to Kelly, like that to Astaire in 1949, was therefore a token of recognition and gratitude. And, appropriately, **An American In Paris** represented the culmination of Kelly's efforts to establish what he called the 'integrated musical', in which the musical numbers would function as an integral part of the story rather than as pleasant diversions from a generally inane plotline. Not only did he choreograph and star in the film, it was he who proposed as leading lady a vivaciously pretty young ballerina from Paris, Leslie Caron.

Kelly was also the inspirational force behind the film's magnificent climactic ballet lasting seventeen-and-a-half minutes and based on the orchestral scherzo which gave the film its title. At a cost of almost half-a-million dollars, this sequence was ravishingly designed in the manner of such Impressionist and Post-Impressionist painters as Utrillo, Renoir, Dufy, Toulouse-Lautrec, Rousseau and Van Gogh. Despite the studio's concern that restless audiences would balk at such a lengthy passage of pure choreography, it became the film's undisputed highlight and prompted similar ballets in numerous musicals to come (in particular, the wonderfully garish Mickey Spillane parody 'Girl Hunt' in Minnelli's **The Band Wagon**). Kelly himself was to take the process to its logical conclusion in 1954 with his feature-length ballet extravaganza, *sans* dialogue, **Invitation To The Dance**.

It's arguable that Humphrey Bogart is now, posthumously, a more adulated star than in his own lifetime. Though, following his breakthrough performance in

LEFT *One of the many* tableaux dansantes *based on French Impressionist and Post-Impressionist paintings in the final 18-minute ballet in* An American In Paris, *danced superbly by Gene Kelly and Leslie Caron (in her screen debut)*

1941 as Sam Spade in Huston's **The Maltese Falcon**, he enjoyed nearly two decades of popularity, it was not until his premature death from cancer in 1957 that his unique brand of cynical idealism made him the idol of a whole generation of young people in both the United States and Europe. Typically, it was not the self-image which Bogie indelibly stamped on film history – the one honest, unafraid man who walks down those 'mean streets' immortalized by Chandler and Hammett – to which Hollywood paid tribute. In **The African Queen** (based on a novel by C.S. Forester) he played a drunken, disheveled steamboat captain in the Congo who is persuaded by a prim, Bible-quoting spinster (Katharine Hepburn) to destroy a German gunboat during World War I. The film's huge box-office success could be attributed in part to its skilful blending of comedy, drama and thrills, in part to the inspired pairing of Hepburn and Bogart, the missionary and the sinner, between whom an unlikely romance begins to blossom. If **The African Queen** is, perhaps, less than a certified classic, it is the very next best thing: a film impossible not to enjoy.

Twice a runner-up, to **An American In Paris** and Bogart, **A Streetcar Named Desire** finally came into its own with the presentation of the Best Actress Oscar to Vivien Leigh. The film, curiously, can be compared to **The African Queen** in that it, too, centers on the confrontation of an (ostensibly) ladylike heroine and a hero brimming over with crude animal energies and appetites. There, however, the resemblance ends. Williams' drama, set in New Orleans (where, until recently, it was still possible to take a streetcar to the city's Desire district), recounts the tragic collision of a faded beauty of the Old South, Blanche DuBois, whose flirtatiously aristocratic mannerisms conceal a debilitating sexual maladjustment, and her brutishly proletarian brother-in-law (Brando). The English Leigh had already convincingly impersonated a Southern belle in **Gone With The Wind**; but, though she had enjoyed a personal triumph in the London stage production of Williams' play, it was only when her then husband, Laurence Olivier, was obliged to take up residence in Hollywood for the filming of William Wyler's **Carrie** that she agreed to repeat her performance on the screen. As we have learned from biographies of this exquisite actress, she was not without psychological problems of her own; and her performance as Blanche DuBois, one of the finest (if most mannered and fluttery) in Hollywood's history, was no doubt lent a poignant edge by the emotional instability to which so many of her friends and colleagues have since testified.

The film, tensely and Oscar-winningly directed by Kazan, featured the entire New York stage cast (with the exception of Tandy): Brando, Karl Malden and Kim Hunter (who won twin Oscars as Best Supporting Actor and Actress), Rudy Bond, Nick Dennis, Peg Hillias, Wright King, Richard Garrick and Ann Dere. In short, another fruitful union between Hollywood and Broadway was achieved.

BELOW *Marlon Brando, in his second screen role, as the mumbling, brooding brute Stanley Kowalski in* A Streetcar Named Desire, *affronts his ladylike sister-in-law Blanche DuBois* (Vivien Leigh). *Best Actress winner Leigh in her faded Southern belle-of-the-ball gown, was perfect as one of Tennessee Williams' most tragic creations*

WINNERS 1951

Nominations Announced: February 11, 1952
Awards Ceremony: March 20, 1952
RKO Pantages Theatre

Best Picture
AN AMERICAN IN PARIS, MGM: ARTHUR FREED,
Producer

Actor
HUMPHREY BOGART in *The African Queen*, Horizon/UA

Actress
VIVIEN LEIGH in *A Streetcar Named Desire*,
Feldman/Warner Bros.

Supporting Actor
KARL MALDEN in *A Streetcar Named Desire*

Supporting Actress
KIM HUNTER in *A Streetcar Named Desire*

Directing
GEORGE STEVENS for *A Place In The Sun*, Paramount

Writing
(Motion Picture Story)
SEVEN DAYS TO NOON, Boulting Bros/Mayer-Kingsley-
Distinguished Films (British): PAUL DEHN and JAMES
BERNARD
(Screenplay)
A PLACE IN THE SUN: MICHAEL WILSON and HARRY
BROWN
(Story and Screenplay)
AN AMERICAN IN PARIS: ALAN JAY LERNER

Cinematography
(Black-and-White)
A PLACE IN THE SUN: WILLIAM C. MELLOR
(Color)
AN AMERICAN IN PARIS: ALFRED GILKS
Ballet photography: JOHN ALTON

Art Direction-Set Decoration
(Black-and-White)
A STREETCAR NAMED DESIRE: RICHARD DAY
Set Decoration: GEORGE JAMES HOPKINS
(Color)
AN AMERICAN IN PARIS: CEDRIC GIBBONS and
PRESTON AMES
Set Decoration: EDWIN B. WILLIS and KEOGH GLEASON

Sound Recording
THE GREAT CARUSO, MGM: DOUGLAS SHEARER,
Sound Director

Film Editing
A PLACE IN THE SUN: WILLIAM HORNBECK

Music
(Scoring of a Dramatic or Comedy Picture)
A PLACE IN THE SUN: FRANZ WAXMAN
(Scoring of a Musical Picture)
AN AMERICAN IN PARIS: JOHNNY GREEN and SAUL
CHAPLIN
(Best Song)
IN THE COOL, COOL, COOL OF THE EVENING from
Here Comes The Groom, Paramount
Music: HOAGY CARMICHAEL
Lyrics: JOHNNY MERCER

Costume Design
(Black-and-White)
A PLACE IN THE SUN: EDITH HEAD
(Color)
AN AMERICAN IN PARIS: ORRY-KELLY, WALTER
PLUNKETT and IRENE SHARAFF

Short Subjects
(Cartoons)
TWO MOUSEKETEERS, MGM. (Tom & Jerry): FRED
QUIMBY, Producer
(One-reel)
WORLD OF KIDS, Warner Bros. (Vitaphone Novelties):
ROBERT YOUNGSON, Producer
(Two-reel)
NATURE'S HALF ACRE, Disney/RKO Radio. (True-Life
Adventure): WALT DISNEY, Producer

Documentary
(Short Subjects)
BENJY, made by FRED ZINNEMANN with the
co-operation of Paramount for the Los Angeles
Orthopaedic Hospital
(Features)
KON-TIKI, Artfilm/RKO Radio (Norwegian): OLLE
NORDEMAR, Producer

Special Effects
(From 1951 to 1953 Special Effects classified as an 'other'
Award, not necessarily given each year).
WHEN WORLDS COLLIDE, Paramount

Honorary Awards
RASHOMON (Japanese) – the most outstanding foreign
language film released in the United States in 1951.
(statuette)
GENE KELLY in appreciation of his versatility as an actor,
singer, director and dancer, and specifically for his brilliant
achievements in the art of choreography on film. (statuette)

Irving G. Thalberg Memorial Award
ARTHUR FREED

1952

ONE YEAR THAT could be said to be a turning point in Oscar's history was 1952. After years of having rejected the advances of television, the Academy succumbed at last – the Awards ceremony, which had always been Hollywood's night, a private party during which the industry could honor its own, went public. On March 19, 1953, 80,000,000 TV viewers across the continent tuned in to Oscar night – by far the greatest single audience in the five-year history of American television.

In fact, it was, for the cinema, a marriage on the rebound. Only weeks before the ceremony was due to be held, four major studios (Warner Bros., Columbia, Universal-International and Republic) decided to withdraw financial backing from the event; and since the NBC-RCA organization had simultaneously made a tempting $100,000 bid for the radio and TV rights, the Academy realized that it had received an offer it could not afford to refuse and gratefully capitulated. In spite of first night nerves, the show unfolded with fewer hitches than has often been the case since, with cameras smoothly switching back and forth between the Pantages Theater in Hollywood and the International Theater in New York, between the Tinseltown Master of Ceremonies Bob Hope (himself the recipient of an honorary Oscar "for his contribution to the laughter of the world") and Conrad Nagel in the Big Apple.

For the first time, the invited guests probably found themselves at a disadvantage. Obstructed by the multiplicity of TV cameras, floodlights and monitoring screens, the ubiquitous technicians and the dense undergrowth of wiring, they had a less complete view of the proceedings than the ordinary punter comfortably ensconced in his living room. And, since the event had been split up between the East and West Coasts, the live audience, too, was obliged – for part of the time, at least – to watch the presentations on an enormous rear-projection screen, placed in the center of the stage. Notwithstanding these minor irritations, however, the evening was pronounced as much of a success for the cinema as for its smaller, but increasingly tenacious, rival. Hollywood had begun to discover that it could not only learn to live with television, but also to exploit the medium's extraordinary audience as a means of publicizing its own products.

Appropriately for such a star-studded (and spectator-studded) evening, the Best Picture Award went to Cecil B. DeMille's circus spectacular, **The Greatest Show On Earth**. This was a surprise hardly less than that of the previous year's winner. It was not merely that most of the informed betting had been laid on Fred Zinnemann's classic Western, **High Noon**. DeMille, though one of Hollywood's most consistently money-making directors, and one of the few whose name meant more on a billboard than that of many stars, had always kept a remarkably low profile in the Oscar stakes. In a career spanning nearly half a century, from silent two-reelers to his last and costliest production, **The Ten Commandments** in 1956, he was only twice nominated for an Academy Award. For a consummate showman like DeMille, critics were dispensable. Since, in such films as **The Sign Of The Cross** (1932), **Cleopatra** (1934), **The Plainsman** (1937) and **Samson And Delilah** (1949), he had established a direct *rapport* with mass audiences, he could ignore the judgement of the critical Establishment that his work was vulgar and mindless. He took the idea of 'the big screen' literally: his films were defiantly larger-than-life, with their monstrously outsize sets, breathtaking crowd scenes (rare was a DeMille film which did not boast its 'cast of thousands') and epic themes. In the year when the cinema definitively hitched itself to television's rising star, there was a kind of ironic justice to its honoring a director who represented everything to which the more modest medium could never aspire.

Since DeMille's films always had been three-ring circuses, whatever their subject-matter, no one ought to have been surprised that he eventually chose the Big Top

BELOW *John Ford won his fourth Academy Award as Best Director for his rollicking Irish comedy* The Quiet Man. *Watching the discomfiture of bully Victor McLaglen (nominated for a supporting Oscar) are Barry Fitzgerald (left) and John Wayne (right)*

ABOVE *Dorothy Lamour (center), one of the many artistes of the Big Top in* The Greatest Show On Earth. *The clown in the background is James Stewart. The Best Picture was produced and directed by the Barnum of Hollywood Cecil B. DeMille*

itself as a setting. The preparation of **The Greatest Show On Earth** required three intense years of planning and research, during which the 70-year-old director himself accompanied the Ringling Brothers and Barnum and Bailey circus on its annual cross-country tour. Location shooting took place at the circus' winter headquarters in Florida and during actual performances staged for paying customers. In only his second film appearance, Charlton Heston was cast as the circus manager; and Betty Hutton, who played an aerialist, spent three months practising the perilous techniques she was required to display on the screen. Besides a stupendous train-wreck sequence, the film's fittingly DeMillean climax, it featured two unusual gimmicks. Though unlisted in the credits, Bob Hope and Bing Crosby appeared as a droll pair of popcorn-munching spectators; and James Stewart, playing a suspected

criminal on the run from the police, did not once remove his traditional clown's make-up throughout the two-and-a-half hour running time. Once dubbed "the founder of Hollywood", Cecil Blount DeMille was finally receiving due homage from the industry he had helped to create. The Best Director Oscar, however, went to John Ford for his Irish romance, **The Quiet Man**.

Though small in scale when compared to **The Greatest Show On Earth**, and relatively unviolent by contemporary standards, **High Noon** was as taut and gripping as a countdown to zero. Its themes of cowardice and responsibility, of what Hemingway called "grace under pressure", would not have seemed incongruous in a drama by Ibsen; and it was one of the few Westerns capable of attracting into the cinema even those spectators who would not normally admit to affection for the genre. Telling its story of a recently retired Marshal who finds himself alone and friendless when news reaches town of the impending arrival – by the noon train – of a desperado he had once 'sent up', to join three sidekicks already waiting at the station, **High Noon** respected the unities of time and place. The minutes ticking inexorably away in the small town coin-

cided exactly with those on one's wristwatch. There were no flashbacks, no subplots – no escape.

Ousted for the Best Picture Award, it nevertheless managed to secure a statuette for its star, Gary Cooper – an ageing Coop still possessed of the mythic aura which he assumed with such easy masculine (though never aggressively macho) elegance and humor. The project had started out as a modest, low-budget feature made by a fairly untested director and starring an actor whose fortunes were, in the early 50s, at a low ebb. No one – least of all, its producer Stanley Kramer – had expected much of it, critically or commercially. Its ascension to Oscar-winning prestige, and its current status as one of Hollywood's finest genre movies, should therefore be ascribed to its own, still potent, cinematic mastery.

LEFT *Fifty-one-year-old Gary Cooper in his Oscar-winning performance (and perhaps his best) as the lone Marshal in* High Noon *forced to face four outlaws on his wedding day. 'Do not forsake me, oh my darlin' sings Tex Ritter (Best Song) on the soundtrack. His darlin' was the young Grace Kelly (illustrated) in her second screen role*
BELOW *Best Actress winner Shirley Booth was the frumpish Lola Delaney in* Come Back Little Sheba. *Here she is seen admiring her alcoholic husband, Burt Lancaster, who is optimistically hoping to give up drink. The photo on the dressing-table depicts a happier time*

Winner of the Best Actress Award was Shirley Booth for her moving performance as Burt Lancaster's sluttish wife in Daniel Mann's **Come Back, Little Sheba** (based on William Inge's play). Though her debut screen appearance, it was a role she had played on Broadway for over a thousand performances; and she generously confessed to a reporter before the ceremony, "I don't think it's fair if I win. There is all the difference in the world between playing a character more than a thousand times, as I did, and getting your lines on the set in the morning and having to face the camera with them in the afternoon." Yet her searing portrait of a woman unwittingly driving her husband to alcoholism could not be denied, and there was never much doubt that she would carry off the Oscar.

It turned out to be a rather fraught moment for her, however. Dashing up the red-carpeted stairs of the International Theater to collect her prize, she all but tripped over her own gown (in front of that 80,000,000 viewing audience). And, in her breathless acceptance speech, she pronounced these strangely prophetic words: "I guess this is the peak". As it turned out, Hollywood never knew quite how to handle Shirley Booth, who made only four more feature films there, not one of them an outstanding hit. It was, coincidentally enough, television which was to make her a household name. She achieved her most enduring popularity as the daffy heroine of a long-running comedy show, *Hazel*.

WINNERS 1952

Nominations Announced: February 9, 1953
Awards Ceremony: March 19, 1953
RKO Pantages Theatre

Best Picture
THE GREATEST SHOW ON EARTH, DeMille/Paramount:
CECIL B. DeMILLE, Producer

Actor
GARY COOPER in *High Noon*, Kramer/UA

Actress
SHIRLEY BOOTH in *Come Back, Little Sheba*,
Wallis/Paramount

Supporting Actor
ANTHONY QUINN in *Viva Zapata!* 20th Century-Fox

Supporting Actress
GLORIA GRAHAME in *The Bad And The Beautiful*, MGM

Directing
JOHN FORD for *The Quiet Man*, Argosy/Republic

Writing
(Motion Picture Story)
THE GREATEST SHOW ON EARTH: FREDERIC M.
FRANK, THEODORE ST JOHN and FRANK CAVETT
(Screenplay)
THE BAD AND THE BEAUTIFUL: CHARLES SCHNEE
(Story and Screenplay)
THE LAVENDER HILL MOB, Rank-Ealing/U-I (British):
T.E.B. CLARKE

Cinematography
(Black-and-White)
THE BAD AND THE BEAUTIFUL: ROBERT SURTEES
(Color)
THE QUIET MAN: WINTON C. HOCH and ARCHIE
STOUT

Art Direction-Set Decoration
(Black-and-White)
THE BAD AND THE BEAUTIFUL: CEDRIC GIBBONS and
EDWARD CARFAGNO
Set Decoration: EDWIN B. WILLIS and KEOGH GLEASON
(Color)
MOULIN ROUGE, Romulus/UA: PAUL SHERIFF
Set Decoration: MARCEL VERTES

Sound Recording
BREAKING THE SOUND BARRIER, London Films/UA
(British): LONDON FILM SOUND DEPARTMENT

Film Editing
HIGH NOON: ELMO WILLIAMS and HARRY GERSTAD

Music
(Scoring of a Dramatic or Comedy Picture)
HIGH NOON: DIMITRI TIOMKIN

(Scoring of a Musical Picture)
WITH A SONG IN MY HEART, 20th Century-Fox: ALFRED
NEWMAN
(Best Song)
HIGH NOON (DO NOT FORSAKE ME, OH MY DARLIN')
from *High Noon*
Music: DIMITRI TIOMKIN
Lyrics: NED WASHINGTON

Costume Design
(Black-and-White)
THE BAD AND THE BEAUTIFUL: HELEN ROSE
(Color)
MOULIN ROUGE: Romulus/UA: MARCEL VERTES

Short Subjects
(Cartoons)
JOHANN MOUSE, MGM. (Tom & Jerry): FRED QUIMBY,
Producer
(One-reel)
LIGHT IN THE WINDOW, Art/20th Century-Fox. (Art
Series): BORIS VERMONT, Producer
(Two-reel)
WATER BIRDS, Disney/RKO Radio. (True-Life
Adventure): WALT DISNEY, Producer

Documentary
(Short Subjects)
NEIGHBOURS, National Film Board of Canada/Mayer-
Kingsley (Canadian): NORMAN McLAREN, Producer
(Features)
THE SEA AROUND US, RKO Radio: IRWIN ALLEN,
Producer

Special Effects
PLYMOUTH ADVENTURE, MGM

Honorary Awards
FORBIDDEN GAMES (French) – Best Foreign Language
Film first released in the United States during 1952.
(statuette)
GEORGE ALFRED MITCHELL for the design and
development of the camera which bears his name and for
his continued and dominant presence in the field of
cinematography. (statuette)
JOSEPH M. SCHENCK for long and distinguished service
to the motion picture industry. (statuette)
MERIAN C. COOPER for his many innovations and
contributions to the art of motion pictures. (statuette)
BOB HOPE for his contribution to the laughter of the world,
his service to the motion picture industry, and his devotion
to the American premise. (statuette)

Irving G. Thalberg Memorial Award
CECIL B. DeMILLE

1953

IT WAS A supporting actor who provided the sole sensation of 1953. In the early 1950s Frank Sinatra suffered a series of setbacks: CBS abruptly canceled his TV show, RCA Records unceremoniously dropped him, a recent divorce property settlement (enabling him to marry Ava Gardner) had left him deep in debt and, frighteningly, a haemorrhage of blood vessels in his vocal apparatus was beginning to affect the quality of his voice. It was for all of these reasons, and against his agent's advice, that he agreed to play the secondary role of Private Maggio in Fred Zinnemann's **From Here To Eternity** for the insultingly low fee of $8000. As for so many involved with this film, it proved to be a watershed for Sinatra. His touching, vibrant performance as a carefree young soldier who falls victim to the sadistic attentions of Sergeant Fatso Judson (Ernest Borgnine) won him a Best Supporting Actor Oscar; and his career was galvanized to such an extent that he soon acquired the affectionate nickname of 'Chairman of the Board of Show Business'.

Otherwise, the year was not a vintage one. Zinnemann's film collected, as had been foreseen, the lion's share of the evening's awards. Its final count of eight Oscars (Best Picture, Supporting Actor and Actress, Director, Screenplay, Cinematography, Sound and Film Editing) matched the all-time record held by **Gone With The Wind**. Not one of the other winners belied pre-ceremony forecasts. And poor William Holden, named Best Actor for his appearance in Billy Wilder's black comedy **Stalag 17**, found himself obliged to reduce his acceptance speech to a bare minimum so that the show's TV sponsor, Oldsmobile, could insert extra commercials. Holden later grumbled to a journalist: "They told me to say 'thank you' and get off. I think they could have held off the closing commercials a little longer so that everyone could know how much Billy Wilder was responsible." Despite the irritating frequency with which the evening was interrupted by commercial breaks, it had become impossible by this stage to finance the ceremony from within the industry itself. But the show's organizers were incensed that economic considerations had left it looking embarrassingly truncated and determined that in future the television broadcast would be, as it is today, open-ended – sometimes with unwelcome results.

Until the invasion of the Top Ten charts by Spielberg,

BELOW *Enjoying themselves in a Honolulu nightclub away from the stresses of the Pearl Harbor barracks are soldiers Montgomery Clift (far right) and Frank Sinatra (second right) with Donna Reed in* From Here To Eternity, *the eight-Oscar winner*

Lucas and diverse other 'movie brats' of the 1980s, **From Here To Eternity** continued to figure prominently among the major commercial hits of film history. This condensation of James Jones' mammoth chronicle of life on a Hawaiian military base just before Pearl Harbor is best remembered, perhaps, for its love scene on the beach between Burt Lancaster and Deborah Kerr, which became for a while (as numerous parodies bear witness) the movie equivalent of a well-thumbed page in some slightly *risqué* bestseller. What is most striking about the scene when viewed with hindsight is not its 'torrid' semi-nudity, fairly tame by present-day standards, but the fact that it set a style in romantic soft-core eroticism for years to come (e.g. William Holden and Jennifer Jones on the beach in **Love Is A Many Splendored Thing**, 1955), before filtering down to TV commercials.

It was a scene which totally changed the public image of Deborah Kerr and revitalized her flagging career. After years of playing demure English roses in such films as **Black Narcissus, The Hucksters** and **Young Bess**, Kerr must have seemed odd casting for the plum role of a warm-blooded but sex-starved Captain's wife falling in love with a lowly Sergeant, but the risk paid off handsomely for Zinnemann (who had rejected the studio's proposed casting of Joan Crawford). Another performer obliged to play against type in the film was Donna Reed, an insipidly wholesome ingenue whom Zinnemann decided to cast as a nightclub singer-cum-prostitute. Obviously hungry for meatier roles than had ever come her way, Reed gave such an emotionally unrestrained performance that she won the Best Supporting Actress Oscar. In her case, unfortunately, the award was nothing more than an isolated highlight in an otherwise uneventful career; and she achieved lasting popularity only on television, with her long-running *Donna Reed Show*.

Though, in the 50s, it was necessary to cleanse Jones' raunchy novel of language and situations still considered too suggestive for cinematic adaptation, screenwriter Daniel Taradash did a magnificent job of transferring its multiple narrative strands to the screen, and there is not an ounce of fat on the film's 118-minute running time. Frequently revived on TV and the art-house circuit, **From Here To Eternity** is as watchably tense and dramatic now as when it was made.

William Holden's Oscar, too, came as a reward for audacious casting against type. Holden had often complained of the kind of role in which his sunny, clean-cut, All-American good looks had condemned him: "I got into a rut playing all kinds of nice-guy meaningless roles in meaningless movies in which I found no interest or enjoyment." He defined his characteristic screen persona as 'Nice Willie': "He had a great big smile and a great big

RIGHT *The celebrated erotic beach scene in* From Here To Eternity. *The fact that the English, and hitherto ladylike, Deborah Kerr played the adulterous army wife caught up in an affair with Burt Lancaster probably added to the* frisson *felt by audiences*

ABOVE *Best Actor winner William Holden as the selfish wheeling and dealing internee of* Stalag 17, *who nevertheless turns out to be the hero in Billy Wilder's enjoyable comedy-drama. The role of Sgt Sefton won the reliable Holden his only Oscar*

laugh and he laughed at everything everyone said. I hated his guts", he said with feeling.

No one could have described Holden's role in **Stalag 17** as a variation on his Nice Willie character. Based on a Broadway play, Wilder's raucous comedy-drama was set in a German P.O.W. camp during World War II and exploited the most traditional theme of such films: the desire to escape. Inside the camp, however, there lurks a spy; and, as far as its inmates are concerned, the obvious suspect is its resident 'Bilko', a scheming, wheeling-and-dealing sergeant whose only interest in their escape plan is laying odds on its chance of succeeding or failing. Needless to say, the sergeant has wholly redeemed himself by the film's thrilling climax; but not before the usually bland and folksy Holden had etched in a memorable portrait of wisecracking, cigar-chewing cynicism. Since Wilder's film allowed him not only to kill off Nice Willie but enshrined him for several years in succession as one of Hollywood's most sought-after actors, one can well understand why Holden was distressed at being prevented from paying proper tribute to his director when accepting his Oscar.

ABOVE *Elfin beauty Audrey Hepburn, the Best Actress winner, as the incognito Princess in* Roman Holiday *sleeping innocently as her surprised beau, newspaperman Gregory Peck, discovers her in the morning. She successfully traded on her gamine charms for a further fourteen years*

Only a year later, Holden was again to appear under Wilder's direction in the comedy **Sabrina**, playing opposite 1953's winner for Best Performance by an Actress, Audrey Hepburn (the third side of that film's triangle was formed by another recent winner, Humphrey Bogart). William Wyler's **Roman Holiday**, a delightfully frothy comedy about a lonely European princess traveling incognito and her romantic encounter with an American journalist (Gregory Peck), was actually Hepburn's seventh film; but it was the first she had to carry on her frail shoulders and it transformed her outright into one of the most bewitching of modern stars. "Only the absolutely determined people succeed," she once asserted. Yet her own career strikes one as a living contradiction of that claim. Hepburn seemed to do nothing to become a star except remain, as long as possible, her own uniquely gamine self. Her big break on Broadway, playing the title role in an adaptation of Colette's *Gigi*, came by chance when she was spotted in Monte Carlo by the sexagenarian author herself. "*There* is Gigi," said Colette – and so it proved to be. And little in her (British) film career prior to **Roman Holiday** intimated that she was capable of rising

to the occasion of a major starring role. What the film called for, however, was less of measurable acting ability than that indefinable 'star quality' of which Hepburn undeniably possesses oodles. As one astute critic later remarked, "Hepburn's appeal, it becomes clearer with every appearance, is largely to the imagination; the less acting she does, the more people can imagine her doing." Her Oscar was awarded not so much for a performance as for sheer *presence*.

Incidentally, the films with which Hepburn has been associated seem to lead as charmed an existence as she herself. Immediately after the release of **Roman Holiday**, the story of Princess Margaret's ill-fated affair with Captain Peter Townsend hit the world's headlines, thereby providing Wyler's fictional account of a similar entanglement with extensive free publicity.

WINNERS 1953

Nominations Announced: February 15, 1954
Awards Ceremony: March 25, 1954
RKO Pantages Theatre

Best Picture
FROM HERE TO ETERNITY, Columbia: BUDDY ADLER, Producer

Actor
WILLIAM HOLDEN in *Stalag 17*, Paramount

Actress
AUDREY HEPBURN in *Roman Holiday*, Paramount

Supporting Actor
FRANK SINATRA in *From Here To Eternity*

Supporting Actress
DONNA REED in *From Here To Eternity*

Directing
FRED ZINNEMANN for *From Here To Eternity*

Writing
(Motion Picture Story)
ROMAN HOLIDAY: IAN McLELLAN HUNTER
(Screenplay)
FROM HERE TO ETERNITY: DANIEL TARADASH
(Story and Screenplay)
TITANIC, 20th Century-Fox: CHARLES BRACKETT, WALTER REISCH and RICHARD BREEN

Cinematography
(Black-and-White)
FROM HERE TO ETERNITY: BURNETT GUFFEY
(Color)
SHANE, Paramount: LOYAL GRIGGS

Art Direction-Set Decoration
(Black-and-White)
JULIUS CAESAR, MGM: CEDRIC GIBBONS and EDWARD CARFAGNO
Set Decoration: EDWIN B. WILLIS and HUGH HUNT
(Color)
THE ROBE, 20th Century-Fox: LYLE WHEELER and GEORGE W. DAVIS
Set Decoration: WALTER M. SCOTT and PAUL S. FOX

Sound Recording
FROM HERE TO ETERNITY, Columbia
Sound Department: JOHN P. LIVADARY, Sound Director

Film Editing
FROM HERE TO ETERNITY: WILLIAM LYON

Music
(Scoring of a Dramatic or Comedy Picture)
LILI, MGM: BRONISLAU KAPER
(Scoring of a Musical Picture)
CALL ME MADAM, 20th Century-Fox: ALFRED NEWMAN
(Best Song)
SECRET LOVE from *Calamity Jane*, Warner Bros.
Music: SAMMY FAIN
Lyrics: PAUL FRANCIS WEBSTER

Costume Design
(Black-and-White)
ROMAN HOLIDAY: EDITH HEAD
(Color)
THE ROBE: CHARLES LeMAIRE and EMILE SANTIAGO

Short Subjects
(Cartoons)
TOOT, WHISTLE, PLUNK AND BOOM, Disney/Buena Vista (Special Music Series): WALT DISNEY, Producer
(One-reel)
THE MERRY WIVES OF WINDSOR OVERTURE, MGM. (Overture Series): JOHNNY GREEN, Producer
(Two-reel)
BEAR COUNTRY, Disney/RKO Radio. (True-Life Adventure): WALT DISNEY, Producer

Documentary
(Short Subjects)
THE ALASKAN ESKIMO, Disney/RKO Radio: WALT DISNEY, Producer
(Features)
THE LIVING DESERT, Disney/Buena Vista: WALT DISNEY, Producer

Special Effects
THE WAR OF THE WORLDS, Paramount

Honorary Awards
PETE SMITH for his witty and pungent observations on the American scene in his series of *Pete Smith Specialties*. (statuette)
JOSEPH I. BREEN for his conscientious, open-minded and dignified management of the Motion Picture Production Code. (statuette)
20TH CENTURY-FOX FILM CORPORATION in recognition of their imagination, showmanship and foresight in introducing the revolutionary process known as CinemaScope. (statuette)
BELL AND HOWELL COMPANY for their pioneering and basic achievements in the advancement of the motion picture industry. (statuette)

Irving G. Thalberg Memorial Award
GEORGE STEVENS

IN 1951, MARLON Brando had been nominated for his performance in **A Streetcar Named Desire**, in 1952 for **Viva Zapata!** and in 1953 for **Julius Caesar** (in which he played Mark Antony). "I coulda been a contender..." the three-time loser might ruefully have murmured. In 1954, however, he found himself among the champions. For his performance as a tough but sensitive longshoreman in Elia Kazan's **On The Waterfront** (Kazan had directed him in both *Streetcar* and *Zapata*), this young actor, already regarded by many as the finest of his generation, was named the year's Best for his delivery of, among others, that famous line of dialogue.

Brando's, nevertheless, was a surprise victory. Hollywood is a sentimental little village; and virtually the whole movie community hoped – and expected – that the Oscar would go to one of its favorite sons, Bing Crosby, who had discarded his familiar laidback image to portray an alcoholic actor on the skids in **The Country Girl**. Nor did it help matters that Brando had already acquired the reputation of being the cinema's least conventional, least accommodating star, given to appearing unshaven and disheveled in public, accused of incoherent mumbling on screen and flaunting an indecent lack of respect for Hollywood's most revered codes and values. "Acting is the expression of a neurotic impulse. It is a bum's life. Quitting acting is a sign of maturity" was only one of his blunt, uningratiating public statements. Yet, when the award was announced, and he received a standing ovation from the Pantages Theater, Brando could not have been more charming than if he had been the Old Groaner himself. "It's much heavier than I thought," he disarmingly commented when presented with the statuette.

The evening saw another major upset, another struggle between a popular movie trouper making a belated comeback and a much younger personality on the way up: Judy Garland (nominated for her superb performance in Cukor's musical masterwork **A Star Is Born**) vs Grace Kelly (for her unexpectedly mature characterization as Crosby's frumpish wife in **The Country Girl**). To add poignancy to the 'human element', Garland had given birth to a son just the day before and NBC television installed a camera crew in the corridors of Hollywood's Cedars of Lebanon Hospital to cover her triumph. It failed to happen: 1954 was to be the year of 'Beauty and the Beast', with the cool Miss Kelly taking her appointed place on the stage beside the brooding Mr Brando – a

decision still considered by many as the Academy's greatest oversight.

Yet again, **Gone With The Wind**'s record was matched but not beaten. **On The Waterfront** won Academy Awards in eight different departments (Best Film, Actor, Supporting Actress, Director, Story and Screenplay, Cinematography, Art Direction, Film Editing), though not, curiously, for Leonard Bernstein's hauntingly jagged musical accompaniment. Bernstein subsequently reworked his soundtrack score as an orchestral suite, which can occasionally be heard in the concert hall.

Among the evening's other highlights: the two diminutive performers of **The Little Kidnappers**, Jon Whiteley and Vincent Winter, received a tiny statuette apiece for their performances; the Best Foreign Language Film was judged to be the colorful Samurai epic from Japan, **Gate Of Hell** (directed by Teinosuke Kinugasa), complete with breathtakingly stylized, almost choreographed, battle sequences; and there were special Oscars to Danny Kaye "for his unique talents" and to an actress who had been systematically forgotten by the Academy voters throughout her career, Greta Garbo, ironically "for her unforgettable screen performances". Finally, the show was all but stolen by Bette Davis, who presented Brando with his Oscar. Her shaven head (she was currently filming **The Virgin Queen** as Elizabeth I of England) was bizarrely masked by a sequinned metal helmet.

ABOVE *Grace Kelly, playing against her glamorous, privileged image, won a Best Actress Oscar for* The Country Girl. *Here she is seen behind her alcoholic singer husband Bing Crosby, in the invariable cardigans she wore in the movie. Incidentally, Kelly and Crosby dated for a time*

RIGHT *Best Actor Marlon Brando for* On The Waterfront *played washed-up boxer Terry Molloy who speaks the poignant lines, 'I coulda had class. I coulda been somebody. I coulda been a contender instead of a bum, which is what I am'. Brando proved he had class, was a somebody, and was a champion*

The troubled genesis of **On The Waterfront** recalled that of Zinnemann's **High Noon**. Here was another low-budget production in which not much faith was placed. Two major studios, 20th Century-Fox and United Artists, rejected Budd Schulberg's script before it was accepted by the independent producer Sam Spiegel. Perhaps because the film had thus been freed from studio pressures, the result was shattering: a powerful melodrama of social conscience about a group of dock laborers in the clutches of a venal and unscrupulous union boss (Lee J. Cobb, an Oscar nominee), who eventually confront their exploiters with the aid of a former union henchman (Brando), a liberal priest (Karl Malden, an Oscar nominee) and a courageous young woman (Eva Marie Saint, who won an Oscar as Best Supporting Actress). Though it is possible to question the film's politics (critics have argued that **On The Waterfront** obliquely reflects the slavish capitulation to McCarthyism of both Schulberg and Kazan), there can be no doubting the film's power to hold an audience enthralled. One edgy scene in particular, played in the back seat of an automobile between Brando and his brother, Rod Steiger (yet another nominee) – the scene during which the former makes his celebrated "contender" speech – has been much-anthologized.

Brando's relationship with Hollywood has always been an uncomfortably ambivalent one. Though he began his career as a stage actor, one of the Method School generation, he definitively renounced the theater after establishing himself as a screen star. This was, in part, a question of money: he has never denied that the astronomical fees he could command in Hollywood (notably for two brief but memorable appearances in **The Godfather**, 1972, and **The Formula**, 1980) were a decisive factor in his fidelity to a medium he has often claimed to despise. But it was doubtless also true that Brando's personality was simply too gargantuan to be satisfied with the limited opportunities (and audiences) which would have been offered him by an exclusively theatrical career. By wholeheartedly giving himself up to the movies, he totally changed our perception of the medium: his influence on such actors as Hoffman, Pacino, Nicholson, De Niro and Hackman has been immeasurable. Riding into a Hollywood sunset on the motorcycle of **The Wild One** back in 1953, he laid the groundwork for a new breed of actors who have enriched the American cinema ever since.

It would be hard to imagine a personality more dissimilar to Brando's than that of the year's Best Actress, Grace Kelly. She had been born into a wealthy Philadelphia family: her father was a business tycoon, politician and Olympic champion, her uncle, George Kelly, a once famous Broadway playwright. If she had not early decided on a show business career, she would have almost certainly

ABOVE *Garbo . . . The apotheosis of the Hollywood star. Garbo – Camille, Anna Karenina, Queen Christina, Ninotchka, and Mata Hari of legend – incredibly never received a Best Actress Oscar. Thirteen years after her last movie,* Two-Faced Woman, *she was belatedly presented with a special statuette 'for her unforgettable screen performances'*

lived out a gracious existence as a prominent figure of society; and, as everyone knows, her acting career was curtailed when, during the shooting of Hitchcock's **To Catch A Thief** on the French Riviera, she met and later married Prince Rainier of Monaco, becoming one of the most loved and esteemed of European First Ladies.

It was Hitchcock who most cannily exploited her flawless chic and poised blonde charms in such thrillers as **Rear Window** and **Dial M For Murder** (both 1954). But her Oscar-winning performance came in a role which cast her very much against type – practically a tradition with the Academy in the 50s. In **The Country Girl** she astonished her admirers by appearing in dowdy cardigans, spectacles and 'plain' make-up as Crosby's long-suffering wife; and it would probably not be uncharitable to assume that it was as much for these accoutrements as for her performance in itself that she was nominated. Her ultimate screen appearance was, appropriately, in the Cole Porter musical version of **The Philadelphia Story**, **High Society**, in which she again partnered Bing Crosby. Though there were intermittent rumors of a return to the cinema (e.g. to play the title role in Hitchcock's **Marnie** in 1964), the reaction of her Monacan subjects was uniformly unfavorable to the idea and her retirement became a permanent one. She died, tragically, in a car crash in 1984.

LEFT *A quiet and loving moment between Brando and Eva Marie Saint as a prologue to the violence in* On The Waterfront, *the powerful dockside drama that won its director, Elia Kazan, his second Oscar, and awards for Best Black-and-White Cinematography, Art Direction, and Editing*

WINNERS 1954

Nominations Announced: February 12, 1955
Awards Ceremony: March 30, 1955
RKO Pantages Theatre

Best Picture
ON THE WATERFRONT, Horizon-American/Columbia:
SAM SPIEGEL, Producer

Actor
MARLON BRANDO in *On The Waterfront*

Actress
GRACE KELLY in *The Country Girl*,
Perlberg-Seaton/Paramount

Supporting Actor
EDMOND O'BRIEN in *The Barefoot Contessa*, Figaro/UA

Supporting Actress
EVA MARIE SAINT in *On The Waterfront*

Directing
ELIA KAZAN for *On The Waterfront*

Writing
(Motion Picture Story)
BROKEN LANCE, 20th Century-Fox: PHILIP YORDAN
(Screenplay)
THE COUNTRY GIRL: GEORGE SEATON
(Story and Screenplay)
ON THE WATERFRONT: BUDD SCHULBERG

Cinematography
(Black-and-White)
ON THE WATERFRONT: BORIS KAUFMAN
(Color)
THREE COINS IN THE FOUNTAIN, 20th Century-Fox:
MILTON KRASNER

Art Direction-Set Decoration
(Black-and-White)
ON THE WATERFRONT: RICHARD DAY
Set Decoration: No credits listed
(Color)
20,000 LEAGUES UNDER THE SEA, Disney/Buena Vista:
JOHN MEEHAN
Set Decoration: EMILE KURI

Sound Recording
THE GLENN MILLER STORY, U-I: LESLIE I. CAREY,
Sound Director

Film Editing
ON THE WATERFRONT: GENE MILFORD

Music
(Scoring of a Dramatic or Comedy Picture)
THE HIGH AND THE MIGHTY, Wayne-Fellows/Warner
Bros.: DIMITRI TIOMKIN
(Scoring of a Musical Picture)
SEVEN BRIDES FOR SEVEN BROTHERS, MGM:
ADOLPH DEUTSCH and SAUL CHAPLIN

(Best Song)
THREE COINS IN THE FOUNTAIN from *Three Coins In The Fountain*
Music: JULE STYNE
Lyrics: SAMMY CAHN

Costume Design
(Black-and-White)
SABRINA, Paramount: EDITH HEAD
(Color)
GATE OF HELL, Daiei/Harrison (Japanese): SANZO
WADA

Short Subjects
(Cartoons)
WHEN MAGOO FLEW, United Productions of
America/Columbia: STEPHEN BOSUSTOW, Producer
(One-reel)
THIS MECHANICAL AGE, Warner Bros.: ROBERT
YOUNGSON, Producer
(Two-reel)
A TIME OUT OF WAR, Carnival: DENIS and TERRY
SANDERS, Producers

Documentary
(Short Subjects)
THURSDAY'S CHILDREN, British Information Services
(British): WORLD WIDE PICTURES AND MORSE FILMS,
Producers
(Features)
THE VANISHING PRAIRIE, Disney/Buena Vista: WALT
DISNEY, Producer

Special Effects
(Back to Annual Award)
20,000 LEAGUES UNDER THE SEA

Honorary Awards
GATE OF HELL (Japanese) – Best Foreign Language Film
first released in the United States during 1954. (statuette)
KEMP R. NIVER for the development of the Renovare
Process which has made possible the restoration of the
Library of Congress Paper Film Collection. (statuette)
GRETA GARBO for her unforgettable screen
performances. (statuette)
DANNY KAYE for his unique talents, his service to the
Academy, the motion picture industry, and the American
people. (statuette)
JON WHITELEY for his outstanding juvenile performance
in *The Little Kidnappers*. (miniature statuette)
VINCENT WINTER for his outstanding juvenile
performance in *The Little Kidnappers*. (miniature statuette)
BAUSCH & LOMB OPTICAL COMPANY for their
contributions to the advancement of the motion picture
industry. (statuette)

Irving G. Thalberg Memorial Award
None

1955

"THE ITALIANS ARE coming!" – such might have been the cry heard, *à la* Colin Welland, on Oscar night, March 21, 1956. The Best Film award was carried off by first-time feature director Delbert Mann's **Marty**, a Paddy Chayefsky-scripted comedy-drama about an Italian butcher in the Bronx, shy and physically unattractive, who discovers romance for the first time in his life at the age of 35. Another film nominated for the year's highest honor was **The Rose Tattoo**, based on Tennessee Williams' play about a widowed Italian housewife tempted into a love affair for the first time since her husband's death: the film lost out to **Marty**, but its star, Anna Magnani, the actress for whom the play had originally been written, was deservedly named the year's best. And, among the nominees for Best Supporting Performers, there were also two – Marisa Pavan (for **The Rose Tattoo**) and Sal Mineo (for **Rebel Without A Cause**) – of Italian origin.

Magnani was in Rome, asleep in her apartment, when the good news was communicated to her. "If this is a joke," she shrieked into the telephone, "I will get up and kill you whoever you are!" Ernest Borgnine, who had always seemed destined to remain one of nature's supporting actors, was overwhelmed by his Best Actor Oscar for **Marty** and offered his most heartfelt thanks to his mother. Winners of Best Supporting Performance Oscars were Jack Lemmon (for **Mister Roberts**) and Jo Van Fleet (for her brilliantly stylized performance as James Dean's mother in **East Of Eden**).

But the stars who commanded greatest attention, perhaps, were a recently deceased young actor and an actress about to depart from Hollywood altogether. James Dean, already a legendary figure in his own tragically brief lifetime, was a Best Actor nominee for **East Of Eden**. Only six months prior to the ceremony, however, he had been killed in an automobile crash, becoming thereby the first actor ever to receive a posthumous nomination. And Grace Kelly, on hand to present the Oscar to Borgnine, had just announced her engagement to Rainier of Monaco and was about to bid farewell to her Hollywood career. It was, incongruously but touchingly,

BELOW *Julie Harris and James Dean in a gentle scene from* East of Eden, *Elia Kazan's loving adaptation of the second half of John Steinbeck's novel. Dean, the first actor to be nominated posthumously for an Oscar, played an adolescent lacking affection, who discovers that his mother (Jo Van Fleet, the Best Supporting Actress) is the madam of a brothel*

Jerry Lewis, the evening's M.C. in Hollywood, who offered her the film community's very best wishes. Finally, the work judged Best Foreign Picture was **Samurai, The Legend Of Musashi**, a Japanese offering directed by Hiroshi Inagaki.

Marty was what is known in the business as a 'sleeper', which is to say, a film ostensibly without any strong mass audience appeal but which, contrary to everyone's predictions, begins to make pleasant noises at the box-office. It had started life as a television play, directed as on film by Delbert Mann and starring Rod Steiger. (Curiously, the role of Clara, the lonely, retiring young schoolmistress whom Marty meets by chance in a dance-hall, had been taken in the TV production by Nancy Marchand, now better known as the elegant newspaper proprietress Mrs Pynchon in the TV series *Lou Grant*). The independent production company Hecht-Hill-Lancaster ('Lancaster' being Burt) agreed to finance a cinematic adaptation (on a derisively minuscule budget of $343,000) solely as a tax loss: in short, like Zero Mostel in Mel Brooks' comedy **The Producers**, they were actively praying for the film to flop. When, after no more than a few days into its release, it became evident that, far from their writing it off financially, **Marty** was destined to make them a handsome profit, the producers reversed their original intention to let the film slip out unheralded and spent more on advertising and promotion than the shooting itself had cost.

Marty became something of a cult figure. The butchers of America voted him as their Man of the Year; and Borgnine, whose coarsely pudgy features and stocky build had never endeared him to columnists and photographers, suddenly (and, it has to be said, briefly) joined the roster of bankable performers. How can one explain the popularity of an inexpensively produced, black-and-white movie boasting neither stars nor glamorous settings? No doubt because, to a degree that was rare in the Hollywood cinema of the 50s, **Marty** encouraged audiences to relate directly to its protagonist's modest problems and triumphs.

In fact, the film was only superficially 'naturalistic'. Chayefsky's brilliant dialogue, though founded on the idiomatic speech patterns of ordinary, working-class Americans, was as carefully crafted as that of a wisecracking comedy; and a subplot, concerning the strained relations of a widowed aunt with her son and daughter-in-law, was cunningly introduced to underline the fear of loneliness which Marty's hesitant romance instils in his own mother. Yet it was an unusual occurrence for a Hollywood film actually to depict its hero at work – in a job, moreover, as humdrum as butchering. And Marty's mundane yet affecting crises – how to spend a Saturday night

RIGHT *Emest Borgnine, the lonely Bronx butcher* Marty, *looks in the mirror and doesn't like what he sees. His homely looks and affecting performance beat James Cagney (*Love Me Or Leave Me*), James Dean (*East Of Eden*), Frank Sinatra (*The Man With The Golden Arm*), and Spencer Tracy (*Bad Day At Black Rock*) for the Best Actor award*

with 'the boys', how to muster courage enough to invite a girl on a date – were ones with which the vast majority of the male half of the public could ruefully identify. And they would certainly have identified with the film's basic premise, one of the most moving it's possible to imagine: the ultimate victory of a loser over his fate.

For Borgnine, too, **Marty** perhaps represented the victory of a loser over his fate. This decidedly plain, unalluring actor – most of whose past screen appearances had been of a purely contractual order, 'blind dates', as it were – had at last the good fortune to encounter a role made to measure for his particular talents and physique, so that character and actor merged in the harmony of a perfect romance. It was, as it happens, a question of chance. Hecht, Lancaster and Chayefsky were all hoping that Rod Steiger, star of the original TV version, would replay his role on the big screen. Steiger, however, was otherwise engaged, filming Rodgers and Hammerstein's **Oklahoma!** for director Fred Zinnemann, and he reluc-

BELOW *Best Actress winner Anna Magnani and co-star Burt Lancaster on location in Key West, Florida for* The Rose Tattoo. *The film, based on Tennessee Williams' play, was set in the Italian quarter of a steamy town on the American coast, and wonderfully photographed by James Wong Howe who won the black-and-white cinematography Oscar*

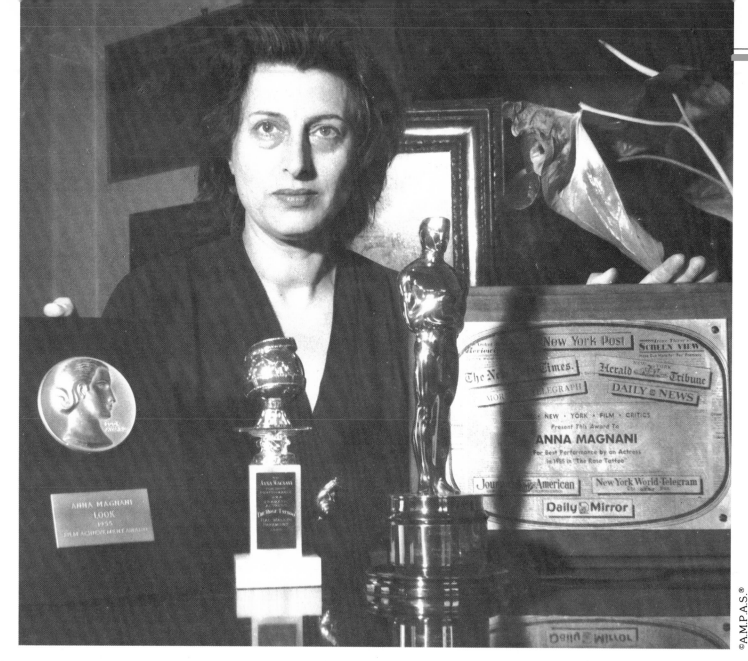

ABOVE *Hot-blooded Italian actress Anna Magnani proudly displays the awards she received for her performance in* The Rose Tattoo, *the first of her four American films. Her trophies are (from left to right) the Look Film Achievement Award, the Golden Globe given by the Hollywood Press Association, the Oscar, and the New York Film Critics Award*

tantly had to decline their offer. Even so, Borgnine's was scarcely a name to conjure with; and, or so legend has it, he was offered the part only when, at a Hollywood reception, a woman guest quite disinterestedly remarked to producer Harold Hecht that, ugly as he was, Borgnine possessed an oddly tender quality which made her yearn to mother him. "That," Hecht said later, "is when I decided to give him the part."

His Oscar apart, Borgnine won the Best Actor Award at the Cannes Film Festival, the New York Film Critics Award and the National Board of Review Award. Though no finer role ever came his way, he was at least grateful no longer to be automatically cast as a heavy; and it was as a comic character, in the popular TV series *McHale's Navy*, that he was to make his most enduring impression on the American public.

In her lifetime, the Italian actress Anna Magnani was often compared to a volcano (indeed, **Volcano** was the title of one of her films), a permanently erupting volcano which only her death in 1973 rendered extinct. Like Borgnine, she in no way conformed to our conventionally idealized conception of a movie star, being slightly plump, short in stature, unkempt in appearance and famous for the deep, dark shadows which circled her heavy-lidded eyes. Unlike Borgnine, however, she was earthy, temperamental and brimming over with a ripe Mediterranean sensuality. If Magnani made just a handful of Hollywood films, it was probably because her overwhelming personality could not comfortably be contained within the rigidly structured genres of the American cinema, and few male actors cared to be upstaged by such a force of nature. At her best, however, working at the full volcanic blast of her histrionic powers, as was the case in **The Rose Tattoo**, Anna Magnani was unquestionably one of the greatest actresses the cinema has ever known.

WINNERS 1955

Nominations Announced: February 18, 1956
Awards Ceremony: March 21, 1956
RKO Pantages Theatre

Best Picture
MARTY, Hecht & Lancaster's Steven Prods/UA: HAROLD HECHT, Producer

Actor
ERNEST BORGNINE in *Marty*

Actress
ANNA MAGNANI in *The Rose Tattoo*, Wallis/Paramount

Supporting Actor
JACK LEMMON in *Mister Roberts*, Orange/Warner Bros.

Supporting Actress
JO VAN FLEET in *East Of Eden*, Warner Bros.

Directing
DELBERT MANN for *Marty*

Writing
(Motion Picture Story)
LOVE ME OR LEAVE ME, MGM: DANIEL FUCHS
(Best Screenplay)
MARTY: PADDY CHAYEFSKY
(Story and Screenplay)
INTERRUPTED MELODY, MGM: WILLIAM LUDWIG and SONYA LEVIEN

Cinematography
(Black-and-White)
THE ROSE TATTOO: JAMES WONG HOWE
(Color)
TO CATCH A THIEF, Paramount: ROBERT BURKS

Art Direction-Set Decoration
(Prior to 1955, Set Decorators were given plaques. Beginning in 1955, Gold Statuettes were given.)
(Black-and-White)
THE ROSE TATTOO: HAL PEREIRA and TAMBI LARSEN
Set Decoration: SAM COMER and ARTHUR KRAMS
(Color)
PICNIC, Columbia: WILLIAM FLANNERY and JO MIELZINER
Set Decoration: ROBERT PRIESTLEY

Sound Recording
OKLAHOMA!, Todd-AO Sound Department: FRED HYNES, Sound Director

Film Editing
PICNIC: CHARLES NELSON and WILLIAM A. LYON

Music
(Scoring of a Dramatic or Comedy Picture)
LOVE IS A MANY-SPLENDORED THING, 20th Century-Fox: ALFRED NEWMAN
(Scoring of a Musical Picture)
OKLAHOMA!, Rodgers & Hammerstein/Magna Theatre: ROBERT RUSSELL BENNETT, JAY BLACKTON and ADOLPH DEUTSCH
(Best Song)
LOVE IS A MANY-SPLENDORED THING from *Love Is A Many-Splendored Thing*
Music: SAMMY FAIN
Lyrics: PAUL FRANCIS WEBSTER

Costume Design
(Black-and-White)
I'LL CRY TOMORROW, MGM: HELEN ROSE
(Color)
LOVE IS A MANY-SPLENDORED THING: CHARLES LeMAIRE

Short Subjects
(Cartoons)
SPEEDY GONZALES, Warner Bros.: EDWARD SELZER, Producer
(One-reel)
SURVIVAL CITY, 20th Century-Fox: EDMUND REEK, Producer
(Two-reel)
THE FACE OF LINCOLN, University of Southern California Presentation/Cavalcade: WILBUR T. BLUME, Producer

Documentary
(Short Subjects)
MEN AGAINST THE ARCTIC, Disney/Buena Vista: WALT DISNEY, Producer
(Features)
HELEN KELLER IN HER STORY, Hamilton: NANCY HAMILTON, Producer

Special Effects
THE BRIDGES AT TOKO-RI, Paramount

Honorary Award
SAMURAI, THE LEGEND OF MUSASHI (Japanese) – Best Foreign Language Film first released in the United States during 1955. (statuette)

Irving G. Thalberg Memorial Award
None

1956

THE ACADEMY AWARDS ceremony for 1956 sprang all kinds of odd little surprises. Voted Best Film was a three-hour epic produced by a man who had never worked in the cinema before, Mike Todd's **Around The World In 80 Days**. Best Actor was a virtually unknown, completely bald gypsy who claimed to have been born in Outer Mongolia but had actually seen the light of day on Sakhalin, a small island east of Siberia and north of Japan – Yul Brynner, for his performance as the King of Siam in **The King And I**. Best Actress was Ingrid Bergman (playing the ambiguous title role in **Anastasia**), whose Oscar symbolized her return to the fold after years of being ostracized by Hollywood. And, for the second year in succession, the late James Dean was a posthumous nominee, on this occasion for his eccentric portrayal of Jett Rink in George Stevens' (Best Director for the year) mammoth Texan drama **Giant**: his is, needless to say, a record which has never been, and is unlikely ever to be, matched by any other actor.

Elsewhere, confusion reigned among the screenplay categories, as a consequence of the blacklisting House UnAmerican Activities Committee and its abiding influence on the Hollywood community. The winner of an Oscar for the Best Motion Picture Story was one 'Robert Rich', the scenarist of **The Brave One**, a modestly affecting account of a young Mexican's attachment to his pet bull. 'Rich' was not present at the Pantages Theater to collect his prize, which was picked up by Jesse Lasky Jr. To the Academy's mortification, however, it subsequently transpired that 'Robert Rich' was a pseudonym for Dalton Trumbo, a blacklisted writer and one of the legendary 'Hollywood Ten', imprisoned by a grand jury for refusing to testify before the Committee on matters pertaining to membership in the Communist Party. It was not until 1960, and his screenplays for **Spartacus** and **Exodus**, that Trumbo's own name could be publicly credited. In the Best Adaptation category, too, the Academy learned to its chagrin that it had made an embarrassing gaffe. One of the nominees, for William Wyler's **Friendly Persuasion**, was Michael Wilson, who had delivered his screenplay just before being blacklisted by the industry on the same grounds as Trumbo. Wilson was, at the eleventh hour, declared ineligible for an award; and he resurfaced as a credited scenarist only with Vincente Minnelli's **The Sandpiper** in 1965.

The Best Foreign Language Film Oscar (selected this year for the first time from among five contenders) went to Federico Fellini's sentimental parable of circus life **La Strada**; an honorary award was presented to the much-loved singer and comedian Eddie Cantor "for distinguished service to the film industry"; and, bizarrely, one of the nominees for Best Motion Picture Story was the distinguished French novelist, dramatist, philosopher and future Nobel Prize recipient, Jean-Paul Sartre. In the cartoon category, Walt Disney, recipient of more Oscar statuettes than any other artist in Hollywood's history, found himself upstaged by the jazzily angular graphics of U.P.A., creators of, among others, the myopic Mr Magoo.

Mike Todd's filmography was surely the most laconic of any major Oscar winner. One film: **Around The World In 80 Days**. Yet, into the spectacular adaptation of Jules Verne's classic novel (about a phlegmatic Englishman who wagers that he will circle the globe in exactly 80 days), Todd packed more stars, more changes of scenery, more adventures and more surprises than could be boasted of by producers with far more prolific careers. Perhaps the most eye-catching novelty of all was the film's dazzling array of 'cameo players'. Apart from the quartet of principals – David Niven as the staid, methodical clubman, the Mexican comedian Cantinflas as his resourceful valet Passepartout, Shirley MacLaine as the Indian Princess Aouda and Robert Newton as the Scotland Yard detective Inspector Fix – there were no fewer than 44 well-known faces, many of them appearing on-screen for only a minute or two. These included John Gielgud as the perfect 'gentleman's gentleman', Marlene Dietrich as a dance-hall hostess (her fabulous legs displayed to advantage by the wide-screen process Todd-AO), Buster Keaton, George Raft, Noel Coward, Frank Sinatra, Ronald Colman and Charles Boyer. If ever a film merited an Oscar for Best Supporting Cast, it was **Around The World In 80 Days**.

It is also fondly remembered for its epigrammatic script (on which the humorist S.J. Perelman collaborated); its witty setpiece highlights (e.g. Cantinflas, from an air balloon, scooping crisp white snow off an Alpine peak to ice his master's champagne); its catchy theme song by Victor Young; and, last (it was screened at the end of the film) but not least, its extraordinary cartoon credit-title sequence by Saul Bass, retelling the entire plot a second time around. Todd was never allowed to repeat his success: in 1958, on his way to receive an award as 'Showman of the Year', he was killed when his private plane (named 'Lucky Liz' after his wife, Elizabeth Taylor) crash-landed in the New Mexico desert.

Though Yul Brynner's filmography was a long and intermittently interesting one (including **The Brothers Karamazov, The Buccaneer**, both 1958, **The Sound And The Fury**, 1959, and **The Magnificent Seven**, 1960), he will always be recalled for one role, a role he played from the very beginning to the very end of his career – that in **The King And I**. Of part-gypsy ancestry, Brynner had led a famously chequered early life, as a balalaika musician in a Parisian nightclub, a trapeze artist with the internation-

ABOVE *David Niven (right) as the globe-trotting Englishman Phileas Fogg and Mexican comedian Cantinflas as his valet Passepartout, on top of the world in Mike Todd's Best Picture winner* Around The World In Eighty Days. *The trip took three hours of screen time to complete*

RIGHT *A scene from the first Foreign Language film to win an Oscar in competition, Federico Fellini's* La Strada. *Fellini's wife Giulietta Masina (background left) played – wonderfully – a half-witted peasant girl sold to an itinerant strong man (Anthony Quinn, foreground right)*

ally famous Cirque d'Hiver, a student at the Sorbonne, a radio commentator in the United States during World War II and, in both directing and acting capacities, as one of the pioneers of American television. He had even acted in a single film before his breakthrough role, **Port Of New York** (1949), a B-movie thriller in which he was cast as a villainous narcotics dealer. His career totally changed direction, however, when he was offered the lead in the Broadway production of Rodgers and Hammerstein's musical **The King And I** and, almost as significantly, was required to shave his head for the part. Perhaps out of superstition, Brynner never allowed his hair to grow back and, when occasionally necessary, would sport a toupee. Apart from his Oscar-winning performance in Walter Lang's film version, he played the imperious but lonely Siamese monarch in numerous revivals right up to his death in 1985, and it would be difficult to imagine another actor filling the role so compellingly, with such a striking blend of personal magnetism and self-deflating humor.

Nineteen-fifty-six was very much Brynner's year. Not only did he win an Oscar for **The King And I**, but also figured prominently in two other award-winning films, Cecil B. DeMille's **The Ten Commandments** (as the Pharaoh Rameses II) and Anatole Litvak's **Anastasia** (as a scoundrelly White Russian attempting to pass off an amnesiac, half-mad woman as the missing daughter of Tsar Nicholas II of Russia). The heroine of the film – possibly, just as possibly not, Anastasia – was played to the hilt by Ingrid Bergman, who thus came in from the cold after almost a decade of exile from Hollywood. Bergman's reputation had remained at such a low ebb in

ABOVE *One of the few intimate moments from Cecil B. DeMille's Biblical epic* The Ten Commandments, *whose sole Oscar went to John Fulton's special effects, the most spectacular of which was the parting of the Red Sea. Pictured are Yul Brynner (left) as the Pharaoh, Rameses II, and Charlton Heston as Moses*

the United States – a Colorado Senator had even publicly denounced her as "a powerful influence for evil" – that 20th Century-Fox was extremely nervous about employing her: its president, Spyros Skouras, feared that the American public had still to forgive Bergman her adulterous affair with Roberto Rossellini and her illegitimate child. It was the film's producer, the maverick non-conformist Darryl F. Zanuck, who insisted that only she could incarnate Anastasia and that a great performance would instantly erase the taint of scandal from the public's memory. Not for the first time, Zanuck's instinct paid off. When the Oscar was accepted on her behalf by Cary Grant (Bergman could not attend because of a theatrical engagement in Paris), he said, "Dear Ingrid, if you can hear me or see this, I want you to know we all send you our love and admiration." The episode – an episode which, in truth, reflected more badly on Hollywood than on the actress herself – was finally closed.

LEFT *Best Actress Ingrid Bergman as* Anastasia *(or was she?) in a poverty-stricken and amnesiac state before being taken up and passed off as the last surviving daughter of the executed Tsar Nicholas of Russia. The award was Hollywood's way of 'forgiving her sins', and it was a triumphant return to American films after eight years in exile*

WINNERS 1956

Nominations Announced: February 18, 1957
Awards Ceremony: March 27, 1957
RKO Pantages Theatre

Best Picture
AROUND THE WORLD IN 80 DAYS, Todd/UA: MICHAEL TODD, Producer

Actor
YUL BRYNNER in *The King And I*, 20th Century-Fox

Actress
INGRID BERGMAN in *Anastasia*, 20th Century-Fox

Supporting Actor
ANTHONY QUINN in *Lust For Life*, MGM

Supporting Actress
DOROTHY MALONE in *Written On The Wind*, U-I

Directing
GEORGE STEVENS for *Giant*, Giant/Warner Bros.

Writing
(Motion Picture Story)
THE BRAVE ONE, King Bros/RKO Radio: ROBERT RICH (pseudonym for Dalton Trumbo)
(Best Screenplay – adapted)
AROUND THE WORLD IN 80 DAYS: JAMES POE, JOHN FARROW and S.J. PERELMAN
(Best Screenplay – original)
THE RED BALLOON, Films Montsouris/Lopert (French): ALBERT LAMORISSE

Cinematography
(Black-and-White)
SOMEBODY UP THERE LIKES ME, MGM: JOSEPH RUTTENBERG
(Color)
AROUND THE WORLD IN 80 DAYS: LIONEL LINDON

Art Direction-Set Decoration
(Black-and-White)
SOMEBODY UP THERE LIKES ME: CEDRIC GIBBONS and MALCOLM F. BROWN
Set Decoration: EDWIN B. WILLIS and KEOGH GLEASON
(Color)
THE KING AND I: LYLE R. WHEELER and JOHN DeCUIR
Set Decoration: WALTER M. SCOTT and PAUL S. FOX

Sound Recording
THE KING AND I, 20th Century-Fox
Studio Sound Department: CARL FAULKNER, Sound Director

Film Editing
AROUND THE WORLD IN 80 DAYS: GENE RUGGIERO and PAUL WEATHERWAX

Music
(Scoring of a Dramatic or Comedy Picture)
AROUND THE WORLD IN 80 DAYS: VICTOR YOUNG
(Scoring of a Musical Picture)
THE KING AND I: ALFRED NEWMAN and KEN DARBY
(Best Song)
WHATEVER WILL BE, WILL BE (QUE SERA, SERA) from *The Man Who Knew Too Much*, Filwite/Paramount
Music and Lyrics: JAY LIVINGSTON and RAY EVANS

Costume Design
(Black-and-White)
THE SOLID GOLD CADILLAC, Columbia: JEAN LOUIS
(Color)
THE KING AND I: IRENE SHARAFF

Short Subjects
(Cartoons)
MISTER MAGOO'S PUDDLE JUMPER, UPA/Columbia: STEPHEN BOSUSTOW, Producer
(One-reel)
CRASHING THE WATER BARRIER, Warner Bros.: KONSTANTIN KALSER, Producer
(Two-reel)
THE BESPOKE OVERCOAT, Romulus (John and James Woolf)/Arthur: JACK CLAYTON, Producer

Documentary
(Short Subjects)
THE TRUE STORY OF THE CIVIL WAR, Camera Eye: LOUIS CLYDE STOUMEN, Producer
(Features)
THE SILENT WORLD, Filmad-FSJYC/Columbia (French): JACQUES-YVES COUSTEAU, Producer

Special Effects
THE TEN COMMANDMENTS, Motion Picture Associates/Paramount: JOHN FULTON

Foreign Language Film Award
(New Category)
(Prior to 1956 an Honorary Award voted by the Board of Governors.)
LA STRADA, A Ponti-De Laurentiis Prod (Italy): DINO DE LAURENTIIS and CARLO PONTI, Producers

Honorary Award
EDDIE CANTOR for distinguished service to the film industry. (statuette)

Irving G. Thalberg Award
BUDDY ADLER

Jean Hersholt Humanitarian Award
(New Category)
Y. FRANK FREEMAN

1957

THE 1957 ACADEMY Awards ceremony proved to be the smoothest, best-coordinated and most sheerly entertaining for some years. Because of negative reactions from the television public to Oldsmobile's incessant commercial breaks, the industry decided that it would have to finance and sponsor the show itself, with a rare display of solidarity from major studios, independent production companies and exhibitors alike. The 70 celebrities who participated all offered their services free of charge; and 90 million viewers were able to watch – live on their screens – such Hollywood luminaries as Burt Lancaster, Kirk Douglas, Rock Hudson, Rosalind Russell,

David Niven, James Stewart and the 65-year-old but still indestructibly charismatic Mae West. Highlights of the evening were two gloriously droll song-and-dance duets worthy of inclusion in any Hollywood musical: Hudson and West's campy rendition of 'Baby, It's Cold Outside', and a delightful number parodying the award itself, 'It's Great Not To Be Nominated', sung (if that's the word to describe it!) by Lancaster and Douglas.

To add to an already potent brew, the event was brushed by both tragedy and scandal. Two of the nominees for Best Actress were Elizabeth Taylor (for **Raintree County**) and that durable high-gloss platinum blonde Lana Turner (for 20th Century-Fox's **Peyton Place**, from the Grace Metalious bestseller). A shadow was cast over Oscar night by the death of Taylor's husband, Mike Todd, in an air crash only four days before the ceremony; and, ten days later, Turner's daughter Cheryl

BELOW *East is East and West is West . . . Two officers confront one another in* The Bridge On The River Kwai, *the Best Picture winner. Best Actor Alec Guinness (left) as the brave and stubborn English colonel who won't give in to the orders of his Japanese captor played by veteran actor Sessue Hayakawa (Oscar-nominated)*

ABOVE *Glamorous blond Lana Turner (right) received her only Oscar nomination, after twenty years of service as a screen sex goddess, for her role as the mother of teenage Diane Varsi (illustrated, also nominated) in* Peyton Place, *a tale of lust, greed and violence simmering beneath the surface of a small New England Town. Lloyd Nolan, also pictured, was the local doctor*

Crane hit the headlines by fatally stabbing her mother's current companion, an underworld hoodlum named Johnny Stompanato. Cheryl was acquitted on the grounds of justifiable homicide; a sheaf of torrid love letters was read out in court; and Miss Turner herself might easily have won an Oscar for her patently sincere but virtuoso performance as a tragically distressed mother.

The evening's clear winner was David Lean's **The Bridge On The River Kwai**, securing seven Oscars (for Best Picture, Actor, Director, Screenplay, Cinematography, Musical Score – including the British military march 'Colonel Bogey', destined to enter the international hit-parade – and Editing). Another film with an

Oriental setting, Joshua Logan's somewhat sudsy soap opera of East-West romance, **Sayonara** (which starred Marlon Brando), monopolized the Best Supporting Performance category, with Red Buttons and the Japanese actress Miyoshi Umeki earning twin statuettes. It was also a year in which the voting system was radically altered. Whereas, before, the original nominations had been made by 12,000 people selected from within the film industry, with the final votes to be decided by the Academy's official 1,800 members, in 1957 these members alone were responsible for both nominations and awards. And as there had been criticism that the ceremony was gradually becoming topheavy, the number of categories was significantly reduced – from 31 to 23.

The Bridge On The River Kwai was based on a bestselling novel by Pierre Boulle about the infamous Burma Road in World War II. Out of that novel David Lean fashioned what might be described as a bestselling movie, thrilling its spectators with setpieces of almost unparalleled brilliance and spectacle while, at the same time, forcing them to question their received ideas of individual courage and responsibility. Few war films can boast as subtle and complex a plotline. Its account of a British officer (a haunting study in stiff-necked self-absorption from Alec Guinness) driving the P.O.W.s under his command to construct a magnificent bridge as a form of therapy is invested with a rich subtext of ambiguities. So wholeheartedly does the Colonel give himself up to his bridge-building, such is the pride he takes in his achievement, that it eventually becomes an end in itself. Forgotten is the fact that such a bridge can only aid the enemy's movement of supplies and troops. And when the British High Command is determined to destroy it, the audience actually finds itself assailed with pangs of remorse. Such is the film's diabolic cunning that we have been encouraged to identify with Guinness's character to the point where we, too, resist the demolition of his beloved structure.

Superbly cast, with an outstanding appearance by Sessue Hayakawa (a veteran of silent movies) as Guinness's Japanese opposite number, a man whose cruelty and ruthlessness conceal a profound fear of 'losing face', **The Bridge On The River Kwai** was distinguished by a visual and narrative sweep rare in the modern cinema. To take one example from among many, it will be difficult to forget the arrival on foot of the British P.O.W.s inside the Japanese camp, proudly raising their weary heads and whistling 'Colonel Bogey'. Such a moment produces a direct physical effect on the spectator: in a quite literal sense, it sends a cold shiver through the spine.

The film made the already distinguished and brilliantly gifted Alec Guinness into an international star, turned William Holden into a millionaire (in lieu of the substantial fee he would normally have commanded he had opted for a percentage of the profits) and must have seemed, with its bouquet of Oscars and its enduring reputation, a worthy compensation for the gruelling rigors of the three-month shoot in Burma.

Strangely enough, the central role of the demented martinet was initially offered to Charles Laughton (no doubt as a companion piece to his Captain Bligh in **Mutiny On The Bounty**). Laughton turned it down, later generously admitting, "I never understood the part until I saw Guinness play it." (Laughton was himself a nominee in 1957 for his ripely eccentric performance as a crotchety old barrister in Billy Wilder's **Witness For The Prosecution**.) To start with, Guinness himself was no more enthusiastic about the project: "The first time I didn't like the script; second, I thought it was anti-British; third, I just didn't like the role." His reticence may also have derived from the fact that he had generally been associated with humorous characters, most notably in an almost unbroken cycle of Ealing comedies. Yet, in **The Bridge On The River Kwai**, an ambiguously steely quality infected the

RIGHT *Alec Guinness, Best Actor winner, in one of the stiffest of stiff upper lip moments from David Lean's seven-Oscar winning* The Bridge On The River Kwai. *It remains the brilliantly subtle English actor's only Oscar to date. Guinness, who was knighted in 1959, has appeared in six of Lean's last twelve pictures*

ABOVE *Joanne Woodward, named Best Actress for her third film and first starring role as the triple schizophrenic in* The Three Faces Of Eve *displays three distinct personalities: drab housewife, mature sophisticated woman and good-time girl (pictured here). Lee J. Cobb (right) was the patient, probing psychiatrist helping her to deal with her problems*

tight-lipped but boyishly sunny smile with which one had become familiar from such films as **The Lavender Hill Mob** and **The Man In The White Suit**; and his characterization was all the more resonant for having been achieved without the sometimes dubious benefit of wigs and elaborate make-up. (Coincidentally, it was by accepting a percentage offer similar to Holden's for **Kwai** that Guinness, in his turn, became a multimillionaire; but then, the film in question was **Star Wars**!)

Joanne Woodward is a quintessentially modern actress, expert at capturing the social, sexual and psychological pressures which beset women in a male-dominated world, and she most frequently acts in a register of 'heightened ordinariness'. Thus she excels at playing spinsters and slatterns, but always contrives to avoid the whiny self-righteousness inherent in such roles by her radiant and never humorless presence. Her sole Academy Award (to date) was won for the extraordinary title role (or roles) of **The Three Faces Of Eve**, a semi-fictionalized case-history of a celebrated victim of split personality. In fact, the film was flat, melodramatic and often risibly superficial and, notwithstanding the challenge

which it posed, Woodward's performance can hardly be considered among her best. Schizophrenia was a modish theme in the 50s and it is likely that, on this occasion, the Oscar went to the virtuosity rather than the insight, of her performance. Woodward herself seems to have been aware of the problem. As she said, "I don't feel it was either my most difficult or my best performance, but of course I'm grateful for it."

Though very much a star after Oscar night, she had not regarded herself as one before. In what was undoubtedly a unique case in the ceremony's 30-year history, she stepped up to receive her award wearing a home-made gown. When questioned about it, she replied with wholly disarming candor, "I didn't think I had a chance to win, so I didn't want to invest too much."

WINNERS 1957

Nominations Announced: February 17, 1958
Awards Ceremony: March 26, 1958
RKO Pantages Theatre

Best Picture
THE BRIDGE ON THE RIVER KWAI, Horizon/Columbia:
SAM SPIEGEL, Producer

Actor
ALEC GUINNESS in *The Bridge On The River Kwai*

Actress
JOANNE WOODWARD in *The Three Faces Of Eve*, 20th
Century-Fox

Supporting Actor
RED BUTTONS in *Sayonara*, Goetz/Warner Bros.

Supporting Actress
MIYOSHI UMEKI in *Sayonara*

Directing
DAVID LEAN for *The Bridge On The River Kwai*

Writing
(Rules changed this year to two awards for Writing instead of
three awards as previously given.)
(Best Screenplay – based on material from another medium)
THE BRIDGE ON THE RIVER KWAI: PIERRE BOULLE
(pseudonym for Carl Foreman and Michael Wilson)
(Best Story and Screenplay – written directly for the screen)
DESIGNING WOMAN, MGM: GEORGE WELLS

Cinematography
(Rules changed this year to one Award instead of separate
awards for black-and-white and color.)
THE BRIDGE ON THE RIVER KWAI: JACK HILDYARD

Art Direction-Set Decoration
(Rules changed this year to one Award instead of separate
awards for black-and-white and color.)
SAYONARA: TED HAWORTH
Set Decoration: ROBERT PRIESTLEY

Sound
(Prior to 1957, 30th Year, known as Sound Recording.)
SAYONARA, Warner Bros. Studio Sound Department:
GEORGE GROVES, Sound Director

Film Editing
THE BRIDGE ON THE RIVER KWAI: PETER TAYLOR

Music
(Rules changed this year to one Award for Music Scoring
instead of separate awards for scoring a Dramatic or
Comedy Picture and Scoring of a Musical Picture.)
(Scoring)
THE BRIDGE ON THE RIVER KWAI: MALCOLM
ARNOLD

(Best Song)
ALL THE WAY from *The Joker Is Wild*, AMBL/Paramount
Music: JAMES VAN HEUSEN
Lyrics: SAMMY CAHN

Costume Design
(Rules changed this year to one Award instead of separate
awards for black-and-white and color.)
LES GIRLS, Siegel/MGM: ORRY-KELLY

Short Subjects
(Rules changed this year to two awards for Short Subjects
instead of three as previously given.)
(Cartoons)
BIRDS ANONYMOUS, Warner Bros.: EDWARD SELZER,
Producer
(Live Action Subjects)
THE WETBACK HOUND, Disney/Buena Vista: LARRY
LANSBURGH, Producer

Documentary
(No Short Subject Documentary nominations voted this
year.)
(Features)
ALBERT SCHWEITZER, Hill & Anderson/Louis De
Rochemont Associates: JEROME HILL, Producer

Special Effects
THE ENEMY BELOW, 20th Century-Fox Audible:
WALTER ROSSI

Foreign Language Film Award
(Rules changed this year: award given to Production
Company, not the individual producer.)
THE NIGHTS OF CABIRIA, Dino De Laurentiis Production
(Italy)

Honorary Awards
CHARLES BRACKETT for outstanding service to the
Academy. (statuette)
B.B. KAHANE for distinguished service to the motion
picture industry. (statuette)
GILBERT M. ('Broncho Billy') ANDERSON, motion picture
pioneer, for his contributions to the development of motion
pictures as entertainment. (statuette)
THE SOCIETY OF MOTION PICTURE AND TELEVISION
ENGINEERS for their contributions to the advancement of
the motion picture industry. (statuette)

Irving G. Thalberg Memorial Award
None

Jean Hersholt Humanitarian Award
SAMUEL GOLDWYN

1958

"THERE'S NO BUSINESS like show business" – and there's no disaster like a show business disaster! That was the ultimate lesson of the 1958 Academy Awards ceremony, held on April 6, 1959. Everything was running according to plan until the spectacular finale, a massed rendering of Irving Berlin's show business hymn by more than 90 of Hollywood's top stars, including Cary Grant, Bette Davis, James Cagney, Laurence Olivier, John Wayne, Rock Hudson, Doris Day, Sophia Loren and Ingrid Bergman. The song itself was well-appreciated by the vast TV audience, estimated at 70,000,000 – the only snag was that it came to a close fully 20 minutes before the show was due to go off the air.

In the past, it had sometimes been difficult to squeeze all of the proceedings into the allotted running time. On this occasion, by contrast, an unparalleled array of Hollywood talent – "more stars than there are in Heaven", as MGM used to boast of its stable of contract artists – found themselves standing on a sumptuously bedecked stage with absolutely nothing to do. It was the classic actor's nightmare. Jerry Lewis, one of the show's M.C.s, desperately endeavored to save the situation by indulging in some half-hearted, and unenthusiastically received, clowning, a few of the embarrassed performers wondered whether or not to launch into yet another refrain of Berlin's song – until they were all rescued from further mortification by NBC's welcome emergency decision to bring the shambles to an abrupt end and insert a 15-minute programme filler.

For those who left the Pantages Theater with Oscars under their arms, of course, not even the disastrous climax could diminish their elation. None was more elated than Susan Hayward who, despite regular nominations (for **Smash Up – Story Of A Woman**, 1947, **My Foolish Heart**, 1949, **With A Song In My Heart**, 1952, and **I'll Cry Tomorrow**, 1955), had always been a bridesmaid, never a bride. It finally happened with **I Want To Live**, for her meatily dramatic portrayal of Barbara Graham, a gangster's moll executed in San Quentin prison in 1955. Hayward had patently sought an Oscar the way other women yearn to have a child: as one Hollywoodite wryly commented after the ceremony, "Thank heavens, now we can all relax. Susie got what she's been chasing for twenty years!" Winner of the Best Actor award was David Niven for Delbert Mann's film version of two one-act plays by Terence Rattigan, **Separate Tables**.

Niven was a popular choice precisely because, unlike Hayward, he had never given an aggressive, pushy, Oscar-grabbing performance in his life; and it was felt only right that, from time to time, Hollywood should honor those amiable, dependable and often underrated performers whose appeal was better measured in terms of an entire career than for one showy characterization. That might apply, too, to Bugs Bunny who, after years of being upstaged by the Disney menagerie, won his very first Academy Award for the Warner Bros. short **Knighty Knight Bugs**.

The record held by **Gone With The Wind** – and only twice matched – was finally beaten. By the end of the evening, Vincente Minnelli's **Gigi** had scored a grand total of nine Oscars: for Best Picture, Director, Screenplay,

Gigi attained a kind of perfection in virtually every department. The score by Alan Jay Lerner and Frederick Loewe rivaled their own **My Fair Lady** (and, indeed, teasingly resembled it at times); Cecil Beaton's costume and set design arguably surpassed his work on the earlier musical, as his lavishly idealized evocation of Belle Époque Paris also managed to appear warm, human and lived-in (something that could not honestly be claimed of his scrumptious but slightly stiff designs for **My Fair Lady**); and the performers, though Oscar-less, could only have been bettered in Heaven itself. Taking the part played by Audrey Hepburn in a non-musical stage version of Colette's novella, Leslie Caron looked as though her whole life had been lived in preparation for the role of the pretty

BELOW *Susan Hayward (foreground center) finally won her longed-for Best Actress Oscar for her performance as Barbara Graham, the prostitute who went to the gas chamber in* I Want To Live. *Here, good-time girl Graham is letting herself go before her imprisonment – and nobody in Hollywood could let themselves go like Miss Hayward*

ABOVE *The elegant Vincente Minnelli musical* Gigi *won Oscars in almost every category (nine in all) except acting. Nevertheless Maurice Chevalier (right), as the elderly roué uncle of Louis Jourdan (in carriage), the eligible man about town who captures the heart of the blossoming young Gigi (Leslie Caron, illustrated) gave a scintillating performance, oozing his characteristic Gallic charm*

Cinematography, Art Direction, Song, Musical Score, Costume Design and Editing. (Unusually, not one of its cast was honored in any category, though Maurice Chevalier received a special Oscar "for his contributions to the world of entertainment for more than a half-century".) It may have lacked the vigor, the sheer unashamed vulgarity and exuberance of one's favorite musicals, but

RIGHT *David Niven was rewarded after twenty-three years in the motion picture business with a Best Actor award for his poignant and accurate portrayal of a bogus army major in* Separate Tables. *Wendy Hiller (right), best known as a stage actress, won her supporting Oscar for her role as owner of the seaside hotel, the setting of the film*

Parisian ingenue coached for courtesanship who finds happiness at last in marriage. But this ideal fusion of character and actor applied to everyone involved in the project: it was almost as though Colette had been thinking of Chevalier, Louis Jourdan, Hermione Gingold and Isabel Jeans when creating her characters on the page.

Gigi's opulent charm was best described by Janet Flanner, the *New Yorker*'s columnist, who wrote: "The film's hothouse scenes of flirtations, champagne drinking, and waltzes in the summer room at Maxim's have been peopled by Vincente Minnelli with some of the most extraordinary-looking young and old women that Paris has seen in a while. There are dark beauties with white

BELOW *The cheeky, wisecracking Warner Bros. cartoon character Bugs Bunny, whose voice was Mel Blanc's, was created in 1936 by Chuck Jones and Friz Freleng. The superstar 'wabbit' gained an Oscar for* Knighty Knight Bugs. *Here, he is with a friend from space in another sparkling adventure,* Bugs Bunny In The 21st Century

skins and white ripe shoulders, such as the Impressionist artists painted; girls by the dozen with hourglass shapes and hats the size of tea trays, loaded with roses found only in Renoir's gardens, or heavy with black ostrich plumes; and one straw-haired comedienne, dressed in canary yellow, with a face as blank and deadpan as a Puvis de Chavannes fresco." That, as Colette herself might have said, is indeed **Gigi**.

On stage, Rattigan's **Separate Tables** comprised separate plays, both set in the same residential hotel in Bournemouth; and it was the dramatist's intention that the same two actors play the leads in each. Initially, this schema was to be adopted for the film version, the proposed stars being Laurence Olivier (doubling as director) and Vivien Leigh. When the producer, Harold Hecht, decided that the more realistic medium of the cinema would expose the artifice of such a construction, Olivier and Leigh dropped out and David Niven was offered the juicy role of a self-styled military man paying bashful court to a repressed, mother-dominated spinster (Deborah Kerr) until suddenly arrested for molesting women in a cinema. (To an English journalist Rattigan, a homosexual himself, revealed the character as originally conceived had been apprehended making advances to a young man.) And since Niven had played, for much of his professional life, the kind of nonchalant, devil-may-care individual that Rattigan's bogus Major would wish to have been, he was, paradoxically, both typecast and cast against type. The film's most poignant moment was that of his re-entry into the hotel's dining-room after his arrest to be welcomed, at first timorously, then more convivially, by the other guests; and, for all that Niven's performance remained obstinately in a minor key, it was a well-deserved Oscar.

As for Susan Hayward, she was probably unfamiliar with the expression 'in a minor key'. To borrow from the hyperbolic idiom of the Hollywood publicity machine, she was never more at ease than when 'exploding across the screen', her characteristic persona being of a feisty lady, tough but sentimental at heart, gamely struggling against adversity. That certainly was the nature of her role in Robert Wise's drama **I Want To Live** (which, given her clammy, screen-hugging performance, might have been retitled 'I Want To Win An Oscar'). Minute by minute, then second by agonizing second, we follow Barbara Graham's arrest, her trial and conviction, and, after every avenue of appeal and clemency has been fruitlessly explored, her death in the gas chamber at San Quentin. The film was certainly a harrowing experience – never had a Hollywood movie portrayed in such macabre detail the meticulous preparations which precede any form of capital punishment. But it was possible to wonder whether it was not the character and her plight, rather than the actress and her performance, that audiences found so unbearably moving. And it can be argued that Wise's sensationalist treatment of the subject was intent less on indicting an unjust penal system than on voyeuristically leering at its heroine and her predicament.

WINNERS 1958

Nominations Announced: February 23, 1959
Awards Ceremony: April 6, 1959
RKO Pantages Theatre

Best Picture
GIGI, Freed/MGM: ARTHUR FREED, Producer

Actor
DAVID NIVEN in *Separate Tables*, Clifton/UA

Actress
SUSAN HAYWARD in *I Want To Live!*, Figaro/UA

Supporting Actor
BURL IVES in *The Big Country*, Anthony-Worldwide/UA

Supporting Actress
WENDY HILLER in *Separate Tables*

Directing
VINCENTE MINNELLI for *Gigi*

Writing
(Best Screenplay – based on material from another medium)
GIGI: ALAN JAY LERNER
(Best Story and Screenplay – written directly for the screen)
THE DEFIANT ONES, Kramer/UA: NATHAN E.
DOUGLAS and HAROLD JACOB SMITH

Cinematography
(Rules changed again this year to two awards.)
(Black-and-White)
THE DEFIANT ONES: SAM LEAVITT
(Color)
GIGI: JOSEPH RUTTENBERG

Art Direction-Set Decoration
GIGI: WILLIAM A. HORNING and PRESTON AMES
Set Decoration: HENRY GRACE and KEOGH GLEASON

Sound
SOUTH PACIFIC, Todd-AO Sound Department: FRED
HYNES, Sound Director

Film Editing
GIGI: ADRIENNE FAZAN

Music
(Rules changed again this year to two awards: one award for
Scoring of a Dramatic or Comedy Picture, and one award
for Scoring of a Musical Picture.)
(Scoring of a Dramatic or Comedy Picture)
THE OLD MAN AND THE SEA, Leland Hayward/Warner
Bros.: DIMITRI TIOMKIN
(Scoring of a Musical Picture)
GIGI: ANDRE PREVIN
(Best Song)
GIGI from *Gigi*
Music: FREDERICK LOEWE
Lyrics: ALAN JAY LERNER

Costume Design
GIGI: CECIL BEATON

Short Subjects
(Cartoons)
KNIGHTY KNIGHTY BUGS, Warner Bros.: JOHN W.
BURTON, Producer
(Live Action Subjects)
GRAND CANYON, Disney/Buena Vista: WALT DISNEY,
Producer

Documentary
(Short Subjects)
AMA GIRLS, Disney/Buena Vista: BEN SHARPSTEEN,
Producer
(Features)
WHITE WILDERNESS, Disney/Buena Vista: BEN
SHARPSTEEN, Producer

Special Effects
TOM THUMB, Galaxy/MGM Visual: TOM HOWARD

Foreign Language Film Award
MY UNCLE (*Mon Oncle*), Specta-Gray-Alter/Films del
Centaure (France)

Honorary Award
MAURICE CHEVALIER for his contributions to the world of
entertainment for more than half a century. (statuette)

Irving G. Thalberg Memorial Award
JACK L. WARNER

Jean Hersholt Humanitarian Award
None

1959

T HE YEAR WAS practically a one-man show – the man being **Ben-Hur**. William Wyler's spectacular remake of one of MGM's greatest silent successes carried off no fewer than eleven Oscars, setting a new record (not only in the total itself but in the fact that the film lost out in only a single nomination – that for Best Screenplay). Apart from its Best Picture award, it was voted supreme in the following categories: Actor, Supporting Actor, Director, Cinematography, Art Direction, Sound, Musical Score, Film Editing, Special Effects and Costume Design. Budgeted at the (for the period) almost unheard-of sum of $15,000,000, which meant that its break-even figure was twice as high, it represented the greatest calculated risk in the history of Metro-Goldwyn-Mayer. Had it flopped, the studio would have had no other recourse than to call in the receivers. In the event, its eleven Oscars acted as magnets at the box-office, and MGM lived on to produce movies for a good many more years.

It's always thrilling to see records broken, of course; but, as far as the ceremony itself was concerned, a certain monotony began to set in as, in category after category, one or other of the **Ben-Hur** alumni would mount the stage to receive an Oscar. There can be few artists in any medium who have been thanked as often and as profusely, in the space of three hours, as was Wyler on the night of April 4, 1960. In consequence, some of the warmest ovations were reserved for those few winners not associated with the film: the French star Simone Signoret (for **Room At The Top**), the first actress ever to receive an Oscar for a performance in a British or foreign film; Neil Paterson for Best Screenplay from another medium (**Room At The Top**), and Russell Rouse, Clarence Green, Stanley Shapiro and Maurice Richlin for the original screenplay of the sunny Doris Day-Rock Hudson charmer **Pillow Talk**; a tear-stained Shelley Winters (Best Supporting Actress), winning her first Oscar, after 20 years of hoping and praying, for George Stevens' **The Diary Of Anne Frank**; and Buster Keaton, one of the cinema's most sublime clowns, who received a special Academy Award "for his unique talents which brought immortal comedies to the screen".

In general, there was a rather subdued quality to the ballyhoo surrounding the event. Hollywood was undergoing one of its periodic crises of finance and identity; and, during the run-up to Oscar night, a protracted actors' strike had almost totally halted production. Unemploy-

ment was rife. A rumble of discontent could be felt not far beneath the glittering façade of the film industry's capital city. And, doubtless because of the chaotic lack of organization which had marred the previous year's ceremony, fewer celebrities than usual had agreed to participate this year. Not, then, truly vintage Oscar – except, of course, if you happened to have become involved with the filming of **Ben-Hur**.

"The more I thought about it," said Wyler about being offered MGM's costliest production, "the more I saw the possibilities. There were interesting elements. The tremendous enmity between hero and villain was nothing new, but here the antagonism grew out of a great childhood friendship. Ben-Hur and Messala had grown up together and their reunion after many years offered the possibility for a great emotional scene. On the other hand, Ben-Hur and the commander of the Roman fleet started as the bitterest of enemies only to become the best of friends. Basically, of course, it was an adventure yarn."

BELOW *In the first of her mature character roles, Shelley Winters won the Best Supporting Actress Oscar in* The Diary of Anne Frank. *She and her husband (Lou Jacobi, illustrated) were two Jews hiding, with the Frank family, in unbearably cramped conditions in an attic above an Amsterdam warehouse during the Nazi occupation*

THE MOST HONORED MOTION PICTURE IN ACADEMY AWARDS HISTORY

In fact, when subsequently interviewed about the film, Wyler tended to play down the element of spectacle – most notably, the chariot-race sequence, which had not been filmed by him at all but by a second-unit team led by Andrew Marton and the former stuntman Yakima Canutt. Yet it was the spectacle which made **Ben-Hur** such a consistently engrossing entertainment, on a scale which had never even been equaled by DeMille at his most extravagant. The stunning sets constructed for the film on the outskirts of Rome were actually visible from several spots within the city itself; and, during the nine months of shooting (Wyler once compared himself to one of the galley slaves in the naval battle scene), no visit to the classical wonders of the Eternal City was complete without a trip out to the **Ben-Hur** set. Almost 5,000 VIPs from the worlds of show business, politics, high finance and high society were offered guided tours around the life-size reconstruction of ancient Rome.

The breathtaking chariot race contained one of the most dangerous stunts ever attempted on the screen. In order to show audiences clearly that the vehicles of the rival charioteers, Ben-Hur and his boyhood friend Messala, were virtually interlocked, Marton decided to chain the camera car to the two chariots. "I didn't have time to

ABOVE *Although the chariot race in* Ben-Hur *is one of the most exciting and spectacular sequences ever filmed, there were many other eye-catching moments in the record-breaking eleven-Oscar winner, notably this scene with Charlton Heston, a suffering galley slave in the foreground*
TOP RIGHT *Best Actor winner Charlton Heston (right), as the Patrician Jew* Ben-Hur *who eventually converts to Christianity, face to face with his boyhood friend, Messala (Stephen Boyd), now the Roman commander. The two later oppose one another in the chariot race. The film is the only remake to have won the Best Picture award*

realize that if one horse stumbled," he later nervously confessed, "the whole contraption – horses, chariots, stars, camera car – would crash and pile up in disaster." Miraculously, in contrast to the original **Ben-Hur**, which had suffered several major casualties, no fatal accidents were recorded during the filming.

Apart from its near-dozen Oscars, **Ben-Hur** won the New York Film Critics award, the Directors Guild award, the British Film Academy award, and countless other

prizes throughout the world. In financial terms, moreover, it was a total triumph, earning $66 million for MGM on its initial release and making an immediate dent in *Variety*'s list of all-time box-office champs.

In blockbuster films actors are, if not dispensable, then decidedly secondary. To begin with, they tend to be dwarfed by the scenery and swallowed up by the thousands of extras. Which is no doubt why Charlton Heston has been associated primarily – though not always willingly – with Biblical or historical epics. **Ben-Hur** apart, one might mention DeMille's **The Greatest Show On Earth** and **The Ten Commandments** (in which he played Moses), Wyler's Western super-production **The Big Country**, George Stevens' **The Greatest Story Ever Told**, Nicholas Ray's Boxer Rebellion drama **Fifty-Five Days At Peking**, Anthony Mann's **El Cid** (in the title role, naturally) and Carol Reed's **The Agony And The Ecstasy** (in which he impersonated Michelangelo). Not only does he possess a resolutely uncontemporary face – high cheekbones, deep-set eyes – his massively rugged frame made him, in a sense, the human equivalent of the scenery around him. It would, in short, be difficult to dwarf an actor as imposing as Heston. Though he occasionally expressed a wistful longing to broaden his appeal – "Why does Cary Grant get all those pictures set entirely in penthouses?" he would plaintively sigh – Heston's physique cast him once and for all in the classic mold; and it is to his credit (and Wyler's) that, in the most expensive and spectacular epic of all, he left such a powerful impression of his own presence that his peers in the industry awarded him their highest accolade.

Simone Signoret, who died in 1985 after a long and debilitating illness, was by common consent one of the greatest of all film actresses. Yet the Oscar which was awarded her for a moving performance as the lonely middle-aged Frenchwoman courted, loved and abandoned by Laurence Harvey's Joe Lampton in **Room At The Top** paid tribute to a type as much as to a talent. Signoret was French – in both an evocatively figurative as well as a literal sense. Her warm, somewhat overripe beauty and world-weary sensuality epitomized 'Frenchness' in every corner of the globe. It therefore wasn't surprising that, when the 'thawing' British cinema of the late 50s and early 60s required an actress of mature sex appeal, it would turn to Signoret. Even when her once delicately ravishing features lost their bloom and became blowsy, she retained a quality that no British or American actress could hope to emulate. Signoret herself summed it up admirably when interviewed on the subject of her Oscar-winning performance: "It sustained both sexes. It was very reassuring to women of 40 and over. And men liked it because a lot of them have had an affair with an older woman, or wanted to."

BELOW *French star Simone Signoret brought sex into the British cinema as the tragic mistress of Laurence Harvey (right) in* Room At The Top, *and won the Best Actress award. Harvey was nominated for his performance as the ruthlessly ambitious Joe Lampton, his most famous role*

WINNERS 1959

Nominations Announced: February 22, 1960
Awards Ceremony: April 4, 1960
RKO Pantages Theatre

Best Picture
BEN-HUR, MGM: SAM ZIMBALIST, Producer

Actor
CHARLTON HESTON in *Ben-Hur*

Actress
SIMONE SIGNORET in *Room At The Top*,
Romulus/Continental (British)

Supporting Actor
HUGH GRIFFITH in *Ben-Hur*

Supporting Actress
SHELLEY WINTERS in *The Diary Of Anne Frank*, 20th
Century-Fox

Directing
WILLIAM WYLER for *Ben-Hur*

Writing
(Best Screenplay – based on material from another medium)
ROOM AT THE TOP: NEIL PATERSON
(Best Story and Screenplay – written directly for the screen)
PILLOW TALK, Arwin/U-I
Story: RUSSELL ROUSE and CLARENCE GREENE
Screenplay: STANLEY SHAPIRO and MAURICE RICHLIN

Cinematography
(Black-and-White)
THE DIARY OF ANNE FRANK: WILLIAM C. MELLOR
(Color)
BEN-HUR: ROBERT L. SURTEES

Art Direction-Set Decoration
(Rules changed this year to two awards.)
(Black-and-White)
THE DIARY OF ANNE FRANK: LYLE R. WHEELER and
GEORGE W. DAVIS
Set Decoration: WALTER M. SCOTT and STUART A.
REISS
(Color)
BEN-HUR: WILLIAM A. HORNING and EDWARD
CARFAGNO
Set Decoration: HUGH HUNT

Sound
BEN-HUR, MGM Studio Sound Department: FRANKLIN
E. MILTON, Sound Director

Film Editing
BEN-HUR: RALPH E. WINTERS and JOHN D. DUNNING

Music
(Scoring of a Dramatic or Comedy Picture)
BEN-HUR: MIKLOS ROZSA
(Scoring of a Musical Picture)
PORGY AND BESS, Goldwyn/Columbia: ANDRE PREVIN
and KEN DARBY
(Best Song)
HIGH HOPES from *A Hole In The Head*, Sincap/UA
Music: JAMES VAN HEUSEN
Lyrics: SAMMY CAHN

Costume Design
(Rules changed this year to two awards.)
(Black-and-White)
SOME LIKE IT HOT, Ashton & Mirisch/UA: ORRY-KELLY
(Color)
BEN-HUR: ELIZABETH HAFFENDEN

Short Subjects
(Cartoons)
MOONBIRD, Storyboard: EDWARD HARRISON and
JOHN HUBLEY, Producers
(Live Action Subjects)
THE GOLDEN FISH, Les Requins Associes/Columbia
(French): JACQUES-YVES COUSTEAU, Producer

Documentary
(Short Subjects)
GLASS, Netherlands Government/Arthur-Go Pictures (The
Netherlands): BERT HAANSTRA, Producer
(Features)
SERENGETI SHALL NOT DIE, Okapia/Transocean
(German): BERNARD GRZIMEK, Producer

Special Effects
BEN-HUR:
Visual: A. ARNOLD GILLESPIE and ROBERT
MacDONALD
Audible: MILO LORY

Foreign Language Film Award
BLACK ORPHEUS, Dispatfilm & Gemma Cinematografica
(France)

Honorary Awards
LEE DE FOREST for his pioneering inventions which
brought sound to the motion picture. (statuette)
BUSTER KEATON for his unique talents which brought
immortal comedies to the screen. (statuette)

Irving G. Thalberg Memorial Award
None

Jean Hersholt Humanitarian Award
BOB HOPE

1960

AS SHIRLEY MACLAINE, one of 1960's Academy Awards nominees, phrased it, "I lost to a tracheotomy." The tracheotomy was Elizabeth Taylor's. After two successive nominations for performances in steamy Tennessee Williams adaptations (as the sexually frustrated Maggie in **Cat On A Hot Tin Roof**, 1958, and as Katharine Hepburn's mentally disturbed niece in **Suddenly Last Summer**, 1959), she finally secured her Oscar for a quite unremarkable performance as an expensive call girl in Daniel Mann's **Butterfield 8** (the title refers to the heroine's telephone number). Even at the time, as MacLaine's comment bears witness, it was widely interpreted as a sentimental gesture made less in recognition of her talent than of her recent, near-fatal bout of pneumonia.

But Taylor's tracheotomy was undoubtedly the star of the show. The actress herself looked suitably wan and fatigued; and when her name was announced by Yul Brynner, she had to be assisted on to the stage by her new husband, the crooner Eddie Fisher. Simply because of its inaudibil-

ity, her acceptance speech – a mere whispered "thank you" – received a standing ovation from the audience. And if this might appear to be casting a cynically beady eye on the proceedings, it's perhaps necessary to add that, in the event of MacLaine winning after all, the show's organizers had assigned Miss Taylor to the task of presenting her rival's Oscar.

Nothing else in the evening's entertainment rose to such a height of melodramatic suspense. From a mixed bag of contenders (**The Alamo, Elmer Gantry, Sons And Lovers** and **The Sundowners**) it was Billy Wilder's acid-sketched comedy **The Apartment** which was justifiably voted Best Picture (also Director, Story and Screenplay, Art Direction and Film Editing). Richard Brooks' **Elmer Gantry**, a colorful, rumbustious film version of the Sinclair Lewis novel, generated Oscars for Best Actor (Burt Lancaster) and Best Supporting Actress (Shirley Jones, very much cast against type as an easygoing prostitute); and Peter Ustinov was judged Best Supporting Actor for his portrayal of a wily slavemaster in **Spartacus**. (So protracted was the shooting of Stanley Kubrick's epic that, as Ustinov recounted, when one of his children was asked what his father did for a living, he innocently replied, "**Spartacus**.")

For the first time in a decade the ceremony was held, not in the Pantages Theater, but at the Civic Auditorium in Santa Monica, which was located almost 20 miles from Hollywood Boulevard (though handily close to many of the stars' homes). Once more, it was sponsored by commercial advertisers; once more, too, Bob Hope was the evening's M.C. And illness as a theme was raised again when James Stewart appeared on stage to accept an honorary Oscar on behalf of the absent Gary Cooper "for his many memorable screen performances and the international recognition he, as an individual, has gained for the motion picture industry". Stewart made a highly emotional speech, almost as though he himself were being honored, thereby fueling rumors that Cooper was gravely ill. So tenacious were these rumors that, two days later, it was officially announced that the actor was in a terminal stage of cancer. The famous star died just one month later.

For most of his professional career, Billy Wilder has been hounded by accusations of cynicism and tastelessness. And it is certainly true that, in his comedies, he has never shied away from any subject that might risk a controversial reaction: the aftermath of World War II (**A Foreign Affair**), adultery (**The Seven Year Itch**), transvestism (**Some Like It Hot**), the Berlin Wall (**One, Two, Three**), prostitution (**Irma**

LEFT *The ravishing Elizabeth Taylor, as a high class but unhappy New York prostitute in* Butterfield 8, *is seen drowning her sorrows. The two men with whom she is actually involved were played by Laurence Harvey and her real-life fourth husband Eddie Fisher*
FAR LEFT *Master of a school for gladiators, Best Supporting Actor Peter Ustinov taunts one of his best graduates Spartacus (Kirk Douglas, left) in Stanley Kubrick's tale of a slave's revolt. The picture also won Oscars for color cinematography, art direction-set decoration, and costume design. Douglas is modeling an example of the latter . . . !*

ABOVE *It is astonishing that none of the superb cast of Billy Wilder's* The Apartment *won an Oscar. Nominated were Jack Lemmon (left), Shirley MacLaine (center), at their best, and Jack Kruschen (a supporting nominee). Also excellent were Fred MacMurray, Ray Walston and Edie Adams*

La Douce) and death (**Avanti!**). His detractors, however, are often the same critics who excoriate more typical Hollywood fare for its mealymouthed blandness.

The best of Wilder's work has the courage to treat serious themes seriously – if within a framework of comedy; and few of his films have depicted the ravages of contemporary urban alienation with such sardonic wit as **The Apartment**. It told the story of C.C. Baxter (Jack Lemmon), a promising insurance clerk in a large company who – at first sporadically, then on a more and more systematic basis – lends his drab New York apartment to four of his superiors for their illicit, adulterous lovemaking. Despite finding himself often excluded from his own modest hearth, Baxter has no complaints with the set-up, since each tryst implies a corresponding promotion for himself. Until one day, the young woman brought to his apartment is the company elevator

girl (Shirley MacLaine), in whom he himself had begun to take a fond interest . . .

The Apartment is not merely a masterpiece, it is something of a little miracle. Shot in sober black-and-while, brilliantly played by every member of the cast, scripted with all of Wilder's abrasive wit and underlying humanity, it maintained throughout an extraordinary balance between comedy and drama, cynicism and human warmth, fiction and reality. It's a film which is guaranteed to age well.

Though, during the 50s, Burt Lancaster's name was often mentioned in connection with the Academy Awards, it was, paradoxically, as a producer. The independent production company of which he was a partner, Hecht-Hill-Lancaster, had been responsible for such critically acclaimed (and Oscar-winning) films as **Marty, Sweet Smell Of Success, Bachelor Party** and **Separate Tables**. The last time he had been nominated as an actor was in 1953 for **From Here To Eternity**; but he finally won his Oscar for a role that might have been written for him, that of the rabble-rousing, womanizing preacher Elmer Gantry in Richard Brooks' film version of Sinclair Lewis' novel. The project had been cherished by Brooks for several years – since 1947, in fact –

and he had never envisaged any other actor for the title role. Lancaster was, supremely, a *physical* presence – not unsurprisingly, since he had begun his show business career as a circus acrobat and his agility had already been displayed to advantage in two early swashbucking roles (**The Flame And The Arrow** and **The Crimson Pirate**) and again in Carol Reed's **Trapeze**. That same physicality, that wiry animal energy, was no less evident in **Elmer Gantry**. With their spellbinding gesticulation and literally 'daredevil' antics, hell-and-damnation revivalists are also acrobats of a kind; and it was percipient of Brooks, way back in 1947, to sense

BELOW *The role of the whoring, drinking, silver-tongued con-man Elmer Gantry was perfectly suited to the dynamic, athletic talents of Burt Lancaster whose grinning mouth seemed to dominate the film.*

ABOVE *Best Actor Burt Lancaster, the rabble-rousing evangelist Elmer Gantry, in an encounter with his former girlfriend turned prostitute Shirley Jones (Best Supporting Actress). The film's director Richard Brooks won the Oscar for Best Screenplay adapted from another medium for faithfully recapturing the essence of Sinclair Lewis' novel of the American Midwest*

that the virtually unknown Lancaster would so completely fill the role. The result, in any case, was a revelation, one of the great hypnotic, barnstorming performances recorded on film. One finds oneself emerging from the cinema almost willing to be converted.

As already remarked, Elizabeth Taylor's performance in **Butterfield 8** was not one of her best; and it would be fair to say that, though most Academy Awards have generated a degree of controversy, hers was generally regarded as one of the weakest ever to find itself on top of the heap. Taylor herself harbored few illusions about either film or performance: "I still think it stinks. I have never seen it and I have no desire ever to see it." In fact, **Butterfield 8** had been a

strictly contractual obligation as far as she was concerned; and it was only because MGM threatened to make life difficult for her that she finally, reluctantly, agreed to the project. Her mind was doubtless on her next film but one, 20th Century-Fox's proposed epic of **Cleopatra**. Taylor had not exactly been a stranger to the headlines – her marriages to Conrad Hilton Jr, Michael Wilding, Mike Todd, Eddie Fisher and several more to come; her much-publicized attachments to Montgomery Clift and James Dean, both of whom were to meet premature deaths; Mike Todd's death and her own illness – but, as she falteringly stepped up to collect her Oscar on April 17, 1961, no one could have predicted that, with **Cleopatra** and her co-star Richard Burton in the offing, she was about to enter a whole new dimension of public exposure.

WINNERS 1960

Nominations Announced: February 27, 1961
Awards Ceremony: April 17, 1961
Santa Monica Civic Auditorium

Best Picture
THE APARTMENT, Mirisch/UA: BILLY WILDER, Producer

Actor
BURT LANCASTER in *Elmer Gantry*,
Lancaster-Brooks/UA

Actress
ELIZABETH TAYLOR in *Butterfield 8*,
Afton-Linebrook/MGM

Supporting Actor
PETER USTINOV in *Spartacus*, Bryna/U-I

Supporting Actress
SHIRLEY JONES in *Elmer Gantry*

Directing
BILLY WILDER for *The Apartment*

Writing
(Best Screenplay – based on material from another medium)
ELMER GANTRY: RICHARD BROOKS
(Best Story and Screenplay – written directly for the screen)
THE APARTMENT: BILLY WILDER and I.A.L. DIAMOND

Cinematography
(Black-and-White)
SONS AND LOVERS, Company of Artists/20th
Century-Fox: FREDDIE FRANCIS
(Color)
SPARTACUS: RUSSELL METTY

Art Direction-Set Decoration
(Black-and-White)
THE APARTMENT: ALEXANDER TRAUNER
Set Decoration: EDWARD G. BOYLE
(Color)
SPARTACUS: ALEXANDER GOLITZEN and ERIC
ORBOM
Set Decoration: RUSSELL A. GAUSMAN and JULIA
HERON

Sound
THE ALAMO, Goldwyn Studio Sound Department:
GORDON E. SAWYER, Sound Director; and Todd-AO
Sound Department: FRED HYNES, Sound Director

Film Editing
THE APARTMENT: DANIEL MANDELL

Music
(Scoring of a Dramatic or Comedy Picture)
EXODUS, Carlyle-Alpina/UA: ERNEST GOLD

(Scoring of a Musical Picture)
SONG WITHOUT END (THE STORY OF FRANZ LISZT),
Goetz-Vidor/Columbia: MORRIS STOLOFF and HARRY
SUKMAN
(Best Song)
NEVER ON SUNDAY from *Never On Sunday*,
Melinafilm/Lopert (Greek)
Music and Lyrics: MANOS HADJIDAKIS

Costume Design
(Black-and-White)
THE FACTS OF LIFE, Panama & Frank/UA: EDITH HEAD
and EDWARD STEVENSON
(Color)
SPARTACUS: VALLES and BILL THOMAS

Short Subjects
(Cartoons)
MUNRO, Rembrandt/Film Representations: WILLIAM L.
SNYDER, Producer
(Live Action Subjects)
DAY OF THE PAINTER, Little Movies/Kingsley-Union:
EZRA R. BAKER, Producer

Documentary
(Short Subjects)
GIUSEPPINA, Hill/Schoenfeld (British): JAMES HILL,
Producer
(Features)
THE HORSE WITH THE FLYING TAIL, Disney/Buena
Vista: LARRY LANSBURGH, Producer

Special Effects
THE TIME MACHINE, Galaxy/MGM:
Visual: GENE WARREN and TIM BAAR

Foreign Language Film Award
THE VIRGIN SPRING, Svensk Filmindustri (Sweden)

Honorary Awards
GARY COOPER for his many memorable screen
performances and the international recognition he, as an
individual, has gained for the motion picture industry.
(statuette)
STAN LAUREL for his creative pioneering in the field of
cinema comedy. (statuette)
HAYLEY MILLS for *Pollyanna*, the most outstanding
juvenile performance during 1960. (miniature statuette)

Irving G. Thalberg Memorial Award
None

Jean Hersholt Humanitarian Award
SOL LESSER

1961

T HE 1961 ACADEMY Awards ceremony would not itself have deserved an Oscar for drama, excitement or spectacle. It was a flat, ho-hum affair which a high proportion of the nominees did not even bother to attend. The musical **West Side Story**, as widely predicted, monopolized the evening's honors, almost matching the record established (and to this day maintained) by **Ben-Hur** with ten Oscars: for Best Picture, Supporting Actor, Supporting Actress, Director (or rather, uniquely, Directors: Robert Wise and the choreographer Jerome Robbins were co-credited in this category), Art Direction, Cinematography, Sound, Musical Score, Film Editing and Costume Design. (Robbins also received an honorary Oscar "for his brilliant achievements in the art of choreog-

raphy on film".) The two principal acting awards went to non-Americans: Best Actor to Maximilian Schell for his performance as one of the Nuremberg Trial lawyers in Stanley Kramer's **Judgment At Nuremberg** and Sophia Loren as a much-abused Italian mother in Vittorio De Sica's **Two Women**.

De Sica's film, though given wide distribution (and massive publicity) in the United States by the flamboyant impresario Joseph E. Levine, was wholly Italian in origin and language, and therefore released abroad in either a dubbed or subtitled version. It was felt by numerous movie journalists that not only should the Oscar remain an exclusively American award (a status already compromised by several British winners) but that no performance could properly be judged by a spectator unable to experience a direct relation between voice, gesture and language. The glamorous Miss Loren, moreover, was so little convinced that she would win that she declined to fly to Hollywood for the ceremony, and heard of her victory

BELOW *Stanley Kramer's 178-minute* Judgment At Nuremberg *was up for eight awards, including Best Picture, Director, Cinematography, and Supporting Actor and Actress (Montgomery Clift and Judy Garland). The two winners were Maximilian Schell (left with Richard Widmark), who beat Spencer Tracy for Best Actor, and screenwriter Abby Mann*

only by telephone in Rome. Cracked the evening's M.C., Bob Hope, "It must be wonderful to have talent enough just to send for an Oscar."

There was the usual quota of minor hiccups and surprises. One of the nominees for Best Supporting Actor, the pugnacious George C. Scott (for Robert Rossen's **The Hustler**), made Hollywood headlines by publicly rejecting the tribute paid him. He tactlessly suggested that "the competition is made more important than the artist's work itself" and dismissed the Academy Awards ritual as a nauseating, self-congratulatory "meat parade". On this occasion, Scott was not actually voted the winner; but the Academy subsequently called his bluff with an Oscar for **Patton** (1970). As good as his word, Scott contemptuously declined the bait. A man with a diametrically opposed opinion of the importance of being Oscar was

Stan Berman. Styling himself a "professional gate-crasher", Berman contrived to elude the police guards stationed outside the theatre, sashayed up the red-carpeted aisle and onto the stage to present a home-made statuette to an astonished Bob Hope.

From its breathtaking opening sequence, filmed not on a Hollywood back lot but on the sidewalks of New York, to the climactic moment when the murdered Tony (Richard Beymer) is isolated in a solitary pool of light, **West Side Story**, Leonard Bernstein's dynamic updating

BELOW *Natalie Wood as the Puerto Rican 'Juliet' on her fire escape balcony in the 'Tonight' number from the ten-Oscar winning* West Side Story. *Natalie, whose singing was dubbed in the movie by Marni Nixon, gained her Oscar nomination this year for* Splendor In The Grass

ABOVE *The dynamic Puerto Rican dancer Rita Moreno ironically extolling the virtues of 'America' in* West Side Story *watched by fellow Sharks, including George Chakiris (far right). Both Moreno and Chakiris won Best Supporting awards*

of Shakespeare's *Romeo and Juliet* made an immediate and unforgettable impact on audiences all over the world. Though originally a theatrical spectacle, it more properly belonged to a cinematic world of tenement slums and gang warfare, and few musicals have so seamlessly effected the transition from stage to screen.

The basis of Shakespeare's tragedy was, of course, fairly universal and *Romeo and Juliet* has, over the years, undergone an extraordinary number of transformations (a celebrated instance was Peter Ustinov's Cold War political satire *Romanoff and Juliet*). None has worked as well, however, as this tale of two fiercely opposed street gangs, the Jets and the Sharks, the former home-grown American whites, the latter Puerto Rican immigrants, strutting and swaggering through Manhattan's Lower West Side, settling territorial disputes with the time-honored ritual of the 'rumble'. When Tony meets the Puerto Rican Maria (Natalie Wood) at a community dance, and the lights dim, their romance promises to be no less 'star-crossed' than that of their illustrious models.

Unusually for a musical (the word, after all, is a contraction of 'musical comedy'), **West Side Story** accepted the challenge of an unhappy ending. Yet a musical, whatever

more subtle claims it may make on our attention, must be a joyous and confident entertainment or it is nothing. With a host of memorable numbers – such songs as the lyrical 'Tonight', the sentimental, almost hymn-like ballad 'Maria', and the indestructibly chirpy 'I Feel Pretty' have become modern standards – and the most energetic ballet ever seen in the cinema, Bernstein's masterpiece conclusively demonstrated that a downbeat plot need not stifle the sheer physical exuberance we have come to expect of the genre.

West Side Story, finally, broke new ground for a musical in the fact that its immense popularity was not only confined, as had often been the case, to the American and British markets. Probably because dialogue played second fiddle, as it were, to music, it became a solid and, indeed, durable international hit.

Maximilian Schell was what might be called one of the unlucky Academy Award winners. There are, it's claimed, 'good' Oscars and 'bad' Oscars: a good one will raise an actor's career to new and hitherto unsuspected heights, a bad one risks stunting his growth. Schell, perhaps the least-known performer (in Hollywood's terms) ever to win a Best Actor award, was thereafter offered a series of undistinguished roles in which he might have been replaced by any number of German or Austrian emigrés. Films like **The Reluctant Saint** (1962), Vittorio De Sica's catastrophically turgid version of Sartre's **The Condemned of Altona** (1963), Jules Dassin's lightweight com-

ABOVE *Vittorio De Sica's* Two Women, *filmed in Italian in Italy, gained for Sophia Loren (left) her only Oscar to date. The title refers to Loren and her 13-year-old daughter (Eleanora Brown) trying to survive in the dark days of 1943. With her in this scene, French star Jean-Paul Belmondo*

edy thriller **Topkapi** (1964) and **Krakatoa, East Of Java** (1969) were all very differently received by critics and public, but none of them will be remembered for his contribution. His dark matinee-idol good looks were possibly too dated for the changing cinema of the 60s and 70s; and though he earned further Oscar nominations for **The Man In The Glass Booth** (1975, another film about a Nazi war criminal on trial) and Fred Zinnemann's **Julia** (1977), his reputation will ultimately rest on his work as a director.

The high-watermark of Schell's acting career, however, remains his disturbing portrayal of the defence attorney in **Judgment At Nuremberg**, a man who finds that his professional obligation to secure acquittal for his clients leads him into dubiously grey areas of ethical responsibility. As too often with Stanley Kramer, the film was bloated, overlong and incongruously star-studded – with Spencer Tracy, Marlene Dietrich, Burt Lancaster, Montgomery Clift, Judy Garland and Richard Widmark (Garland and Clift were both nominated for Best Supporting Performances, which was felt unjust to their less

charismatic, less starry rivals in that category). And it was Schell's performance which injected a refreshing and much-needed sense of authenticity.

Sophia Loren's Oscar for an Italian film confirmed one's suspicions that, despite her Hollywood stardom, the American cinema never properly learned how to exploit her voluptuously earthy appeal. In films like **Boy On A Dolphin, The Pride And The Passion, Legend Of The Lost** (all 1957), **Desire Under The Elms, The Key** and **Houseboat** (all 1958), films of varying quality and appeal, she was so indiscriminately cast that she appeared a caricature of herself. Notwithstanding an uneven filmography, however, Loren remained much loved by the American public and it was thanks to her no less than to its powerful narrative that De Sica's **Two Women**, subtitles and all, became one of the few foreign films to enjoy real commercial success in the United States. Appearing at the very end of the Italian neo-realist movement (out of which such classics as **Bicycle Thieves, Umberto D, Open City** and **La Terra Trema** had emerged), it told the story of a widowed mother and her teenage daughter surviving enemy attack, deprivation and ultimately rape in the Italian countryside of the wartime years. On home ground, then, and minus the tinsely image fabricated for her by Hollywood, Loren confirmed Jean Cocteau's aphorism: 'A bird sings best on its family tree.'

WINNERS 1961

Nominations Announced: February 26, 1962
Awards Ceremony: April 9, 1962
Santa Monica Civic Auditorium

Best Picture
WEST SIDE STORY, Mirisch-B & P Enterprises/UA:
ROBERT WISE, Producer

Actor
MAXIMILIAN SCHELL in *Judgment At Nuremberg*,
Kramer/UA

Actress
SOPHIA LOREN in *Two Women*, Champion-Les Films
Marceau Cocinor & Societe Generale De
Cinematographic/Embassy (Italo-French)

Supporting Actor
GEORGE CHAKIRIS in *West Side Story*

Supporting Actress
RITA MORENO in *West Side Story*

Directing
JEROME ROBBINS and ROBERT WISE for *West Side Story*

Writing
(Best Screenplay – based on material from another medium)
JUDGMENT AT NUREMBERG: ABBY MANN
(Best Story – written directly for the screen)
SPLENDOR IN THE GRASS, NBI/Warner Bros.: WILLIAM INGE

Cinematography
(Black-and-White)
THE HUSTLER, Rossen/20th Century-Fox: EUGEN SHUFTAN
(Color)
WEST SIDE STORY: DANIEL L. FAPP

Art Direction-Set Decoration
(Black-and-White)
THE HUSTLER: HARRY HORNER
Set Decoration: GENE CALLAHAN
(Color)
WEST SIDE STORY: BORIS LEVEN
Set Decoration: VICTOR A. GANGELIN

Sound
WEST SIDE STORY, Todd-AO Sound Department: FRED
HYNES, Sound Director; and Goldwyn Studio Sound
Department: GORDON E. SAWYER, Sound Director

Film Editing
WEST SIDE STORY: THOMAS STANFORD

Music
(Scoring of a Dramatic or Comedy Picture)
BREAKFAST AT TIFFANY'S,
Jurow-Shepherd/Paramount: HENRY MANCINI

(Scoring of a Musical Picture)
WEST SIDE STORY: SAUL CHAPLIN, JOHNNY GREEN,
SID RAMIN and IRWIN KOSTAL
(Best Song)
MOON RIVER from *Breakfast At Tiffany's*
Music: HENRY MANCINI
Lyrics: JOHNNY MERCER

Costume Design
(Black-and-White)
LA DOLCE VITA, Riama/Astor (Italian): PIERO GHERARDI
(Color)
WEST SIDE STORY: IRENE SHARAFF

Short Subjects
(Cartoons)
ERSATZ (The Substitute), Zagreb/Herts-Lion International
(Live Action Subjects)
SEAWARDS THE GREAT SHIPS, Templar/Schoenfeld

Documentary
(Short Subjects)
PROJECT HOPE, MacManus/John &
Adams/Ex-Cell-O/Klaeger: FRANK P. BIBAS, Producer
(Features)
LE CIEL ET LA BOUE (Sky Above And Mud Beneath),
Ardennes & Arthur/Rank (French): ARTHUR COHN and
RENE LAFUITE, Producers

Special Effects
THE GUNS OF NAVARONE, Foreman/Columbia
Visual: BILL WARRINGTON
Audible: VIVIAN C. GREENHAM

Foreign Language Film Award
THROUGH A GLASS DARKLY, Svensk Filmindustri
(Sweden)

Honorary Awards
WILLIAM L. HENDRICKS for his outstanding patriotic
services in the conception, writing and production of the
Marine Corps film *A Force In Readiness*, which has brought
honor to the Academy and the motion picture industry.
(statuette)
FRED L. METZLER for his dedication and outstanding
service to the Academy of Motion Picture Arts and Sciences.
(statuette)
JEROME ROBBINS for his brilliant achievements in the art
of choreography on film. (statuette)

Irving G. Thalberg Memorial Award
STANLEY KRAMER

Jean Hersholt Humanitarian Award
GEORGE SEATON

1962

THERE COULD BE detected a hint of sadism in one aspect of the 1962 ceremony, held at the Santa Monica Civic Auditorium on April 8, 1963. One of the nominees for Best Actress was Anne Bancroft, whose absence from the event was due to the fact that she was currently playing the title role of Brecht's **Mother Courage** in New York; and the star assigned to accept the Oscar on her behalf, should she win it, was Joan Crawford. Bancroft was duly named Best Actress (for her performance as Annie Sullivan, Helen Keller's teacher and mentor, in Arthur Penn's shattering film version of **The Miracle Worker**), and Crawford, a glamorously silver-haired matron dripping with diamonds, duly picked up the award. In fact, she seemed exceedingly gratified to be doing so, positively beaming at the audience. Which is where the element of sadism comes in. For one of Bancroft's fellow-nominees was Bette Davis for her outrageously over-the-top playing of a former child screen star in Robert

Aldrich's Gothick thriller **What Ever Happened To Baby Jane?** Davis's un-nominated co-star and bitter rival in that film was, of course, the same Joan Crawford who was so radiantly happy to be accepting an Oscar on behalf of the deservedly fortunate Anne Bancroft.

Named Best Film was **Lawrence Of Arabia**, with producer Sam Spiegel and director David Lean repeating the earlier triumph of **The Bridge On The River Kwai**. Both *Kwai* and *Lawrence* captured seven Oscars apiece – in the latter case, for Best Picture, Director, Cinematography, Art Direction, Sound, Film Editing and Musical Score. Though the film's T.E. Lawrence, an ethereally handsome young British stage actor named Peter O'Toole, lost out to veteran Gregory Peck in the Best Actor stakes, the role turned him overnight into an international star. Indeed, critics were to carp that he continued to play self-indulgent variations on the character for several years to come – notably, in Richard Brooks' **Lord Jim** of 1965. (Still Oscarless, O'Toole has been nominated seven times, holding the weird distinction of being nominated twice for the same role, that of King Henry II in **Becket**, 1964, and **The Lion In Winter**, 1968.)

Among the other awards, Ed Begley was voted Best Supporting Actor for his creepy portrayal of a vicious Southern politician in **Sweet Bird Of Youth** (the betting

BELOW *A tempestuous scene from* Sweet Bird Of Youth *in which corrupt town boss Ed Begley (Best Supporting Actor winner) gets his daughter Shirley Knight to leave a political meeting after his men have beaten up a protester*

Registered Tr

ABOVE *Irish-born actor Peter O'Toole (in white) as* Lawrence Of Arabia *spectacularly leads his Arab troops against the Turks. Both O'Toole and Omar Sharif, in his first English-speaking role, were nominated for Best Actor and Best Supporting Actor, and both shot to international fame*

had been on Omar Sharif for **Lawrence Of Arabia**) and the 16-year-old Patty Duke Best Supporting Actress for playing – or rather, *being* – the child Helen Keller in **The Miracle Worker**. Master of Ceremonies was Frank Sinatra, who almost missed his cue. Since he had failed to attach an official Academy sticker to his car, he was forced to find parking space himself and eventually made a dash to the theater on foot.

In view of a subsequent multi-Oscar winner, it's interesting to note that, following the commercial and critical success of **The Bridge On The River Kwai**, Sam Spiegel and David Lean had planned to film the life of . . . Gandhi. Richard Attenborough has no doubt since felt grateful that the project was cancelled when Spiegel acquired the rights to T.E. Lawrence's biographical memoir *Seven Pillars of Wisdom* and hired the dramatist Robert Bolt to shape the complexities of the great man's life into a manageable screenplay. Bolt did a superb job (even if, after its initial release, *Lawrence* was shorn of 20 minutes from its three hour-40 minutes running time). Though purists cavilled at the liberties taken with histori-

cal fact, at the total absence from the film of Lawrence's later, mystery-shrouded life in England and, especially, at the way Bolt glossed over the ambiguities of his sexual psychology, the majority of critics concurred in finding the film the most intelligent blockbuster to have reached the screen since the D.W. Griffith classics from the very dawn of the medium.

It remains David Lean's best, and certainly most personal, work. For once this patrician director deserved to be praised as more than a 'brilliant technician'. Inspired by the equivocal personality of his hero, responding like Lawrence himself to the glittering harmonies of sun and steel and sand (the desert, perhaps the true star of the film, was magnificently caught in all its shifting moods by the cinematographer Freddie Young), he made a film in which the spectacle was cunningly used to reveal conflict and character – an 'integrated epic', as one refers to an 'integrated musical'.

The narrative began at the end – with Lawrence's death in England in a motorcycle accident and the memorial service held in his honor – then, by flashback, retraced the major stages of his tumultuous military career: his posting to Cairo during World War I as a young intelligence officer; his friendship with Sherif Ali (Omar Sharif); his capture, torture and, though this is less evident in the film, rape by the Turkish Bey (José Ferrer); and the central role he played in the dismantling of the Ottoman Empire.

ABOVE AND RIGHT *Best Actress winner Anne Bancroft and Best Supporting Actress Patty Duke in two contrasting scenes from* The Miracle Worker *that illustrate the progression of the teaching of the deaf-blind-mute Helen Keller: Annie Sullivan locked in struggle with her young pupil whom she is trying to teach to fold a table napkin; and a moment of calm when she succeeds in getting the girl to understand the word 'water'*

LEFT *Tall and handsome Gregory Peck at last received an Oscar – for his role as the small-town lawyer defending a black wrongly accused of murder in* To Kill A Mockingbird. *His court room speech at the end was a tour de force*

Lawrence Of Arabia was therefore a spectacle, a travelogue, a history lesson, an adventure movie and, above all, a study in character.

Like Peter O'Toole, Gregory Peck has been a much nominated actor: for **The Keys Of The Kingdom** (1945), **The Yearling** (1946), **Gentleman's Agreement** (1947), **Twelve O'Clock High** (1949) and **To Kill A Mockingbird**. It was **Mockingbird** which, in 1962, finally clinched it. He himself said, "I can honestly say that in twenty years of making movies, I never had a part that came close to being the real me until Atticus Finch." Finch was the hero

of the much-esteemed first novel by Harper Lee brought to the screen by a young director from television, Robert Mulligan. It told the story of a gentle, avuncular, soft-spoken Alabama lawyer (Peck) entrusted with the formidable task of defending a young black falsely accused of rape while struggling to raise his own two motherless children in a hostile environment of bigotry and economic depression. Though the youngsters – Mary Badham and Philip Alford, both non-professionals, both local Alabamans – all but stole the film, Peck gave by far the best performance of his career. Too often stolid and expressionless, acting with his tight-set jaw the way others act with their eyes, he had been presented with the role of his life and did not fail to make the most of it. Without ever forfeiting his still boyish charm – despite the horn-rimmed spectacles, pipe and crumpled seersucker suit that came with the part – he managed to create a portrait of strength, dignity and intelligence that was thankfully devoid of sanctimoniousness.

Strength, dignity and intelligence were only three of the qualities required of Annie Sullivan, a teacher of the blind whose name will forever be linked with that of her most celebrated pupil, Helen Keller. Partially blind herself, Sullivan was employed by the Keller family to turn their wretched savage of a daughter into an obedient, controllable 'vegetable'. Their hopes rose no higher than that. What Sullivan's heroically patient efforts achieved was, of course, a great woman, one who continues to be an inspiration to the disabled and non-disabled alike. William Gibson's play **The Miracle Worker** had already made a Broadway star out of a minor B-movie actress, Anne Bancroft; and the film-maker Arthur Penn, refusing to succumb to the temptation to opt for a more famous name, sensibly offered the screen role to Bancroft again. She read all of the existing literature on both Sullivan and Keller, spent weeks mastering the deaf-and-dumb alphabet, and even rode blindfold on a roller-coaster in order to understand what it must feel like to lose one's sensory bearings. Though she has done much fine work since (in Jack Clayton's **The Pumpkin Eater**, 1964, John Ford's **Seven Women**, 1966, Mike Nichols' **The Graduate**, 1967, and Herbert Ross' **The Turning Point**, 1977), it was Bancroft's finest hour; and it is impossible to remain unmoved – in particular, by the scene in **The Miracle Worker** where, after a violent battle of wills between teacher and pupil, she finally succeeds in instilling a sense of language (the single word 'water') into her apparently hopeless charge.

WINNERS 1962

Best Picture
LAWRENCE OF ARABIA, Horizon
(GB)-Spiegel-Lean/Columbia: SAM SPIEGEL, Producer

Actor
GREGORY PECK in *To Kill A Mockingbird*,
U-I-Pakula-Mulligan-Brentwood/U-I

Actress
ANNE BANCROFT in *The Miracle Worker*, Playfilms/UA

Supporting Actor
ED BEGLEY in *Sweet Bird Of Youth*, Roxbury/MGM

Supporting Actress
PATTY DUKE in *The Miracle Worker*

Directing
DAVID LEAN for *Lawrence Of Arabia*

Writing
(Best Screenplay – based on material from another medium)
TO KILL A MOCKINGBIRD: HORTON FOOTE
(Best Story and Screenplay – written directly for the screen)
DIVORCE – ITALIAN STYLE, LuxVides-Galatea/Embassy:
ENNIO DE CONCINI, ALFREDO GIANNETTI and PIETRO
GERMI

Cinematography
(Black-and-White)
THE LONGEST DAY, Zanuck/20th Century-Fox: JEAN
BOURGOIN and WALTER WOTTITZ
(Color)
LAWRENCE OF ARABIA: FRED A. YOUNG

Art Direction-Set Decoration
(Black-and-White)
TO KILL A MOCKINGBIRD: ALEXANDER GOLITZEN
and HENRY BUMSTEAD
Set Decoration: OLIVER EMERT
(Color)
LAWRENCE OF ARABIA: JOHN BOX and JOHN STOLL
Set Decoration: DARIO SIMONI

Sound
LAWRENCE OF ARABIA, Shepperton Studio Sound
Department: JOHN COX, Sound Director

Film Editing
LAWRENCE OF ARABIA: ANNE COATES

Music
(Note: Title of Awards changed)

(Music Score – substantially original)
LAWRENCE OF ARABIA: MAURICE JARRE
(Scoring of Music – adaptation or treatment)
Meredith Willson's THE MUSIC MAN, Warner Bros.: RAY
HEINDORF
(Best Song)
DAYS OF WINE AND ROSES from *Days of Wine and Roses*,
Manulis-Jalem/Warner Bros.
Music: HENRY MANCINI
Lyrics: JOHNNY MERCER

Costume Design
(Black-and-White)
WHATEVER HAPPENED TO BABY JANE?, Seven Arts &
Aldrich/Warner Bros.: NORMA KOCH
(Color)
THE WONDERFUL WORLD OF THE BROTHERS
GRIMM, MGM & Cinerama: MARY WILLS

Short Subjects
(Cartoons)
THE HOLE, Storyboard/Brandon: JOHN and FAITH
HUBLEY, Producers
(Live Action Subjects)
HEUREUX ANNIVERSAIRE, CAPAC/Atlantic: PIERRE
ETAIX and J.C. CARRIERE, Producers

Documentary
(Short Subjects)
DYLAN THOMAS, TWW/Janus (Welsh): JACK
HOWELLS, Producer
(Features)
BLACK FOX, Image/Heritage: LOUIS CLYDE STOUMEN,
Producer

Special Effects
THE LONGEST DAY:
Visual: ROBERT MacDONALD
Audible: JACQUES MAUMONT

Foreign Language Film Award
SUNDAYS AND CYBELE, Terra-Fides-Orsay-Trocadero
(France)

Honorary Awards
None

Irving G. Thalberg Memorial Award
None

Jean Hersholt Humanitarian Award
STEVE BROIDY

1963

THE BRITISH ENJOYED another bumper Oscar year in 1963. There were 27 nominations related to British films, 20 from among the acting nominees, 10 for a single film, Tony Richardson's bawdy adaptation of the Henry Fielding classic, **Tom Jones**. Disappointingly, **Tom Jones**, in the event, succeeded in winning only four Academy awards: for Best Picture, Director, Screenplay (by the dramatist John Osborne) and Musical Score; and though the film's stylized visuals were crucial to its appeal, its editor, cinematographer and costume designer were not even nominated. Four Oscars was the evening's rather meager record, shared by a film which should not have figured in the Oscar lists at all, Joseph L. Mankiewicz's florid and foolish historical epic **Cleopatra**, starring Elizabeth Taylor, Richard Burton and Rex Harrison.

Cleopatra had all but bankrupted the studio which produced it, 20th Century-Fox (despite the fiasco of **Heaven's Gate** and when inflation is also taken into account, it remains the greatest commercial disaster in Hollywood's history); and its extraordinary inclusion in the Best Picture category was widely and accurately interpreted as a generous gesture on the Academy's part to help Fox recoup even a little of its costs.

The Best Actor category notched up a first: the first major Oscar ever won by a black performer, in this case Sidney Poitier for **Lilies Of The Field**. He was not the first black to be nominated in the big two categories: that honor went to Dorothy Dandridge for her vibrant portrayal of the title role in Otto Preminger's **Carmen Jones** (1954), and Poitier himself had already been a nominee for Stanley Kramer's **The Defiant Ones** (1958). Nor was he the first black to possess a gold statuette: the endearing Hattie McDaniel had been voted Best Supporting Actress in 1939 for her resourceful Mammy in **Gone With The Wind**. However, 1963 was the breakthrough year, and,

BELOW *One of the most spectacular scenes from the multi-million dollar* Cleopatra, *in which Rex Harrison (left, nominated) as Julius Caesar welcomes the Queen of Egypt (Elizabeth Taylor, right) to Rome. The otherwise disastrous picture won four Oscars – for cinematography, art direction, costume design and special effects*

TOP *Paul Newman (nominated) as the feckless amoral Hud meets resistance from Patricia Neal's sexy housekeeper. The award-winning Miss Neal was one of a moving quartet of players that included Melvyn Douglas and Brandon de Wilde*
ABOVE *Known as a debonair and witty romantic lead in the 30s and 40s, Melvyn Douglas returned to the screen after eleven years' absence to play tough elderly gentlemen. In Hud, he won the Best Supporting actor award as the uncompromising patriarch owner of a cattle farm*

as Poitier tellingly remarked, "It was a long journey to this moment."

Best Actress was Patricia Neal for Martin Ritt's 'contemporary' Western **Hud**. Neal, based in England (she was then married to the author of children's books and elegant horror tales, Roald Dahl), refused to be carried away by all the excitement, as she was several months pregnant and literally feared a miscarriage. The honored Supporting performers were the 53-year-old Melvyn Douglas, a former screen lounge lizard, for **Hud** and the 72-year-old character actress Margaret Rutherford for **The V.I.P.s**. Said the deliciously eccentric Rutherford, "I like to feel that this will be the starting point of a new little phase for me in films." It was.

Unfortunately, with the profusion of British actors mostly unfamiliar to American audiences, the fact that no major stars were among the recipients and that too many nominees, for one reason or another, were otherwise engaged on Oscar night, the show was generally regarded as one of the dullest in recent years. There were no scandals, no real surprises and, finally, not much excitement. Even a disaster might have helped to enliven the sluggish proceedings; everything, alas, ran as smoothly as possible.

An 18th-century classic of English literature may seem unlikely material for one of the cinema's biggest box-office hits, but such was the case with Tony Richardson's **Tom Jones**. Based on Fielding's picaresque tale of a lusty, rambunctious young squire, and blessed with a witty script by John Osborne, it caught the imaginations of audiences all over the world, launching its leading performer (Albert Finney) on the path to international stardom and making its director one of the industry's 'hottest' properties. It was the kind of British film which surfaces once or twice in a decade, whose very Britishness represents the primary source of its appeal. What **Tom Jones** offered the spectator was delicately photographed rustic settings, a range of lively, uninhibited performances, a raucously sexy yarn and some of the most amusing sight gags in recent years.

There was, in truth, no real 'plot' to speak of: the film simply related the sentimental education, in and out of bed, of its perky young stud of a hero. And it was often Richardson's clever play with cinematic devices that provoked the loudest laughter. He deployed a barrage of modish visual tricks, but so lightheartedly as to suggest that nothing need to be taken at face value. Thus, the account of Tom's childhood was narrated in the style of a silent film, with appropriate grimaces, a tinkling piano accompaniment and melodramatic intertitles. There was a hilarious use of both slow and accelerated motion. One character, when suddenly confronted with the possibility of a little incestuous lovemaking, knowingly glances at the camera. And Tom himself is ultimately rescued from death on the gallows by another cinematic device – the freeze frame.

No less memorable were the performances, from such stalwarts of the English theatrical tradition as Hugh Griffith and Edith Evans. Susannah York made an exquisite impression as a genteel heroine with her faint yet tangible aura of unstated sexuality. As for the title role, Albert Finney could not be faulted, notably in a now famous scene with Joyce Redman in which a *tête-à-tête*, finger-lickin' supper of chicken, lobster, mutton and oysters is gradually transformed into a feast of a very different kind.

Tom Jones was not only, to date, the most commercially successful film in the chequered history of the British cinema, it heralded the advent of the so-called 'Swinging Sixties', a period when British films had little difficulty competing on the world market.

It was Sidney Poitier who forged the essential link be-

BELOW *Albert Finney (Tom) and Susannah York (Sophia Weston) in a rare romantic moment from* Tom Jones. *It was the only picture in Academy history to boast three supporting actress nominees (Diane Cilento, Edith Evans and Joyce Redman)*

ABOVE *Sidney Poitier, the first black winner of an Oscar for 24 years, as the footloose handyman Homer Smith in* Lilies Of The Field. *With him is Lilia Skala as one of a group of refugee nuns he helps*

tween the cheerful if ultimately demeaning black stereotypes represented in films of the 30s and 40s by the likes of Stepin Fetchit and Hattie McDaniel, and the arrival of such sassy, jive-talking superstars of the 80s as Richard Pryor and Eddie Murphy. Inevitably, with his self-consciously 'soulful' dignity, he came to appear a rather dated, even dubious, model to young black audiences in America; but this is a fate often reserved for transitional figures, and Poitier's immense influence on the future of black artists in the cinema can neither be belittled nor denied. The presentation of his award was the most warmly applauded of all on Oscar night, April 13, 1964, the Academy audience no doubt feeling that recognition of Hollywood's black performers was long overdue.

A pity, then, that Poitier should have been honored for his work in a film as mawkish as **Lilies Of The Field**, in which he played a vagrant handyman inveigled by some white nuns into building a new chapel for their order. Though played in almost as sentimental a style as the whole film, Poitier's performance was thankfully not devoid of humor and grit; and, for a career which already included such superior films as **Blackboard Jungle** (1955), **Something Of Value** (1957), **The Defiant Ones**

(1958) and **Porgy And Bess** (1959), no one was ready to begrudge him his Oscar.

Though Patricia Neal was hardly a household name in 1963, Martin Ritt envisaged no other actress for the role of a cynical, world-weary housekeeper in **Hud** (opposite Paul Newman). "It was a tough part to cast," he told one interviewer. "This woman had to be believable as a housekeeper and still be sexy. It called for a special combination of warmth and toughness, while still being very feminine. Pat Neal was it." And perhaps the most telling indication of her gifts was the fact that, though the role was quite a brief one in terms of her screen exposure, and Neal herself was no topliner, the Academy did not hesitate to include her in the Best Actress, rather than Best Supporting Actress, category.

Only one year later, it must have appeared as though her career had come to an end. Already no stranger to personal affliction (her infant son was struck by an automobile and suffered severe brain damage, her daughter died of measles at the age of 13), Neal suffered a series of near-fatal strokes which left her partially paralyzed, confined to a wheelchair and incapable of articulate speech. Over the years, however, she made an astonishing recovery, one complete enough for her to return to the cinema: she was nominated for an Oscar in 1968 for **The Subject Was Roses**. It is a testament as much to her talent as to her courage that the nomination was not wholly sentimental in origin.

WINNERS 1963

Nominations Announced: February 24, 1964
Awards Ceremony: April 13, 1964
Santa Monica Civic Auditorium

Best Picture
TOM JONES, Woodfall/UA-Lopert: TONY RICHARDSON, Producer

Actor
SIDNEY POITIER in *Lilies Of The Field*, Rainbow/UA

Actress
PATRICIA NEAL in *Hud*, Salem-Dover/Paramount

Supporting Actor
MELVYN DOUGLAS in *Hud*

Supporting Actress
MARGARET RUTHERFORD in *The V.I.P.s*, MGM

Directing
TONY RICHARDSON for *Tom Jones*

Writing
(Best Screenplay – based on material from another medium)
TOM JONES: John Osborne
(Best Story and Screenplay – written directly for the screen)
HOW THE WEST WAS WON, MGM & Cinerama: JAMES R. WEBB

Cinematography
(Black-and-White)
HUD: JAMES WONG HOWE
(Color)
CLEOPATRA, 20th Century-Fox-MCL-WALWA/20th Century-Fox: LEON SHAMROY

Art Direction-Set Decoration
(Black-and-White)
AMERICA AMERICA, Athena/Warner Bros.: GENE CALLAHAN
(Color)
CLEOPATRA: JOHN DeCUIR, JACK MARTIN SMITH, HILYARD BROWN, HERMAN BLUMENTHAL, ELVEN WEBB, MAURICE PELLING and BORIS JURAGA
Set Decoration: WALTER M. SCOTT, Paul S. FOX and RAY MOYER

Sound
HOW THE WEST WAS WON, MGM Studio Sound Department: FRANKLIN E. MILTON, Sound Director

Film Editing
HOW THE WEST WAS WON: HAROLD F. KRESS

Music
(Music Score – substantially original)
TOM JONES: JOHN ADDISON
(Scoring of Music – adaptation or treatment)
IRMA LA DOUCE, Mirisch-Phalanx/UA: ANDRE PREVIN

(Best Song)
CALL ME IRRESPONSIBLE from *Papa's Delicate Condition*, Amro/Paramount
Music: JAMES VAN HEUSEN
Lyrics: SAMMY CAHN

Costume Design
(Black-and-White)
Federico Fellini's *8½*, Cineriz/Embassy: PIERO GHERARDI
(Color)
CLEOPATRA: IRENE SHARAFF, VITTORIO NINO NOVARESE and RENIE

Short Subjects
(Cartoons)
THE CRITIC, Pintoff-Crossbow/Columbia: ERNEST PINTOFF, Producer
(Live Action Subjects)
AN OCCURRENCE AT OWL CREEK BRIDGE, Films Du Centaure-Filmartic/Cappagariff-Janus: PAUL DE ROUBAIX and MARCEL ICHAC, Producers

Documentary
(Short Subjects)
CHAGALL, Auerbach-Flag: SIMON SCHIFFRIN, Producer
(Features)
ROBERT FROST: A LOVER'S QUARREL WITH THE WORLD, WGBH Educational Froundation: ROBERT HUGHES, Producer

Special Visual Effects
(New Category)
(For the 36th Awards Year the Academy Board of Governors, in recognition of the fact that the best visual effects and the best audible effects each year did not necessarily occur in the same picture, voted to discontinue the Special Effects Award and created two new awards.)
CLEOPATRA: EMIL KOSA, Jr

Sound Effects
(New Category)
IT'S A MAD, MAD, MAD, MAD WORLD, Casey/UA: WALTER G. ELLIOTT

Foreign Language Film Award
Federico Fellini's *8½*, Cineriz/Embassy (Italy)

Honorary Awards
None

Irving G. Thalberg Memorial Award
SAM SPIEGEL

Jean Hersholt Humanitarian Award
None

1964

A CURSORY GLANCE AT the major trio of Academy Award results for 1964 would suggest a clear-cut victory for a single film: Best Picture, **My Fair Lady**; Best Actor, Rex Harrison; and Best Actress, Julie Andrews. It was not as straightforward as that, however. In fact, Andrews earned her Oscar, not for **My Fair Lady**, but for Walt Disney's enchanting blend of cartoon and live-action, **Mary Poppins** (based on the classic children's books of P.L. Travers). And thereby hangs a rather sorry tale. When Warner Bros. purchased the film rights to Alan Jay Lerner and Frederick Loewe's **My Fair Lady**, Broadway's longest-running musical to date, producer Jack Warner decided that, in view of the show's unheard-of price tag of $5,500,000, the screen version could not be entrusted to an actress who, even if she were the current toast of Broadway, had never before appeared in a film, much less in a starring role. (Indeed, Warner even briefly toyed with the idea of replacing Harrison with either Richard Burton or Cary Grant.)

Even before the $17,000,000 movie version went into production, many industry observers publicly expressed their disapproval of the snub which Andrews had received and claimed that Warner had been extremely short-sighted in his approach to the adaptation. And since Andrews was concurrently offered the title role in **Mary Poppins**, winning not only a nomination but the Best Actress statuette itself, they would seem to have been vindicated; especially as the cinematic Eliza Doolittle, Audrey Hepburn, was not even nominated, an omission felt by some to represent an implicit criticism of Warner's handling of the affair.

Miss Hepburn agreed nevertheless to attend the ceremony, only to discover that, each time **Poppins** was voted a winner, the TV cameras would zoom into her exquisitely poised features to capture the merest hint of a frown. (Andrews was subjected to the same treatment.) As for Harrison, he tactfully murmured thanks and affection to ". . . two fair ladies". Though the rival movies had been neck-and-neck in the nominations race (**Poppins** with 13, **Fair Lady** with 12), it was **My Fair Lady** which emerged as the evening's overall victor with eight Oscars: for Best Picture, Actor, Director, Musical Score, Costume Design, Cinematography, Art Direction and Sound. It was, incredibly, a first Oscar for the veteran film-maker George Cukor, whose reputation as an 'actors' director' was underlined by the fact that five stars (James Stewart,

ABOVE *Rex Harrison (left) as Professor Higgins, Audrey Hepburn as Eliza Doolittle (center) and Wilfrid Hyde White as Colonel Pickering celebrating 'The Rain In Spain' in the year's Best Picture winner,* My Fair Lady

Ingrid Bergman, Ronald Colman, Judy Holliday and, this year's winner, Rex Harrison) had won Oscars under his coaching and 14 others had been nominated – something of a record. And though the two films which dominated the event had both been financed by American studios, they were indelibly British in both style and atmosphere, which prompted M.C. Bob Hope to remark, "The losers will now join hands and march on the British embassy."

What is there left to say about **My Fair Lady**? As one Hollywood wag commented on the immensely enjoyable screen version, "Jack Warner has miraculously managed to turn gold into gold." The film's principal flaw, ironically, remained the casting of Audrey Hepburn, who made a

game attempt at playing a Cockney flower girl but was visibly a lady from the beginning – which removed much of the plot's credibility. On the other hand, with the casting of Harrison, the film quite simply became, its many other qualities apart, a documentary record of one of the greatest of all musical comedy performances, with familiarity breeding, for the actor, an ever more subtly attuned reading of the role and, for the spectator, an ever increasing admiration.

Cukor directed tastefully, making a real showstopper out of 'Get Me to the Church on Time' with the sublime Stanley Holloway as the dustman Doolittle (another second choice: Warner had expressed a preference for James Cagney!), while other highlights included the 'Ascot Gavotte', whose elegant Edwardian ladies and gentlemen were decked out by designer Cecil Beaton in glorious black-and-white, 'The Rain in Spain' (sung by Hepburn, Harrison and Wilfrid Hyde White as Colonel

BELOW *Russian-born actress Lila Kedrova in her first English-speaking film won the Best Supporting Actress Oscar as the pathetic ageing prostitute in* Zorba The Greek. *Anthony Quinn (right) had to be content with only a nomination in the title role*

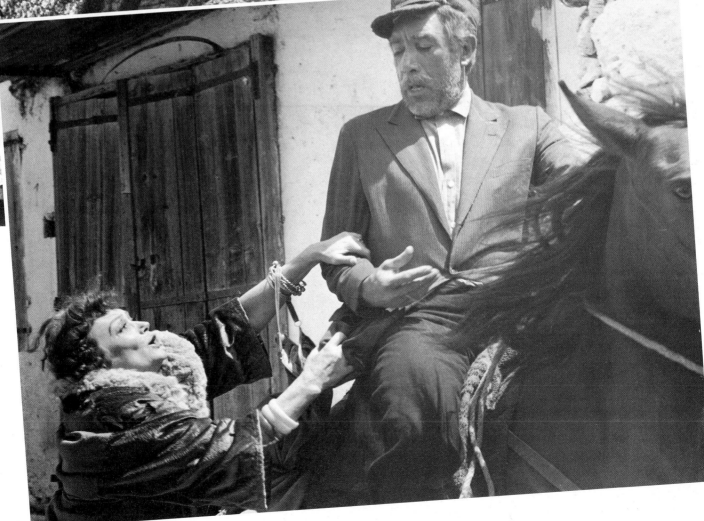

Pickering) and, perhaps most memorable of all, Harrison's unexpectedly touching rendition of 'I've Grown Accustomed to Her Face'. Gladys Cooper was cast as Mrs Higgins, Isobel Elsom as Mrs Eynsford Hill and Jeremy Brett as her lovesick son Freddy. The unforgettable score was transferred absolutely intact from the stage production (something of a novelty for film musicals); Hepburn's vocals were dubbed in by Marni Nixon, who has frequently been called upon to perform such a thankless chore; and, of course, the ending left Higgins and Eliza facing the future together, a very radical deviation from Shaw's original **Pygmalion**, from which the musical had been adapted.

One curious fact is worth noting: **Pygmalion** itself had already been brought to the screen by Gabriel Pascal in 1938, with Leslie Howard (the film's co-director) and Wendy Hiller. On that occasion, its scenario was judged the year's best – winning an unlikely Oscar for the dramatist Bernard Shaw. Crusty to the last, the formidable GBS considered the award an insult!

The fact that Rex Harrison is now as closely associated with **My Fair Lady** as Yul Brynner with **The King And I** tends to obscure a fundamental difference between the two roles: whereas Brynner's launched him into international stardom, Harrison's represented practically the culmination of a long and, by any standard, distinguished

BELOW *Audrey Hepburn (foreground) as the cockney flower girl Eliza Doolittle at Covent Garden in* My Fair Lady *before her transformation into a lady. None of the eight awards went to ⱥⁿⱥⱥ ⱥⱥ the cast,* Rex Harrison *and the real star was Cecil Beaton's Oscar-winning costume design*

career on both stage and screen. Though his very first film appearance came as early as 1929, in a totally forgotten British farce entitled **Get Your Man**, his most productive period was the 40s, with such British films as **Major Barbara** (1941, another Shavian adaptation by Gabriel Pascal) and **Blithe Spirit** (1945, from Noël Coward's play); and, in the United States, **Anna And The King of Siam** (1946, in which, coincidentally, he played the same monarch as Brynner), **The Ghost And Mrs Muir, The Foxes Of Harrow** (1947) and Preston Sturges' frenetic comedy **Unfaithfully Yours** (1948, and recently remade with Dudley Moore). It was in 1948, too, that Harrison's Hollywood prestige was temporarily blighted by his involvement in the suicide of the actress Carole Landis, as a result of which unhappy incident he was saddled with the rather vulgar nickname of 'Sexy Rexy'.

Knowing himself to be a poor singer, Harrison was at first deeply reluctant to commit himself to the role of Higgins. Yet it was, paradoxically, his vocal inadequacy which made the performance so uniquely graceful, affecting and funny. He was, more or less, the first of the genre's 'talk-singers', merely stylizing or heightening his own limited vocal range to accord with a musical accompaniment. But though he represented a model for a host of non-singing musical comedy stars (notably, Richard Burton in *Camelot* in the theater), none has ever rivaled the inimitable quality – as though 'talk-singing' were simply a more *civilized* form of vocalizing – that he so uniquely brought to **My Fair Lady**.

As for Julie Andrews, her reputation as a singer has arguably damaged her hopes of a broader-based career. Even if, after the disappointment of being rejected for Warners' **My Fair Lady**, she was eternally grateful for the opportunity of **Mary Poppins**, the part was not without its drawbacks. It could be said that, because of her identification with the film, the expression 'a Mary Poppins' has entered the language; but the characterization it suggests, that of everyone's favorite nanny, is one that Andrews has been striving to shake off since she completed the film. Brisk and pretty, with a charming, bell-like soprano voice and a tendency to enunciate her dialogue so clearly that she could be lip-read from a hundred yards away, she has sometimes found it a strain personifying the more realistic and gritty type of character she so patently craves to play. Thus, already concerned to avoid typecasting, she followed **Mary Poppins** with **The Americanization Of Emily** in the same year, a curious Paddy Chayefsky-scripted comedy about a British war widow who falls helplessly in love with a smooth American naval officer.

On Oscar night, however, it was Mary Poppins all the way. Even Andrews' acceptance speech was uttered in a nanny-like tone: "I know you Americans are famous for your hospitality, but this is really ridiculous."

WINNERS 1964

Nominations Announced: February 23, 1965
Awards Ceremony: April 5, 1965
Santa Monica Civic Auditorium

Best Picture
MY FAIR LADY, Warner Bros.: JACK L. WARNER, Producer

Actor
REX HARRISON in *My Fair Lady*

Actress
JULIE ANDREWS in *Mary Poppins*, Disney

Supporting Actor
PETER USTINOV in *Topkapi*, Filmways/UA

Supporting Actress
LILA KEDROVA in *Zorba The Greek*, Rochley/International Classics

Directing
GEORGE CUKOR for *My Fair Lady*

Writing
(Best Screenplay – based on material from another medium)
BECKET, Wallis/Paramount: EDWARD ANHALT
(Best Story and Screenplay – written directly for the screen)
FATHER GOOSE, Universal-Granox/Universal
Story: S.H. BARNETT
Screenplay: PETER STONE and FRANK TARLOFF

Cinematography
(Black-and-White)
ZORBA THE GREEK: WALTER LASSALLY
(Color)
MY FAIR LADY: HARRY STRADLING

Art Direction-Set Decoration
(Black-and-White)
ZORBA THE GREEK: VASSILIS FOTOPOULOS
(Color)
MY FAIR LADY: GENE ALLEN and CECIL BEATON
Set Decoration: GEORGE JAMES HOPKINS

Sound
MY FAIR LADY, Warner Bros. Studio Sound Department:
GEORGE R. GROVES, Sound Director

Film Editing
MARY POPPINS: COTTON WARBURTON

Music
(Music Score – substantially original)
MARY POPPINS: RICHARD M. SHERMAN and ROBERT B. SHERMAN

(Scoring of Music – adaptation or treatment)
MY FAIR LADY: ANDRE PREVIN
(Best Song)
CHIM-CHIM-CHER-EE from *Mary Poppins*
Music and Lyrics: RICHARD M. SHERMAN and ROBERT B. SHERMAN

Costume Design
(Black-and-White)
THE NIGHT OF THE IGUANA, Seven Arts/MGM:
DOROTHY JEAKINS
(Color)
MY FAIR LADY: CECIL BEATON

Short Subjects
(Cartoons)
THE PINK PHINK, Mirisch-Geoffrey/UA: DAVID H.
DePATIE and FRIZ FRELENG, Producers
(Live Action Subjects)
CASALS CONDUCTS: 1964, Thalia/Beckman: EDWARD
SCHREIBER, Producer

Documentary
(Short Subjects)
NINE FROM LITTLE ROCK, United States Information
Agency/Guggenheim
(Features)
Jacques-Yves Cousteau's WORLD WITHOUT SUN,
Filmad-Les Requins Associes-Orsay-CEIAP/Columbia:
JACQUES-YVES COUSTEAU, Producer

Special Visual Effects
MARY POPPINS: PETER ELLENSHAW, HAMILTON
LUSKE and EUSTACE LYCETT

Sound Effects
GOLDFINGER, Eon/UA: NORMAN WANSTALL

Foreign Language Film Award
YESTERDAY, TODAY AND TOMORROW,
Champion-Concordia (Italy)

Honorary Award
WILLIAM TUTTLE for his outstanding make-up
achievement for *7 Faces Of Dr Lao*. (statuette)

Irving G. Thalberg Memorial Award
None

Jean Hersholt Humanitarian Award
None

1965

THE CLIMAX OF **The Oscar**, a movie about the efforts of an unscrupulous young actor to forge a Hollywood reputation for himself, was set, as its title would suggest, at the Academy Awards ceremony. Frank, played by Stephen Boyd, has been nominated for the Best Actor Oscar, and nervously awaits the Academy's decision. When the envelope is unsealed, the celebrity assigned to make the presentation breathlessly announces, "And the winner is Frank . . .". Boyd half-rises from his seat – whereupon the voice continues, ". . . Sinatra!" Collapse of hopeful loser.

Much the same kind of suspense was generated during the 1965 Oscar ceremony, held at the Santa Monica Civic Auditorium on April 18, 1966. The principal contenders for the Best Actress Award were both British and both named Julie – Andrews, for **The Sound Of Music**, and Christie, for **Darling**. Naturally, the local press found such a strange coincidence irresistible, and hastened to plant rumors of a feud between the two actresses. To counter such calumnies, Julie and Julie planned to arrive at the theater in the same limousine – a project scotched by the fact that their respective films had been produced by different studios, neither one of which cared to offer free publicity to the opposition.

In the event, it was Julie Christie who triumphed, for her portrayal of an ambitious young model in a cynical, fashion-obsessed milieu. Had her rival won, she would have been the first to match a record established by Luise Rainer for two Best Actress Oscars in succession (**The Great Ziegfeld**, 1936, and **The Good Earth**, 1937). As it was, she accepted defeat as gracefully as, the previous year, she had accepted victory, hugging her tearfully overjoyed fellow-Brit and calmly remarking, "It's almost a relief not to have won again."

In the Best Picture race, **The Sound Of Music** and **Doctor Zhivago** had entered the nominations heat neck-and-neck: ten apiece. It was to remain a tie to the end, with five Oscars for the Rodgers and Hammerstein musical (Best Picture, Director, Musical Score, Editing and Sound), five to the Russian epic (Best Screenplay, Cinematography, Art Direction, Original Musical Score and Costume Design). Though Christie had not been nominated for her luminous performance as Lara, the heroine of David Lean's sweeping adaptation of the Boris Pasternak novel, she herself regarded it as the better of the two: "I wish I had made **Darling** after **Zhivago**," she said with a candor

to which Hollywood was unaccustomed. "It would have been quite different."

Best Supporting performers were the veteran trouper Martin Balsam for **A Thousand Clowns** and second-time winner Shelley Winters, playing a mother again, for **A Patch of Blue**. The evening's M.C., Bob Hope, received yet another honorary award (not a statuette but a gold medal) "for unique and distinguished service to the motion picture industry and the Academy"; director William Wyler won the Irving Thalberg Memorial Award; and the most televised personality in attendance happened not to be a movie star at all but the President's daughter, Lynda Bird Johnson, escorted by an actor better-known as a playboy, George Hamilton.

It is appropriate that the title of one of the most commercially successful musicals of all time – grossing almost $200,000,000 worldwide – should so succinctly sum up the genre's appeal: **The Sound Of Music**. It wasn't only Rodgers and Hammerstein's score, however, that prompted several spectators to revisit the movie again and

BELOW *Shelley Winters as the blowsy, overbearing mother of blind girl Elizabeth Hartman in* A Patch Of Blue, *won her second supporting actress award, having won her first for* The Diary Of Anne Frank *six years previously*

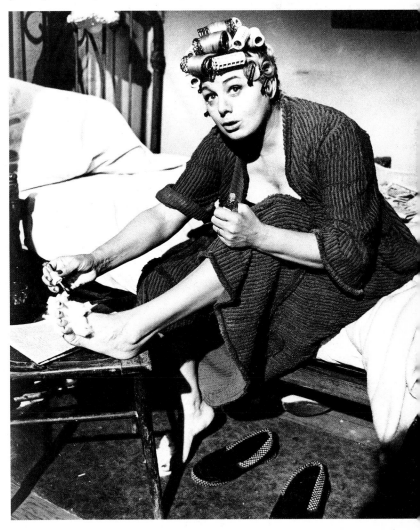

again, and one Englishwoman to travel the length and breadth of the United Kingdom to catch its every screening. **The Sound Of Music** offered an unbeatable range of ingredients. There was the delicious Miss Andrews, then on the very crest of her popularity; an unsophisticated but eminently hummable collection of tunes; some ravishing views of Salzburg and the Tyrol filling out the Todd-AO screen; and, not least, a good, strong storyline, involving nuns and children, Nazis and dogs – all under the expert control of director Robert Wise.

The plot, of course, centered on the internationally celebrated Trapp Family Singers. Julie Andrews played Maria, a young postulant nun who quits her convent – temporarily, she believes – to take up a position as governess to the seven children of an attractive but tetchy widower, Captain von Trapp (Christopher Plummer). After various misadventures and misunderstandings, she renounces her vocation to stay on as the Captain's wife. And the charm of the movie's romantic scenes (with a narrative development not unlike that of an earlier Rodgers and Hammerstein hit, **The King And I**), derived from the incongruous matching of the endearingly level-headed governess with the unbending but lonely martinet whose crusty exterior she soon succeeds in melting.

Given such material, the film could hardly fail to make equally musical noises at box-offices around the world. It might be schmaltzy, but musical comedy audiences have always possessed a sweet tooth and it would have been churlish not to enter into the spirit of it all when the camera soared high over the Alps and Andrews opened up her heart with the title song. It helped, too, that the score was a chocolate box packed with such soft-centered goodies as 'Maria', 'Climb Every Mountain' and 'My Favorite Things' (all of them now standards). For many moviegoers, **The Sound of Music** could henceforth be accounted as one of their 'favorite things'.

Despite charismatic performances by Christopher Plummer and Omar Sharif respectively, neither **The Sound Of Music** nor **Doctor Zhivago** received a Best Actor nomination. That particular Oscar was won by an actor who, for most of his career, had played a series of tough, scowling heavies in minor thrillers and Westerns, Lee Marvin. During these years, in which he only very gradually built up a reputation, the most to which Marvin might reasonably have aspired was a Best Supporting Actor award; and he would doubtless have been astonished to learn that the Oscar, when it came, would be for Best Actor – and in a comedy! Elliot Silverstein's **Cat Ballou** was a consistently funny spoof Western in which Marvin was allowed to exploit his untapped comic gifts in the dual role of a grizzled, alcoholic old gunfighter (when informed that his eyes are bloodshot, he replies,

LEFT *Christopher Plummer as Captain von Trapp caught between Eleanor Parker (left), his fiancee, and Julie Andrews, the governess to his seven children. Previous year's winner Andrews was nominated for her bright and tuneful performance*

"You ought to see 'em from my side!") and his murderous twin brother. Though a small-budget feature, which producer Harold Hecht released without any initial barrage of publicity, it benefited enormously from that greatest publicist of all, word-of-mouth, and soon turned into a 'cult' film among American college students, who responded to its outrageous humor and irreverence. Marvin (perhaps surprisingly, the son of a well-to-do New York family with somewhat artistic inclinations, and a man of no mean culture himself) received the warmest ovation of the evening – no doubt because the Academy audience was particularly touched by the idea of an actor

ABOVE Darling *was the last word to describe Julie Christie's ambitious, vain, and selfish model, a role which won her the Best Actress Oscar. Here she gets what she deserves from one of the men she has used, TV interviewer Dirk Bogarde*
LEFT *Lee Marvin, as the drunken, has-been gunfighter in* Cat Ballou, *tries to protect Jane Fonda from a vicious gunman. She turns outlaw and he turns hero. He was also the hero of the Awards ceremony when he carried off the Best Actor award*

whose very status in the film industry had been changed by the bestowal of an Oscar.

It was John Schlesinger's **Billy Liar** (1963) which turned Julie Christie into an international star – in spite of the fact that her role, though important, was a relatively brief one. As the dream girl in Tom Courtenay's life who attempts to persuade him to leave his home town in the provinces for the siren attractions of London, she dazzled a whole generation of filmgoers as a mini-skirted apparition who seemed to represent everything that was carefree and youthful about the changing society of England. She was viewed as the very embodiment of the 'Swinging Sixties', she was ravishingly beautiful in a completely uncosmeticized style and the Americans went mad about

her. As she said of that period, "You could be someone without having to be glamorous. I know I wasn't, and I was criticized quite a lot for that in England – perhaps not in America, because they were too gaga over English people then to criticize."

Her celebrity was consecrated in **Darling**, a film written by Frederic Raphael especially for her; and in a not notably sympathetic role, she contrived to appear both ice-cold and radiant – which was quite a feat!

Of late, Christie has lived in semi-retirement from the cinema, preferring to devote her energies to the feminist movement and the campaign for nuclear disarmament, of which she is a strong and active supporter. But she never did identify with the heroine of **Darling**: "Whatever I am, I'm *not* Diana," she once protested. "I don't have the energy for all that kind of thing."

WINNERS 1965

Nominations Announced: February 21, 1966
Awards Ceremony: April 18, 1966
Santa Monica Civic Auditorium

Best Picture
THE SOUND OF MUSIC, Argyle/20th Century-Fox:
ROBERT WISE, Producer

Actor
LEE MARVIN in *Cat Ballou*, Hecht/Columbia

Actress
JULIE CHRISTIE in *Darling*, Anglo-Amalgamated/Embassy

Supporting Actor
MARTIN BALSAM in *A Thousand Clowns*, Harrell/UA

Supporting Actress
SHELLEY WINTERS in *A Patch Of Blue*,
Berman-Green/MGM

Directing
ROBERT WISE for *The Sound Of Music*

Writing
(Best Screenplay – based on material from another medium)
DOCTOR ZHIVAGO, Sostar-MGM (British)/MGM:
ROBERT BOLT
(Best Story and Screenplay – written directly for the screen)
DARLING: FREDERIC RAPHAEL

Cinematography
(Black-and-White)
SHIPS OF FOOLS, Columbia: ERNEST LASZLO
(Color)
DOCTOR ZHIVAGO: MGM: FREDDIE YOUNG

Art Direction-Set Decoration
(Black-and-White)
SHIPS OF FOOLS: ROBERT CLATWORTHY
Set Decoration: JOSEPH KISH
(Color)
DOCTOR ZHIVAGO: JOHN BOX and TERRY MARSH
Set Decoration: DARIO SIMONI

Sound
THE SOUND OF MUSIC, 20th Century-Fox Studio Sound
Department: JAMES P. CORCORAN, Sound Director; and
Todd-AO Sound Department: FRED HYNES, Sound
Director

Film Editing
THE SOUND OF MUSIC: WILLIAM REYNOLDS

Music
(Music Score – substantially original)
DOCTOR ZHIVAGO: MAURICE JARRE

(Scoring of Music – adaptation or treatment)
THE SOUND OF MUSIC: IRWIN KOSTAL
(Best Song)
THE SHADOW OF YOUR SMILE from *The Sandpiper*,
Filmways-Venice/MGM
Music: JOHNNY MANDEL
Lyrics: PAUL FRANCIS WEBSTER

Costume Design
(Black-and-White)
DARLING: JULIE HARRIS
(Color)
DOCTOR ZHIVAGO: PHYLLIS DALTON

Short Subjects
(Cartoons)
THE DOT AND THE LINE, MGM: CHUCK JONES and
LES GOLDMAN, Producers
(Live Action Subjects)·
THE CHICKEN (Le Poulet), Renn/Pathe Contemporary:
CLAUDE BERRI, Producer

Documentary
(Short Subjects)
TO BE ALIVE!, Johnson Wax: FRANCIS THOMPSON INC,
Producer
(Features)
THE ELEANOR ROOSEVELT STORY, Glazier/American
International: SIDNEY GLAZIER, Producer

Special Visual Effects
THUNDERBALL, Broccoli-Saltzman-McClory/UA: JOHN
STEARS

Sound Effects
THE GREAT RACE, Patricia-Jalem-Reynard/Warner Bros:
TREGOWETH BROWN

Foreign Language Film Award
THE SHOP ON MAIN STREET, Ceskoslovensky Film
Production (Czechoslovakia)

Honorary Award
BOB HOPE for unique and distinguished service to our
industry and the Academy. (gold medal)

Irving G. Thalberg Memorial Award
WILLIAM WYLER

Jean Hersholt Humanitarian Award
EDMOND L. DePATIE

1966

THE 1966 ACADEMY Awards ceremony almost didn't take place – and many subsequently felt it might have been better that way. Two weeks before the event, a strike was called by A.F.T.R.A., the theatrical union on which depended all live broadcasts on television. If it were to remain unsettled by April 10, 1967, the ceremony could not be televised – and, in view of the revenue which the sale of TV rights generated annually for the Academy, it might not be held at all. Eventually, the film industry decided that, with or without television coverage, the event would go ahead as planned – it was not prepared to capitulate so abjectly to its rival medium. The decision was a wise one: A.F.T.R.A. called off the strike only three hours before Oscar night got under way, and 65 million viewers (a far smaller audience than usual) were able to watch the proceedings.

Following such last-minute suspense, however, the ceremony itself turned out to be a dreary anti-climax. In terms of entertainment, to be sure, it offered viewers a few delectable moments: a brief but poignant valedictory fling by Fred Astaire and Ginger Rogers, publicly teamed for the last time; an exuberantly fizzy rendering of the very 60s number 'Georgy Girl' by Mitzi Gaynor; and, in a rather different register, the first Hollywood appearance of Patricia Neal since the series of debilitating strokes she had suffered two years before.

It was the evening's *raison d'être*, the presentation of Oscars, which proved so disappointingly under par. To begin with, only one winner cited in any of the four acting categories was present to receive his award: Walter Matthau, as Best Supporting Actor for his witty, wily performance as a shyster lawyer in Billy Wilder's **The Fortune Cookie**. Paul Scofield, winner for **A Man For All Seasons**, remained in England ("I didn't expect to get it. I had made up my mind that Richard Burton would get it"); Elizabeth Taylor, awarded her second Oscar for **Who's Afraid Of Virginia Woolf?**, was vacationing in the South of France with husband and fellow-nominee Burton; and Sandy Dennis, Best Supporting Actress for **Who's Afraid Of Virginia Woolf?**, was in New York. The fact that two Redgrave sisters were up for a Best Actress award (Vanessa for **Morgan – A Suitable Case For Treatment** and Lynn for the serio-comic title role of **Georgy Girl**) might have generated a little suspense – except that neither had been perceived as having the slightest chance of winning. And, again and again, acceptance speeches were made

ABOVE *Best Actor Paul Scofield (left) standing by his principles as Sir Thomas More in* A Man For All Seasons, *in opposition to Nigel Davenport as the Duke of Norfolk (right) and King Henry VIII (Robert Shaw). It was the distinguished English stage actor's greatest screen success*

on behalf of, rather than by, the winners. Perhaps because it had seemed probable for a while that the event's only spectators would be the invited audience, Hollywood's luminaries showed scant interest in what is generally considered the industry's greatest night.

The films of the year, by the nomination count, were Mike Nichols' acerbic screen adaptation of Edward Albee's **Who's Afraid Of Virginia Woolf?** (13 nominations, including one in each of the four acting categories) and Fred Zinnemann's biopic of Sir Thomas More, **A Man For All Season** (eight nominations). It was, unexpectedly, Zinnemann's film which came up trumps with a total of six

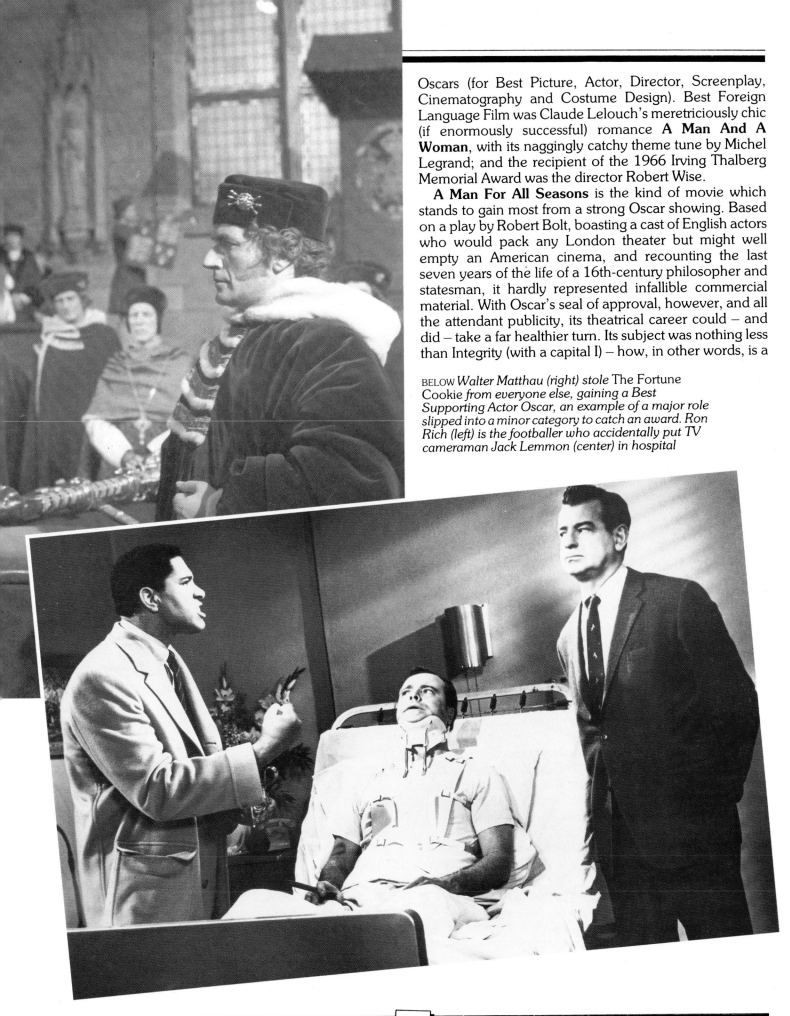

Oscars (for Best Picture, Actor, Director, Screenplay, Cinematography and Costume Design). Best Foreign Language Film was Claude Lelouch's meretriciously chic (if enormously successful) romance **A Man And A Woman**, with its naggingly catchy theme tune by Michel Legrand; and the recipient of the 1966 Irving Thalberg Memorial Award was the director Robert Wise.

A Man For All Seasons is the kind of movie which stands to gain most from a strong Oscar showing. Based on a play by Robert Bolt, boasting a cast of English actors who would pack any London theater but might well empty an American cinema, and recounting the last seven years of the life of a 16th-century philosopher and statesman, it hardly represented infallible commercial material. With Oscar's seal of approval, however, and all the attendant publicity, its theatrical career could – and did – take a far healthier turn. Its subject was nothing less than Integrity (with a capital I) – how, in other words, is a

BELOW *Walter Matthau (right) stole* The Fortune Cookie *from everyone else, gaining a Best Supporting Actor Oscar, an example of a major role slipped into a minor category to catch an award. Ron Rich (left) is the footballer who accidentally put TV cameraman Jack Lemmon (center) in hospital*

man of honor to remain faithful to his own deeply-held convictions in the face of pressure from his masters? In Sir Thomas More's case, the master was the King himself – Henry VIII (played by Robert Shaw with a kind of volatile arrogance); and by refusing to sacrifice his principles to expediency, he found himself on the executioner's block.

Though very much an inner drama, a struggle of wills and a clash of personalities, **A Man For All Seasons** was neither wordy nor static. Shot not in a studio but in English country homes and palaces, it looked absolutely splendid (especially when one considers that its budget – just under $2,000,000 – was already a paltry one for the 60s); and the decision of producer Mike Frankovich and director Zinnemann to use English actors rather than American stars invested the film with a sense of authenticity that was unusual for historical dramas made in Hollywood. Scofield apart, there was a brusque, sensitive performance from Wendy Hiller as More's long-suffering wife, a meltingly charming one from Susannah York as his daughter and, especially, a magnificently eloquent cameo from Orson Welles as Cardinal Wolsey.

In certain respects, as Shirley Booth once observed, it can be considered unjust to offer an Academy Award to an actor or actress repeating, on film, a performance played many times in a long-running stage hit. It is as though – unlike the actor who originates a screen role and who may rehearse each scene a mere half-dozen times before stepping in front of the camera – theatrical performers working in the cinema have profited from anything up to 2,000 'rehearsals' during a stage run. The most intelligent of them, however, quickly realize that the new medium will make new demands upon them – that, whereas actors on the stage must *project*, actors in the cinema are *projected*. A stage performance must renounce its broader effects to become less overtly expressive, more introspective. There is, after all, no third row in the gallery to which they have to play.

This was certainly the case with Paul Scofield's

ABOVE *Elizabeth Taylor in a typically verbally abusive moment from her second Oscar-winning role as the loud-mouthed, shrewish wife of a self-loathing University professor (Richard Burton, right) in* Who's Afraid Of Virginia Woolf?

Thomas More in **A Man For All Seasons**. Faced with mounting pressure to endorse Henry VIII's marriage to Anne Boleyn, More cunningly bests his adversaries until, as a last resort, the charge of 'perjury' is used to justify his death sentence. He is a man who finds himself caught between conflicting loyalties – to his family, his monarch, his nation, his religious beliefs and, ultimately, his own life. And though, in the theatre, Scofield has on occasion hovered perilously close to hamminess, he contrived on film to convey this inner conflict with the most economic of means – a melancholic half-smile, an ironic curl of the lips, a peculiar inflection of the voice. It was a magnificent performance (even if its subtlety also demonstrated why the actor has been so neglected by the cinema) and, as one reviewer wrote, "not so much an instance of repeating a performance as of perfecting one".

Elizabeth Taylor and Richard Burton must have seemed unlikely, not to say ludicrous, casting for the roles of George and Martha, the lonely, tormented, mutually destructive couple of Edward Albee's Pulitzer Prize-winning drama **Who's Afraid of Virginia Woolf?** Burton was the man whom Taylor married twice and divorced twice, in whose company she was seen everywhere, and with whom she appeared in no fewer than 11 films. Most of these were unspeakably bad – pointless, pretentious vehicles for a couple whose interest, as far as the general public was concerned, derived almost entirely from the publicity they so assiduously courted. Exception must be made, nevertheless, of **Virginia Woolf**, in which Burton gave his last good screen performance (prior to **1984**) and Taylor, astounding as his raddled, foul-mouthed wife, this time fully deserved her Oscar.

With both Burton and Taylor at their considerable best, it seemed likely that, for the first time in the Academy's history, a husband-and-wife couple would carry off the top acting prizes. It did not happen; Taylor, in consequence, sulked for two whole weeks before, finally, gracefully accepting her Oscar from Lord Mountbatten at a British Film Academy Award reception in London.

WINNERS 1966

Nominations Announced: February 20, 1967
Awards Ceremony: April 10, 1967
Santa Monica Civic Auditorium

Best Picture
A MAN FOR ALL SEASONS, Highland/Columbia: FRED ZINNEMANN, Producer

Actor
PAUL SCOFIELD in *A Man For All Seasons*

Actress
ELIZABETH TAYLOR in *Who's Afraid Of Virginia Woolf?*, Chenault/Warner Bros.

Supporting Actor
WALTER MATTHAU in *The Fortune Cookie*, Phalanx-Jalem-Mirisch/UA

Supporting Actress
SANDY DENNIS in *Who's Afraid Of Virginia Woolf?*

Directing
FRED ZINNEMANN for *A Man For All Seasons*

Writing
(Best Screenplay – based on material from another medium)
A MAN FOR ALL SEASONS: ROBERT BOLT
(Best Story and Screenplay – written directly for the screen)
A MAN AND A WOMAN, Les Films 13/Allied Artists
Story: CLAUDE LELOUCH
Screenplay: PIERRE UYTTERHOEVEN and CLAUDE LELOUCH

Cinematography
(Black-and-White)
WHO'S AFRAID OF VIRGINIA WOOLF?: HASKELL WEXLER
(Color)
A MAN FOR ALL SEASONS: TED MOORE

Art Direction-Set Decoration
(Black-and-White)
WHO'S AFRAID OF VIRGINIA WOOLF?: RICHARD SYLBERT
Set Decoration: GOERGE JAMES HOPKINS
(Color)
FANTASTIC VOYAGE, 20th Century-Fox: JACK MARTIN SMITH and DALE HENNESY
Set Decoration: WALTER M. SCOTT and STUART A. REISS

Sound
GRAND PRIX, MGM Studio Sound Department: FRANKLIN E. MILTON, Sound Director

Film Editing
GRAND PRIX, Douglas-Lewis-Frankenheimer-Cherokee/ MGM: FREDERIC STEINKAMP, HENRY BERMAN, STEWART LINDER and FRANK SANTILLO

Music
(Original Music Score)
BORN FREE, Open Road-Atlas/Columbia: JOHN BARRY
(Scoring of Music – adaptation or treatment)
A FUNNY THING HAPPENED ON THE WAY TO THE FORUM, Frank/UA: KEN THORNE
(Best Song)
BORN FREE from *Born Free*
Music: JOHN BARRY
Lyrics: DON BLACK

Costume Design
(Black-and-White)
WHO'S AFRAID OF VIRGINIA WOOLF? IRENE SHARAFF
(Color)
A MAN FOR ALL SEASONS: ELIZABETH HAFFENDEN and JOAN BRIDGE

Short Subjects
(Cartoons)
HERB ALPERT AND THE TIJUANA BRASS DOUBLE FEATURE, Hubley/Paramount: JOHN and FAITH HUBLEY, Producers
(Live Action Subjects)
WILD WINGS, British Transport/Manson: EDGAR ANSTEY, Producer

Documentary
(Short Subjects)
A YEAR TOWARD TOMORROW, Sun Dial Films for Office of Economic Opportunity: EDMOND A. LEVY, Producer
(Features)
THE WAR GAME, BBC Production for the British Film Institute/Pathe Contemporary: PETER WATKINS, Producer

Special Visual Effects
FANTASTIC VOYAGE, 20th Century-Fox: ART CRUICKSHANK

Sound Effects
GRAND PRIX: GORDON DANIEL

Foreign Language Film Award
A MAN AND A WOMAN, Les Films 13 (France)

Honorary Awards
Y. FRANK FREEMAN for unusual and outstanding service to the Academy during his thirty years in Hollywood. (statuette)
YAKIMA CANUTT for achievements as a stunt man and for developing safety devices to protect stunt men everywhere. (statuette)

Irving G. Thalberg Memorial Award
ROBERT WISE

Jean Hersholt Humanitarian Award
GEORGE BAGNALL

1967

T HE 1967 ACADEMY Awards ceremony, the 40th in its history, was held under unusually somber circumstances. The assassination of Martin Luther King, only one of a tragic series in recent American history, caused the event to be postponed for forty-eight hours — until April 10, 1968. And, for the same reason, the annual post-Oscar ball sponsored by the Governor of California was canceled altogether. Oscar night did not seem particularly relevant to these uncertain days of vague social unease, political upheaval and, of course, the Vietnam War rumbling away inconclusively on the other side of the globe yet brought home with a vengeance to the American people on nightly TV news broadcasts: the attendant hoopla of the movie industry's Night of Nights was reduced to what was considered a decent minimum.

Bob Hope again presided over the event, between flights out to South-East Asia to entertain the troops; and, because of some energetic hustling by the Academy president Gregory Peck, no fewer than 18 out of the 20 acting nominees were on hand to hear the announcements. It was unfortunate, then, that the Best Actress Oscar went, in a surprise decision, to one of the only two performers who could not make it: Katharine Hepburn, for Stanley Kramer's comedy of racial coexistence **Guess Who's Coming To Dinner** (which constituted her very last collaboration on screen with Spencer Tracy, also a nominee but, by this time, a posthumous one). Best Actor was Rod Steiger for his colorful performance as a viciously bigoted sheriff in Norman Jewison's atmospheric thriller **In The Heat Of The Night**. (Curiously, Sidney Poitier, who presented Hepburn's Oscar, was co-star to both her and Steiger, as well as the star of a third 1967 film, **To Sir With Love**, but had received no nomination at all.)

The race for the Best Picture Oscar was considered one of the most even and open-ended in years. 20th Century-Fox's leaden fantasy with Rex Harrison, **Dr Dolittle**, could safely be discounted; but, of the others, Arthur Penn's **Bonnie And Clyde**, Mike Nichols' **The Graduate, Guess Who's Coming To Dinner** and **In The Heat Of The Night**, all had their share of devotees and detractors and none had emerged the clear favorite. In the end, it was the dark horse, **In The Heat Of The Night**, which first crossed the winning tape, with Ocars for Best Picture, Best Actor, Screenplay, Editing and Sound. **The Graduate** secured a single Oscar (for director Nichols), **Bonnie And Clyde** the same meager total, and **Guess Who's Coming To Dinner**

just two. Best Supporting Performers were George Kennedy, an actor who specialized in playing brutish hoodlums, for **Cool Hand Luke**, and Estelle Parsons, a theatrical actress making a memorable screen debut as Warren Beatty's neurotic sister-in-law in **Bonnie And Clyde**.

Finally, the two highlights of the evening were a filmed review of Oscar's forty years, introduced, decade by decade, by Katharine Hepburn, Olivia de Havilland, Grace Kelly and Anne Bancroft; and Angela Lansbury's very 'twenties' rendition of one of the nominated songs, 'Thoroughly Modern Millie'.

Films centered on racial tensions are almost invariably structured around a direct confrontation between an individual black and an individual white, and Norman Jewison's **In The Heat Of The Night** was no exception to the rule. There were two factors, however, which raised it far above the well-intentioned but often flabby dramas in which Hollywood has worn its socially conscious heart on

BELOW *George Kennedy (right) and Paul Newman in one of many highly charged scenes from Stuart Rosenberg's prison chain-gang drama,* Cool Hand Luke. *Newman was nominated for Best Actor, Kennedy won for Best Supporting Actor*

ABOVE *Sidney Poitier (left), the young black doctor in* Guess Who's Coming To Dinner, *wants to marry Katharine Houghton (center). Here, they discuss their plans with her parents, Spencer Tracy and Katharine Hepburn. Hepburn won the Best Actress award, Tracy the sad honor of a posthumous nomination*

its sleeve: the film was also an engrossing thriller, the murderer's identity unmasked only in the climactic scene; and, most significantly, black and white found themselves for once working on the same side. Ironically, following the discovery that a local white industrialist has been killed, Virgil Tibbs (Poitier), a Philadelphia-based police detective on a visit to his Mississippi hometown, is arrested by the local police chief (Steiger) on the assumption that a black out late at night, and a stranger as well, must have committed the crime. Naturally, having entered into uneasy collaboration with each other, the two men cannot help but acquire a no less uneasy respect for each other's deductive skills. Tibbs is gradually allowed to shed a little of the hatred and resentment he continues to feel in a bigoted community from which he was driven in his youth; and Steiger's cigar-chewing, law-unto-himself police chief evolves no less gradually into a man honest and baffled enough to question his own prejudices and overcome them.

Though no classic of film history – not only the solution but the basic situation is too neatly contrived and developed – **In The Heat Of The Night** was a sassy, atmospheric and consistently absorbing entertainment reminiscent of certain cheerfully unpretentious dramas produced by Warner Bros. in the 30s. It benefited from fluid and smokily beautiful color cinematography by Haskell Wexler and a nervy jazz score by the musician Quincy Jones. It was, in a sense, a key film of the period, since it demonstrated that Hollywood could tackle more serious and urgent themes without being forced to reduce the entertainment quotient which was still the industry's stock-in-trade; and its success, both commercial and critical, prompted a pair of sadly less distinguished sequels, **They Call Me Mister Tibbs!** (1970) and **The Organization** (1971), neither of them able to be considered in the slightest degree award-worthy.

The Academy Awards have, on more than one occasion, confused over-acting with great acting, as if a superior performance could be produced by the mere inflation of an actor's histrionic abilities. A case in point is Rod Steiger, who had studied as a young man at the modishly prestigious Actors Studio in New York, the home of what was widely to be known as the Method school. He

RIGHT *Sidney Poitier and Rod Steiger made powerful adversaries-cum-colleagues in Norman Jewison's* In The Heat Of The Night, *the year's Best Picture, for which Steiger won the Best Actor award*

was to remain profoundly influenced by the Stanislavskian techniques in practice there, applying them even in films where they tended to clash incongruously with the more instinctual styles of his co-performers. With a film like **In The Heat Of The Night**, however, this became a positive asset, so to speak, since its narrative was based precisely on a notion of confrontation. The clammy and claustrophobic mannerisms which have marred many a Steiger performance, the self-indulgent tics on which he has sometimes slavishly depended, were wholly integrated into a psychology and were tellingly juxtaposed with the more natural, understated style of Poitier. Much of the failure of the film's two sequels stemmed from the absence of Steiger and the inability of their screenwriters and directors to create adversaries for Tibbs as powerfully etched, yet as real and vulnerable, as the racist cop of **In The Heat Of The Night**.

Steiger never won another Oscar (though he had twice before been nominated); and, beset of late by marital problems, chronic depression, alcoholism and radical heart surgery, he would seem virtually to have retired from screen acting.

Said Katharine Hepburn of the role which she played in **Guess Who's Coming To Dinner**, "She's a normal, middle-aged, unspectacular, unglamorous creature with a good brain and a warm heart who's doing the best she can to do the decent thing in a difficult situation. In other words, she is a good wife, our most unsung and important heroine. I'm glad she's coming back in style. I modeled her after my mother." Since there can exist few women in the world less normal, middle-aged, unspectacular and unglamorous than Hepburn, it is a measure of her infinite warmth and humanity on the screen that, for two hours or so, she managed to convince audiences that she was the being she described. And though the central theme of Stanley Kramer's comedy-drama was interracial marriage, for audiences the supreme pleasure of the film – indeed, the principal reason for seeing it – was the ninth and ultimate screen reunion of Hepburn with her lifetime companion, Spencer Tracy. Perhaps because she was aware that Tracy was close to death – he died only 10 days after the film shoot had been completed – she invested their exchanges with a depth of emotion rare in a mainstream commercial comedy. On paper, **Guess Who's Coming To Dinner** may have appeared to be a film about marriage; in fact, it was a film about love.

BELOW *Estelle Parsons (right), a fine Broadway actress and superb screen character actress who appeared in few films, well-merited her Best Supporting Actress Oscar as the neurotic Blanche Barrow, Clyde's sister-in-law in* Bonnie And Clyde. *With her here, Gene Hackman and, back to camera, Warren Beatty*

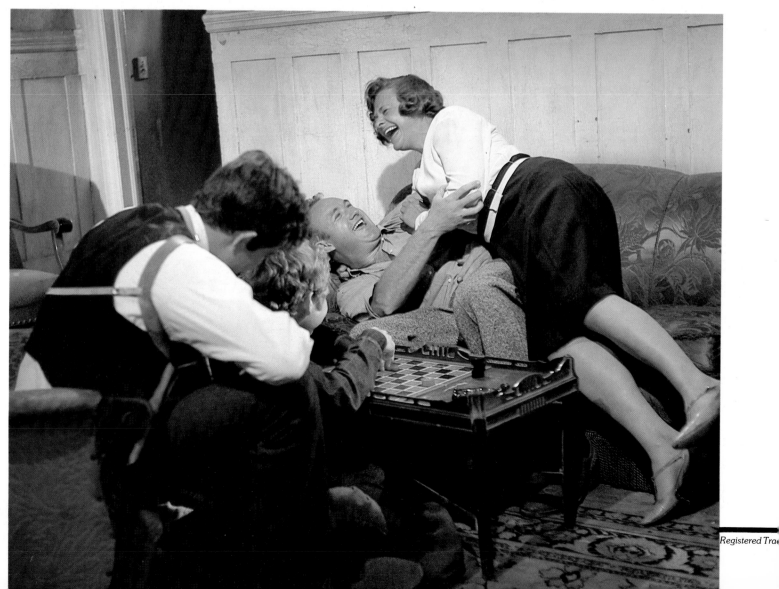

WINNERS 1967

Nominations Announced: February 19, 1968
Awards Ceremony: Postponed from April 8 to April 10,
1968 because of the death of Dr Martin Luther King
Santa Monica Civic Auditorium

Best Picture
IN THE HEAT OF THE NIGHT, Mirisch/UA: WALTER
MIRISCH, Producer

Actor
ROD STEIGER in *In The Heat Of The Night*

Actress
KATHARINE HEPBURN in *Guess Who's Coming To
Dinner*, Columbia

Supporting Actor
GEORGE KENNEDY in *Cool Hand Luke*, Jalem/Warner
Bros.–Seven Arts

Supporting Actress
ESTELLE PARSONS in *Bonnie And Clyde*, Tatira-Hiller/
Warner Bros.–Seven Arts

Directing
MIKE NICHOLS for *The Graduate*, Nichols-Turman/
Embassy

Writing
(Best Screenplay – based on material from another medium)
IN THE HEAT OF THE NIGHT: STIRLING SILLIPHANT
(Best Story and Screenplay – written directly for the screen)
GUESS WHO'S COMING TO DINNER: WILLIAM ROSE

Cinematography
(Rules changed this year to one Award for Cinematography
instead of separate awards for black-and-white and color.)
BONNIE AND CLYDE: BURNETT GUFFEY

Art Direction-Set Decoration
(Rules changed this year to one Award instead of separate
awards for black-and-white and color.)
CAMELOT, Warner Bros.–Seven Arts: JOHN TRUSCOTT
and EDWARD CARRERE
Set Decoration: JOHN W. BROWN

Sound
IN THE HEAT OF THE NIGHT, Goldwyn Studio Sound
Department

Film Editing
IN THE HEAT OF THE NIGHT: HAL ASHBY

Music
(Original Music Score)
THOROUGHLY MODERN MILLIE, Hunter-Universal/
Universal: ELMER BERNSTEIN

(Scoring of Music – adaptation or treatment)
CAMELOT: ALFRED NEWMAN and KEN DARBY
(Best Song)
TALK TO THE ANIMALS from *Doctor Dolittle*, Apjac/20th
Century-Fox
Music and Lyrics: LESLIE BRICUSSE

Costume Design
(Rules changed this year to one Award instead of separate
awards for black-and-white and color.)
CAMELOT: JOHN TRUSCOTT

Short Subjects
(Cartoons)
THE BOX, Murakami-Wolf/Brandon: FRED WOLF,
Producer
(Live Action Subjects)
A PLACE TO STAND, TDF Production for the Ontario
Department of Economics and Development/Columbia:
CHRISTOPHER CHAPMAN, Producer

Documentary
(Short Subjects)
THE REDWOODS, King Screen: MARK HARRIS and
TREVOR GREENWOOD, Producers
(Features)
THE ANDERSON PLATOON, French Broadcasting
System: PIERRE SCHOENDOERFFER, Producer

Special Visual Effects
DOCTOR DOLITTLE: L.B. ABBOTT

Sound Effects
(Not given as an Annual Award after this year.)
THE DIRTY DOZEN, MKH/MGM: JOHN POYNER

Foreign Language Film Award
CLOSELY WATCHED TRAINS, Barrandov
(Czechoslovakia)

Honorary Award
ARTHUR FREED for distinguished service to the Academy
and the production of six top-rated Awards telecasts.
(statuette)

Irving G. Thalberg Memorial Award
ALFRED HITCHCOCK

Jean Hersholt Humanitarian Award
GREGORY PECK

1968

N 1968 THE Academy numbered 3030 members, each of whom had a single vote to cast in the various categories (excepting those regarded as technical or specialized); and a simple majority decision was all that was required for an Oscar to be awarded. It would therefore take the skills of a mathematician (or a highly sophisticated pocket calculator) to compute the odds against a tie – yet a tie is precisely what occurred on the 41st Oscar night, April 14, 1969. When Ingrid Bergman, making one of her rare public appearances in Hollywood, unsealed the envelope containing the name of the year's Best Actress, she began to read out, "The winner is . . .". Then, her features a mask of

bewilderment, she came to an abrupt halt. After a suspenseful moment of hesitation, she exclaimed, "It's a tie!" Barbra Streisand (for her impersonation of the vaudeville queen Fanny Brice in William Wyler's **Funny Girl**) and Katharine Hepburn (for *her* impersonation of Eleanor of Acquitaine in **The Lion In Winter**) had each obtained exactly the same number of votes.

This freakish score represented an absolute first for the ceremony. To be sure, Fredric March and Wallace Beery had already tied for the 1931-32 Best Actor trophy; but, as we have seen, the voting in the early 30s was not based on a majority decision. Hepburn's victory, moreover, brought a number of other new records in its wake. Not only was she the first (and, to date, sole) performer ever to win a trio of major Oscars, but her tally of 11 nominations was the highest ever recorded in the Academy's history. Hepburn, as usual, declined to attend the event, her Oscar being accepted on her behalf by the film's director Anthony Harvey. Streisand *was* present – indeed, ultra-present in an eye-catching (and light-catching) transparent pajama suit.

In a surprise decision, the Best Actor award went to someone usually thought of (if at all) as bland and inexpressive, Cliff Robertson, for his extraordinary perfor-

LEFT *The ageing queen, Eleanor of Aquitaine, bundled up against the medieval cold in* The Lion In Winter, *which won Katharine Hepburn her third Oscar. She would win a fourth Best Actress award for* On Golden Pond *thirteen years later*
ABOVE *The year's Best Actor, Cliff Robertson, was* Charly, *seen here in menial employment befitting his retarded mentality.* Charly *is turned into a genius by medical science, but slips back again to his former sad state*

ABOVE *Fagin (Ron Moody, center) addresses the young 'pupils' at his school for pickpockets in Carol Reed's* Oliver!, *the year's Best Picture. Moody was nominated for Best Actor for the role he originally created on stage. Best Supporting nominations were earned, too, by Mark Lester (right) in the title role and Jack Wild (second left) as the Artful Dodger*

mance as the mentally retarded **Charly** in Ralph Nelson's film drama of that title. And the Best Picture was judged to be Carol Reed's jolly adaptation of the Lionel Bart musical **Oliver!** (based, it hardly needs qualifying, on Dickens' *Oliver Twist*). Though uncited in both major and minor acting categories, **Oliver!** received a total of five Academy Awards (Best Picture, Director, Musical Score, Art Direction and Sound – with a bonus sixth for Onna White's choreography); and the exclamation mark which completed its title began to bear a decided resemblance to Oscar himself. Best Supporting Performers were Jack Albertson (repeating his Tony Award-winning stage per-

formance in **The Subject Was Roses**) and the corncrake-voiced veteran actress and writer Ruth Gordon (for her eccentrically Bohemian witch in Roman Polanski's **Rosemary's Baby**).

The event's other major 'first' was its change of venue (and style) after almost two decades at Santa Monica. It was held in the 3,400-seat Dorothy Chandler Pavilion at the Los Angeles Music Center and directed by the former dancer Gower Champion (partner and husband of Marge). Under Champion's direction, the show became smoother, snappier and more spectacular (winners had much less distance to cover on their way to the stage, song-and-dance numbers were 'integrated' into the award-giving process), besides being glitteringly star-studded (there were no fewer than ten M.C.s – Bergman, Tony Curtis, Diahann Carroll, Henry Fonda, Burt Lancaster, Walter Matthau, Sidney Poitier, Rosalind Russell, Frank Sinatra and Natalie Wood). For the first time, too, the ceremony received not only a national but an international TV airing (albeit in a truncated, 50-minute version), with an audience estimated at approximately 500,000,000 viewers.

Perhaps the most famous (and certainly uncuttable) line of dialogue in *Oliver Twist* is Oliver's own plaintive "Please, sir, I want more" in the poorhouse. For those 'who want more', Carol Reed's musical version provided it. The film offered more of everything that spectators seek, too often vainly, from a musical: elaborate sets, with a lavish, if somewhat prettified, recreation of Dickensian London, all insalubrious alleys and grimy marketplaces; hit songs (notably 'As Long As He Needs Me', 'Consider Yourself', 'Food, Glorious Food', 'I'd Do Anything' and 'Who Will Buy'); and colorful characters (played by such stalwarts of the British cinema as Ron Moody, Harry Secombe, Hugh Griffith and Peggy Mount) – not to mention Bullseye, an endearingly mournful mongrel owned and abused by Bill Sikes (Oliver Reed, the director's nephew) but praised by one reviewer as "the most memorable dog since the Hound of the Baskervilles." Little Oliver himself

BELOW *The versatile Ruth Gordon – she wrote, too, in collaboration with her husband Garson Kanin – was voted Best Supporting Actress for her chilling portrayal as the not-so-friendly neighbor in* Rosemary's Baby. *Here, she is conferring with Ralph Bellamy (center) and John Cassavetes*

Charly was very much Cliff Robertson's personal project – one he had been nurturing for several years. It started life as a short story, *Flowers For Algernon*, by Daniel Keyes. Keyes then transformed the story into a full-length novel, which in turn became *The Two Worlds Of Charlie Gordon*, a TV drama for which Robertson, in the title role, was nominated for an Emmy (television Oscar). Sensing that it was the role capable of rescuing his hitherto run-of-the-mill career from the doldrums, Robertson purchased the film rights and expended all his energies in setting up a production. The gamble paid off handsomely. Though **Charly** received less than rave reviews and was a sluggish box-office earner to begin with, Robertson's virtuoso performance and his subsequent Oscar turned it into a solid if minor success.

Robertson played the mentally retarded hero whom an experimental medical operation transforms into a genius – but only temporarily. The notion of making a romantic melodrama (Charly enjoys a brief fling with his therapist) out of mental disability was a dangerous one; and, from the audience's point of view, the principal challenge which the film posed was that of identifying with a character whose level of intelligence is either far below or far above the average. It was to Robertsons's credit that he carried it off so persuasively, and to Oscar's credit that it recognized and honored the achievement.

There are performers whose physique tends to typecast them in historical roles (e.g. Charlton Heston), others who cannot appear anything but contemporary (e.g. Jane Fonda). Katharine Hepburn's style might be described as timeless. Thus there was no incongruity in her winning an Oscar in 1967 for her harassed suburban wife and mother in **Guess Who's Coming To Dinner** and another in 1968 for her witty, patrician, strong-willed Eleanor of Aquitaine, the estranged wife of King Henry II (Peter O'Toole), in **The Lion In Winter**.

As for Barbra Streisand, Hepburn's co-winner, her pungent Brooklyn accent, flamboyant showbiz mannerisms and sheer Jewish chutzpah define her as indelibly of the 20th century. Streisand's Oscar for **Funny Girl**, a musical dramatization of the life and unhappy loves of Fanny Brice, was awarded less to a mere performer than to a force of nature. Like Brice, Streisand is a classic 'ugly duckling', with a gawky physique and an imperfect face, marred by a famously long and prominent nose. She has the kind of features only a mother – or a camera – could love. In **Funny Girl** the camera loved her (even if, reportedly, her co-stars loathed her), the public loved her and Oscar loved her. And she loved Oscar: "The first script of **Funny Girl** was written when I was only 11 years old," she exulted at the ceremony. "Thank God it took so long to get it right!"

(chronologically, the eighth in English-speaking film history) was played by nine-year-old, blond and apple-cheeked Mark Lester and the Artful Dodger, his equally diminutive mentor and tormentor, by Jack Wild.

In this musical treatment, as one might have expected, Dickens' once radical tale of the foundling who first finds acceptance in Fagin's den of thieves before being rescued for middle-class comfort and respectability lost much of the original's sense of moral outrage and social injustice, of villainy and terror (vividly present in the most famous screen version, directed by David Lean in 1948 and starring Alec Guinness as Fagin). Yet chocolate-box prettification is what invariably happens to musical versions of classic novels, and few have appeared as delightfully, unashamedly pretty as **Oliver!**. Not least, it had become increasingly rare for an Oscar-winning film to be safely recommendable to cinemagoers of all ages.

WINNERS 1968

Nominations Announced: February 24, 1969
Awards Ceremony: April 14, 1969
Dorothy Chandler Pavilion, Los Angeles County
Music Centre

Best Picture
OLIVER!, Romulus/Columbia: JOHN WOOLF, Producer

Actor
CLIFF ROBERTSON in *Charly*, American Broadcasting-Selmur/Cinerama

Actress (tie awards)
KATHERINE HEPBURN in *The Lion In Winter*, Haworth/Avco Embassy
BARBRA STREISAND in *Funny Girl*, Rastar/Columbia

Supporting Actor
JACK ALBERTSON in *The Subject Was Roses*, MGM

Supporting Actress
RUTH GORDON in *Rosemary's Baby*, Castle/Paramount

Directing
CAROL REED for *Oliver!*

Writing
(Best Screenplay – based on material from another medium)
THE LION IN WINTER: JAMES GOLDMAN
(Best Story and Screenplay – written directly for the screen)
THE PRODUCERS, Glazier/Avco Embassy: MEL BROOKS

Cinematography
Franco Zeffirelli's ROMEO AND JULIET, BHE-Verona-De Laurentiis/Paramount: PASQUALINO DE SANTIS

Art Direction-Set Decoration
OLIVER!: JOHN BOX and TERENCE MARSH
Set Decoration: VERNON DIXON and KEN MUGGLESTON

Sound
OLIVER!: Shepperton Studio Sound Department

Film Editing
BULLITT, Solar/Warner Bros.–Seven Arts: FRANK P. KELLER

Music
(Best Original Score – for a motion picture (not a musical))
THE LION IN WINTER: JOHN BARRY
(Best Score of a Musical Picture – original or adaptation)
OLIVER!: JOHN GREEN
(Best Song)
THE WINDMILLS OF YOUR MIND from *The Thomas Crown Affair*, Mirisch-Simkoe-Solar/UA
Music: MICHEL LeGRAND
Lyrics: ALAN and MARILYN BERGMAN

Costume Design
Franco Zeffirelli's ROMEO AND JULIET: DANILO DONATI

Short Subjects
(Cartoons)
WINNIE THE POOH AND THE BLUSTERY DAY, Disney/Buena Vista: WALT DISNEY, Producer
(Live Action Subjects)
ROBERT KENNEDY REMEMBERED, Guggenheim/National General: CHARLES GUGGENHEIM, Producer

Documentary
(Short Subjects)
WHY MAN CREATES, Bass: SAUL BASS, Producer
(Features)
JOURNEY INTO SELF, Western Behavioral Sciences Institute: BILL McGAW, Producer

Special Visual Effects
2001: A SPACE ODYSSEY, Polaris/MGM: STANLEY KUBRICK

Foreign Language Film Award
WAR AND PEACE, Mosfilm (Russia)

Honorary Awards
JOHN CHAMBERS for his outstanding make-up achievement for *Planet Of The Apes*. (statuette)
ONNA WHITE for her outstanding choreography achievement for *Oliver!*. (statuette)

Irving G. Thalberg Memorial Award
None

Jean Hersholt Humanitarian Award
MARTHA RAYE

"I HAVE SPENT NEARLY 50 years chasing this elusive fellow with good performances and bad, so I was extremely delighted when he was handed to me by Barbra Streisand." John Wayne began his film career in that first Oscar season of 1927-28, but it took the Academy 42 years to grant Hollywood's most consistent box-office performer a Best Actor award. He won it, in the end, in 1969 for his portrayal of Rooster Cogburn, the hulking, one-eyed, drunken, mean-tempered old marshal hired by a young girl, Mattie (Kim Darby), to capture her father's killers, in Henry Hathaway's **True Grit**. "If I'd known," Wayne, otherwise known as The Duke, quipped, "I'd have put the eye-patch on 35 years earlier."

Wayne's 139th film (out of an eventual total of 151), it is scarcely his greatest – indeed, as in several of his later movies, the role he played can be partly construed as a parody, albeit an affectionate one, of his established over-the-top macho persona. That this particular Oscar was a belated 'career' award is in little doubt, and today it is hard to believe that none of Wayne's finest performances – in **Stagecoach** (1939), **Red River** (1948), **She Wore A Yellow Ribbon** (1949), **The Quiet Man** (1953), **The Searchers** (1956) and **The Man Who Shot Liberty Valance** (1962) – were nominated for Oscars. The Duke's only previous nomination, in fact, was for his gung-ho officer fighting the Japanese in **The Sands Of Iwo Jima** in 1949, although **The Alamo** (1960), which he produced, directed, and in which he played Davy Crockett, was nominated for Best Film.

The award finally came at a point when Wayne's popularity had been shaken by his making of **The Green Berets** (1968), his hawkish espousal of US intervention in Vietnam and a film loathed by every liberal-thinking Ameri-

BELOW *'It wasn't a case of upstaging one another, but it was let's see who can really act better in this scene,' explained Dustin Hoffman (right) of his working relationship with fellow nominee Jon Voight (left) in the year's Best Picture,* Midnight Cowboy

ABOVE *John Wayne (right) as the ageing, hard-drinking, one-eyed marshal, and folk singer Glen Campbell as a brash Texas Ranger in* True Grit. *It was the umpteenth time Wayne was on the trail of badmen, but it was the first time he won an Oscar for his pains*
RIGHT *Paul Newman (left) and Robert Redford (right) as the legendary outlaws* Butch Cassidy And The Sundance Kid. *The picture's four Oscars went to screenplay, cinematography, music score and song, but it was the successful tandem of Newman and Redford that really brought in the shekels*

can. The accolade revitalized his career and by 1971 the sexagenarian star was the film industry's biggest money-maker again.

True Grit has its moments. The old warhorse Cogburn is characteristically cantankerous, uncouth and, of course, brave and – beneath the boorish exterior – a romantic. Wayne's greatest attribute in such roles, though he himself would have denied it, was the way his arrogant, often brutal heroes, men soured by bitter experience, could conceal a tender heart and an unusual gentleness (which occasionally lapsed into pathos). Although in **True Grit** he will chiefly be remembered for leaping his equally ancient mount over a fence and for taking his reins in his teeth and charging down on his quarries with guns blazing in both hands, it is for his kinder side that Mattie grows to love him. Wayne reprised the role in **Rooster Cogburn**, his penultimate film, in 1975.

Among those up with Wayne for Best Actor at the 1969 awards – the first to be held on a Tuesday instead of the traditional Monday – were Jon Voight (his first nomination) and Dustin Hoffman (his second, following **The**

Graduate) who, respectively, played Joe Buck and Ratso in **Midnight Cowboy**, which was selected as Best Film of the year. At the helm was John Schlesinger – previously nominated for **Darling** in 1965 – who won for Best Director, following the success of his fellow Englishman Carol Reed for **Oliver!** the year before, but for a very different type of film.

Midnight Cowboy was a significant Oscar-winner because, in the era of permissiveness hitherto neglected by the Academy, it dealt with sex in an almost offhand manner. Although Julie Christie had won the Best Actress award for her 'swinging' model in **Darling** and Mike Nichols had been judged Best Director for **The Graduate** (with its adultery and strip joints), it was **Midnight Cowboy** which confirmed that the Academy had 'adult' tastes.

It seemed there was altogether a new maturity about the Oscar-voters' attitude towards sex on the screen. Bob Hope (M.C. again) joked about nudity during the Awards evening, but in a famous closing speech, endorsed by Academy president Gregory Peck, he seriously suggested that Hollywood would never again be content with depicting "a lollipop world", but would from now on "hold a mirror up to nature". The ceremony also included film of directors such as Nichols, Fellini and Kurosawa talking about cinema's new-found freedom. The showbiz Bible *Variety* editorialized:

"It's a new ballgame; the artists and scientists of the

BELOW *Maggie Smith as the eccentric Scottish schoolmistress addresses her 'gels' on extra-curricular subjects like fascism in* The Prime of Miss Jean Brodie. *Miss Maggie Smith, in her prime aged 35, won the Best Actress Award*

ABOVE *Gig Young as the oily Master of Ceremonies accompanying the Dance Marathon with his own Talk Marathon in* They Shoot Horses, Don't They? *Young, who won the Best Supporting award at his third attempt, committed suicide in 1978 after shooting his bride of three weeks*

world's cinema center are unhesitant about saying to all the world that there's to be no hesitation about subject matter. As a matter of fact there's pride, pride in that a picture can get away from the lollipops and still be inoffensive and commercially pleasing. **Midnight Cowboy . . .** deals, among other things, with male whoredom. The voting majority of the Academy said yes, this is the legitimate victory."

Schlesinger's film tells the story of a naive blond Texan youth (Voight), gauchely clad in what he imagines to be the outfit of a stud – fringed leathers and stetson – who has come to New York to set himself up servicing women. He is befriended by Ratso, a tubercular, down-and-out Bronx hustler, for much of the film about to expire in the gutter, who offers him shelter; together they fight for survival on the pernicious, violent back streets. The film wades knee-deep in urban sleaze and offers nudity and degradation, but it probably won its awards more for its human story than the trappings of seaminess. Joe's plans to become a stud go pathetically wrong; eventually he has to pawn his transistor radio to keep Ratso alive. In a world of dog-eat-dog – Sylvia Miles was Oscar-nominated for

her playing of a hooker who outfoxes Joe – compassion and dignity, however small, must be seen to rule the day, in movies at least, and the film, despite its X-certificate, ultimately has a regenerative power.

Waldo Salt claimed **Midnight Cowboy**'s third Oscar for his screenplay, adapted from James Leo Herlihy's novel. The film scarcely ushered in an age of rampant sexual freedom in top-notch Hollywood movies – although **Ryan's Daughter, Women In Love, Klute** and **The Last Picture Show**, winners in various categories in the next two years, all had moments of tasteful eroticism.

Four of 1969's Oscars went to **Butch Cassidy And The Sundance Kid** – an altogether more modern Western than **True Grit** – which shared with **Midnight Cowboy** the 'buddy-buddy' mentality that would reap rich rewards for the **Butch Cassidy** team of director George Roy Hill (a nominee this year) and stars Robert Redford and Paul Newman with **The Sting** in 1973. **Butch Cassidy** won for William Goldman's witty Best Original Screenplay; Conrad Hall's superb photography, famous for its sepia tint in the opening sequence; Burt Bacharach's Best Original Score; and his and Hal David's Best Song, the much-loved 'Raindrops Keep Fallin' On My Head', to which Paul Newman and Katharine Ross fool around on an early model of the bicycle.

Maggie Smith's Best Actress award for **The Prime Of Miss Jean Brodie**, directed by Ronald Neame, was, perhaps, the surprise in this year's Oscar package. A performer who had divided her attention between the London stage – excelling as Desdemona to Olivier's *Othello* at the National Theatre – and a mixed bag of films, she had first attracted attention on screen in **The VIPs** (1963), which she stole from Elizabeth Taylor and Richard Burton with her portrayal of a lovelorn secretary. She was then nominated for an Oscar for her performance in the film version of **Othello** in 1965. Her playing of Jean Brodie, though, was a revelation. An arch, elitist teacher at an Edinburgh school for girls, she is also inflated with the notion that she is in her intellectual 'prime', is sexually unfulfilled, mannered and posturing – and deeply vulnerable. She infuses her 'gels' with a virtual neo-fascist doctrine of their superiority, but receives her comeuppance when one of them runs off to die in the Spanish Civil War, and another runs off with her intended, art master Robert Stephens (the actress's then husband).

After winning for this bravura performance of a good but misguided woman, Maggie Smith would receive two more nominations in the next decade. She missed out as Best Actress for her aunt in the 1972 film of Graham Greene's **Travels With My Aunt**, but – to her own astonishment – won as Best Supporting Actress for her sharp comic caricature of, topically, an English actress arrived in Hollywood for the Oscar ceremony (but not winning) in Neil Simon's **California Suite**. Perhaps no other star in Hollywood history – with the possible exception of Luise Rainer – has pleased the Academy twice with so slender a body of film to her credit: just two outstanding roles played to near perfection.

WINNERS 1969

Nominations Announced: February 16, 1970
Awards Ceremony: April 7, 1970
Dorothy Chandler Pavilion, Los Angeles County
Music Center

Best Picture
MIDNIGHT COWBOY, Hellman-Schlesinger/UA:
JEROME HELLMAN, Producer

Actor
JOHN WAYNE in *True Grit*, Wallis/Paramount

Actress
MAGGIE SMITH in *The Prime Of Miss Jean Brodie*, 20th
Century-Fox

Supporting Actor
GIG YOUNG in *They Shoot Horses, Don't They?*,
Chartoff-Winkler-Pollack/ABC/Cinerama

Supporting Actress
GOLDIE HAWN in *Cactus Flower*, Frankovich/Columbia

Directing
JOHN SCHLESINGER for *Midnight Cowboy*

Writing
(Best Screenplay – based on material from another medium)
MIDNIGHT COWBOY: WALDO SALT
(Best Screenplay – based on material not previously
published or produced)
BUTCH CASSIDY AND THE SUNDANCE KID,
Hill-Monash/20th Century-Fox: WILLIAM GOLDMAN

Cinematography
BUTCH CASSIDY AND THE SUNDANCE KID: CONRAD
HALL

Art Direction-Set Decoration
HELLO, DOLLY!, Chenault/20th Century-Fox: JOHN
DeCUIR, JACK MARTIN SMITH and HERMAN
BLUMENTHAL
Set Decoration: WALTER M. SCOTT, GEORGE HOPKINS
and RAPHAEL BRETTON

Sound
HELLO, DOLLY!; JACK SOLOMON and MURRAY
SPIVACK

Film Editing
Z, Reggane-ONCIC/Cinema V: FRANÇOISE BONNOT

Music
(Best Original Score – for a motion picture (not a musical)
BUTCH CASSIDY AND THE SUNDANCE KID: BURT
BACHARACH

(Best Score of a Musical Picture – original or adaptation)
HELLO, DOLLY!
Adaptation: LENNIE HAYTON and LIONEL NEWMAN
(Best Song)
RAINDROPS KEEP FALLIN' ON MY HEAD from *Butch
Cassidy And The Sundance Kid*
Music: BURT BACHARACH
Lyrics: HAL DAVID

Costume Design
ANNE OF THE THOUSAND DAYS, Wallis-Universal:
MARGARET FURSE

Short Subjects
(Cartoons)
IT'S TOUGH TO BE A BIRD, Disney/Buena Vista: WARD
KIMBALL, Producer
(Live Action Subjects)
THE MAGIC MACHINES, Fly-By-Night/Manson: JOAN
KELLER STERN, Producer

Documentary
(Short Subjects)
CZECHOSLOVAKIA 1968, Sanders-Fresco Film Makers
for United States Information Agency: DENNIS SANDERS
and ROBERT M. FRESCO, Producers
(Features)
ARTHUR RUBINSTEIN – THE LOVE OF LIFE, Midem:
BERNARD CHEVRY, Producer

Special Visual Effects
MAROONED, Frankovich-Sturges/Columbia: ROBBIE
ROBERTSON

Foreign Language Film Award
Z (Algeria)

Honorary Award
CARY GRANT for his unique mastery of the art of screen
acting with the respect and affection of his colleagues.
(statuette)

Irving G. Thalberg Memorial Award
None

Jean Hersholt Humanitarian Award
GEORGE JESSEL

1970

THE NOMINEES FOR the Best Actor Oscar in 1970 were Melvyn Douglas in **I Never Sang For My Father**, James Earl Jones in **The Great White Hope**, Jack Nicholson in **Five Easy Pieces**, Ryan O'Neal in the year's box-office smash, **Love Story**, and George C. Scott in **Patton**. Before she announced the winner, Goldie Hawn suggested that it was the best *performance* rather than the best performer that won the Academy's accolade: "It is the specific achievement that is being honored. That is a pertinent distinction to be kept in mind." She followed this with a shrill "Oh my God!" and called out the name of George C. Scott, who – as in 1961 when he won his second Best Supporting Actor nomination for **Hud** (the first was for **Anatomy Of A Murder** in 1959) – had asked to have his nomination withdrawn and said that he would refuse the Oscar if he was chosen.

Scott regarded the awards ceremony as a "meat parade" – and he has also refused an Emmy. "Life isn't a race," he stated, "and because it is not a race I don't consider myself in competition with my fellow actors for awards or recognition. That is why I have rejected the nomination and Oscar for playing Patton." The Academy had no intention of striking his name off its illustrious roster of winners, however, and Frank McCarthy, who also collected the Best Film award as producer of **Patton**, accepted Scott's unwanted trophy with a nod to the voters' fair-mindedness. Scott *did* accept the New York Critics prize for his work in **Patton**, however, and his wife, who collected it for him, quoted the prickly star as saying: "This was the only film acting award worth having."

Patton was a huge panorama of the tyrannical, controversial and strangely anachronistic US commander General George S. Patton Jr's campaigns in North Africa, Sicily, Normandy and Czechoslovakia during World War II. The first war film to win the Best Film Oscar since 1962's **Lawrence Of Arabia**, **Patton** took five additional awards: for Franklin J. Schaffner's direction (he, too, missed the ceremony, being on location in Spain with **Nicholas and Alexandra**), for Francis Ford Coppola and Edmund H. North's Best Original Story and Screenplay, and for art direction, editing and sound.

RIGHT *George C. Scott, one of Hollywood's most controversial stars, was 'Blood and Guts' Patton, one of the most controversial of American commanders in World War II. By declining his Oscar, Scott became the first refusenik actor in the Academy's history*

Known originally as **Patton: A Salute To A Rebel** in America and as **Patton: Lust For Glory** in Britain, Schaffner's film was one of the most intelligent war epics of its period, and yet all its paraphernalia of combat and troop movements hinges on Scott's gargantuan performance – conceived like a Shakespearean tragic hero – in the central role. Indeed, McCarthy has claimed that there are only 11 minutes of actual battle scenes in the film.

The story follows Patton's progress from Tunis to the conquest of Sicily – where he slaps a fatigued soldier and is relieved of his command – to England and to Normandy where, in charge of the Third Army, he lifts the siege of Bastogne during the Battle of the Bulge. Then, pushing into Czechoslovakia and sniffing a glorious victory, he is forced by Eisenhower to make way for Montgomery's Northern Front, enabling the Russians to seize Prague. After the war, Patton's forces occupy Bavaria, but his unconcealed resentment of the Russians and his refusal to dismiss Nazis from civil office leads to his downfall and bitter departure.

Based by Coppola on Patton's diaries, the autobiography of General Omar Bradley (Patton's deputy and later his superior, a quieter, deeper thinker, played by Karl Malden) and Ladislas Farago's *Patton: Ordeal and Triumph*, the script, licked into structural shape by North, presented Patton as a huge, ebullient warlord, a driven

BELOW *Best Supporting Actor John Mills (left) as the village idiot, Sarah Miles (center) as the village flirt, and Trevor Howard (right) as the village priest meet on an Irish beach (photographed by Oscar-winner Freddie Young) in* Ryan's Daughter

ABOVE *In Airport, Best Supporting Actress Helen Hayes (foreground center) was a screaming success as an aged stowaway on board an airliner which included among its passengers mad bomber Van Heflin (foreground right), in his last role*

man to whom war and victory are all, but an enigma of flawed humanity. For all his triumphs, Patton is lonely, wrong-headed and a political embarrassment. As played by Scott, Patton is magisterial, magnetic, and at times profoundly vain and stupid. He offends everyone from Montgomery to the Russian allies; he has to humiliate himself by publicly apologizing for hitting the soldier – then marches off to triumph in France; he kisses his wounded men and wonders why the corpses won't get up to fight again.

Scott – his head shaved, his craggy features cast in expressions of baleful contempt or red-faced rage – was worried during filming whether he was succeeding in the part. He said he was playing it because Patton "was a professional and I admire professionalism. And for whatever else he was, good or bad, he was an individual." In the final analysis, Scott's portrayal of this monstrous, patriotic, rebellious romantic was sublime.

Director Schaffner, too, must be acknowledged for his technical craftsmanship and his ability to contain Scott's performance within the wider context of what is a superbly realized movie.

If **Patton** ruled the roost in 1970, there were other epics to consider, too. **Ryan's Daughter**, David Lean's first film since **Dr Zhivago** (1965), didn't get Best Film or Best Director nominations, however, having been critically torn apart at the time of its release – an unjust treatment for a beautifully visualized film that led to a self-imposed 14-year exile from films for the deeply wounded Lean. But John Mills – funny, touching and tragic as the crippled village idiot, a wordless sage fool – took the Best Supporting Actor Oscar for his performance in Lean's film, a paean to romance and Ireland which won Freddie Young the Best Cinematography award.

Mills was the only Oscar-winning actor present at the ceremony. Helen Hayes, whose little old lady stowaway in **Airport** won her the Best Supporting Actress award (making her the first star to achieve the 'double' – she was Best Actress for **The Sin Of Madelon Claudet**, her first talkie, in 1931/2), was absent and so was Best Actress Glenda Jackson. Meanwhile, there was only one award apiece for the $50 million-grossing **Love Story** (Best Original Score by Francis Lai) and **M*A*S*H** (Ring Lardner's Best Screenplay Adaptation), and nothing at all for **Little Big Man** or **Five Easy Pieces**.

Glenda Jackson's Oscar, for her Gudrun Brangwen in Ken Russell's **Women In Love**, was the fourth in six years in that category for an English actress, following Julie Andrews in **Mary Poppins** (1964), Julie Christie in **Darling** (1965), and Maggie Smith in **The Prime Of Miss Jean Brodie** (1969); only Katharine Hepburn's wins for **Guess Who's Coming To Dinner** (1967) and **The Lion In Winter** (1968) had waved the American flag.

The 34-year-old Miss Jackson, a Presbyterian Liverpudlian builder's daughter who took ballet lessons as a girl, went to RADA, worked in Boots the Chemist, and got her first big opportunity at the Royal Shakespeare Company when Peter Brook cast her as the murderous Charlotte Corday in **Marat/Sade**, a role she repeated on screen. Perhaps it was the powerful sexuality she demonstrated in her stage work that led Ken Russell to offer her Gudrun in his film of D.H. Lawrence's novel – although it could equally well have been her unnerving northern flatness.

Set in a Midlands coal town, **Women In Love** concerns two tempestuous love affairs – between Gudrun and the mine-owner's son Gerald Crich (Oliver Reed), and between Gudrun's sister Ursula (Jennie Linden) and the school inspector Rupert Birkin (Alan Bates). Despite the bonds of macho physicality created between the friends Gerald and Rupert, and that of pantheistic romantic love between soul mates Rupert and Ursula, it is Gudrun's single-minded emancipation and lack of sexual fulfilment that dominate the film. And Jackson, acid-tongued and aggressive, gave film audiences their first real indication of her formidable, if unendearing, screen presence.

Gudrun's disdain and taunting of Gerald, who is in love with her but insensitive, is a little like her taunting of a bull in a field where she dances with Ursula early on in the film. Eventually he climbs up to her bedroom and makes love to her like a rapist. When the four of them go away on an alpine holiday, she takes another lover and leaves Gerald to die in the snow.

It was a commanding performance by the actress, but one which led her to become stereotyped as a bitchy nymphomaniac – Russell cast her as a voracious sexual

RIGHT *Best Actress Glenda Jackson (left) and Jenny Linden as the two emancipated Brangwen sisters in* Women In Love, *Oscar-nominated director Ken Russell's version of the D.H. Lawrence novel. The film's success put both Russell and Jackson on the international map*

weapon turned on an impotent Tchaikovsky for her next film, **The Music Lovers** (1971), and she was a liberated woman struggling to continue her affair with her bisexual lover in John Schlesinger's **Sunday, Bloody Sunday** (1971), for which she gained another Best Actress nomi-nation. Even in her first comedy, **A Touch Of Class** (1973), which brought her a second Oscar, she is a tough sexual opponent. Indeed, television and the stage, rather than the cinema, have given this genuinely great actress a wider range of roles over the years.

WINNERS 1970

Nominations Announced: February 22, 1971
Awards Ceremony: April 15, 1971
Dorothy Chandler Pavilion, Los Angeles County
Music Center

Best Picture
PATTON, 20th Century-Fox: FRANK McCARTHY, Producer

Actor
GEORGE C. SCOTT in *Patton*

Actress
GLENDA JACKSON in *Women In Love*, Kramer-Rosen/UA

Supporting Actor
JOHN MILLS in *Ryan's Daughter*, Faraway/MGM

Supporting Actress
HELEN HAYES in *Airport*, Ross Hunter-Universal

Directing
FRANKLIN J. SCHAFFNER for *Patton*

Writing
(Best Screenplay – based on material from another medium)
M*A*S*H, Aspen/20th Century-Fox: RING LARDNER Jr
(Best Story and Screenplay – based on factual material or material not previously published or produced)
PATTON: FRANCIS FORD COPPOLA and EDMUND H. NORTH

Cinematography
RYAN'S DAUGHTER: FREDDIE YOUNG

Art Direction-Set Decoration
PATTON: URIE McCLEARY and GIL PARRONDO
Set Decoration: ANTONIO MATEOS and PIERRE-LOUIS THEVENET

Sound
PATTON: DOUGLAS WILLIAMS and DON BASSMAN

Film Editing
PATTON: HUGH S. FOWLER

Music
(Best Original Score)
LOVE STORY, Love Story/Paramount: FRANCIS LAI
(Best Original Song Score)
LET IT BE, Beatles-Apple/UA
Music & Lyrics: THE BEATLES

(Best Song)
FOR ALL WE KNOW from *Lovers And Other Strangers*, ABC/Cinerama
Music: FRED KARLIN
Lyrics: ROBB ROYER and JAMES GRIFFIN (aka ROBB WILSON and ARTHUR JAMES)

Costume Design
CROMWELL, Allen/Columbia: NINO NOVARESE

Short Subjects
(Cartoons)
IS IT ALWAYS RIGHT TO BE RIGHT?, Bosustow/Schoenfeld:
NICK BOSUSTOW, Producer
(Live Action Subjects)
THE RESURRECTION OF BRONCO BILLY, University of Southern California/Universal: JOHN LONGENECKER, Producer

Documentary
(Short Subjects)
INTERVIEWS WITH MY LAI VETERANS, Laser: JOSEPH STRICK, producer
(Features)
WOODSTOCK, Wadleigh-Maurice: BOB MAURICE, Producer

Special Visual Effects
TORA! TORA! TORA!, 20th Century-Fox: A.D. FLOWERS and L.B. ABBOTT

Foreign Language Film Award
INVESTIGATION OF A CITIZEN ABOVE SUSPICION, Vera Films (Italy)

Honorary Awards
LILLIAN GISH for superlative artistry and for distinguished contribution to the progress of motion pictures. (statuette)
ORSON WELLES for superlative artistry and versatility in the creation of motion pictures. (statuette)

Irving G. Thalberg Memorial Award
INGMAR BERGMAN

Jean Hersholt Humanitarian Award
FRANK SINATRA

1971

IT WAS "FOR the incalculable effect he has had in making motion pictures the art form of his century" that 82-year-old Charles Chaplin was awarded a special Oscar in 1972. But, in truth, Hollywood was genuflecting a little late in the day. Twenty years earlier, Chaplin had been hounded out of America after years of public disapproval of his marital affairs, and violent smear campaigns against his pacifism because he had ignored a subpoena to testify before the House Un-American Activities Committee during the red scare (even though he had denied any Communist affiliations). Vowing never to return to America, Chaplin made his home in Switzerland. The Academy Award ceremony was, then, honored when this great artist returned expressly to collect his award, and the 1971 show was, in a sense, dedicated to him. A four-minute ovation from the assembled 2,900 guests greeted the frail old man, who bowed and blew kisses to them "Words are so futile, so feeble," he said, "I can only say thank you for the honor of inviting me here. You are wonderful, sweet people."

Apart from Chaplin, the 1971 Oscar ceremony belonged to **The French Connection**, which won five of the gold statuettes, two more than its nearest rival, the musical **Fiddler On The Roof**. As well as the award for the Best Film, it won for William Friedkin's direction, for Ernest Tidyman's Screenplay Adaptation, for Jerry Greenberg's editing – most impressive during the famous car chase – and for Gene Hackman's outstanding performance as James 'Popeye' Doyle, which brought him the coveted Best Actor award.

The French Connection is based on a real-life two-and-a-half year investigation by two New York narcotics squad officers, Egan and Grosso – Doyle and Russo (Roy Scheider, a Best Supporting Actor candidate) in the film – who, in 1961, seized 120 lbs of heroin worth $32 million.

BELOW *Best Supporting Actress Cloris Leachman, as the desperately lonely small-town housewife in Peter Bogdanovich's* The Last Picture Show, *reaches out for some love from young Timothy Bottoms, many years her junior. Ellen Burstyn, also in the film, was nominated for the same award*

ABOVE *Gene Hackman won the Best Actor award for his world-weary, obsessive and violent New York cop, 'Popeye' Doyle, in the Best Picture winner,* The French Connection. *The real-life officer on whom the role was based had a bit part in the movie*

Friedkin's film was a key thriller and audience-pleaser of its time, which offered a sometimes flashy, sometimes downbeat and realistic version of those events with violence added – Egan and Grosso killed no one but Doyle shoots one of his quarries *and*, by mistake, a hated colleague – as well as one of the most exciting car chases ever filmed and a vicious, obsessive cop as a hero.

'The French Connection' refers to a meeting point for French drug traffickers entering New York and, with knowledge of a huge consignment coming over from Marseilles, Doyle and Russo persuade their chief to let them track it down. Forced to accept the unwanted help of Federal officers Mulderig and Klein, they trail suspect Sal Boca, a Brooklyn candy-store owner, who leads them to recently arrived Frenchmen Nicoli and Charnier (Fernando Rey), the latter a criminal genius. Although the case is then closed, Nicoli attempts to shoot Doyle and

then leaps on a train which speeds above ground and below it with Doyle in ferocious pursuit in his car. A breathtaking sequence of location photography, with the action carving a groove of destruction through the city, it ends with Doyle cornering and killing Nicoli.

The case is reopened and the heroin located in a car belonging to a French TV personality, one of Charnier's contacts. The police close in and Doyle ends up shooting Mulderig by mistake in the gun battle which eliminates most of the drug ring. Charnier escapes, but Doyle cannot let the case go . . .

The French Connection was left ripe for a sequel which duly followed in 1975. Directed by John Frankenheimer, **French Connection II** takes Doyle off to Marseilles where Charnier has him plugged full of heroin. After 'cold turkey', though, Doyle – after another chase sequence, this time on foot – catches up with Charnier and kills him, murder being an option Charnier eschewed when he had 'Popeye' at his mercy.

This darker *film noir* continuation of the **French Connection** saga was in many ways a better film than its predecessor, but it didn't win any Oscars because sequels seldom do. Hackman's first incarnation of 'Popeye' Doyle was rare for its total lack of concession to audience sympathy. Doyle is crude, foul-mouthed and not even conventionally good-looking, and in his ambiguous pursuit of law and order thoroughly convincing – for Hackman is a master.

He studied with the real Eddie Egan in Harlem during his research for the film, and when it came to it did most of his own stunt driving, too. But the actor had this to say about 'Popeye' Doyle: "Most cops like the idea of a movie showing something of the reality they know, with a hero who is a very right-wing conservative – let's be honest, Doyle is a fascist." The role made Hackman a major star (though he had already been twice nominated as Best Supporting Actor), and the Oscar reputedly put his price for a film up from $200,000 to $500,000.

As well as **The French Connection**, Roy Scheider appeared, as a pimp, in another dark American thriller in 1971, Alan J. Pakula's **Klute**, for which Jane Fonda won the Best Actress award after previously being nominated for **They Shoot Horses, Don't They?** (1969). On Oscar night 1971, it was feared that Fonda, if she won, might use the occasion as a political platform, for she had campaigned hard and controversially for America's withdrawal from Vietnam. She had also considered refusing the Oscar as a protest, but she collected the statuette, contenting herself with: "There's a great deal to say, but I'm not going to say it tonight."

In **Klute**, ex-policeman John Klute (Donald Sutherland) comes from Pennsylvania to New York in search of a friend, Tom Gruneman, with just a letter to a prostitute as a clue. Gruneman was a client of a hip, sexy, upwardly mobile call-girl, Bree Daniels (Fonda). Bree is a classy but cynical operator, a consummate actress in bed, but she is hovering on the edge of her nerves. There have been disturbing 'breather' calls made to her . . .

Klute visits her, is rebuffed, and then begins to tail her as she goes to work, calling on her 'tricks' in mini-skirt and thigh-high boots. He becomes fascinated, takes a room in her apartment block, and spies on her at night. But someone else is watching her from above, and when she screams Klute comes to the rescue.

He watches over her like a father. Then one night she comes to him, scared, and they make love. But it was a game, and once it's over she gets up and goes back to her apartment. Her friend Arlyn is murdered, but Bree still takes chances – the suspense alone is killing her. One night she goes to a deserted garment factory, seeking help from an old client. But she is alone in the dark when tracked down by the killer, Cable, an ex-partner of Tom's. He aims to kill her too. He makes her listen to a tape of Arlyn's death. But Klute has been unable to stop following her and he arrives in time.

A stylized, 70s *film noir* from Pakula, **Klute** is a very

RIGHT *Best Actress Jane Fonda, suitably attired in kinky gear for her job as a call girl, takes a call in* Klute. *Donald Sutherland, as the private eye of the title, was a member of Fonda's Anti-War Troupe which toured military camps at the time*

Best Supporting Actor Ben Johnson (right), in The Last Picture Show, *was the owner of the fleapit movie theater, the only entertainment in the small Texas town. The theater had to close down – hence the film's title – much to the distress of teenager Sam Bottoms*

dark vision indeed, charged with neurosis and paranoia. Sutherland's gazing detective seems as much a dangerous sexual – and certainly an emotional – threat to Bree as her terrorizer. Although the film was named for his character, it belonged to Fonda – and it is the key work in her transition from sex symbol to great screen actress. She is many things in this film: liberated woman, *femme fatale*, little girl lost and victim. Her immersion in her part was total and her technique perfect, whether pretending to fake the depravity her johns require – "Don't be ashamed, nothing is wrong, let it all hang out!" – or so paralyzed with fear at the hands of her would-be assassin that she lets the mucus flow from her nostrils. It was a dynamic piece of actorly self-discovery, an indisputable Oscar-worthy performance. For Fonda, too, who spent time with prostitutes as part of her research, it reinforced her feminism and, indeed, critical battles have since been fought over **Klute**'s role in women's cinema.

Both the Best Supporting Actress and Actor of 1971 came from Peter Bogdanovich's superb black-and-white homage to the rural Texas of the 50s, **The Last Picture Show**. Set on the eve of the Korean War, it tells of the closure of a small-town cinema and the rites of passage of two friends, Sonny (Timothy Bottoms) and Duane (Jeff Bridges). Both Cloris Leachman as Ruth, the neglected wife of the football coach, who falls in love with Sonny, and Ellen Burstyn as Lois, the mother of Duane's girl Jacy, were Oscar nominees. They were both splendid, but it was Leachman who won for her tender portrayal of a lonely woman.

Ben Johnson, a beloved member of the old John Ford stock company, here gave a marvelous performance as Sam the Lion, the cinema owner who, on a fishing trip with Sonny, delivers a touching soliloquy reminiscing about a youthful idyll in which he went nude swimming with a girl – Lois. Shortly after he dies offscreen.

Johnson gave one of the warmest, most honest, Oscar acceptance speeches for years. He said he left his written speech at home because, "the longer I worked on it the phonier it got. What I'm about to say will start a controversy around the world: this couldn't have happened to a nicer feller."

WINNERS 1971

Nominations Announced; February 22, 1972
Awards Ceremony: April 10, 1972
Dorothy Chandler Pavilion, Los Angeles County
Music Center

Best Picture
THE FRENCH CONNECTION,
D'Antoni-Schine-Moore/20th Century-Fox:
PHILIP D'ANTONI, Producer

Actor
GENE HACKMAN in *The French Connection*

Actress
JANE FONDA in *Klute*, Gus/Warner Bros.

Supporting Actor
BEN JOHNSON in *The Last Picture Show*, BBS/Columbia

Supporting Actress
CLORIS LEACHMAN in *The Last Picture Show*

Directing
WILLIAM FRIEDKIN for *The French Connection*

Writing
(Best Screenplay – based on material from another medium)
THE FRENCH CONNECTION: ERNEST TIDYMAN
(Best Story and Screenplay – based on factual material or
material not previously published or produced)
THE HOSPITAL, Gottfried-Chayefsky-Hiller/UA:
PADDY CHAYEFSKY

Cinematography
FIDDLER ON THE ROOF, Mirisch-Cartier/UA: OSWALD
MORRIS

Art Direction-Set Decoration
NICHOLAS AND ALEXANDRA, Horizon/Columbia:
JOHN BOX, ERNEST ARCHER, JACK MAXSTED and GIL
PARRONDO
Set Decoration: VERNON DIXON

Sound
FIDDLER ON THE ROOF: GORDON K. McCALLUM and
DAVID HILDYARD

Film Editing
THE FRENCH CONNECTION: JERRY GREENBERG

Music
(Best Original Dramatic Score)
SUMMER OF '42, Mulligan-Roth/Warner Bros.: MICHEL
LEGRAND

(Best Scoring: Adaptation and Original Song Score)
FIDDLER ON THE ROOF
Adaptation: JOHN WILLIAMS
(Best Song)
THEME FROM SHAFT from *Shaft*, Shaft/MGM
Music & Lyrics: ISAAC HAYES

Costume Design
NICHOLAS AND ALEXANDRA: YVONNE BLAKE and
ANTONIO CASTILLO

Short Subjects
(The designation of this category was changed from
'Cartoons' to 'Animated Films')
(Animated Films)
THE CRUNCH BIRD, Maxwell-Petok-Petrovich/Regency:
TED PETOK, Producer
(Live Action Films)
SENTINELS OF SILENCE, Concord/Paramount: MANUEL
ARANGO and ROBERT AMRAM, Producers

Documentary
(Short Subjects)
SENTINELS OF SILENCE: MANUEL ARANGO and
ROBERT AMRAM, Producers
(Features)
THE HELLSTROM CHRONICLE, Wolper/Cinema 5:
WALON GREEN, Producer

Special Visual Effects
(Not given as an Annual Award after this year.)
BEDKNOBS AND BROOMSTICKS, Disney/Buena Vista:
ALAN MALEY, EUSTACE LYCETT and DANNY LEE

Foreign Language Film Award
THE GARDEN OF THE FINZI-CONTINIS, Lucari-Cohn
(Italy)

Honorary Award
CHARLES CHAPLIN for the incalculable effect he has had
in making motion pictures the art form of this century.
(statuette)

Irving G. Thalberg Memorial Award
None

Jean Hersholt Humanitarian Award
None

1972

THE CEREMONY FOR the 1972 Academy Awards was a less than graceful affair, of which the highlight – or low point – was the refusal for the second time in three years by the star chosen as Best Actor to accept his Oscar. Unlike George C. Scott, though, Marlon Brando – winning for his portrayal of Don Vito Corleone in Francis Ford Coppola's **The Godfather** – used his non-appearance as a platform for airing a personal grievance. Spurning the award on his behalf was a native Amerindian girl called Sacheen Littlefeather, who came on stage in tribal dress to read excerpts of a letter from Brando complaining about America's treatment of Indians and especially by Hollywood in Westerns: "The motion picture industry has been as responsible as any for degrading the Indian and making a mockery of his character, describing him as hostile, savage and evil." Brando's proxy address also cited current troubles at the Wounded Knee reservation, and suggested that his presence there might be more helpful to its Indian residents than an appearance at the Dorothy Chandler Pavilion.

The gesture was greeted with a mixture of derision and applause by the celebrity audience – but if the Academy was offended, it didn't bear a grudge against the actor. Brando – who had previously won the award for his work in **On The Waterfront** in 1954 – was nominated again in 1973, for the eighth time, for **Last Tango In Paris**.

The Academy's president, Daniel Taradash, had got the 1972 party underway with a snide dig at film critics "who can't act, direct, write or produce pictures", a self-congratulatory pat on the back for the industry's awards that went sadly awry. These ill-chosen words were followed by Charlton Heston failing to turn up – he had a flat tyre – to read a mock-biblical passage guying all his roles as a monolithic he-man in Christian epics. The joke was lost when Clint Eastwood – who later in the proceedings took a swipe at Brando by asking if anyone would like to say a word on behalf of all the movie cowboys killed by Indians – had to step into the breach and read from cue cards until Heston finally turned up.

Aside from these embarrassments – watched by some 80 million Americans on television – the greatest area of controversy was the actual allocation of the Oscars. Eight went to Bob Fosse's musical **Cabaret** and three to **The Godfather**. How, it was argued afterwards, could **Cabaret** win for Best Direction, Best Actress, Best Supporting Actor, Best Cinematography, Best Art Direction, Best Editing, Best Sound and Best Scoring and yet not for Best Picture? Albert S. Ruddy, who eventually collected

BELOW *Veteran Broadway actress Eileen Heckart (left) gained her Best Supporting Actress Oscar for* Butterflies Are Free, *as the overpowering, overpossessive mother of blind songwriter Edward Albert, with whom kooky would-be actress Goldie Hawn (right) is in love*

Registered Tra

that top prize for **The Godfather**, commented that he had wondered if he would ever get on stage at all.

The Godfather's other Oscar was for Best Screenplay Adaptation, and there is no disputing the brilliance of Coppola's reworking, with Mario Puzo, of the latter's novel about the ageing head of a Mafia dynasty who plays godfather to New York's Sicilian immigrants. Conceived by Paramount as the first of a run of annual moneyspinners that would carry the rest of the year's productions, the film was an immediate box-office smash that quickly recouped its budget, made immense profits and announced the arrival of the movie-brat generation of directors – led by Coppola – in Hollywood.

A sprawling three-hour epic showing the power struggles and business activities of America's top crime syndicates, dominated by the Corleone family, **The Godfather** is leisurely in pace and matter-of-fact, sometimes surreal in its depiction of violence: a film producer's unwillingness to do Corleone a favor is rewarded with the gift, left in his bed, of his favorite horse's severed head; the succession to power of Michael Corleone (Al Pacino) is consecrated by the simultaneous Catholic baptism of his godson and his men's wiping out of the family's enemies. But for all its cold-bloodedness, the movie is most powerful in

ABOVE *Liza Minnelli's bravura singing, dancing and acting as the 'divinely decadent' Sally Bowles brought Broadway pazzaz into pre-war Berlin, and plenty of heart to Bob Fosse's* Cabaret, *winning her one of the picture's eight Oscars in the process*

conveying the codes of loyalty, love, masculine honor and wifely subservience, enterprise and corporate self-interest which bind the family together – perhaps as reactionary a symbol of American life that has ever been placed on screen.

The Godfather is a serious dramatic masterpiece – but it is also a visual one, whose rich tones – especially Gordon Willis' extraordinary chiaroscuro photography of the interiors – deserved (but didn't get) acknowledgement from the Academy's voters.

Marlon Brando's Corleone is one of the great achievements of his career. He had gone so far as to test for the role at his own expense, Paramount not originally intending him for it, but in the film the authority is all his. His barely stated movements and slow, rasping words make little concession to emotion as he dispenses life and death, though here is a giant man also aware of his mortality and the limitations of his heirs. His own death as an elderly, shuffling grandfather is drily handled by Coppola,

233

ABOVE *Al Pacino (left) as Michael Corleone, heir-apparent to the soon-to-be-killed Mafia chief (Marlon Brando, right) in* The Godfather. *Pacino, nominated as Best Supporting Actor, and for Best Actor in* Serpico *(1973),* The Godfather Part II *(1974) and* Dog Day Afternoon *(1975), has yet to win*
RIGHT *Marlon Brando won (and refused) his second Academy award for his meticulous impersonation of aged Mafia chief Don Vito Corleone in* The Godfather, *Francis Ford Coppola's Best Picture*

but Brando's detail of the half-consumed orange bared in his mouth as he expires is a touch of bizarre actorly genius.

The Best Actor contenders in 1972 were no match for Don Corleone. Michael Caine and Laurence Olivier's nominations for their performances in the over-theatrical two-handed matinee thriller **Sleuth** would at least enable Joseph L. Mankiewicz (nominated in the Best Director category) to boast that this was the only time that the entire cast of a film had been so honored!

Best Supporting Actor nominees Al Pacino, James Caan and Robert Duvall, all from **The Godfather**, canceled each other out and the award went to Joel Grey for

ABOVE *Joel Grey (on ladder) as the lewd, sexually ambivalent MC, and the scantily-clad girls of the Kit Kat Club in* Cabaret. *Grey, in his first film for eleven years, won the Best Supporting Actor award for the role he had created on Broadway*

his sly, camp master of ceremonies in pre-war Berlin's Kit Kat Club in **Cabaret**. In that same film, her fourth as an adult, Liza Minnelli, daughter of Judy Garland and Vincente Minnelli (Best Director for **Gigi** in 1958), won the Best Actress Oscar for her wild, electrifying Sally Bowles – immortalized in black bowler, spidery mascara and suspenders. The role was clearly tailored – and the songs were written – for Liza's brash, exuberant style, and she was perfect as the nightclub dancer stranded in Germany on the eve of Europe's cataclysm; though she is not as decadent as she thinks she is and, indeed, in her scenes with Michael York she is both vulnerable and touching.

As played by Liza (at 19, the youngest winner of a Tony award and an Oscar nominee for **The Sterile Cuckoo** in 1969), Sally is a character that spills over from life, her nervous hysteria and flamboyance owing not a little to perceptions of Judy Garland's ragged stardom and the

actress's own traumatic childhood and turbulent private life. Like Liza and Judy, Sally is a trouper to the end. The Academy must surely have been aware of the in-built legends that inflected **Cabaret** when they awarded Minnelli her Oscar.

Exquisitely directed and choreographed by Bob Fosse, the film is otherwise a 70s update on the Kurt Weill-Brecht world of *The Threepenny Opera* and Josef von Sternberg's **The Blue Angel**, as well as being a rude and welcome antidote to the sugary musicals that had continued to diminish the genre since the mid-60s (only Fosse's **Sweet Charity** had previously suggested that a musical could be both sexy and popular). It well deserved its technical awards. Veteran cinematographer Geoffrey Unsworth's long-awaited Oscar was probably due to his low-lit atmospherics in the sleazy club, though his sharp, bright images of the Hitler youth in blazing sunshine is a disturbing visual *hommage* to Aryanism.

Best Supporting Actress of 1972, Eileen Heckart – the dominating mother of a blind songwriter loved by a kook (Goldie Hawn) in **Butterflies Are Free** – had previously been nominated for **The Bad Seed** in 1956.

WINNERS 1972

Nominations Announced: February 12, 1973
Awards Ceremony: March 27, 1973
Dorothy Chandler Pavilion, Los Angeles County
Music Center

Best Picture
THE GODFATHER, Ruddy/Paramount: ALBERT S. RUDDY, Producer

Actor
MARLON BRANDO in *The Godfather*

Actress
LIZA MINNELLI in *Cabaret*, ABC/Allied Artists

Supporting Actor
JOEL GREY in *Cabaret*

Supporting Actress
EILEEN HECKART in *Butterflies Are Free*, Frankovich/Columbia

Directing
BOB FOSSE for *Cabaret*

Writing
(Best Screenplay – based on material from another medium)
THE GODFATHER: MARIO PUZO and FRANCIS FORD COPPOLA
(Best Story and Screenplay – based on factual material or material not previously published or produced)
THE CANDIDATE. Redford-Ritchie/Warner Bros.: JEREMY LARNER

Cinematography
CABARET: GEOFFREY UNSWORTH

Art Direction-Set Decoration
CABARET: ROLF ZEHETBAUER and JURGEN KIEBACH
Set Decoration: HERBERT STRABEL

Sound
CABARET: ROBERT KNUDSON and DAVID HILDYARD

Film Editing
CABARET: DAVID BRETHERTON

Music
(Best Original Dramatic Score)
LIMELIGHT, Chaplin/Columbia: CHARLES CHAPLIN, RAYMOND RASCH and LARRY RUSSELL
(Best Scoring: Adaptation and Original Song Score)
CABARET
Adaptation: RALPH BURNS
(Best Song)
THE MORNING AFTER from *The Poseidon Adventure*, Allen/20th Century-Fox
Music & Lyrics: AL KASHA and JOEL HIRSCHHORN

Costume Design
TRAVELS WITH MY AUNT, Fryer/MGM: ANTHONY POWELL

Short Subjects
(Animated Films)
A CHRISTMAS CAROL, Williams/ABC: RICHARD WILLIAMS, Producer
(Live Action Films)
NORMAN ROCKWELL'S WORLD . . . AN AMERICAN DREAM, Concepts Unlimited/Columbia: RICHARD BARCLAY, Producer

Documentary
(Short Subjects)
THIS TINY WORLD, Huguenot van der Linden: CHARLES and MARTINA HUGUENOT VAN DER LINDEN, Producers
(Features)
MARJOE, Cinema X/Cinema 5: HOWARD SMITH and SARAH KERNOCHAN, Producers

Foreign Language Film Award
THE DISCREET CHARM OF THE BOURGEOISIE, Silberman (France)

Honorary Awards
CHARLES S. BOREN, Leader for 38 years of the industry's enlightened labor relations and architect of its policy of non-discrimination. With the respect and affection of all who work in films
EDWARD G. ROBINSON who achieved greatness as a player, a patron of the arts and a dedicated citizen . . . in sum, a Renaissance man. From his friends in the industry he loves

Special Achievement
(New Category)
(Created as an 'other' Award – not necessarily given each year – to honor achievements formerly recognized in the Special Visual Effects and Sound Effects categories.)
Visual Effects: L.B. ABBOTT and A.D. FLOWERS for *The Poseidon Adventure*

Irving G. Thalberg Memorial Award
None

Jean Hersholt Humanitarian Award
ROSALIND RUSSELL

1973

AVID NIVEN WAS on stage, about to introduce Elizabeth Taylor, when it happened. A moustacheoed man broke through a cyclorama (causing $4,000 worth of damage), ran behind the suave star waving a V-sign in the air, and then exited at the back of the stage. And then he put his clothes on.

The Awards ceremony's first streak – at the height of the craze – came courtesy of a Hollywood adman called Robert Opel, who had acquired a yellow pass enabling him to get behind the scenes at the Dorothy Chandler Pavilion. He was later marched away by an Academy press representative, claiming, "I have nothing to hide." The Oscar TV crew had focused directly and discreetly on the upper half of Opel's torso. Niven, recovering with aplomb, commented: "Isn't it fascinating that probably the only laugh this man will ever get in his life is by stripping off his clothes and showing his shortcomings?"

Miss Taylor, suntanned and in yellow, then came on to present the Best Picture award to Tony Bill and Michael and Julia Phillips, producers of **The Sting**, which stole the statuette from under the nose of **The Exorcist**. The only horror film ever to have been nominated for the top prize, the latter had been expected to sweep the board but ended up with only two Oscars, for Robert Knudson and Chris Newman's sound (marvelous in its delivery of the unseen Mercedes McCambridge's rasping voice of Satan) and William Peter Blatty's screenplay from his own novel. With its scenes of the possessed adolescent (Linda Blair) vomiting green bile, spitting out foul imprecations, and stabbing herself in the genitals with a crucifix, **The Exorcist** was a supremely disturbing chiller, but scarcely a film the cautious Academy could endorse as its favorite. Accordingly, its director William Friedkin, leading lady Ellen Burstyn, and supporting players Blair, and Jason Miller were all nominated but walked away empty-handed.

The Sting took seven awards. Reteaming Best Director George Roy Hill and stars Robert Redford and Paul Newman from **Butch Cassidy And The Sundance Kid**, it could hardly fail. It is an engaging tale of two confidence tricksters in 30s Chicago, small-timer Johnny Hooker (Redford, whose boyish grin helped him to a Best Actor nomination) and big-timer Henry Gondorff (Newman). They team up after Hooker's partner has been murdered by swindled racketeer Doyle Lonnegan (Robert Shaw). 'The Sting' is the duo's biggest con. Already 'done' by

Gondorff in a card game en route by train from New York to Chicago, Lonnegan is given bogus information by Johnny on how to cheat Gondorff's phony betting operation. From then on, it gets very complicated with several false trails that lead nowhere except to Hooker and Gondorff's outrageous heist – and with Scott Joplin's piano rags building up a delightful atmosphere of smooth, apparently guileless cross and double-cross. For these, Marvin Hamlisch won the Best Music Score Adaptation Oscar. Indeed, it was Hamlisch's *annus mirabilis* – he also took home Oscars for his melancholy score and title song (with lyricists Alan and Marilyn Bergman) for **The Way We Were**, starring Redford and Best Actress nominee Barbra Streisand as star-crossed lovers.

Although it has dated as a comedy drama, **The Sting** still looks impressive, and cornered the awards for editing and art direction – a superbly constrasting view of both seedy and sumptuous Chicago, ranging from flashy apartments to sordid backstreets which, despite the jokey tenor of the script never leaves any doubt that this is the Depression. Edith Head, first lady of Hollywood costume

BELOW *Best Actor Jack Lemmon (standing), at the end of his tether in* Save The Tiger*, argues about an arson plot with Jack Gilford, his partner in an LA garment factory. Veteran vaudeville comedian Gilford was nominated as Best Supporting Actor for his dramatic performance*

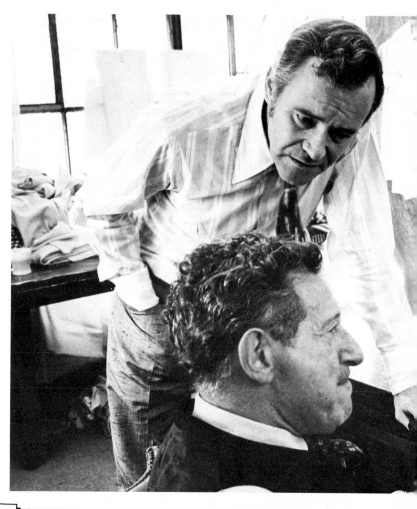

Confidence trickster Robert Redford (nominated, center) being taken for a ride by big-time racketeer Robert Shaw (right) and a crony in the gangster-ridden Chicago of the 30s recreated in the seven-Oscar winning The Sting
BELOW LEFT *Paul Newman (seated) on a winning streak in* The Sting, *the movie that turned up trumps for Best Director George Roy Hill, and resuscitated the piano rags of Scott Joplin*

design, accepted her eighth and last Oscar for dressing the stars. This remarkable woman was, astoundingly, Oscar-nominated every year from the inception of the Best Costume Design award in 1948 until 1966; in nine of those years she was nominated twice; and in 1963 three times – a staggering 33 times in all.

Best Actor in 1973 was Jack Lemmon, whose Oscar for **Save The Tiger** made him the first recipient of both actor awards (he won the 1955 supporting prize for **Mister Roberts**). One of the cinema's finest performers, Lemmon had been previously nominated as Best Actor for **Some Like It Hot** (1959), **The Apartment** (1960) and **Days Of Wine And Roses** (1962). A week before the 1973 ceremony, he spoke at a live TV dinner tribute to James Cagney. He was on prescribed medication for minor surgery the following day, and the effect of wine on this made his speech 'discursive' – his wife sobered him up by throwing water at him. This minor incident apparently didn't endear Lemmon to the censorious Academy, but he got the Oscar anyway, and showed his elation: "I had a

speech prepared – in 1959. There has been a lot of controversy over this award, but I think it's one hell of an honor and I am thrilled."

Lemmon has no peer as a menopausal male struggling to come to terms with an identity he doesn't want, and over the years his portrayals of this type have moved increasingly away from comedy to heavy drama. **Save The Tiger**, directed by John G. Avildsen, gave him an ideal role as rag-trade executive, Harry Stoner, whose disenchantment and haggardness double during one day of crisis. Harry has fallen into cynical and corrupt business practices – he fixes up a buyer with a prostitute and has a scheme to burn down a warehouse for the insurance money, against the wishes of his partner Phil (Best Supporting Actor nominee Jack Gilford). Whether tearing around trying to sort out the mess caused by the randy buyer's subsequent heart attack, or lost in a wartime reverie at an evening fashion show, Harry is weighed down by the futility and frustration of life, and Lemmon called upon a wide range of moods and feelings to engage our sympathy.

Sixty-one years separated the ages of 1973's Best Supporting Actor and Actress, 71-year-old John Houseman and 10-year-old Tatum O'Neal – the youngest-ever reci-

BELOW *British actress Glenda Jackson, winning her second award in four years, catches up on her feminist reading in* A Touch of Class, *no doubt hoping it will help her cope more easily with her adulterous affair with insurance agent George Segal*

ABOVE *Ryan O'Neal (left) finds the nine-year-old orphaned daughter of an old flame a burden in* Paper Moon – *until she becomes a valuable asset in a con game. Ryan's daughter, Tatum O'Neal (right) was named Best Supporting Actress. Nominated in the same category, in the same film, was Madeline Kahn as the belly dancer Trixie Delight*

pient of a competitive Oscar. Houseman, one of Hollywood and Broadway's most distinguished producers, had turned to acting late in his career, and his award for the despotic university professor in James Bridges' **The Paper Chase** was both popular and deserved. Tatum O'Neal, daughter of actress Joanna Moore and Ryan O'Neal, the latter her co-star in Peter Bogdanovich's **Paper Moon**, gave a thoroughly winning performance as Addie, a shrewd, cigarette-smoking, wisecracking nine-year-old con girl teaching her father a few tricks in Depression Kansas. Only when her father becomes romantically involved with a floozie (Madeline Kahn, who was one of Tatum's co-nominees) does she show her age in a fit of childish jealousy.

Glenda Jackson won the Best Actress Oscar for the second time in four years for her Vickie Allessio in Melvin Frank's light sex comedy **A Touch Of Class**, the first time an actress playing a comedy role proper had won the award since Judy Holliday in **Born Yesterday** (1950).

A series of coincidences lead Vickie (a rag-trade pirate, like Lemmon's Harry Stoner) and American insurance agent Steve Blackburn (George Segal), who is married with children, into an affair that is consummated in a dirty weekend in Marbella (the best sequence in the film) during which Steve, in bed, hilariously dislocates his back. They make a tempestuous couple, although the affair prospers for a while in their London flat, until Steve – beset on all sides by wife, children and mistress – calls it off.

This kind of witty sex-war saga was very popular in the early 70s and **A Touch Of Class** is rooted in that era, consequently seeming limp today. It was very much Segal's kind of film, however, and whereas he is at home here, Jackson patently is not, despite her Oscar. Sylvia Miller wrote in the *Monthly Film Bulletin*: '. . . it is unedifying to see Glenda Jackson's tense, harpy-like personality constrained by a strait-jacket of tame naughtiness and sentimentality. Sarcastic rather than wry, brittle rather than suave, Miss Jackson is not equipped for lightness.' But Jackson, absent from the ceremony, was the winner. She has made better films without acknowledgement.

Finally in 1973 there was a special award for the now frail Groucho Marx ("and the unequaled achievements of the Marx Brothers"). If she wasn't there in person, the late Margaret Dumont – Groucho's long-suffering straight-woman – was there in spirit, acknowledged by the star who insulted her through seven Marx Brothers movies. And, awaiting soap-opera stardom in **Dallas**, was one of the ceremony's decorative 'Oscar guardians' – a young starlet called Victoria Principal.

WINNERS 1973

Nominations Announced: February 19, 1974
Awards Ceremony: April 2, 1974
Dorothy Chandler Pavilion, Los Angeles County
Music Center

Best Picture
THE STING, Universal-Bill/Phillips-George Roy Hill
Production/Zanuck-Brown Presentation,
Universal: TONY BILL, MICHAEL and JULIA PHILLIPS,
Producers

Actor
JACK LEMMON in *Save The Tiger*,
Filmways-Jalem-Cirandinha/Paramount

Actress
GLENDA JACKSON in *A Touch Of Class*, Brut/Avco
Embassy

Supporting Actor
JOHN HOUSEMAN in *The Paper Chase*,
Thompson-Paul/20th Century-Fox

Supporting Actress
TATUM O'NEAL in *Paper Moon*, Directors
Company/Paramount

Directing
GEORGE ROY HILL for *The Sting*

Writing
(Best Screenplay – based on material from another medium)
THE EXORCIST, Hoya/Warner Bros.: WILLIAM PETER
BLATTY
(Best Story and Screenplay – based on factual material or
material not previously published or produced)
THE STING: DAVID S. WARD

Cinematography
CRIES AND WHISPERS, Svenska
Filminstitutet-Cinematograph AB/New World:
SVEN NYKVIST

Art Direction-Set Decoration
THE STING: HENRY BUMSTEAD
Set Decoration: JAMES PAYNE

Sound
THE EXORCIST: ROBERT KNUDSON and CHRIS
NEWMAN

Film Editing
THE STING: WILLIAM REYNOLDS

Music
(Best Original Dramatic Score)
THE WAY WE WERE, Rastar/Columbia: MARVIN
HAMLISCH
(Best Scoring: Original Song Score and/or Adaptation)
THE STING
Adaptation: MARVIN HAMLISCH
(Best Song)
THE WAY WE WERE from *The Way We Were*
Music: MARVIN HAMLISCH
Lyrics: ALAN and MARILYN BERGMAN

Costume Design
THE STING: EDITH HEAD

Short Subjects
(Animated Films)
FRANK FILM, Mouris: FRANK MOURIS, Producer
(Live Action Films)
THE BOLERO, Miller: ALLAN MILLER and WILLIAM
FERTIK, Producers

Documentary
(Short Subjects)
PRINCETON: A SEARCH FOR ANSWERS, Krainin-Sage:
JULIAN KRAININ and DeWITT L. SAGE Jr, Producers
(Features)
THE GREAT AMERICAN COWBOY, Merrill-Rodeo:
KEITH MERRILL, Producer

Foreign Language Film Award
DAY FOR NIGHT, Les Films Du Carrosse-PECF (Paris)-
PIC (Rome). (France)

Honorary Awards
HENRI LANGLOIS for his devotion to the art of film, his
massive contributions in preserving its past and his
unswerving faith in its future
GROUCHO MARX in recognition of his brilliant creativity
and for the unequalled achievements of the Marx Brothers in
the art of motion picture comedy

Irving G. Thalberg Memorial Award
LAWRENCE WEINGARTEN

Jean Hersholt Humanitarian Award
LEW WASSERMAN

1974

THE CONTROVERSIAL ANTI-war film **Hearts And Minds** was loudly applauded for winning the 1974 Best Documentary Oscar, but in his acceptance speech Bert Schneider (who co-produced with Peter Davis), set the cat among the pigeons by reading a congratulatory telegram bearing "greetings of friendship" from the Vietcong government in South Vietnam. Bob Hope, one of four M.C.s, insisted on the Academy issuing an official disclaimer to this announcement, and Frank Sinatra read it: "We are not responsible for any political references made on this programme tonight. And we are sorry they were made." Warren Beatty countered, when introducing the Best Picture nominees, by calling ol' Blue Eyes, "You old Republican, you."

Francis Ford Coppola had two Oscars to his name before this ceremony, for the Best Story and Screenplay of **Patton** (1970) and the Best Adapted Screenplay of **The Godfather** (1972) (shared with Edmund H. North and Mario Puzo respectively). **The Godfather Part II** brought him three more awards – as producer of the Best Film (his surveillance thriller **The Conversation** was also nominated), for its direction, and for writing the Best Screenplay Adaptation, again with Puzo, who went up to collect the statuette. Added to this, Coppola had the joy of seeing his father, Carmine Coppola, share with Nino Rota the Oscar for Best Original Dramatic Score. Coppola Sr thanked his son for employing him on **The Godfather Part II** and himself for siring him.

Had Best Supporting Actress nominee Talia Shire – Coppola's sister – taken an Oscar for her headstrong Connie Corleone in the film, it would have completed a memorable family hat-trick. But she lost out to Ingrid Bergman, winning for her shy Swedish spinster helping her fellow passengers commit **Murder On The Orient Express**. "It's always nice to win an Oscar," said Miss Bergman. It was her third – following her Best Actress awards for 1944's **Gaslight** and 1955's **Anastasia** – and with it she emulated Helen Hayes' feat of winning in both actress categories; Maggie Smith and Meryl Streep have since followed suit.

There were two more honors for **The Godfather Part II** – for Angelo Graham and Dean Tavoularis's Best Art Direction, and for Robert De Niro – whose fellow nominees as Best Supporting Actor included co-stars Michael V. Gazzo and Lee Strasberg. **The Godfather** had had three Best Supporting Actor nominees in 1972,

among them Al Pacino, who brilliantly extended his role as Michael, Don Vito Corleone's son and heir, in **The Godfather Part II** and was this time unlucky as a Best Actor nominee.

Coppola's Best Director prize was awarded to him by Goldie Hawn and Robert Wise, and in his speech he gave special thanks to Gordon Willis – a surprising omission from the Best Cinematography nominations – whose sunlit Sicilian and Cuban exteriors, and moody lighting whenever the burdened Michael is in frame, were as vital

to the film's seamlessness as both prequel and sequel to **The Godfather** as De Niro's performance as the razor-sharp young Vito seizing his moments in 20s New York.

A far more self-consciously analytical film than its predecessor, however, **The Godfather Part II** – spanning six decades – sees Coppola attempting to de-romanticize the godfather myth. Vito Corleone's own passage from orphaned waif to neighborhood Robin Hood to respected patriarch is virtually reversed a generation later as rotten strains in the family – perhaps most insidiously represented by the weak, flash Fredo (John Cazale), whose envy of Michael's position leads him to betray him to Jewish Mafia boss Hyman Roth (Strasberg) – ultimately threaten to destroy it and, as loyalties unpeel, to leave Michael isolated. Perhaps Michael's failing is that whereas his father was *truly* motivated by the family codes of duty, fidelity and honor he, while preserving these, has leaned more towards corporate power, wealth and bourgeois respectability. It is as if the Mafia doctrine, as practised by Vito with his pure Sicilian origins, offers a nobler way of life than Michael's big-business approach, tainted as it is by the sick and corrupt heart of America.

Is **The Godfather Part II** a better film than **The Godfather**? Possibly not, since it is incomplete without our knowledge of the latter (Coppola later edited them together for NBC TV), although apart from that it is a considerable achievement by one of the world's greatest directors. Coppola's handling of the Corleones' business and dynastic affairs and the set-pieces (notably the opening party, the street festival with Vito prowling across the

ABOVE *Robert De Niro, one of the screen's most supremely gifted actors, finally gained Academy recognition for his role as the young immigrant Corleone in* The Godfather Part II *which won him the Best Supporting Actor award*
RIGHT *The star-studded group of passengers aboard the train for* Murder On the Orient Express *included Lauren Bacall (left) as the loquacious Mrs Hubbard, here speaking her mind to shy Swedish missionary Greta Ohlsson. Miss Ohlsson was really glittering star Ingrid Bergman, who was voted the year's Best Supporting Actress*

rooftops to assassinate the 'Black Hand', and the little stage melodrama) is near perfect. The acting, too, is a joy.

The Best Actor of 1974 turned out to be 55-year-old Art Carney for his performance in **Harry And Tonto**. He was presented with his award by Glenda Jackson, a double Oscar-winning actress making her first appearance at the ceremony. In the film, sensitively directed by Paul Mazursky, Carney was touching as a 72-year-old widower who is evicted from his apartment on Manhattan's West Side and, with his orange cat Tonto, makes an odyssey across the US to California.

A journey of experience, in which we come to sympathize with the old man rather than his more conventional or supposedly hipper offspring he visits en route, **Harry And Tonto** also provides — through Carney's convincing central performance — a rare glimpse into the wisdom and pain of old age, and the transience of belonging.

It was not a major film, but neither was Carney's Oscar a sentimental gesture. He won it on merit in his fourth screen role (originally intended for James Cagney), having worked his way up to the movies after years as a straight man on radio, television — where he was Ed Norton in **The Honeymooners** in Jackie Gleason's show — and on Broadway. Although he already had four Emmys for his TV work, Art Carney said of Oscar night, "It was the greatest moment of my life."

Harry's daughter in **Harry And Tonto** was played by Ellen Burstyn, who won the 1974 Best Actress Oscar in the title role of **Alice Doesn't Live Here Anymore**. The film's director, Martin Scorsese, collected the award on behalf of the actress who was on stage in *Same Time, Next Year* in New York; her performance in the play won her a Tony, and an Oscar nomination when she brought it to the screen in 1978. She was nominated, too, for her

MEL & RUBY

work in **The Last Picture Show** (1971), **The Exorcist** (1973), and **Resurrection** (1980).

Burstyn – like Carney a graduate of Jackie Gleason's TV show – was a former model, shop assistant, singer and dancer who had had a hard struggle to establish herself as a major actress. She eventually made it to Broadway in *Fair Game* in 1957; ten years with Lee Strasberg and the Actors Studio developed her talent.

Alice is a bruised widow – who was an unfulfilled wife – struggling to come to terms with her independence as she brings up her 12-year-old son Tom (Alfred Lutter). It's difficult not to see something of Burstyn herself in the role – at the same time she was a three-times divorcee with a son the same age as Tom. She was also largely instrumental in getting the film off the ground at Warner Bros. and in choosing crew-members.

Alice nurtures a childhood dream of becoming a singer so, after her husband's death, she sells up and heads with Tom to her native Monterey, but ends up in Phoenix.

ABOVE *Best Actress winner Ellen Burstyn (right), with fellow worker Diane Ladd, suffers the tribulations of a hash joint waitress in Martin Scorsese's* Alice Doesn't Live Here Anymore

After a liaison with a violent philanderer (Harvey Keitel), she and the boy flee to Tucson, where she becomes a waitress and befriends a divorced farmer, David (Kris Kristofferson). Burstyn is at her most persuasive as a woman who – in her confusion and frustration – must decide whether to go it alone or become dependent, once again, on a man. David proposes to her, but the ending is left deliberately vague – although it seems that Alice will stay on with him, for the moment at least.

So, in the year when two families – the Corleones and the Coppolas – dominated the Oscars with corporate strength, it was the stories of two lonelier individuals on voyages of self-discovery – Harry heading to LA, and Alice for Monterey – that earned the particular affection of the Academy voters.

WINNERS 1974

Nominations Announced: February 24, 1975
Awards Ceremony: April 8, 1975
Dorothy Chandler Pavilion, Los Angeles County
Music Center

Best Picture
THE GODFATHER PART II, Coppola/Paramount:
FRANCIS FORD COPPOLA, Producer; GRAY
FREDERICKSON and FRED ROOS, Co-Producers

Actor
ART CARNEY in *Harry And Tonto*, 20th Century-Fox

Actress
ELLEN BURSTYN in *Alice Doesn't Live Here Anymore*,
Warner Bros.

Supporting Actor
ROBERT DE NIRO in *The Godfather Part II*

Supporting Actress
INGRID BERGMAN in *Murder On The Orient Express*, GW
Films/Paramount

Directing
FRANCIS FORD COPPOLA for *The Godfather Part II*

Writing
(Best Original Screenplay)
CHINATOWN, Evans/Paramount: ROBERT TOWNE
(Best Screenplay adapted from other material)
THE GODFATHER PART II
Screenplay: FRANCIS FORD COPPOLA and MARIO
PUZO

Cinematography
THE TOWERING INFERNO, Allen/20th
Century-Fox/Warner Bros.:
FRED KOENEKAMP and JOSEPH BIROC

Art Direction-Set Decoration
THE GODFATHER PART II: DEAN TAVOULARIS and
ANGELO GRAHAM
Set Decoration: GEORGE R. NELSON

Sound
EARTHQUAKE, Universal-Robson-Filmakers:
RONALD PIERCE and MELVIN METCALFE Sr

Film Editing
THE TOWERING INFERNO: HAROLD F. KRESS and
CARL KRESS

Music
(Best Original Dramatic Score)
THE GODFATHER PART II: NINO ROTA and CARMINE
COPPOLA

(Best Scoring: Original Song Score and/or Adaptation)
THE GREAT GATSBY Merrick/Paramount
Adaptation: NELSON RIDDLE
(Best Song)
WE MAY NEVER LOVE LIKE THIS AGAIN from *The
Towering Inferno*
Music & Lyrics: AL KASHA and JOEL HIRSCHHORN

Costume Design
THE GREAT GATSBY: THEONI V. ALDREDGE

Short Films
(Name changed from 'Short Subjects'.)
(Animated Films)
CLOSED MONDAYS, Lighthouse: WILL VINTON and
BOB GARDINER, Producers
(Live Action Films)
ONE-EYED MEN ARE KINGS, CAPAC (Paris): PAUL
CLAUDON and EDMOND SECHAN, Producers

Documentary
(Short Subjects)
DON'T, RA Films: ROBIN LEHMAN, Producer
(Features)
HEARTS AND MINDS,
Touchstone-Audjeff-BBS/Zucker-Jaglom-
Rainbow: PETER DAVIS and BERT SCHNEIDER,
Producers

Foreign Language Film Award
AMARCORD, FC (Rome)-PECF (Paris). (Italy)

Honorary Awards
HOWARD HAWKS, a master American filmmaker whose
creative efforts hold a distinguished place in world cinema.
JEAN RENOIR, a genius who, with grace, responsibility and
enviable devotion through silent film, sound film, feature,
documentary and television, has won the world's
admiration

Special Achievement
Visual Effects: FRANK BRENDEL, GLEN ROBINSON and
ALBERT WHITLOCK for *Earthquake*

Irving G. Thalberg Memorial Award
None

Jean Hersholt Humanitarian Award
ARTHUR B. KRIM

1975

ALL FIVE MAJOR awards in 1975 were swept up by **One Flew Over The Cuckoo's Nest**- Best Picture, Director, Actor, Actress and Screenplay. It was the first time this feat had been achieved since **It Happened One Night** in 1934 (not 1937 as Saul Zaentz's co-producer, Michael Douglas, mis-dated that Columbia classic in his acceptance speech.) Apart from that forgivable slip, this was an auspicious occasion for writer/actor Douglas, son of Kirk, whose first foray into production **One Flew Over The Cuckoo's Nest** was.

The film's success also signified the start of three triumphant years for United Artists, which had begun the 70s with a financial crisis. The company won the Best Film Oscars again in 1976 and 1977, for **Rocky** and **Annie Hall** respectively, although the corporate bubble would burst

a few years later with the financial disaster of **Heaven's Gate**. For the moment, however, the studio could sit back and wait for the money to roll in for their garlanded champ – and it did. *Variety*'s analysis of **One Flew Over The Cuckoo's Nest** gross receipts in 15 cities before and after the Oscar haul revealed a 70 per cent leap.

The film was adapted by Lawrence Hauben and Bo Goldman from Ken Kesey's novel, itself a counter-culture classic, and was directed on a shoestring by the Czech Milos Forman. A film-maker critically esteemed for two films he had made in his native country, the satires **Loves Of A Blonde** (1965) and **The Firemen's Ball** (1967), Forman had arrived in New York in 1969, following the Soviet invasion of Czechoslovakia, to complete the script of his first American feature, **Taking Off** (1971). The Immigration Board, acting on a complaint from the Screen Directors' Guild, nearly prevented him from working in America, but Forman's colleagues Sidney Lumet, Paddy Chayefsky, Mike Nichols and Buck Henry successfully pleaded his case. Forman was disappointed when **Taking Off**, a generation-gap comedy-drama, failed commercially, however, and with a Broadway flop

BELOW *Jack Nicholson as the life-giving, anarchic Randle P. McMurphy in* One Flew Over The Cuckoo's Nest. *Milos Forman's film earned nine nominations and won five Oscars, including Best Picture, Actor, Actress and Director*

to his credit and the threat of expulsion hanging over him he came close to a nervous breakdown. It was then that Zaentz and Douglas approached him to direct **One Flew Over The Cuckoo's Nest**.

"Of course I said yes. I loved the novel from the start and thought it would make a wonderful movie. This showed me that it's much more comfortable to slip into a state of acute depression in America than back home."

The movie was a personal triumph for Forman – one which perfectly demonstrated his special skill in dealing with conflicts between different sets of people, each of whom is well-intentioned but who clash because their ideas and methods are at odds. Randle P. McMurphy – brilliantly played by Jack Nicholson – is a convicted criminal sent from a penal work-farm to a State mental hospital (part of the film was shot at Oregon State Hospital) for observation. Dismayed by the crushed spirits and lethargy of his fellow inmates, the charming, anarchic McMurphy revitalizes them by taking them on illicit sea trips and to parties with girls, but comes up against the cold, unyielding face of the system, as represented by the iron Nurse Ratched (Louise Fletcher). Forman skilfully switches from gentle comedy to farce to chilling tragedy, with McMurphy finally lobotomized for attempting to throttle the nurse – the establishment relentless in its exacting of revenge on transgressors.

Nicholson's extraordinary performance remains central to the actor's career-long identification with the role of the rebel outsider in American society. After four previous nominations – for Best Supporting Actor in **Easy Rider** (1969), as Best Actor in **Five Easy Pieces** (1970), **The Last Detail** (1973) and **Chinatown** (1974) – McMurphy deservedly won him his first Academy Award. Even though he dies, smothered in an act of compassion by the chief (Will Sampson) whose regeneration is the result of McMurphy's crazy, infectious energy, his explosion into a fatal rage against the nurse communicated with film audiences the world over.

Fletcher equally deserved her Best Actress Oscar. An actress with a stop-start career, mostly on TV, she had seemingly abandoned it altogether in the mid-60s when she went to live in London with her then husband, producer Jerry Bick. Back in America in 1974, she got a part in Robert Altman's **Thieves Like Us** and her performance impressed Forman, who cast the actress, at 40, in her first important screen role, although she later said: "When I asked Milos what he'd seen in me, he replied, 'It is something to do with your chin,' which I do not take as a compliment."

In fact, half a dozen better-known actresses, including Anne Bancroft and Angela Lansbury, turned down the role of Nurse Ratched because they regarded her as monstrous. Fletcher later said of the movie, "I felt lonely, lousy and horrible making it because it scared me." But there is no denying the utter conviction she brought to it: Nurse Ratched, though implacable, is not merely a callous woman either, for there is no doubt that she and McMurphy strike sexual sparks off one another as they lock wills.

Fletcher gave a moving acceptance speech when she went up to collect her Oscar – in sign language, the first one ever on the Academy Award stage. This was for the benefit of her parents; her father had been deaf since being struck by lightning at the age of seven, and her mother since a childhood illness. It was "a lovely moment," wrote Addison Verrill, "that would have brought tears to the eyes of Nurse Ratched."

One Flew Over The Cuckoo's Nest has proved the

ABOVE *Nurse Ratched (Louise Fletcher) and patient Randle P. McMurphy (Jack Nicholson) in one of their taut confrontations in Milos Forman's* One Flew Over The Cuckoo's Nest. *The movie won all the major awards for the year*

RIGHT *Goldie Hawn (left), Lee Grant (seated) and Warren Beatty in* Shampoo, *which dealt with the sexual exploits of a West Coast hairdresser (Beatty) and his clients. Miss Grant won the Best Supporting Actress award for her performance*

ABOVE *Much loved old-timer George Burns (left) was a popular choice as Best Supporting Actor for* The Sunshine Boys. *His 'elderly' co-star is Walter Matthau, skilfully made-up for his role*

highpoint of this actress' career, although it might be worth noting that she is capable of a fine line in comedy, as demonstrated in **The Cheap Detective** (1978), as well as in tragedy.

Will Sampson can consider himself unlucky not to have been nominated for a Best Supporting actor award for his giant Indian – mute, it seems, from choice – who bursts away from the asylum at the end; Brad Dourif, who played the stuttering inmate whose fatal tryst with one of McMurphy's whores brings on the terrible climax of **One Flew Over The Cuckoo's Nest**, was. He lost out, however, to a moving performance by George Burns, the slightly more sympathetic of two curmudgeonly old comics – a long-separated double act reunited after 11 years for a TV gala – in Herbert Ross's **The Sunshine Boys.** Walter Matthau, though he had only marginally the bigger part, was nominated for a Best Actor award.

Despite the Academy's tendency to nominate hitherto unrewarded actors in the twilight of their careers, there is little doubt that Burns – who at 80 became the oldest performer to win an Oscar, and whose age remains the key joke in his TV act – won on merit. It might be argued that Matthau had to age considerably to play Willie Clark (the bane of nephew Richard Benjamin's life) and therefore had a harder task than Burns, who more or less played Al Lewis straight, but there are no question marks against the latter's mastery of comic timing and understatement, and the pair of them delivered Neil Simon's barbs, insults and *non sequiturs* to marvelous effect. Burns had first appeared on the screen, with his partner and wife Gracie Allen, in 1932, and thought he'd given up movies in 1939. So this Oscar-winning performance was the comeback of comebacks.

Best Supporting Actress for 1975 was Lee Grant (a nominee in 1951 and 1970), memorable as a politician's wife pulling her panties off over her boots as she gets ready for her hairdresser lover (Warren Beatty), in Hal Ashby's **Shampoo**, a sex-and-social comedy that hasn't stood the test of time. Stanley Kubrick's lavish, beautifully conceived – but ultimately soulless – 18th-century costume drama, **Barry Lyndon**, missed out in the major categories but scooped the year's technical awards (Best

Cinematography, Art Direction and Set Decoration, Costume Design and Music Scoring Adaptation). Robert Altman's sprawling portmanteau satire on singers, fans and politicians converging on the Grand Old Opry in **Nashville** – now regarded as a masterpiece – deserved more than just one Oscar (for Keith Carradine's laidback song 'I'm Easy'). But nothing – not even Best Actress nominee Ann-Margret cavorting around in a swamp of baked beans in **Tommy** – could deflect the true glory away from **One Flew Over The Cuckoo's Nest**.

WINNERS 1975

Nominations Announced: February 17, 1976
Awards Ceremony: March 29, 1976
Dorothy Chandler Pavilion, Los Angeles County
Music Center

Best Picture
ONE FLEW OVER THE CUCKOO'S NEST, Fantasy/UA:
SAUL ZAENTZ and MICHAEL DOUGLAS, Producers

Actor
JACK NICHOLSON in *One Flew Over The Cuckoo's Nest*

Actress
LOUISE FLETCHER in *One Flew Over The Cuckoo's Nest*

Supporting Actor
GEORGE BURNS in *The Sunshine Boys*, Stark/MGM

Supporting Actress
LEE GRANT in *Shampoo*, Rubeeker/Columbia

Directing
MILOS FORMAN for *One Flew Over The Cuckoo's Nest*

Writing
(Best Original Screenplay)
DOG DAY AFTERNOON, Warner Bros.: FRANK PIERSON
(Best Screenplay adapted from other material)
ONE FLEW OVER THE CUCKOO'S NEST
Screenplay: LAWRENCE HAUBEN and BO GOLDMAN

Cinematography
BARRY LYNDON, Hawk/Warner Bros.: JOHN ALCOTT

Art Direction-Set Decoration
BARRY LYNDON: KEN ADAM and ROY WALKER
Set Decoration: VERNON DIXON

Sound
JAWS, Universal-Zanuck-Brown: ROBERT L. HOYT,
ROGER HEMAN, EARL MADERY and JOHN CARTER

Film Editing
JAWS: VERNA FIELDS

Music
(Best Original Score)
JAWS: JOHN WILLIAMS
(Best Scoring: Original Song Score and/or Adaptation)
BARRY LYNDON
Adaptation: LEONARD ROSENMAN

(Best Original Song)
I'M EASY from *Nashville*,
ABC-Weintraub-Altman/Paramount
Music & Lyrics: KEITH CARRADINE

Costume Design
BARRY LYNDON: ULLA-BRITT SODERLAND and
MILENA CANONERO

Short Films
(Animated Films)
GREAT, Grantstern – British Lion: BOB GODFREY,
Producer
(Live Action)
ANGEL AND BIG JOE, Salzman: BERT SALZMAN,
Producer

Documentary
(Short Subjects)
THE END OF THE GAME, Opus: CLAIRE WILBUR and
ROBIN LEHMAN, Producers
(Features)
THE MAN WHO SKIED DOWN EVEREST, Crawley: F.R.
CRAWLEY; JAMES HAGER and DALE HARTLEBEN,
Producers

Foreign Language Film Award
DERSU UZALA, Mosfilms (USSR)

Honorary Award
MARY PICKFORD in recognition of her unique
contributions to the film industry and the development of
film as an artistic medium

Special Achievement
Sound Effects: PETER BERKOS for *The Hindenburg*,
Wise-Filmakers-Universal
Visual Effects: ALBERT WHITLOCK and GLEN
ROBINSON for *The Hindenburg*

Irving G. Thalberg Memorial Award
MERVYN LeROY

Jean Hersholt Humanitarian Award
JULES C. STEIN

1976

WILLIAM FRIEDKIN – OSCAR-winning director of **The French Connection** in 1971 – attempted, as producer of the 1976 Academy Award gala, to streamline the whole unwieldy business. Out went the telecast shots of the stars arriving in their limos and the crowds of fans awaiting them; out went the dual presenters, envelope routines and superfluous starlet attendants. *Variety* described the sets as "futuristic" – an improvement on old Hollywood decor – perhaps in keeping with **Logan's Run**, a meretricious movie that won the award for Best Special Visual Effects.

What Friedkin hadn't bargained for was a surfeit of bad taste in the 'humor' of some of the presenters. Freed from the constraints of the scripted cue-card patter, several of them were very vulgar indeed. Richard Pryor deadpanned some dubious black jokes and mouthed a 'Holy Shit'; Marty Feldman made some quips about God and Oscar's private parts, failed to call out the nominees for Best Live Action Short (this was left to the *winners* to do), and sent one of the awards toppling to the floor. Worst of all, according to *Variety*, was the writer Norman Mailer, introduced by Jane Fonda to present the screenplay Oscars. Mailer's story about Voltaire attending a gay whorehouse seemed both inappropriate and uncalled for. Much more palatable was Red Skelton's comedy routine and a stunning opening musical number by Ann-Margret which exuded class.

Three of the year's acting Oscars went to performers in the same film, **Network**, only the second time this has happened since the Supporting Actor and Actress awards were introduced in 1936. No film has claimed four Oscar-winning performances, but in 1951 **A Streetcar Named Desire** – with wins for Best Actress Vivien Leigh, Karl Malden and Kim Hunter – had missed out only on the Best Actor prize, with nominee Marlon Brando losing out to Humphrey Bogart in **The African Queen.**

Network went one spot higher by seizing the top two acting awards – Peter Finch was Best Actor, Faye Dunaway was Best Actress – and a supporting award, too, for stage actress Beatrice Straight, who had just one scene in the film as William Holden's neglected wife. Holden – Best Actor in 1953 for **Stalag 17** – was nominated beside Finch as Best Actor; and Ned Beatty, **Network**'s angry chairman of the board, was a Best Supporting Actor nominee – but wasn't fortunate enough to complete the quartet of on-screen winners.

Sidney Lumet, one of the best American directors never to win an Academy Award, received his third nomination for **Network**, and its writer Paddy Chayefsky won his third screenplay award. Seldom has an Oscar-winning script been so vicious. A satire on commercial television, **Network** must still cause the heads of America's broadcast stations to wake shivering in the night. Finch played Howard Beale, an anchor-man at the fictitious UBS network who is fired because his ratings have been slipping. Appearing live before the cameras on his last appearance, Beale goes crazy, cruelly mocks his bosses and threatens to commit suicide in front of the nation, immortalizing the line, "I'm mad as hell and I'm not going to take it anymore."

It was a tyrannical, ranting performance from Finch, and had an awful prophetic truth about it. His biographer Trader Faulkner wrote, "Peter Finch released within himself a force, a terrible rage which suddenly seemed to be using him. The force releasing itself through him was of a far greater dimension than the conception of the character as it had been written. As a result of this role Finch was rocketed to total American stardom . . . only to burn out like a meteor."

Finch, who had also been nominated for his homosexual doctor in **Sunday, Bloody Sunday** in 1971, died in early 1977. He was the third actor to be posthumously nominated, following James Dean for **East Of Eden** (1955) and **Giant** (1956) and Spencer Tracy for **Guess Who's Coming To Dinner** (1967), but the first to win. Liv Ullmann announced his award, and it was Chayefsky who urged the actor's widow, Eletha, carrying a small bouquet, to come and collect it in perhaps the most emotional moment of the 1976 ceremony. When Jack Nicholson introduced the clips from the Best Film nominees, that from **Network** unfortunately showed Finch at his moment of collapse – a dark instance of art mocking life.

ABOVE *British actor Peter Finch was rewarded with the Best Actor Oscar for his powerful performance as an executive victim of the rat-race in* Network. *With him, Best Actress Faye Dunaway who played the ballsy, heartless, woman-in-a-man's-world* RIGHT *William Holden was nominated for Best Actor in* Network, *but lost out to fellow star Peter Finch. Beatrice Straight, however, not well-known to movie audiences, captured the supporting actress award*

Faye Dunaway received her Best Actress statuette from last year's winner Louise Fletcher, having previously been nominated for her Bonnie Parker in **Bonnie And Clyde** (1967) and her Evelyn Mulwray in **Chinatown** (1974). For all Finch's histrionics and William Holden's subtler playing of a weary and sentimental news chief, it was Dunaway who gave Chayefsky's script its rapier thrust. Frequently an implacable bitch in her films, Dunaway was superb as the ruthless programming executive, Diane Christenson, who manipulates Beale into his tragic announcement in order to rocket the ratings, which it does. "She was the nerve centre of the film," David Thomson commented in his *Biographical Dictionary of the Cinema*, "agitated, sensation-seeking and as cold as TV itself. At the same time, she was a believable neurotic career-woman . . ."

The other Oscar-winning actor in 1976 was Jason Robards Jr for his over-the-top portrayal of *Washington Post* editor Ben Bradlee in **All The President's Men**, the heavily tipped Watergate drama which also won for William Goldman's Best Screenplay Adaptation, Best Art Direction and Best Sound and was a candidate, too, for Best Film, and Best Direction by Alan J. Pakula. But everything lost out in the Best Picture stakes to the rags-

to-riches story of the decade, **Rocky**, which also won for direction and editing, and earned Best Actor and Best Original Screenplay nominations for its young creator Sylvester Stallone, a Best Actress nod for Talia Shire as Rocky's shy girlfriend Adrian, and Best Supporting Actor nominations for Burgess Meredith and Burt Young as Rocky's manager and Adrian's brother.

In his book *Adventures in the Screen Trade*, William Goldman cited three reasons for **Rocky**'s success — its good reviews, its spectacular business and its heroic fulfilment of the American Dream in the way Stallone got it made and turned himself into an overnight phenomenon. Everyone likes a winner, and both Stallone and Rocky Balboa fitted the bill.

Rocky's arrival is Hollywood folklore now. Stallone was a 'difficult' child but had enough athletic prowess to win a scholarship to an American college in Switzerland, later studying drama at the University of Miami. He worked off-Broadway, as a cinema usher, did a commercial for Rapid Shave and a soft-core porn film, **A Party At**

ABOVE *Bloody but unbowed, Rocky Balboa (Sylvester Stallone, left) takes on world heavyweight champion Apollo Creed (Carl Weathers) in* Rocky, *the year's Best Picture, and the first of what would be a fortune-grossing series about the underdog-made-good*

Kitty And Studs. But he was also writing scripts, played a subway thug menacing Woody Allen in **Bananas**, and in 1974 got a lead part in the New York comedy **The Lords Of Flatbush**. More small parts followed in Hollywood, but Stallone was short of cash and his wife was expecting a baby. In three days he drafted a script for a boxing movie, **Rocky**, and instead of selling it to independent producers Robert Chartoff and Irwin Winkler for $265,000 held out for $70,000, a percentage of the profits and the lead part.

Directed by John G. Avildsen, who was at home with the film's low $1 million budget and duly earned himself the Best Director Oscar for his tight, economical handling of Stallone's screenplay, **Rocky** became the first sport film to win the Best Picture award. It is the story of a down-at-heel, punch-drunk young club fighter with little hope of making the big-time who, as part of a publicity stunt, gets a crack at Apollo Creed's world heavyweight title in Philadelphia.

Rocky, who by day works for a loan shark, is chosen as Creed's fall-guy – 'the Italian Stallion' as he is billed will be allowed to go three rounds with the champ before being knocked out. But Rocky, encouraged by his manager and his love for Adrian, throws himself into his training like never before. And he manages to go the distance, drawing with Creed in the superbly filmed fight climax.

The message was clear – a punk from the backstreets *can* be a contender, or even a champion. But the simple naivety of the story was artfully contrived by Stallone, who'd accurately guessed that America would respond to this 50s-style fable dressed up for the 1970s. There would be three more *Rockys*, with Stallone in the director's chair, but by the time of **Rocky IV** in 1985 the character had become a figure of absurdity and there were no more Oscars in sight. Meanwhile, Stallone – with **Rambo** in tow – laughed all the way to the bank.

WINNERS 1976

Nominations Announced: February 10, 1977
Awards Ceremony: March 28, 1977
Dorothy Chandler Pavilion, Los Angeles County
Music Center

Best Picture
ROCKY, Chartoff-Winkler/UA: IRWIN WINKLER and
ROBERT CHARTOFF, Producers

Actor
PETER FINCH in *Network*, Gottfried-Chayefsky/MGM-UA

Actress
FAYE DUNAWAY in *Network*

Supporting Actor
JASON ROBARDS in *All The President's Men*,
Wildwood/Warner Bros.

Supporting Actress
BEATRICE STRAIGHT in *Network*

Directing
JOHN G. AVILDSEN for *Rocky*

Writing
(Best Screenplay – written directly for the screen)
NETWORK
Story & Screenplay: PADDY CHAYEFSKY
(Best Screenplay – based on material from another medium)
ALL THE PRESIDENT'S MEN
Screenplay: WILLIAM GOLDMAN

Cinematography
BOUND FOR GLORY, Bound For Glory/UA: HASKELL
WEXLER

Art Direction-Set Decoration
ALL THE PRESIDENT'S MEN: GEORGE JENKINS
Set Decoration: GEORGE GAINES

Sound
ALL THE PRESIDENT'S MEN: ARTHUR PIANTADOSI,
LES FRESHOLTZ, DICK ALEXANDER and JIM WEBB

Film Editing
ROCKY: RICHARD HALSEY and SCOTT CONRAD

Music
(Best Original Score)
THE OMEN, 20th Century-Fox: JERRY GOLDSMITH
(Best Original Song Score and Its Adaptation or Best
Adaptation Score)
BOUND FOR GLORY
Adaptation: LEONARD ROSENMAN

(Best Original Song)
EVERGREEN (LOVE THEME) from *A Star Is Born*,
Barwood-Peters/First Artists/Warner Bros.
Music: BARBRA STREISAND
Lyrics: PAUL WILLIAMS

Costume Design
FELLINI'S CASANOVA, APEA-Produzioni Europee
Associate SpA/Universal: DANILO DONATI

Short Films
(Animated Films)
LEISURE, Film Australia: SUZANNE BAKER, Producer
(Live Action)
IN THE REGION OF ICE, American Film Institute:
ANDRE GUTTFREUND and PETER WERNER, Producers

Documentary
(Short Subjects)
NUMBER OUR DAYS, Community Television of Southern
California: LYNNE LITTMAN, Producer
(Features)
HARLAN COUNTY, USA, Cabin Creek: BARBARA
KOPPLE, Producer

Foreign Language Film Award
BLACK AND WHITE IN COLOR, Cohn/Société Ivoirienne
de Cinéma (Ivory Coast)

Honorary Awards
None

Special Achievement
Visual Effects: CARLO RAMBALDI, GLEN ROBINSON and
FRANK VAN DER VEER for *King Kong*, De Laurentiis/
Paramount
Visual Effects: L.B. ABBOTT, GLEN ROBINSON and
MATTHEW YURICICH for *Logan's Run*, David/MGM

Irving G. Thalberg Memorial Award
PANDRO S. BERMAN

Jean Hersholt Humanitarian Award
None

1977

THE ACADEMY AWARDS' golden anniversary show began with clips of past and present arrivals at the Dorothy Chandler Pavilion and a dance number, 'Look How Far We've Come', led by Debbie Reynolds and featuring a parade of Academy winners, some of them very old. "It looks like the road company of the Hollywood Wax Museum," quipped Bob Hope, M.C. for the 22nd time, whose lines were especially caustic on this occasion. "Welcome to the real Star Wars," was his opening gambit, followed by, "Sure they have their Oscars, but are they happy?"

Hope was 75 in 1978 and had never won an Oscar himself for his acting, although it was a standing Hollywood joke that he lusted after one of the golden statuettes, which he described as "a bookend with a sneer." "I'm very happy to be here for my annual insult," he said in 1940, his first year as a presenter, and added in 1968, "Welcome to the Academy Awards or – as it's known in my house – Passover." The Academy has, in fact, honored Hope five times with various awards, including a special Oscar in 1952, a Jean Hersholt Humanitarian Award in 1959 – and a joke one-inch statuette in 1946. He also sang the award-winning song from **The Big Broadcast Of 1938** – 'Thanks for the Memory' – which became his personal theme.

A film starring another American comedian (and one of Hope's biggest admirers), but one who had also taken his talent behind the camera, dominated the 1977 Awards ceremony, although on that evening of 3 April 1978 Woody Allen chose to be 3000 miles away, playing Dixieland jazz on his clarinet in Michael's Bar on New York's East Side. Allen's **Annie Hall** was voted Best Picture, he was Best Director (and a Best Actor nominee), Diane Keaton – its leading lady – was Best Actress, while Allen and Marshall Brickman shared the Best Original Screenplay award.

Allen had stated in advance that he wouldn't attend the awards, giving shyness as the reason for his absence (though he has also criticized the notion of films competing against one another). Paradoxically, **Annie Hall** – a major departure from the 'funnier' spoofs he had hitherto

BELOW *Landlord (Marsha Mason) and tenant (Richard Dreyfuss) were the adversaries who became lovers in Neil Simon's* The Goodbye Girl, *a stringent comedy of New York life which won Dreyfuss the Best Actor award. Miss Mason, Mr Simon, and the movie were unlucky nominees*

directed – is a strongly autobiographical film, a 'serious' comedy that parades its maker's own neuroses and the progress of his own true-life love affair with Keaton. It was also the first comedy to be voted the Best Picture since the equally bittersweet **The Apartment** in 1960. **Annie Hall** capitalized on the vogue for sexual anxiety in the late 70s, and the tendency for every American couple to examine their relationship from within – frequently taking it to the analyst's couch. **Annie Hall** was, probably, the sharpest and wittiest film to trace the familiar pattern of falling in love, breaking up, reconciling and parting for a final time.

Woody plays Alvy Singer, a successful Jewish New York comedian who, at a Manhattan tennis club, is introduced to Annie Hall, a nervy songstress. Their subsequent banal chat disguises their hesitancy and self-doubt (cleverly conveyed by 'interior' subtitles). They embark on a 'nervous romance' – as the film's poster describes it – and Alvy seeks, Svengali-style, to further Annie's career and her cultural awareness. We also get glimpses of their earlier lives, in which Woody/Alvy's Jewishness emerges as a social weight for him to carry around. It turns out that he has already been 16 years in analysis when he meets Annie.

Eventually Alvy becomes jealous of Annie's friendship with a recording tycoon (Paul Simon); she moves out, gets lonely, and moves back in. They travel to LA, attend one of the tycoon's parties and, on their way back to New York, agree to part. Alvy desperately tries to win Annie back, but it is too late. He writes a play about their affair in which she returns to him, but when they chance on each other a year later they agree to stay just friends. It is exactly that kind of wish-fulfillment in Alvy's play that also gives the film some of its brightest moments. One brilliantly conceived gag has Alvy losing his temper with a movie-bore waffling ignorantly on about Marshall McLuhan as they stand in a cinema line and immediately producing McLuhan in person to put down the poseur. This kind of pretentiousness and bogus intellectualism is another of Allen's targets in **Annie Hall**, many of the themes of which he repeated in **Manhattan** (1979) and **Stardust Memories** (1980).

This was Diane Keaton's fourth film with Allen – and there would be more. As Annie Hall, she is kooky, affectionate and troubled. Looking back on her role in the film, we remember her less for the intensity of her feelings than for the nostalgic value of her jittery presence among the arty set and her gauche outpourings. It was a warm and touching performance and Keaton – in jacket, scarf and buttonhole – even turned up to collect her Oscar, and appeared overjoyed to do so.

The unlucky Best Actress nominees in 1977 were Marsha Mason in **The Goodbye Girl** (unlucky too, in 1973, 1979 and 1981 when she was nominated in the same category for her work in **Cinderella Liberty, Chapter Two**, and **Only When I Laugh**), Jane Fonda in **Julia**, and Anne Bancroft and Shirley Maclaine for **The Turning Point**, which achieved the dubious distinction of becoming the film to win the most nominations – 11 – without

netting a single award. For **Julia**, though, there was a major consolation, with the Best Supporting Actor award for Jason Robards – entering the record books as the first supporting player to win an Oscar for two years running – its distaff equivalent for Vanessa Redgrave, and a Best Screenplay Adaptation award for Alvin Sargent.

In Fred Zinnemann's stylishly made but evasive study of the pact between playwright Lillian Hellman (Fonda) and her friend Julia, the performances (with Robards as Hellman's lover, thriller-writer Dashiell Hammett) were uniformly excellent. The political commitment of the two women, who unite to smuggle money into Germany to rescue persecuted Jews, perhaps gained extra power from our knowledge of two actresses who have both been politically active. Redgrave chose to make a political

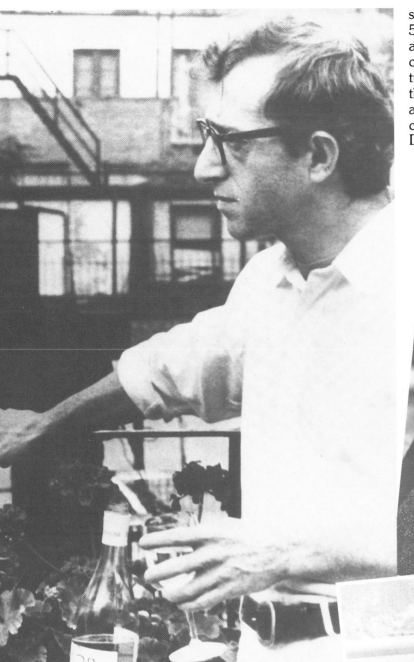

statement in front of an estimated 300,000,000 viewers in 50 countries. She had been much criticized for producing and acting in Roy Battersby's **The Palestinians**, a film considered by many to be anti-Semitic, and she now turned her Oscar acceptance speech into a thank you to those who had voted for her despite Zionist threats against them, and a tribute to Palestinian resistance to fascism and oppression. Outside, a protest by the Jewish Defense League was countered by a PLO demo. Later, in

ABOVE *Diane Keaton, here with Woody Allen in* Annie Hall, *set a new fashion trend as well as winning the Best Actress Oscar. Allen was nominated for his performance, and won for direction, screenplay and Best Picture*

TOP RIGHT *The politically controversial Vanessa Redgrave provokes no disagreement where her sublime screen acting abilities are concerned. Here, in a scene from* Julia, *for which she was named Best Supporting Actress*

RIGHT *Writers Dashiell Hammett (Jason Robards) and Lillian Hellman (Jane Fonda) share one of the few tranquil moments in* Julia. *Miss Fonda was a Best Actress nominee, while Robards was voted Best Supporting Actor for the second successive year*

the auditorium, Paddy Chayefsky rebuked Miss Redgrave: "We are sick and tired of people exploiting the Academy Awards for the propagation of their own personal propaganda. I would suggest to Miss Redgrave that her winning (an Oscar) is not a pivotal moment in history, that no proclamation was needed. Just a simple 'Thank you' would have sufficed."

This was also the year of Darth Vader, Luke Skywalker and Han Solo, but it was the non-human characters – R2-D2 and C-3PO – in George Lucas's box-office champion **Star Wars** that particularly helped the picture to a top haul of seven wins: Best Art Direction, Costume Design, Sound, Editing, Music Score, Visual Effects, Sound Effects Creations. Among these were a third Oscar for composer John Williams, and a Special Achievement Award to Benjamin Burtt for giving the robots and alien creatures their bleeps, burps and whirrs. In the top categories, **Star Wars** was a Best Film nominee, George Lucas was a Best Director nominee and Alec Guinness, who played Ben [Obi-Wan] Kenobi, was up for Best Supporting Actor. **Star Wars**' big rival, **Close Encounters Of The Third Kind**, fared no better in main awards, despite nods for Melinda Dillon as Best Supporting Actress (an award she was desperately unlucky not to win in 1981 when again nominated for **Absence Of Malice**) and Steven Spielberg for Best Direction. In another year, Spielberg's film might have won the lot; but now it had to be content with Frank Warner's Best Sound Effects Editing Oscar and Vilmos Zsigmond's award for his awesome cinematography.

Richard Dreyfuss, surprisingly, was not even nominated for his lead performance in *Close Encounters* but, instead, won the Best Actor Oscar for **The Goodbye Girl**. The youngest man to win the award (he was 29), he was ideally cast as aspiring actor Elliott Garfield who becomes a tenant in the Manhattan tenement apartment of ex-dancer Paula McFadden (Marsha Mason) and her precocious pre-pubescent daughter (Best Supporting Actress nominee Quinn Cummings). It's not a happy set-up: Paula's departing lover has sublet the room without her knowledge, and sparks naturally fly between her and the amiably aggressive Garfield. Directed by Herbert Ross from a screenplay by Neil Simon (Mason's then husband), this unassuming comedy offers up another of Simon's odd couples who find an eventual compatibility – romance blossoms – but not until he has been rudely awakened by having to play a gay Richard III on stage and she has been mugged. The part might have been written for Dreyfuss: chubby, stubborn and capable of great warmth. He was all smiles collecting his Oscar – and as unshaven offscreen as on – though he might have been considering himself lucky to have outflanked his fellow nominees: seventh-time loser Richard Burton (**Equus**), John Travolta (**Saturday Night Fever**), Woody Allen, and Marcello Mastroianni (**A Special Day**).

BELOW *No longer the ravishing sex symbol in full bloom of* Room At The Top *which won her the Best Actress award in 1958, the still nevertheless magnetically powerful Simone Signoret starred in* Madame Rosa, *the Best Foreign Language Film*

WINNERS 1977

Nominations Announced: February 21, 1978
Awards Ceremony: April 3, 1978
Dorothy Chandler Pavilion, Los Angeles County
Music Center

Best Picture
ANNIE HALL, Rollins-Joffe/UA: CHARLES H. JOFFE,
Producer

Actor
RICHARD DREYFUSS in *The Goodbye Girl*,
Stark/MGM-Warner Bros.

Actress
DIANE KEATON in *Annie Hall*

Supporting Actor
JASON ROBARDS in *Julia*, 20th Century-Fox

Supporting Actress
VANESSA REDGRAVE in *Julia*

Directing
WOODY ALLEN for *Annie Hall*

Writing
(Best Screenplay – written directly for the screen)
ANNIE HALL
Story & Screenplay: WOODY ALLEN and MARSHALL
BRICKMAN
(Best Screenplay – based on material from another medium)
JULIA
Screenplay: ALVIN SARGENT

Cinematography
CLOSE ENCOUNTERS OF THE THIRD KIND, Close
Encounters/Columbia:
VILMOS ZSIGMOND

Art Direction-Set Decoration
STAR WARS, 20th Century-Fox: JOHN BARRY, NORMAN
REYNOLDS and LESLIE DILLEY
Set Decoration: ROGER CHRISTIAN

Sound
STAR WARS: DON MacDOUGALL, RAY WEST, BOB
MINKLER and DEREK BALL

Film Editing
STAR WARS: PAUL HIRSCH, MARCIA LUCAS and
RICHARD CHEW

Music
(Best Original Score)
STAR WARS: JOHN WILLIAMS
(Best Original Song Score and Its Adaptation or Best
Adaptation Score)
A LITTLE NIGHT MUSIC, Sascha-Wien-Kastner/New
World
Adaptation: JONATHAN TUNICK

(Best Original Song)
YOU LIGHT UP MY LIFE from *You Light Up My Life*,
Session/Columbia
Music & Lyrics: JOSEPH BROOKS

Costume Design
STAR WARS: JOHN MOLLO

Short Films
(Animated)
SAND CASTLE, National Film Board of Canada:
CO HOEDEMAN, Producer
(Live Action)
I'LL FIND A WAY, National Film Board of Canada:
BEVERLY SHAFFER and YUKI YOSHIDA, Producers

Documentary
(Short Subjects)
GRAVITY IS MY ENEMY, Joseph: JOHN JOSEPH and JAN
STUSSY, Producers
(Features)
WHO ARE THE DeBOLTS? AND WHERE DID THEY GET
NINETEEN KIDS?, Korty-Schulz-Sanrio: JOHN KORTY,
DAN McCANN and WARREN L. LOCKHART, Producers

Foreign Language Film Award
MADAME ROSA, Lira (France)

Visual Effects
STAR WARS: JOHN STEARS, JOHN DYKSTRA,
RICHARD EDLUND, GRANT McCUNE and ROBERT
BLALACK

Honorary Award
MARGARET BOOTH for sixty-two years of exceptionally
distinguished service to the motion picture industry as a film
editor

Special Achievement Awards
Sound Effects: BENJAMIN BURTT Jr for the creation of the
alien, creature, and robot voices in *Star Wars*
Sound Effects Editing Award: CLOSE ENCOUNTERS OF
THE THIRD KIND: FRANK WARNER, Supervising Sound
Effects Editor

Irving G. Thalberg Memorial Award
WALTER MIRISCH

Jean Hersholt Humanitarian Award
CHARLTON HESTON

1978

THE 1978 ACADEMY Awards were expected to be a two-horse race between Warren Beatty and Buck Henry's fantasy **Heaven Can Wait**, a big hit, and Michael Cimino's Vietnam War drama **The Deer Hunter**, nominated nine times apiece. But **Heaven Can Wait** won in just one category, Best Art Direction, as the traumas of America's returning Vietnam veterans moved to the center of the Academy stage.

Hollywood had been reluctant to come to grips with the war, which had ended in 1975, probably because it was an issue that had divided the nation and, in commercial terms, was therefore bound to offend and alienate a major section of the potential audience. The film-making community split itself between the hawks like John Wayne, whose **The Green Berets** was the first and most right-wing of the Vietnam War movies and the doves such as Jane Fonda, who made her **Vietnam Journey** to Hanoi on behalf of the anti-war movement. As it was, both attended the 1978 Awards ceremony in triumph, although for very different reasons. By the late 70s the cinema could no longer afford to turn a blind eye to the war as a major subject, even if it did tend to dress it up in myths. Although neither **The Deer Hunter** nor **Coming Home**, the film which turned out to be its main Oscar rival,

is primarily a combat movie, each reveals the scars, both physical and mental, left behind by Nam and the extent to which US soldiers' experiences there had entered the national consciousness; they won five and three Oscars respectively.

Michael Cimino had directed only one film, **Thunderbolt And Lightfoot** for Clint Eastwood's Malpaso company, before he embarked on **The Deer Hunter**, comparatively an epic, which focuses on the lives of three steelworkers – Michael (Robert De Niro), Nick (Christopher Walken) and Steven (John Savage) – before and after their Vietnam tour. Using the camera as an observer, Cimino allows the narrative to unfold in an almost documentary style, and if **The Deer Hunter** proves a huge and unwieldy exploration of a uniquely tragic American experience, it is also stunning in its detail and drama.

In the first half of the film, two long scenes introduce us to the characters and, perhaps, their potential for dealing with the horrors they will face in the jungle. The movie begins – on the eve of the friends' departure – with Steven's wedding, an elaborate ceremony followed by a huge, high-spirited party, at which Nick is the life and soul, Michael largely a shy bystander attracted to Nick's girl Linda (Meryl Streep) and Steven the gauche and drunken groom. Their deer-hunting expedition the following day in the mountains, with their undrafted buddies, enables Michael, the ace hunter with a single-minded and ruthless instinct for survival, to come to the fore. In the brief sequence in Vietnam – in which the three

BELOW *In a year of hard-hitting material, Alan Parker's harsh, uncompromising indictment of the Turkish prison system,* Midnight Express, *lost out on major awards. Parker, the movie, and John Hurt were nominated, and the film won for Best Screenplay adaptation and Best Score. Illustrated, left to right, prison inmates Randy Quaid, Brad Davis and Hurt*

ABOVE *Michael Cimino's disturbing examination of the effects of the Vietnam War, The Deer Hunter, received nine Academy nominations, and was voted Best Picture. Robert De Niro (center), here with John Savage (right), was a deserved Best Actor nominee, but he lost out to Jon Voight, also playing a Vietnam-scarred soldier*

friends are forced to take part in a game of Russian roulette by their Vietcong captors – it is only Michael's ability to avoid being crushed by the terror of the situation itself, and to meet the enemy on its own terms, that keeps the three from instant death. This was the most savage and talked-about scene from any film released in 1978-79, and it has been strongly criticized for its depiction of the Vietcong as the incarnation of evil, without comment on the American tactics. Later, the film dwells on the return of Michael and Steven – the latter wrecked in body and spirit – to their hometown; while Nick carries on with gamblers' games of Russian roulette in Vietnam.

A powerful indictment of what war does to men – as powerful as **The Best Years Of Our Lives** which did the

same job for World War II and won seven Oscars in 1946 – **The Deer Hunter** finally topples over into crude sentimentality and unctuous patriotism, with Michael and Steven and their friends, having buried Nick who tried one shot too many, sitting around a table and singing 'God Bless America'. The scene typifies Cimino's final lack of restraint – even if it may have endeared him to the patriotic among the Academy's voters.

The Deer Hunter won for Best Picture and Michael Cimino for Best Director. If, ultimately, he deserved it over fellow nominees Beatty and Henry, Hal Ashby for **Coming Home**, Woody Allen for the coldly Bergmanesque **Interiors**, and Alan Parker for **Midnight Express**, then it was because **The Deer Hunter** is very much a director's film – even if it was one that should have warned United Artists about Cimino's undisciplined talent, next to be let loose on **Heaven's Gate**.

That Cimino was presented with his directorial award by Francis Ford Coppola – with actress Ali MacGraw – provides another irony. **The Deer Hunter** was released before Coppola's own masterly Vietnam War epic

Apocalypse Now, which eventually qualified for the 1979 Oscars and, inexplicably, won in only two technical categories. **Apocalypse Now** is a film that addresses many of the questions about the war – notably the American forces' own horrific methods – that **The Deer Hunter** shirks, and without any concessions to sentiment. Coppola's disappointment was a year off, but he had lost out to Cimino in the race to get his film to market and may have realized that the Academy wasn't going to keep the Vietnam War in the Oscar frame for another year. Whatever the reason, he was noticeably nervous at the ceremony and kept scratching his ear.

For a second time Robert De Niro was nominated for a Best Actor award for playing a Vietnam 'vet' – following his urban avenger, Travis Bickle, in **Taxi Driver** in 1976 – and for a second time lost out, although it is hard to believe that his performance as Michael, a work of great interior acting (for the deer hunter has thoughts and feelings beyond words), could have been bettered. Meryl Streep, too, was an unlucky nominee as Best Supporting Actress; her Linda – breaking down in tears at the store where she works – was the only real indication in **The** **Deer Hunter** that women, as well as their menfolk, were scarred by the war. Christopher Walken fared better in the Best Supporting Actor category, Nick's attractive personality making his torment by his Vietcong torturers and his resulting disintegration all the more chilling. **The Deer Hunter** also won for Best Editing and Best Sound.

"Tonight I shall have the Oscar, but for (some) the war still goes on . . . " said Nancy Dowd, summing up the general feeling at the ceremony, as she accepted the prize for Best Original Screenplay, shared with Waldo Salt and Robert Jones for **Coming Home**. It was given to her, with some jubilation, by presenter Jon Voight, whom their work helped to the Best Actor Oscar. Voight's own acceptance speech graciously acknowledged his fellow nominees – De Niro, Beatty, the sentimental nod to Laurence Olivier for **The Boys From Brazil**, and the outsider Gary Busey for **The Buddy Holly Story** – and he gave an

BELOW *This was very much the year when Hollywood examined America's legacy from the Vietnam War. Jane Fonda and Jon Voight won the best acting statuettes for their finely judged performances in Hal Ashby's* Coming Home

over-the-top display of emotion when Olivier was awarded a special Oscar "for the full body of his work, the unique achievements of his entire career and his lifetime of contribution to the art of film".

Voight's performance as a crippled soldier was excellent, even if the film truly belongs to Jane Fonda, winner of her second Best Actress award. (It was the first time since **It Happened One Night** in 1934 that an on-screen romantic pairing had won the top two acting awards). It was through Fonda's efforts that the film got made, and it was the professional culmination of her fight against the war. In **Coming Home** Fonda plays Sally, who becomes a voluntary helper at a Vietnam veterans' hospital when her husband Bob (Bruce Dern) is sent to Vietnam, and befriends Luke Martin (Voight) whose war injuries have confined him to a wheelchair. His fellow patient Billy, brother of Sally's friend Vi (Penelope Milford, nominated as Best Supporting Actress), kills himself and Luke protests by chaining himself to the Marine Recruit Centre. Sally gets him out of jail and they become lovers. Bob, returning home a hero but having wounded himself, confronts Luke, is decorated and he, too, commits suicide.

Unobtrusively directed by Ashby, **Coming Home** was a melodrama that seemed to touch the hearts of the nation, perhaps especially those of the women whose menfolk had suffered or died. The film's central dilemmas – especially those faced by Sally – have profound political resonances that make the picture a classic anti-war statement.

John Wayne was fighting his last battle with cancer during that spring of 1979, when he made his final public appearance at the ceremony to present the Best Film prize. He got the biggest cheer of the evening as, gaunt with his illness, he tottered up the Academy staircase and touched everyone with his speech: "Oscar first came to the Hollywood scene in 1928. So did I. We're both a little weatherbeaten but we're still here and plan to be around a whole lot longer." Wayne died that June.

BELOW *The acidly comic English actress Maggie Smith picks disdainfully at a snack in company with her husband (Michael Caine) in a scene from Neil Simon's* California Suite. *Miss Smith picked up the Best Supporting Actress Oscar for her performance as an Oscar-nominated actress arrived in Hollywood to await her fate . . .*

WINNERS 1978

Nominations Announced: February 20, 1979
Awards Ceremony: April 9, 1979
Dorothy Chandler Pavilion, Los Angeles County
Music Center

Best Picture
THE DEER HUNTER, EMI/Cimino/Universal: BARRY SPIKINGS, MICHAEL DEELEY, MICHAEL CIMINO and JOHN PEVERALL, Producers

Actor
JON VOIGHT in *Coming Home*, Hellman/UA

Actress
JANE FONDA in *Coming Home*

Supporting Actor
CHRISTOPHER WALKEN in *The Deer Hunter*

Supporting Actress
MAGGIE SMITH in *California Suite*, Stark/Columbia

Directing
MICHAEL CIMINO for *The Deer Hunter*

Writing
(Best Screenplay – written directly for the screen)
COMING HOME
Story: NANCY DOWD
Screenplay: WALDO SALT and ROBERT C. JONES
(Best Screenplay – based on material from another medium)
MIDNIGHT EXPRESS, Casablanca-Filmworks/Columbia
Screenplay: OLIVER STONE

Cinematography
DAYS OF HEAVEN, OP/Paramount: NESTOR ALMENDROS

Art Direction – Set Decoration
HEAVEN CAN WAIT, Dogwood/Paramount: PAUL SYLBERT and EDWIN O'DONOVAN
Set Decoration: GEORGE GAINES

Sound
THE DEER HUNTER: RICHARD PORTMAN, WILLIAM McCAUGHEY, AARON ROCHIN and DARRIN KNIGHT

Film Editing
THE DEER HUNTER: PETER ZINNER

Music
(Best Original Score)
MIDNIGHT EXPRESS: GIORGIO MORODER
(Best Original Song Score and Its Adaptation or Best Adaptation Score)
THE BUDDY HOLLY STORY, Innovisions-ECA/Columbia
Adaptation Score: JOE RENZETTI

(Best Original Score)
LAST DANCE from *Thank God It's Friday*, Casablanca-Motown/Columbia
Music & Lyrics: PAUL JABARA

Costume Design
DEATH ON THE NILE, Brabourne-Goodwin/Paramount: ANTHONY POWELL

Short Films
(Animated)
SPECIAL DELIVERY, National Film Board of Canada: EUNICE MACAULAY and JOHN WELDON, Producers
(Live Action)
TEENAGE FATHER, New Visions Inc for the Children's Home Society of California: TAYLOR HACKFORD, Producer

Documentary
(Short Subjects)
THE FLIGHT OF THE GOSSAMER CONDOR, Shedd: JACQUELINE PHILLIPS SHEDD, Producer
(Features)
SCARED STRAIGHT!, Golden West TV: ARNOLD SHAPIRO, Producer

Foreign Language Film Award
GET OUT YOUR HANDKERCHIEFS, Les Films Ariane-CAPAC (France)

Honorary Awards
WALTER LANTZ for bringing joy and laughter to every part of the world through his unique animated motion pictures
LAURENCE OLIVIER for the full body of his work, for the unique achievements of his entire career and his lifetime of contribution to the art of film
KING VIDOR for his incomparable achievements as a cinematic creator and innovator
THE MUSEUM OF MODERN ART DEPARTMENT OF FILM for the contribution it has made to the public's perception of movies as an art form

Special Achievement Award
Visual Effects: LES BOWIE, COLIN CHILVERS, DENYS COOP, ROY FIELD, DEREK MEDDINGS and ZORAN PERISIC, for *Superman*,
Dovemead/Salkind/Warner Bros.

Irving G. Thalberg Memorial Award
None

Jean Hersholt Humanitarian Award
LEO JAFFE

1979

A POOR YEAR FOR Hollywood was reflected by a lack of quality competition for the Academy awards and the domination of the child-custody drama, **Kramer vs Kramer**, which won five of them: Best Film for producer Stanley R. Jaffe, Best Direction and Best Screenplay Adaptation for Robert Benton, Best Actor for Dustin Hoffman, and Best Supporting Actress for Meryl Streep – although why she wasn't judged in the Best Actress category is hard to understand.

Francis Coppola's flawed masterpiece of the Vietnam War, **Apocalypse Now**, was nominated for eight awards but won only for its sound and Vittorio Storaro's cinematography. There was the suspicion that this epic, sensual, $31.5 million version of war – the story of an army captain's terrifying journey into Cambodia, and into the darker recesses of the human soul, to assassinate a crazed Special Forces Officer who has set himself up as a genocidal god – was too strong meat for the Academy. Perhaps its lack of honors could be put down to the success of Vietnam movies the previous year and a need to return to the domestic front. Whatever the reasons, Coppola clearly wasn't expecting to win: he didn't come to the ceremony.

Dustin Hoffman who, in his Oscar acceptance speech paid tribute to several performers (including Best Supporting Actor nominee Robert Duvall, the mad Air Cavalry colonel, Kilgore, in **Apocalypse Now**), was a winner at the fourth attempt, having earlier been nominated for **The Graduate** (1967), **Midnight Cowboy** (1969) and **Lenny** (1974). After financial and artistic problems with

BELOW *Best Actor Dustin Hoffman and little Justin Henry, nominated in the supporting actor category, were father and son in Robert Benton's blockbusting success,* Kramer vs Kramer

his two preceding films, **Straight time** (1977) and **Agatha** (1979), it was **Kramer vs Kramer** which restored his faith in the cinema.

In the film, adapted by Benton from Avery Corman's novel, Hoffman plays a pressured Madison Avenue advertising executive, Ted Kramer, whose wife Joanna (Streep) walks out on him and their six-year-old son Billy (Justin Henry). She is no longer in love with him, and wants to assert her independence. At first, it's a struggle for Ted to look after the child. Morose and missing his mother, Billy creates one memorable showdown with his father when he plays with his Swiss steak dinner and then, ignoring all warnings, fetches out the ice cream. Hoffman, who became estranged from his own first wife during the two-and-a-half year making of **Kramer vs Kramer**, said that the scene grew out of his own experiences with his daughters when they came to visit him: "Whatever I'd say to do, they'd do the opposite. Things I knew they always liked, they'd say they didn't like. I couldn't please them. They were testing me . . . like kids will do when they're angry with the people they love most."

Gradually, a special relationship begins to develop between father and son as they grow to understand one another. For Kramer, a change of values is necessary too. Initially, a shifty, somewhat bland businessman with an eye to upward mobility, he is forced to reassess himself when he can no longer hold down such a high-powered job because of Billy's demands on his time, and finds himself becoming a much more caring parent.

LEFT *Joanna Kramer (Meryl Streep) enjoys a game with the son she has deserted, but comes back to see, in Kramer vs Kramer. Curiously, Miss Streep was nominated (and won) in the Best Supporting category*

Meryl Streep had an even less straightforward role as the mother, emotionally bereft and hovering on the edge of hysteria as she returns, in a memorable confrontation in a café with Ted, to try and win custody of Billy. The father's cause isn't helped by Billy's fall at a playground – with Hoffman bringing some heroism to his role as he snatches the child up and runs all the way to the hospital with him in his arms. In the tearjerking courtroom climax, Joanna finally concedes Billy to his father, although Benton has disposed of any moral dilemma and her rightful

ABOVE *Jack Warden (left), as the US President, and Melvyn Douglas as the dying financier in* Being There. *Always remembered as Garbo's debonair lover in* Ninotchka, *the veteran Douglas won the Best Supporting Actor Oscar, as he had for* Hud *in 1963*
LEFT *Following in the wake of the previous year's clean-up by Vietnam War movies, Francis Coppola's ambitious and probing* Apocalypse Now *was unfortunate in losing out on all major awards. Here, the mad Colonel Kilgore (Robert Duvall, nominated) inspects some of the devastation he has caused*

claims as mother – the role she has ostensibly bequeathed to Ted. In the end, it is she – "accused in court of failing in the single most important relationship in her life" – who commands our sympathy.

Streep deserved her Oscar, and despite a fine performance as Ted's sympathetic neighbor by Jane Alexander – also nominated as Best Supporting Actress, as she was for **All the President's Men** in 1976 (and for Best Actress in 1970's **The Great White Hope**) – it would have been a miscarriage of justice if she had cost the leading lady her accolade. Justin Henry's performance as the child at the centre of the tug-of-war shouldn't be overlooked either; seven when the film was started, he was nominated as Best Supporting Actor alongside the eventual winner, 78-year-old Melvyn Douglas, for **Being There**, Duvall,

Frederic Forrest for **The Rose**, and Mickey Rooney for **The Black Stallion**. Henry had been chosen from about a hundred young applicants by Benton in collaboration with Hoffman. The writer/director had encouraged both leads to get creatively involved in the film above and beyond their performances. Hoffman sat in on the editing and Streep wrote all her own dialogue; it wasn't an easy shoot, however, with both stars later admitting there was friction between them on the set, while acknowledging their admiration for one another.

For the 47-year-old Benton, **Kramer vs Kramer** – originally intended for François Truffaut – was a triumph. Nominated in 1967 (with co-writer David Newman) for his **Bonnie and Clyde** screenplay, and again in 1977 for **The Late Show**, he now won a brace and would pick up a third for his **Places in the Heart** script in 1984. That film would star Sally Field in a Best Actress role, but she won her first in 1979 for her universally applauded performance in Martin Ritt's **Norma Rae**, which was also in the running as Best Film and picked up the Best Song award.

ABOVE *Sally Field, voted Best Actress, was* Norma
Rae, *the millworker who fights for the rights of
workers. Here, she discusses her problems with her
mother (Barbara Baxley)*

Norma Rae is a loomworker given to protesting about
the conditions at the Southern textile mill where her
parents also work. A widow with two children (one by an
ex-lover) to support, she is pleased to be promoted to
spot-checker, but returns to her former job when she
realizes that she is being used to spy on her colleagues.

Friendships with two men change Norma Rae's life:
Reuben (Ron Leibman), a Jewish labor organizer from
New York, and Sonny (Beau Bridges), a divorced former
workmate whose marriage proposal she accepts. Under
Reuben's influence, she becomes an active member of
the newly formed union and fights management intimida-
tion of blacks, despite the lukewarm appreciation of her
fellow workers. Norma Rae is arrested but, bailed out by
Reuben and refusing to be sacked, she eventually wins
her struggle to get the union formally accepted. Not even
Sonny's complaints that she is neglecting her family can
stand in the way of her new-found freedom and maturity.

Best known as TV's Gidget and as a support to her lover
Burt Reynolds in a couple of his comedy vehicles, Sally
Field blossomed as one of Hollywood's best dramatic
actresses with **Norma Rae**. In Martin Ritt's film she is
gutsy and single-minded in her pursuit of both political
and personal justice, and her liberation and enlighten-
ment come only after intense struggles. The clear favorite
for Best Actress, she was overcome with emotion when
she went up to get her award.

In 1963 Field's director, Martin Ritt, had guided Melvyn
Douglas to the Best Supporting Actor award in **Hud**. This
former romantic lead and Garbo escort was nominated as
Best Actor for **I Never Sang For My Father** in 1970, and
crowned his career as one of Hollywood's most distinguished veterans with his 1979 Best Supporting Actor
prize, although having made it to the New York honoring
of the Oscar nominees the week before, he didn't turn up
to collect his statuette.

In **Being There** Douglas was outstanding as the dying
Benjamin Rand, a politically powerful financier who discovers an ignorant, illiterate gardner – injured in an auto
accident and brought home by his wife Eve (Shirley Mac-

Laine) – and believes he is possessed of a remarkable homespun wisdom. He simultaneously encourages this man, Chance, to enter the presidential arena and make love to Eve. The unwitting protegé was brilliantly played by Peter Sellers, who was a Best Actor nominee, in his last film role. Sellers died in 1980, Douglas in 1981.

Bob Fosse's musical, **All That Jazz**, collected four awards – Best Art Direction, Best Costume Design, Best Editing, Best Adaptation Score – but drew a blank in its top drawer nominations.

WINNERS 1979

Nominations Announced: February 25, 1980
Awards Ceremony: April 14, 1980
Dorothy Chandler Pavilion, Los Angeles County
Music Center

Best Picture
KRAMER VS. KRAMER, Jaffe/Columbia: STANLEY R. JAFFE, Producer

Actor
DUSTIN HOFFMAN in *Kramer vs. Kramer*

Actress
SALLY FIELD in *Norma Rae*, 20th Century-Fox

Supporting Actor
MELVYN DOUGLAS in *Being There*, Lorimar-Fernsehproduktion GmbH/UA

Supporting Actress
MERYL STREEP in *Kramer vs. Kramer*

Directing
ROBERT BENTON for *Kramer vs. Kramer*

Writing
(Best Screenplay Written Directly for the Screen – may be based on factual material or on story material not previously published or produced)
BREAKING AWAY, 20th Century-Fox
Story & Screenplay: STEVE TESICH
(Based on Material from Another Medium)
KRAMER VS. KRAMER
Screenplay: ROBERT BENTON

Cinematography
APOCALYPSE NOW, Omni Zoetrope/UA: VITTORIO STORARO

Art Direction-Set Decoration
ALL THAT JAZZ, Columbia/20th Century-Fox:
PHILIP ROSENBERG and TONY WALTON
Set Decoration: EDWARD STEWART and GARY BRINK

Sound
APOCALYPSE NOW: WALTER MURCH, MARK BERGER, RICHARD BEGGS and NAT BOXER

Film Editing
ALL THAT JAZZ: ALAN HEIM

Music
(Best Original Score)
A LITTLE ROMANCE, Pan Arts/Orion: GEORGE DELERUE

(Best Original Song Score and Its Adaptation or Best Adaptation Score)
ALL THAT JAZZ
Adaptation Score: RALPH BURNS
(Best Original Song)
IT GOES LIKE IT GOES from *Norma Rae*
Music: DAVID SHIRE
Lyrics: NORMAN GIMBEL

Costume Design
ALL THAT JAZZ: ALBERT WOLSKY

Short Films
(Animated)
EVERY CHILD, National Film Board of Canada:
DEREK LAMB, Producer
(Live Action)
BOARD AND CARE, Ellis: SARAH PILLSBURY and RON ELLIS, Producers

Documentary
(Short Subjects)
PAUL ROBESON: TRIBUTE TO AN ARTIST, Janus Films
(Features)
BEST BOY, Only Child Motion Pictures: IRA WOHL, Producer

Foreign Language Film Award
THE TIN DRUM, Seitz/Bioskop/Artemis/Hallelujah/GGB 14.KG/Argos (Federal Republic of Germany)

Visual Effects
ALIEN, 20th Century-Fox: H.R. GIGER, CARLO RAMBALDI, BRIAN JOHNSON, NICK ALLDER and DENYS AYLING

Honorary Awards
HAL ELIAS for his dedication and distinguished service to the Academy of Motion Picture Arts and Sciences
ALEC GUINNESS for advancing the art of screen acting through a host of memorable and distinguished performances

Special Achievement Award
Sound Editing: ALAN SPLET for *The Black Stallion*, Omni Zoetrope/UA

Irving G. Thalberg Memorial Award
RAY STARK

Jean Hersholt Humanitarian Award
ROBERT BENJAMIN

1980

One of Hollywood's most popular leading men, Robert Redford, had previously received only one Oscar nomination, for his acting in **The Sting** (1973), but with 1980's **Ordinary People** he won the Best Direction award at the first attempt. (Not since Delbert Mann won for **Marty** in 1955 had this feat been achieved.) Producer Ronald L. Schwary meanwhile collected the Best Picture Oscar for **Ordinary People**. Redford's Wildwood Enterprises had moved swiftly to pick up the rights to Judith Guest's novel while other, bigger companies dallied over it. Redford had earlier shown his commercial acumen when he had fought a two-year battle to acquire Bob Woodward and Carl Bernstein's Watergate exposé, **All The President's Men**, as a film property for Wildwood.

Ordinary People, adapted for the screen by Alvin Sargent who won the Best Screenplay Oscar, shares with other Wildwood films – including **All The President's Men** itself, **The Candidate** (1978) and **The Electric Horseman** (1979) – Redford's commitment to exploring social themes seriously and soberly, and the actions of human beings under severe stress. He chose not to appear in this film himself; here the protagonist is the teenager Conrad (played by newcomer Timothy Hutton), who struggles to come to terms with the drowning of his brother in a sailing accident, for which he holds himself responsible.

Blessed with wealthy, middle-class parents – Calvin (Donald Sutherland), nervous, concerned, a jogger, and

WITH THE 1980 Academy Awards ceremony all set to take place on Monday, 30 March 1981, John W. Hinckley Jr – professing undying love for screen actress Jodie Foster – fired a spray of bullets at President Ronald Reagan in an assassination attempt in Washington. As the President underwent surgery, the Academy and ABC-TV decided that it would be wrong to go ahead with Hollywood's gala night – although encouraging news from the White House meant that the event, to be produced by Norman Jewison, would be postponed for just 24 hours.

Oscar night had been postponed twice before, most recently in 1968, and in 1938 the awards were delayed by heavy storms which damaged many Hollywood studios and left much of Los Angeles flooded. The 1980 ceremony got under way on 31 March with Johnny Carson as the host for the evening. He played down the assassination attempt, even managing a dig at the recuperating president. Referring to the Reagan administration's proposed cuts in spending, he commented: "It's Reagan's strongest attack on the arts since he signed with Warner Brothers – I'll bet he's up and around now."

BELOW *Popular star Robert Redford (left) changed hats to become Best Director of the year's Best Picture,* Ordinary People. *Here, he discusses a scene with his leading actor, Timothy Hutton who, at 19, became the youngest winner of the Best Supporting Actor Oscar*

Registered Tra

ABOVE *Sissy Spacek and Tommy Lee Jones in* Coal Miner's Daughter. *In this intelligent biopic of country-and-western superstar Loretta Lynn, the fragile and appealing Miss Spacek acted and sang her way to the Best Actress award*

Beth (Mary Tyler Moore), shallow and unloving – Conrad finds little solace there, isn't sure how he himself should be reacting, and is made to feel more guilty when a neurotic girlfriend commits suicide. Finally, only by coming to terms with *himself*, and realizing that his father is his friend and the strength in the family, does Conrad find a way through. His mother, though, has left them, unable to deal with the effect the tragedy has had on the family and on her own selfish feelings. This ending was deemed misogynistic by many critics, who found Redford's 'buddy-buddy' solution – creating a new bond between father and son – difficult to take.

Mary Tyler Moore's performance was selfless, however – seldom has such coldness been radiated by an American mother on screen. She was nominated for Best Actress, while pundits drew parallels between the film and the actress' own tragic loss of her son and congratulated her on her bravery. She could console herself for her Oscar miss with the record 24 Emmy awards won by *The Mary Tyler Moore Show*, produced by her own company MTM, and the later equaling of that feat by **Hill Street Blues**, another MTM hit. Judd Hirsch and Hutton – the former with a small part as Conrad's psychiatrist in **Ordi-**

nary People, the latter essentially its leading man – were both nominated as Best Supporting Actor, and Hutton deservedly won, becoming at 19 the youngest recipient of the award. He thanked those who had helped him and movingly paid tribute to his late father, actor Jim Hutton, who had died in 1979: "I wish he were here."

Country singer Loretta Lynn and former middleweight boxing champion Jake La Motta were both in the audience to witness the stars who had played them on screen – Sissy Spacek in **Coal Miner's Daughter** and Robert De Niro in **Raging Bull** – collect the Best Actress and Best Actor awards.

It was Spacek's second nomination following her Oscar bid as the telekinetic teenager in **Carrie** in 1976. A pale, frail-looking blonde, she had apparently been chosen to play the gutsy, black-haired 'Queen of Country' by Loretta Lynn herself, whose insistence on Spacek caused the departure from the project of intended director

Joseph Sargent. English director Michael Apted took over and earned **Coal Miner's Daughter** a Best Film nomination. Spacek, once an aspiring country-rock singer, had agreed to do the film if she could use her own voice: "They'd never heard me utter a single note and I was sure they would never gamble on me trying, but I'll be darned if they didn't give in." As it is, her rendition of Loretta Lynn's songs was superb.

Her characterization, too, showed a full awareness of the frightening but triumphant journey from anonymity to superstardom by an Appalachian mountain girl. Spacek gives us a very special insight into that transition while managing to preserve Lynn's humility – especially through the songs, which are nostalgic for home and the struggles of her father to earn the family a crust. The marriage between Loretta, wed at 13, and 'Doo-little' Lynn (Tommy Lee Jones), whose initial pushiness is soured by

BELOW *The contemporary German beauty Nastassia Kinski made a brave stab at the period Dorset lass Tess in Roman Polanski's visually breathtaking version of Thomas Hardy's novel. The movie won the award for cinematography*

drunken introspection as his wife becomes the breadwinner, is marvellously delineated, too – overcoming as it does the tragic death of Loretta's friend Patsy Cline (Beverly D'Angelo), and Loretta's confessional breakdown at the Grand Old Opry. Ageing from adolescence to middle age, Spacek gave a consummate performance.

Robert De Niro's Jake La Motta earned him his Oscar after previous nominations for **Taxi Driver** (1976) and **The Deer Hunter** (1978), and the Best Supporting Actor award for young Vito Corleone in **The Godfather Part II**. **Raging Bull** – based on the autobiography of La Motta, who advised on the film – was De Niro's fourth outing with director Martin Scorsese. Shot mostly in black and white to capture the authenticity of 1940s boxing footage, the film has the tenacity and realism of a powerful documentary inquiry into 'Bronx Bull' La Motta's rise from a middleweight contender to the championship, and his fall from nightclub owner in the mid-50s to a bloated, down-at-heel bar comic and ham monologuist.

The stories of De Niro's near-fanatical preparation for his roles are legion, and his gaining 60 lbs in weight to play the gross figure that La Motta became – an obscene

parody of the ebullient athlete he once was – has entered movie folklore. He also took boxing lessons, but La Motta, as played by De Niro, is also a contradictory character – a savage in the ring, a bully racked by insecurity and irrational sexual jealousy out of it. He seethes in his inarticulacy, is motivated by victory and a sense of destiny, but finds a need to be punished. "I don't like boxing," said De Niro. "It's too primitive. But Jake is a more complex figure than you think. Take his style: that way of uncovering his face to take blows and tire his opponents. In one way or another there has to be some feeling of guilt to deliberately look to get hit."

De Niro makes us suffer with Jake. His crack-up in a police cell, after being busted as an accessory to statutory rape (and unavailingly ripping the jewels off his championship belt to try and raise the bail money), is excruciatingly painful to watch. Not surprisingly De Niro took an eight-month sabbatical after the film to rid himself of Jake. The award couldn't go to anyone else, really.

Cathy Moriarty as Jake's blank, blonde teenage wife, wrongly suspected by him of infidelity, and Joe Pesci, as his fast-talking manager brother accused by him of the same offense, justified their nominations as Best Supporting Actress and Actor, and Scorsese arguably should have won the Director award – although possibly **Raging Bull's** ferocious fight sequences and frank depiction of its Italian street milieu were too brutally real for the tastes of Academy voters. Thelma Schoonmaker's dynamic cutting won the film its only other Oscar.

That Best Supporting Actress award was won by Mary Steenburgen – one of five first-time nominees – who

TOP *The brilliant Robert De Niro's commitment to truth and realism led him to increase his weight by almost five-stone for the latter sequences in* Raging Bull. *Here, now washed-up boxer Jake La Motta relaxes with his wife (Cathy Moriarty, nominated) and children. Scorsese's superb black-and-white biopic finally earned De Niro the Best Actor Oscar* ABOVE *Mary Steenburgen snatched the Best Supporting Actress award from, among others, Mary Tyler Moore in* Ordinary People, *for her portrayal of Melvin Dummar's wife in* Melvin And Howard

played Lynda, the down-to-earth wife of Melvin Dummar, the born loser left a fortune by Howard Hughes in **Melvin And Howard**, which earned Bo Goldman the Best Original Screenplay Oscar. But missing out in the major categories were Roman Polanski's **Tess**, winner for Best Cinematography, Art Direction and Costume Design; Irvin Kershner's massive hit **The Empire Strikes Back**, winner for Best Sound and Visual Effects; and David Lynch's **The Elephant Man**, a Best Film and Direction nominee, which would have won for Best Make-up if the award had been introduced this year instead of next.

WINNERS 1980

Nominations Announced: February 17, 1981
Awards Ceremony: Postponed from March 30 to March 31,
1981, due to an assassination attempt on President Reagan.
Dorothy Chandler Pavilion, Los Angeles County
Music Center

Best Picture
ORDINARY PEOPLE, Wildwood/Paramount: RONALD L.
SCHWARY, Producer

Actor
ROBER DE NIRO in *Raging Bull*, Chartoff-Winkler/UA

Actress
SISSY SPACEK in *Coal Miner's Daughter*,
Schwartz-Universal

Supporting Actor
TIMOTHY HUTTON in *Ordinary People*

Supporting Actress
MARY STEENBURGEN in *Melvin And Howard*,
Linson/Phillips/Demme-Universal

Directing
ROBERT REDFORD for *Ordinary People*

Writing
(Best Screenplay Written Directly for the Screen – may be
based on factual material or on story material not previously
published or produced)
MELVIN AND HOWARD
Screenplay: BO GOLDMAN
(Best Screenplay Based on Material from Another Medium)
ORDINARY PEOPLE
Screenplay: ALVIN SARGENT

Cinematography
TESS, Renn-Burrill with the participation of the Société
Française de Production (SFP)/Columbia:
GEOFFREY UNSWORTH and GHISLAIN CLOQUET

Art Direction-Set Decoration
TESS
Art Direction: PIERRE GUFFROY and JACK STEVENS

Sound
THE EMPIRE STRIKES BACK, Lucasfilm/20th
Century-Fox:
BILL VARNEY, STEVE MASLOW, GREGG LANDAKER
and PETER SUTTON

Film Editing
RAGING BULL: THELMA SCHOONMAKER

Music
(Best Original Score)
FAME, MGM: MICHAEL GORE
(Best Original Song Score and Its Adaptation or Best
Adaptation Score)
No nominations
(Best Original Song)
FAME from *Fame*
Music: MICHAEL GORE
Lyrics: DEAN PITCHFORD

Costume Design
TESS: ANTHONY POWELL

Short Films
(Animated)
THE FLY, Pannonia (Budapest): FERENC ROFUSZ,
Producer
(Dramatic Live Action)
THE DOLLAR BOTTOM, Rocking Horse/Paramount:
LLOYD PHILLIPS, Producer

Documentary
(Short Subjects)
KARL HESS: TOWARD LIBERTY, Hallé/Ladue: PETER W.
LADUE and ROLAND HALLÉ, Producers
(Features)
FROM MAO TO MOZART: ISAAC STERN IN CHINA,
Hopewell Foundation: MURRAY LERNER, Producer

Foreign Language Film Award
MOSCOW DOES NOT BELIEVE IN TEARS, Mosfilm
(USSR)

Honorary Award
HENRY FONDA, the consummate actor, in recognition of
his brilliant accomplishments and enduring contribution to
the art of motion pictures

Special Achievement Award
Visual Effects: BRIAN JOHNSON, RICHARD EDLUND,
DENNIS MUREN and BRUCE NICHOLSON for *The
Empire Strikes Back*

Irving G. Thalberg Memorial Award
None

Jean Hersholt Humanitarian Award
None

1981

IN 1981 **Chariots Of Fire**, produced by David Puttnam and directed by Hugh Hudson, won the Best Picture award, and the British film renaissance began with its Oscar-winning author Colin Welland (Best Original Screenplay) crying, like Paul Revere alerting the American Revolutionaries of the Redcoats' advance, "The British are coming!" **Gandhi**'s triumph a year later hammered home the point.

With the indigenous industry reaching a creative and financial nadir during the 70s, British films scarcely featured among that decade's Oscar-winners. Although actresses Glenda Jackson, Maggie Smith and Vanessa Redgrave won Oscars in American films, and EMI's **Murder On The Orient Express** enabled Ingrid Bergman to win her first Best Supporting Actress award, only Jackson's earlier Best Actress win for **Women In Love**,

John Mills' supporting actor victory for **Ryan's Daughter** (both 1970), and Oliver Stone's Best Screenplay Adaptation for **Midnight Express** (1978) were *bona fide* British Oscars in the major categories. By 1980, however, there were rumblings of a British revival.

Chariots Of Fire originated with Puttnam's reading a history of the Olympic Games a few years earlier. It was the 1924 event that grabbed his attention and, in particular, the very different motivations of two of Britain's gold medalists, runners Harold Abrahams, who ran for Cambridge, his team, his country and for the excellence of victory and honor in overcoming prejudice (in his case the anti-Semitism that existed at his university), and Eric Liddell, a Scottish missionary who ran for the greater glory of God. Back in England, Puttnam raised development money for a screenplay from Goldcrest, the company that would become the flagship of the British renaissance, and hired first-timer Hugh Hudson – like Puttnam's protegés Alan Parker (**Bugsy Malone** and **Midnight Express**) and Ridley Scott (**The Duellists**), from a background in TV commercials – to direct the film. According to Alexander Walker's book *National Heroes*, 14 weeks were spent in

BELOW *Dudley Moore (right), the millionaire playboy* Arthur *brings toys for his friend, confidant and valet,* Hobson (John Gielgud), *in the comedy which won the Best Supporting award for venerable actor-knight Gielgud*

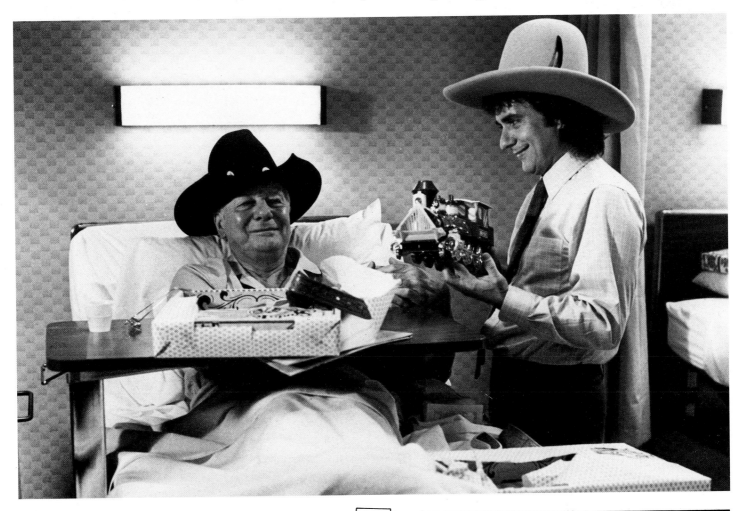

ABOVE *Scottish missionary Eric Liddell (Ian Charleson) exultantly beats Harold Abrahams (Ben Cross) to the finishing post in an early – and only – contest between them in the British triumph, Chariots of Fire*

casting before Ben Cross was chosen as Abrahams, Ian Charleson as Liddell and Ian Holm as Sam Mussabini, the latter's professional coach. Holm would eventually be nominated as Best Supporting Actor, although the award went to his co-star Sir John Gielgud – winning his first Oscar not for *Chariots*, but for his sarcastic English butler in the American comedy **Arthur**.

Chariots Of Fire opened the 1981 New York Film Festival and did excellent business throughout America, where a strong pro-British feeling had been ignited by the Falklands War. The film was no less successful at home where the 20s were in vogue. *Chariots* is in many ways an unusual film. It has very little in the way of a dramatic narrative as it charts Abrahams and Liddell's progress to Paris where they respectively win the 100-yard sprint and 400 yards events. They are rivals whose climactic meeting (apart from an earlier race won by Liddell) doesn't even materialize since Liddell won't compete in the sprint heats which are to be held on the sabbath. The film is more concerned with the different ways in which each man reconciles his conscience to his athletic prowess, but Welland's scenario also questions notions of elitism (of which Abrahams is accused by his Cambridge Masters) and the class system. That it was accused of jingoism and certainly espouses the 'qualities' of patriotism and honor cannot be denied, but it must be remembered that these were qualities much admired in their day and that they must, to some extent, be taken at face value.

With many of the running sequences elegiacally

screened in slow motion and heightened by Vangelis' throbbingly inspirational score – an undisputed Oscar-winner – **Chariots Of Fire** emerged as a hymn to human endeavor. Beautifully dressed by Milena Canonero, **Chariots** was a popular victor and a worthy herald of the re-emergent national cinema. Asked by Alexander Walker in 1984 what he felt at the moment he received his award at the Dorothy Chandler Pavilion, where were seated many powerful figures who had been unhelpful when Puttnam came to them for backing, the producer admitted: "I was thinking how sweet it was to have my revenge. Isn't that what Oscar-winners always think?"

BELOW *Gutsy old Norman Thayer and his wife Ethel, the bickering but devoted protagonists of* On Golden Pond, *were award-winningly played by veterans Katharine Hepburn and Henry Fonda. It was Hepburn's record-breaking fourth Best Actress Oscar but, surprisingly, Fonda's first-ever statuette*

Two of Hollywood's most distinguished veterans won the Best Actor and Actress awards in 1981, although – like Gielgud, who was tied up with a play in England – neither Henry Fonda nor Katharine Hepburn was present to collect their Oscars for their performances as an elderly husband and wife in Mark Rydell's **On Golden Pond** (both director and film were also nominated). Fonda, odds-on favorite over Warren Beatty (**Reds**), Dudley Moore (**Arthur**), Burt Lancaster (**Atlantic City**), and Paul Newman (**Absence Of Malice**), and at 76 the oldest recipient of the award, was ill in hospital and would die a few months after the ceremony. It was collected on his behalf by daughter Jane, herself a supporting nominee for her own role as his daughter in the film. Apart from an honorary award the year before, this was Henry Fonda's only Oscar.

Katharine Hepburn, meanwhile, who became the first performer to win four Best Actress Oscars, from a record 12 nominations, was acting on Broadway in a play written

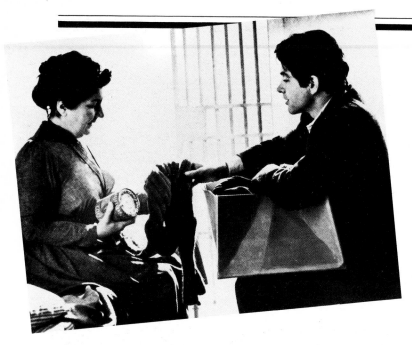

ABOVE *American communist and author John Reed (Warren Beatty) visits fiery anarchist Emma Goldman (Maureen Stapleton), imprisoned for her political agitating in Beatty's sprawling, impressive* Reds. *Distinguished Broadway actress Miss Stapleton was named Best Supporting Actress*

by Ernest Thompson, whose adaptation of **On Golden Pond** from his own play won him a Best Screenplay Oscar. Kate customarily avoided the ceremony; her one appearance at the awards was in 1974 when she came to honor Lawrence Weingarten – who had produced the Hepburn-Tracy vehicle **Adam's Rib** (1949) – winner of the Irving G. Thalberg Memorial Award that year.

The making of **On Golden Pond** was reputedly instrumental in healing a long-standing rift between Henry and Jane Fonda. The film itself follows the same formula. Henry played Norman Thayer Jr, a crusty, 80-year-old former college professor, returning with his wife Ethel to their beloved lakeside holiday cabin in New England, where their daughter Chelsea – on a rare visit – brings her new boyfriend and his 13-year-old son Billy to stay. Norman, growing old, has become aware of his mortality and only Ethel can understand or withstand his caustic humor: Chelsea, never close to Norman, is hurt and resentful; Bill and Billy merely regard the old man's barbs as 'bullshit'.

But when Chelsea and Bill go off to Europe leaving Billy to stay on with her parents, an unlikely friendship develops between the boy and Norman, who has found the son he never had. They go on fishing trips together and a touching bond is created. Chelsea, now married to Bill, returns, and has her face slapped by her mother when she rails against her father again. But the company of youth has mellowed and regenerated Norman; father and daughter are reconciled in a final embrace. Even Norman's heart attack at the end of the film cannot disrupt the new-found tranquility of life at Golden Pond.

A gentle movie, unobtrusively directed by Rydell, with scarcely any action, **On Golden Pond** is a persuasive look at the fear of approaching death without grace and dig-

nity. Henry Fonda, never so moving as when he shows his terror of losing his faculties, is exceptional in his last film role, and Hepburn, the spiritual centre of the story, is marvelous, too: doddery but placid, full of wisdom, and the quiet strength in the family.

Both Fonda and Hepburn earned their awards, and Jane Fonda was unlucky not to win one as well. She lost out to Maureen Stapleton who won for Best Supporting Actress – after three previous nominations – for her portrayal of the disillusioned anarchist Emma Goldman in Best Picture nominee, **Reds**. This 3¼-hour epic about the life of the American communist and journalist John Reed, who witnessed the Russian Revolution in 1917 and wrote the book *Ten Days That Shook The World*, was co-scripted (with English dramatist Trevor Griffiths), directed and produced by Warren Beatty, who starred in the leading role. Beatty was nominated for Best Screenplay, Director, Film and Actor Oscars and **Reds** garnered 12 nominations in all. Beatty's two nominations for **Bonnie And Clyde** (1967), for Best Film and Best Actor, and his four for **Heaven Can Wait** had left him Oscarless; but he won, at last, in his directorial capacity for **Reds**. The magnificent cinematography of Vittorio Storaro – 1979's winner for **Apocalypse Now** – meanwhile brought the film its third Academy Award.

Perhaps the movie should have done better. One can only speculate that had Beatty devoted his energies to a film about Abraham Lincoln or John F. Kennedy he could have cleaned up the 1981 awards, but **Reds**, in any case, remains a towering achievement. Costing $35 million, it paints a broad canvas of Reed's travels from Oregon to Greenwich Village, to the Bolshevik uprising in the streets of Petrograd (shot in Helsinki), to the agitprop rail tour of Russia's southern plains, to his death in Moscow. Perhaps Beatty's most astute stroke was his inclusion of interviews with real-life 'witnesses' who knew Reed, among them writers Henry Miller and Rebecca West, columnist Adela Rogers St Johns and comedian George Jessel. These gave a romantic Hollywood spectacle a firm grounding of historical credibility. It says much for the liberal Beatty's abilities as a producer and director that he was able to get a film about radicalism on the screen in the first place, and that he was able to win over audiences and at least some Academy voters with an account of a creed that 30 years earlier would have had him run out of town.

Albert R. ('Cubby') Broccoli was presented with the Irving G. Thalberg Award for his production work (including 13 James Bond pictures); and Danny Kaye received the Jean Hersholt Humanitarian Award for his charitable activities. Rick Baker's make-up for **An American Werewolf In London** claimed the first ever award in that category, but the memorable moment went to Barbara Stanwyck. One of Hollywood's outstanding actresses, Stanwyck had, incredibly, never won the Oscar, although nominated four times as Best Actress. Now, she received a popular – and overdue – statuette for "an artist of impeccable grace and beauty, a dedicated actress and one of the great ladies of Hollywood".

WINNERS 1981

Nominations Announced: February 11, 1982
Awards Ceremony: March 29, 1982
Dorothy Chandler Pavilion, Los Angeles County
Music Center

Best Picture
CHARIOTS OF FIRE, Enigma/Ladd-Warner Bros.: DAVID PUTTNAM, Producer

Actor
HENRY FONDA in *On Golden Pond*, ITC-IPC/Universal

Actress
KATHARINE HEPBURN in *On Golden Pond*

Supporting Actor
JOHN GIELGUD in *Arthur*,
Rollins/Joffe/Morra-Brezner/Orion

Supporting Actress
MAUREEN STAPLETON in *Reds*, Paramount

Directing
WARREN BEATTY for *Reds*, JRS/Paramount

Writing
(Best Screenplay Written Directly for the Screen)
CHARIOTS OF FIRE
Screenplay: COLIN WELLAND
(Best Screenplay Based on Material from Another Medium)
ON GOLDEN POND
Screenplay: ERNEST THOMPSON

Cinematography
REDS: VITTORIO STORARO

Art Direction-Set Decoration
RAIDERS OF THE LOST ARK, Lucasfilm/Paramount
NORMAN REYNOLDS and LESLIE DILLEY
Set Decoration: MICHAEL FORD

Sound
RAIDERS OF THE LOST ARK: BILL VARNEY, STEVE MASLOW, GREGG LANDAKER and ROY CHARMAN

Film Editing
RAIDERS OF THE LOST ARK: MICHAEL KAHN

Music
(Best Original Score)
CHARIOTS OF FIRE: VANGELIS
(Best Original Song Score and Its Adaptation or Best Adaptation Score)
No nominations

(Best Original Song)
ARTHUR'S THEME (BEST THAT YOU CAN DO) from *Arthur*
Music & Lyrics: BURT BACHARACH, CAROLE BAYER SAGER, CHRISTOPHER CROSS and PETER ALLEN

Costume Design
CHARIOTS OF FIRE: MILENA CANONERO

Make-Up (new category)
AN AMERICAN WEREWOLF IN LONDON,
Lycanthrope/Polygram/Universal: RICK BAKER

Short Films
(Animated)
CRAC, Société Radio-Canada: FREDERICK BACK, Producer
(Live Action)
VIOLET, American Film Institute: PAUL KEMP and SHELLEY LEVINSON, Producers

Documentary
(Short Subjects)
CLOSE HARMONY, Noble: NIGEL NOBLE, Producer
(Features)
GENOCIDE, Schwartzman: ARNOLD SCHWARTZMAN and RABBI MARVIN HIER, Producers

Foreign Language Film Award
MEPHISTO, Mafilm-Objektiv Studio/Dumiok (Hungary)

Visual Effects
RAIDERS OF THE LOST ARK: RICHARD EDLUND, KIT WEST and BRUCE NICHOLSON and JOE JOHNSTON

Honorary Award
BARBARA STANWYCK for superlative creativity and unique contribution to the art of screen acting

Special Achievement Award
Sound Effects Editing: BENJAMIN P. BURTT Jr, and RICHARD L. ANDERSON for *Raiders Of The Lost Ark*

Irving G. Thalberg Memorial Award
ALBERT R. 'CUBBY' BROCCOLI

Jean Hersholt Humanitarian Award
DANNY KAYE

1982

NOT EVEN THAT box-office phenomenon **E.T. The Extra-Terrestrial** could steal any of **Gandhi**'s thunder at the 1982 Academy Awards. Sir Richard Attenborough's epic life of the Mahatma dominated the evening's proceedings with eight Oscars, the biggest haul ever for a British movie and a feat that triumphantly vindicated the British revival heralded a year before by the Best Picture win of **Chariots Of Fire**.

The news was greeted with euphoria in London, especially at Goldcrest, the company that had put up two-thirds of Attenborough's £20 million budget. Attenborough collected two awards as producer and director of the Best Film, and Ben Kingsley – who had appeared in only one movie previously – was chosen as Best Actor for his extraordinary, visionary performance in the title role. John Briley's original screenplay, Billy Williams and Ronnie Taylor's cinematography, John Bloom's editing, Stuart Craig, Bob Laing and Michael Seirton's art direction, and John Mollo and Bhanu Athaiya's costumes won **Gandhi**'s other awards.

Attenborough had first conceived a film about Gandhi 20 years earlier, although he confessed to knowing nothing about the subject when the idea was suggested to him by an unknown Indian called Motilal Kothari, who continued to encourage him until his death in 1970. Lord

Mountbatten, the last Viceroy of India, and India's first prime minister, Pandit Nehru, both of whom are portrayed in the film, lent considerable support. Attenborough dedicated his work to these three men. Nehru's advice was that it would be wrong to deify Gandhi, "He was too great a man for that."

A major difficulty was finding the right actor for the part. Kingsley, an experienced stage actor, was eventually chosen because he not only bore a passing physical resemblance to Gandhi and gave a screen test that Attenborough later described as having "a credibility and magnetism that we could scarcely have contemplated", but also because he was not a known screen face; moreover, he was half-Indian.

Obviously the greatest problem that faced Attenborough, apart from the huge logistical task of actually shooting the picture with its vast crowd scenes, was condensing Gandhi's life into a movie with limited running time. He and Briley dispensed with Gandhi's early life and, apart from the opening sequence which shows his assassination by a fanatical Hindu in 1948 and a funeral procession worthy of D.W. Griffith, trace his story chronologically from his arrival as an attorney in South Africa at the age of 24 in 1893 to that fateful January day in New Delhi when Gandhi, pumped full of bullets, expires with the words "Oh God, oh God" on his lips. Most of the tumultuous events leading up to India's gaining of independence and the creation of Pakistan are

BELOW LEFT *Best Supporting Actress Jessica Lange (left) in the nurse's outfit she wears in a soap opera which co-stars her best 'girlfriend' Dorothy. Dorothy (back to camera) is, of course, Dustin Hoffman in drag in* Tootsie
BELOW *Lou Gossett Jr (center) won the supporting actor award for his tough drill sergeant in conflict with cadet Richard Gere (left) in* An Officer And A Gentleman

seen, but the triumph of the film is in its intimate focus on the spiritual leader of the emergent nation.

The first moment of truth for Gandhi comes when, because of his color, he is thrown off a train travelling to Pretoria. The indignant young barrister embarks on a campaign to establish the equality of all citizens of the Empire, and at his first public meeting burns the passes that symbolize the victimization of the non-white races. A burly policeman rains blows with a truncheon on his head – but the bloodied figure carries on just the same. It is simply and shockingly done, showing the full force of Gandhi's philosophy of non-violent resistance. When repeated *en masse* – as at the Dharasana salt-works years later when rank upon rank of unarmed Indians are beaten to the ground – it leads directly to the first negotiations in England for freeing India.

Before that, we witness Gandhi's moral victory over General Smuts (Athol Fugard) in South Africa following his first of many jail sentences, and his journey through India in 1915 with his friend, the clergyman Charlie

ABOVE *Martin Sheen (left) as the sympathetic crusading American journalist, Walker, who accompanies the Mahatma (Ben Kingsley, right) on his march to make salt at the sea in Richard Attenborough's multi-Oscar winning* Gandhi *which swept the boards this year*

Andrews (Ian Charleson). Fields, rivers and plains flash by and we sense Gandhi finding his destiny in his personal recognition of his country's beauty and poverty.

Taken up by Indian congressmen such as Sardar Patel (Saeed Jaffrey) and Nehru (Roshan Seth) who are building the national movement, Gandhi adheres to his creed of civil disobedience by peaceful non-cooperation. The vestiges of Westernization fall away from him and, except for the little wire spectacles, he wears just a dhoti and a shawl. Kingsley, with his gentle gestures and ever more spindly body, made this frail figure one of great power and dignity.

Acolytes and disciples gather round: the English girl Mirabehn (Geraldine James), the American journalist

Walker (Martin Sheen) who brings Gandhi's message to the world, and Margaret Bourke-White (Candice Bergen), the *Life* photographer who uncovers unique and touching insights into Gandhi the man. There is Gandhi's devoted relationship with his wife Kasturba (Rohini Hattangady); there is a series of confrontations with British officials – brilliantly cast with the cream of the English screen aristocracy (John Mills, John Gielgud, Michael Hordern etc) to convey bigotry and prejudice.

Following Gandhi's epochal march to the sea to make salt as a symbolic declaration of independence, events accelerate. He visits England – including the Lancashire cotton mills – in what is mostly filmed as a black-and-white newsreel; Kasturba dies; independence comes and Nehru's rise to power; the civil war is staunched by the old and weakened Gandhi who ends his last fast with a sip of orange juice – but threatens another if necessary. Then he is shot. The screen goes black, we see a funeral pyre and the leader's ashes are cast on the ocean.

If **Gandhi** is Attenborough's film, one in which he keeps modestly in the background, then it is Kingsley's immaculate impersonation that turns a stolid historical chronicle into a remarkable piece of cinema. In his acceptance speech for the Best Picture Oscar, Attenborough chose to distil the essence of the man Kingsley had so perfectly played. "Gandhi," he said, "simply asked that we should examine the criteria by which we judge the manner of solving our problems. He believed if we could but agree, simplistic though it be, that if we do not resort to violence then the route to solving problems would be much different than the one we take." He added, "All of the films nominated with me say the same thing."

Those films were Steven Spielberg's **E.T.**, winner of four behind-the-scenes honors; Sidney Lumet's **The Verdict**; Constantin Costas-Gavras' **Missing** (he shared the Best Screenplay Adaptation award with Donald Stewart); and Sydney Pollack's **Tootsie**. In this last, Dustin Hoffman, playing an out-of-work actor who poses as a woman to get parts, was nominated for a Best Actor Oscar for his extraordinary drag act. Jessica Lange, who played the girl he falls for, complicatedly, in that film was voted Best Supporting Actress (co-star Teri Garr was a fellow nominee), and was also nominated as Best Actress for her

BELOW *Dustin Hoffman, memorably decked out in cocktail dress for* Tootsie. *The actor's superlative drag performance earned him a Best Actor nomination, but could not wrest the award from Ben Kingsley's* Gandhi

ABOVE *Sophie (Meryl Streep) shares an affectionate moment with her loyal and devoted young friend Stingo (Peter McNichol) in Alan J. Pakula's Sophie's Choice. Miss Streep's startlingly skilful and moving performance as the Polish survivor of Auschwitz, more than deserved its Best Actress Oscar*

portrayal of the tragic film star Frances Farmer in **Frances**. Lou Gossett Jr was picked as Best Supporting Actor for his drill sergeant in **An Officer And A Gentleman**. Best Actor nominees Paul Newman (**The Verdict**) and Peter O'Toole (**My Favorite Year**) missed out for the sixth and seventh times respectively.

Best Actress was Meryl Streep. In the American television series *Holocaust*, Streep had played the Catholic wife of a concentration camp inmate. In **Sophie's Choice**, directed by Alan J. Pakula from William Styron's novel (it was also Pakula's first solo screenplay credit), she is sent through the same hell.

The film begins comfortably enough in New York in 1947, where the young Virginian writer Stingo (Peter MacNicol) befriends the charming, eccentric but unstable couple, Sophie Zawistowska (Streep) and Nathan Landau (Kevin Kline). As the love between the three of them deepens, Stingo learns that Sophie is a Polish Catholic refugee from Auschwitz who was taken in by the Jewish Nathan on reaching Brooklyn.

In flashback, we see Sophie using the knowledge that her father was anti-Semitic to ingratiate herself with the camp commandant to get protection for her young son, and, eventually, to effect her release. Back in the present

it transpires that Nathan, for all his charm and intellect, is a paranoid schizophrenic and dangerous. Stingo runs away with Sophie to Washington – but she chooses to return to a suicide pact with Nathan. She has had one earlier choice to make in Auschwitz – when a German officer asks her to select either her daughter or her son for the gas chambers . . .

Streep is haunting in this cruel and harrowing melodrama, beautifully filmed by Pakula. The scenes in the death camp are as chilling as any that made it to the screens of American main-stream cinema in the early 80s, and it required arguably Hollywood's foremost female talent to convey Sophie's resignation, determination and fatalism at different stages of her private nightmare. She is perhaps at her very best in the America scenes, when the knowledge of what she has been made to do informs her day-to-day existence and renders her strangely beautiful in her ability, still, to love and laugh.

WINNERS 1982

Nominations Announced: February, 1983
Awards Ceremony: April 11, 1983
Dorothy Chandler Pavilion, Los Angeles County
Music Center

Best Picture
GANDHI, Indo-British/Columbia: RICHARD ATTENBOROUGH, Producer

Actor
BEN KINGSLEY in *Gandhi*

Actress
MERYL STREEP in *Sophie's Choice*, ITC-Pakula-Barish-Universal/AFD

Supporting Actor
LOU GOSSETT Jr in *An Officer And A Gentleman*, Lorimar-Elfand/Paramount

Supporting Actress
JESSICA LANGE in *Tootsie*, Mirage/Punch/Columbia

Directing
RICHARD ATTENBOROUGH for *Gandhi*

Writing
(Best Original Screenplay)
GANDHI: JOHN BRILEY
(Best Screenplay Adaptation)
MISSING, Universal/Polygram: CONSTANTIN COSTA-GAVRAS and DONALD STEWART

Cinematography
GANDHI: BILLY WILLIAMS and RONNIE TAYLOR

Art Direction-Set Decoration
GANDHI: STUART CRAIG and BOB LAING
Set Decoration: MICHAEL SEIRTON

Sound
E.T. THE EXTRA-TERRESTRIAL, Universal: ROBERT KNUDSON, ROBERT GLASS, DON DIGIROLAMO and GENE CATAMESSA

Sound Effects Editing
E.T. THE EXTRA-TERRESTRIAL: CHARLES L. CAMPBELL and BENJAMIN BURTT

Film Editing
GANDHI: JOHN BLOOM

Music
(Best Original Score)
E.T. THE EXTRA-TERRESTRIAL: JOHN WILLIAMS

(Best Original Score and Its Adaptation or Best Adaptation Score)
VICTOR/VICTORIA, MGM/UA
Song Score: HENRY MANCINI and LESLIE BRICUSSE
Adaptation: HENRY MANCINI
(Best Original Song)
UP WHERE WE BELONG from *An Officer And A Gentleman*
Music: JACK NITSZCHE and BUFFY SAINTE-MARIE
Lyrics: WILL HENNINGS

Costume Design
GANDHI: JOHN MOLLO and BANU ATHAIYA

Make-Up
QUEST FOR FIRE: International Cinema/20th Century-Fox

Short Films
(Animated)
TANGO, Film Polski: ZBIGNIEW RYBCZYNAKI, Producer
(Live Action)
A SHOCKING ACCIDENT, Flamingo: CHRISTINE OESTREICHER, Producer

Documentary
(Short Subjects)
IF YOU LOVE THIS PLANET, National Film Board of Canada: EDWARD LE LORRAIN and TERRI NASH, Producers
(Features)
JUST ANOTHER MISSING KID, Canadian Broadcasting Corporation: JOHN ZARITSKY, Producer

Foreign Language Film Award
VOLVER A EMPEZAR (TO BEGIN AGAIN), Nickel Odeon S.A. (Spain)

Visual Effects
E.T. THE EXTRA-TERRESTRIAL: CARLO RAMBALDI, DENNIS MUREN and KENNETH F. SMITH

Honorary Award
MICKEY ROONEY in recognition of his 50 years of versatility in a variety of memorable film performances

Jean Hersholt Humanitarian Award
WALTER MIRISCH

1983

DESPITE THE PRODUCERS' attempts in 1983 to trim the oft-criticized lengthy running-time of the Awards ceremony by redesigning the stage of the Dorothy Chandler Pavilion – thereby reducing the winners' 'walking time' to and from the podium – they didn't bargain for the spontaneous overflow of this year's acceptance speeches. The show clocked up a tedious three hours 46 minutes, with lots of film clips and nostalgia helping to drag things out. Meanwhile, the nearest thing to a political protest was a demonstration before the awards by a group called Principles, Equality and Professionalism in Film, whose grievance was that Barbra Streisand hadn't been nominated for her direction of **Yentl**. Out of 274 Best Director nominees in the Academy history, they claimed, only one had been a woman (Lina Wertmüller for **Seven Beauties** in 1976).

It was probably of little consolation to the protesters that what once would have been described as a classic 'woman's picture' collected most of the major Oscars in 1983. As in 1979 (**Kramer vs Kramer**) and 1980 (**Ordinary People**), a superior weepie, Paramount's **Terms Of Endearment**, was voted Best Picture, with its producer James L. Brooks claiming two more awards, for Best Direction and Best Screenplay Adaptation (from Larry McMurtry's novel). "There has been a lot said about the studios that turned it down," said Brooks about **Terms**,

BELOW *James L. Brooks' classy, three-handkerchief weepie,* Terms of Endearment *ran away with all the year's major awards. Here, Best Supporting Actor Jack Nicholson shares a moment with mother (Best Actress Shirley MacLaine, left) and daughter (Debra Winger, also nominated for Best Actress)*

"but I think it's more significant that a Hollywood studio did make it."

Shirley MacLaine, who played 50-year-old mother and grandmother Aurora Greenaway in the film, won the Best Actress Oscar, fending off Debra Winger, who played her daughter Emma, as well as fourth-time loser Jane Alexander (superb as a mother trying to cope with nuclear fall-out in **Testament**), 1982's winner Meryl Streep (**Silkwood**) and Britain's Julie Walters (**Educating Rita**). Similarly, Jack Nicholson beat **Terms** co-star John Lithgow to the Best Supporting Actor Oscar (joining Jack Lemmon and Robert De Niro as the third winner of both actor awards).

Despite Nicholson's bravura performance as Aurora's engagingly crude, licentious and finally caring neighbor and lover, Garrett Breedlove (he's also an astronaut), and Lithgow's quieter depiction of Emma's shy and courteous lover Sam, the film belongs to MacLaine and Winger as the mother and daughter whose ebbing-and-flowing, long-distance relationship over 30 years (20 of which roll by in the first five minutes of screen time) is based on a strong but indefinable love.

Astutely written and directed by the small-screen graduate Brooks, **Terms** is otherwise an eccentric family drama with a rambling plot detailing Emma's marriage to the feckless Flap (Jeff Daniels), Aurora's resistance to that match, and her own oddball lifestyle. Only in the last half-hour of the film, following Emma and Flap's move with their two sons and daughter to Nebraska, and the revelation that Emma has terminal cancer, does the mostly comic scenario switch to melodrama and the audience prepare for tears. But it is excellently done.

MacLaine's performance as Aurora is very striking. All pink frills, flounces and hairpieces, a middle-aged widow waiting to be set sexually alight (which she is by the virile Garrett), she is seemingly dependent on her daughter, but in truth has depths of maturity and resilience such as are only possessed by a mother facing up to her only daughter's death. Stern with her unsuitable suitors and giving as good as she gets to Garrett, she is one of this actress' most marvellous creations. Winger is marvellous, too, as the intense, usually pregnant Emma. Very much her mother's daughter, she deals with Flap's infidelity and her cancer with an aplomb that conceals deep suffering.

But it was MacLaine's Oscar, long overdue. Hitherto nominated four times as Best Actress – for **Some Came Running** (1958), **The Apartment** (1960), **Irma La Douce** (1963) and **The Turning Point** (1977) – she was in tears when she finally took the award: "I have wondered for 26 years what this would feel like. Thank you for terminating the suspense."

Terms Of Endearment wasn't the only multiple award-winner in town. Its five awards came from 11 nominations and it conceded three of the behind-the-scenes awards (for Best Original Score, Sound and Editing) to Philip Kaufman's superbly executed astronaut saga, **The Right Stuff** – which also won for Best Sound Effects Editing. The comparative box-office failure of this space epic

probably damaged its chances as a Best Film nominee. Nor was the Academy in sufficiently sentimental mood to grant Ingmar Bergman the Best Director Oscar for the exquisite film he claimed would be his last, **Fanny And Alexander**, but it did come away with four awards, including Best Foreign Language Film and Best Cinematography by the distinguished Sven Nykvist.

Gene Kelly's honorary Oscar from 1951, destroyed in a fire the previous year, was replaced by the Academy during the ceremony; veteran producer Mike Frankovich was presented with the Jean Hersholt Humanitarian Award by Frank Sinatra; and Linda Hunt, magnificent in the male role of the tiny Chinese-Australian photographer-guide in **The Year Of Living Dangerously**, was a popular choice for Best Supporting Actress.

"I'm very excited, very happy, very everything," said Robert Duvall, voted Best Actor for his performance as Mac Sledge in Bruce Beresford's **Tender Mercies**, which

LEFT *Ingmar Bergman's memorably beautiful elegy to childhood,* Fanny And Alexander, *captured the awards for Best Foreign Film, Costume, Cinematography and Art Direction-Set Decoration. The children were played by Bertil Guve (left) and Pernilla Alwin*

BELOW *Director Peter Weir audaciously cast little Linda Hunt as a male Chinese news photographer in* The Year Of Living Dangerously. *His decision paid off in a Best Supporting Actress Oscar for Miss Hunt*

also won for Best Original Screenplay by Horton Foote (winner for 1962's **To Kill A Mockingbird**, which featured Duvall, in his first film role, as the mentally retarded but kindly Boo Radley). Previously nominated as Best Actor for **The Great Santini** (1980) and as Best Supporting Actor for **The Godfather** (1972) and **Apocalypse Now** (1979), Duvall overcame his British rivals for the award (Albert Finney and Tom Courtenay in **The Dresser**, Michael Caine in **Educating Rita** and Tom Conti in **Reuben, Reuben**) with a downbeat, heartfelt performance as a man on the skids saved by his own hidden resources and the love of a good woman.

Former country star Mac has fallen on hard times and the bottle but a Vietnam widow, Rosa Lee (Tess Harper), takes him on as a handyman at her motel. Her boy Sonny befriends him, Mac and Rosa Lee marry, and soon Mac finds himself becoming involved in the music scene again – where he encounters his ex-wife, singer Dixie, and is reconciled with his daughter Sue Anne. Mac's nerve is stretched again when Sue Anne, eloping with one of Dixie's backing musicians, is killed in a car crash – but he pulls through for the sake of his new family. Duvall is quite superb as a rejuvenated middle-aged man tested by the shadows of the past in a perhaps over-painterly film chock-full of crackerbarrel wisdom.

Finally, one of the cinema's last surviving pioneers, 92-year-old Hal Roach, was presented with an honorary Oscar. Roach started in the business in 1912 (after being a mule-skinner and gold prospector) and became one of the great comedy writer-director-producers of the silent era. Harold Lloyd, Laurel and Hardy, Our Gang, and ZaSu Pitts and Thelma Todd were among the stars who prospered under him. "The first day I worked in motion pictures," said Roach, receiving his statuette from Our Gang's George (Spanky) MacFarland, "I received a dollar a day for car fare and lunch – two sandwiches and a banana." Banana skins, he added, were invaluable to his studio's routines later on in his career. He also paid homage to his fellow professionals: "All these talented people who have been winning Oscars tonight made their money in an old-fashioned way. They earned it."

BELOW *Mac (Robert Duvall) rebuilds his broken life with the devotion of his new wife, Rosa Lee (Tess Harper) and her son (Allan Hubbard) in* Tender Mercies. *An actor of formidable qualities, Duvall was finally rewarded with the Best Actor award*

WINNERS 1983

Nominations Announced: February 20, 1984
Awards Ceremony: April 9, 1984
Dorothy Chandler Pavilion, Los Angeles County
Music Center

Best Picture
TERMS OF ENDEARMENT, Brooks/Paramount: JAMES L. BROOKS, Producer

Actor
ROBERT DUVALL in *Tender Mercies*, Antron Media-Universal/AFD

Actress
SHIRLEY MacLAINE in *Terms Of Endearment*

Supporting Actor
JACK NICHOLSON in *Terms Of Endearment*

Supporting Actress
LINDA HUNT in *The Year Of Living Dangerously*, MGM/UA

Directing
JAMES L. BROOKS for *Terms Of Endearment*

Writing
(Best Original Screenplay)
TENDER MERCIES: HORTON FOOTE
(Best Screenplay Adaptation)
TERMS OF ENDEARMENT: JAMES L. BROOKS

Cinematography
FANNY AND ALEXANDER, Cinematograph AB/Swedish Film Institute/Sweden/Gaumont-France Personafilm-Tobis Filmkunst/BRD/Embassy:
SVEN NYKVIST

Art Direction-Set Decoration
FANNY AND ALEXANDER: ANNA ASP
Set Decoration: SUSANNE LINGHELM

Sound
THE RIGHT STUFF, Chartoff-Winkler/Ladd/Warner Bros.: MARK BERGER, TOM SCOTT, RANDY THOM and DAVID MACMILLAN

Sound Effects Editing
THE RIGHT STUFF: JAY BOEKELHEIDE

Film Editing
THE RIGHT STUFF: GLENN FARR, LISA FRUCHTMAN, STEPHEN A. ROTTER, DOUGLAS STEWART and TOM ROLF

Music
(Best Original Score)
THE RIGHT STUFF: BILL CONTI
(Best Original Song Score and Its Adaptation or Best Adaptation Score)
YENTL, UA/Ladbroke/Harwood/MGM/UA
Original Song Score: MICHEL LEGRAND, ALAN and MARILYN BERGMAN
(Best Original Song)
FLASHDANCE . . . WHAT A FEELING from *Flashdance*, Polygram/Paramount
Music: GIORGIO MORODER
Lyrics: KEITH FORSEY and IRENE CARA

Costume Design
FANNY AND ALEXANDER: MARIK VOS

Short Films
(Animated)
SUNDAE IN NEW YORK, Motionpicker: JIMMY PICKER, Producer
(Live Action)
BOYS AND GIRLS, Atlantis: JANICE L. PLATT, Producer

Documentary
(Short Subjects)
FLAMENCO AT 5.15, National Film Board of Canada: CYNTHIA SCOTT and ADAM SYMANSKY, Producers
(Features)
HE MAKES ME FEEL LIKE DANCIN', Sherick Associates: EMILE ARDOLINO, Producer

Foreign Language Film Award
FANNY AND ALEXANDER (Sweden)

Visual Effects
RETURN OF THE JEDI, Lucasfilm/20th Century-Fox: RICHARD EDLUND, DENNIS MUREN, KEN RALSTON and PHIL TIPPETT

Honorary Award
HAL ROACH in recognition of his unparalleled record of contributions to the motion picture art form

Jean Hersholt Humanitarian Award
M.J. (MIKE) FRANKOVICH

1984

ELEVEN NOMINATIONS EACH for **Amadeus** and **A Passage To India** and seven apiece for **The Killing Fields** and **Places In The Heart** suggested that the 1984 Academy Awards would be a close-run contest. In the event, it was a walkover for **Amadeus**, produced by Saul Zaentz and directed by Milos Forman, who had collaborated to sweep the board nine years earlier with the five-Oscar **One Flew Over The Cuckoo's Nest**.

Amadeus won the Best Picture award; Forman was again Best Director; F. Murray Abraham, as Antonio Salieri, pipped his nominated co-star Tom Hulce – who played Mozart – to the Best Actor post; Peter Shaffer won the Best Screenplay Adaptation award for transforming his long-running Broadway and London stage hit (the winner of five Tonys in 1981); and the film also won for

Best Costume Design, for Art Direction, Sound, and Make-up. Maurice Jarre, whose music for **A Passage To India** won him his third Best Original Score Oscar for a David Lean film (following **Lawrence Of Arabia**, 1962; and **Dr Zhivago**, 1965), acknowledged the supremacy of **Amadeus** in his acceptance speech when he said, "I was lucky Mozart was not eligible this year". As it was, **Amadeus** conductor Neville Marriner and music supervisor John Strauss were awarded a special commendation by the Academy for their work on the film.

Amadeus' triumph at an especially emotional ceremony was a handsome reward for the team of Forman, Zaentz and Shaffer. Forman had seen the 1979 play at its first London preview, let the dramatist know through their mutual agent that he wanted to film it and asked Zaentz to see it in New York. Initially reluctant, Shaffer was persuaded to adapt the work, and the three of them formed a democratic triumvirate, which voted on major decisions such as casting the leads.

Shaffer restructured the play for the screen, which enabled lavish and authentic recreations of Mozart's operas. Much of this rewriting was done in Prague where the film

BELOW *Milos Forman's screen version of* Amadeus *ran away with the 1984 Academy Awards. Previously unknown actor F. Murray Abraham (left) scooped the Best Actor Oscar as court composer Salieri, here with Tom Hulce as Mozart*

ABOVE *Best Supporting Actor winner Haing S. Ngor surveys the horror of* The Killing Fields, *which gave the title to the powerful film dealing with the appalling war in Cambodia*

TOP *Indomitable Edna Spalding (Sally Field) struggles to keep her family, Frank (Yankton Hatten, left) and Possum (Gennie James), together, after the death of her husband in* Places In The Heart. *She is helped by Moze (Danny Glover, right). It was Miss Field's second Best Actress award*

— Forman's first in his native Czechoslovakia since he left for the US in 1969 — was shot. When he went up to collect his Oscar, somewhat hurriedly, Forman thanked his whole company but made special mention of his Czechoslovakian collaborators. Zaentz graciously named all the unlucky nominees — **The Killing Fields, Places In The Heart, A Passage To India, A Soldier's Story** — when he collected the Best Film award, presenter Sir Laurence Olivier having omitted to do so and jumping straight to the winner in the excitement. Zaentz added, "The five pictures nominated this year all had a curious relationship: they were made by film-makers who had to fight to overcome obstacles to film their visions".

The film **Amadeus** was a sumptuous visual spectacle, magnificently empowered by Mozart's music, that is exactly of the type the Academy loves — gorgeous, tasteful and driven by high art, with a tearjerking human tragedy in its climax. It focuses on the rivalry between the composers at the court of the Emperor Joseph II of Austria. Wolfgang Amadeus Mozart, a genius beyond belief (seemingly unaware that any such rivalry exists), is otherwise a scatologically-minded buffoon with a high-pitched giggle and little control of his life; Antonio Salieri is the dignified, supercilious establishment figure whose talent pales beside that of the young prodigy. Salieri is eaten up by his jealousy of Mozart's awesome, God-given abilities — compounded by his distaste for the man — and when he can stand it no longer he dresses up like an avenging angel in black mask and cape and gives Mozart a commission that he knows will kill him.

Finally, Salieri is at Mozart's deathbed, still astounded by his powers of composition but unable to stop himself from draining the last note from him. The shocking moment comes when the dying Mozart speaks of his gratitude and admiration of the man who is killing him, and of his fear that Salieri never liked him. These scenes, and those detailing Mozart's rise and fall, his affectionate marriage to Stanzi (Elizabeth Berridge), and the billowing, flamboyant musical set-pieces, are bookended by the ancient and guilt-ridden Salieri's suicide attempt at the beginning and his ultimate descent into madness at the end. His personal tragedy is that, even in his mania, not an ounce of Wolfie's brilliance lurks within him.

"I didn't want someone familiar like Jack Nicholson or Donald Sutherland that audiences would recognize. So all of us agreed to cast F. Murray Abraham – who *is* Salieri", said Forman. Born in El Paso of Syrian and Italian parents, Abraham came to **Amadeus** via numerous appearances on Broadway, off-Broadway, in TV and films. He was selected to play Salieri after a year of auditions for dozens of candidates. His crazed, religious, half-court lackey, half-Mephistophelean, wholly malevolent Salieri justified his Oscar; although Abraham said that his triumph was "bittersweet" because his role "relies on Tom Hulce's performance. It would be a lie if I told you I didn't know what to say," he added as he collected his award, "because I've been working on this speech for 25 years. I never thought I had a shot at the Oscar. I am not a leading man. Let me tell you who is a leading man – Cary Grant." Hulce's performance as Mozart was indeed deeply affecting and he must have run Abraham close; both were first-time nominees. Other contenders for Best Actor in 1984 were hot favorite Albert Finney, in **Under The Volcano**, outsider Jeff Bridges in **Starman**, and Sam Waterston in **The Killing Fields**.

Waterston gave an emotion-charged performance as Pulitzer-prize winning journalist Sidney Schanberg whose friendship with his interpreter Dith Pran during the disintegration of Cambodia formed the basis of **The Killing Fields**. This superb British film, produced by David Puttnam and directed by Roland Joffé, outpaced David Lean's **A Passage To India** in the Oscar stakes, with Chris Menges' cinematography and Jim Clarke's editing each winning in their categories. **The Killing Fields'** third award went to non-professional, first-time actor Haing S. Ngor.

Ngor, a Cambodian gynaecologist whose own family had been wiped out by the Khmer Rouge during their brutal revolution, was cast as Pran just six weeks before shooting began in Bangkok. His portrayal of his extraordinary countryman, who saves the lives of Schanberg and his fellow journalists, and is then left to save himself from a labor camp and certain death by obliterating all traces of his education (as had Ngor) and escaping into Thailand, is not only remarkable, but one of the most courageous performances in screen history. The on-screen partnership of Ngor and Waterston is said to have curiously reflected that of Pran and Schanberg, and perhaps reflecting the real-life reunion of the characters they were portraying, Waterston's obvious delight at seeing Ngor collect his Oscar was one of the most touching moments captured by the telecast.

Another first-time nominee in 1984 was Dame Peggy Ashcroft, who had begun her film career in the early 1930s. She won for her redoubtable Mrs Moore in **A Passage To India**. The funeral of Sir Michael Redgrave prevented her from attending the Oscar ceremony.

Best Actress of 1984 was Sally Field, repeating her success with **Norma Rae** in 1979. Her performance in **Places In The Heart** – for which directorial nominee Robert Benton won for Best Original Screenplay – was judged better than those of Jessica Lange in **Country** and Sissy Spacek in **The River**, who – like the appositely named Field – played women farmers struggling against rural depression in a male-dominated world. Judy Davis in **A Passage To India** and Vanessa Redgrave in **The Bostonians** were the other nominees. In Hollywood's agrarian year, Field celebrated her success with one of the most embarrassingly over-the-top acceptance speeches Oscar has witnessed: "The first time, I hardly felt it because it was all so new. I haven't had an orthodox career and the first time I didn't feel it. But now I feel it – You like me! You like me!"

Her on-screen performance as Edna Spaulding was a good deal better. Edna is a wife and mother-of-two, widowed in the opening moments of the film, who grittily decides to take on her neighbors during a cotton-picking race. Her friends rally round, her black henchman works heroically (until driven out by the Klan), Edna drives herself to near collapse – but wins the race. Field, comforting mother (but not one to spare the rod), plucky boss and

BELOW *Cambodian interpreter Dith Pran (Haing S. Ngor, right) is finally reunited with American journalist Sidney Schanberg (Sam Waterston), after miraculously surviving dreadful years in the grip of the Khmer Rouge in David Puttnam's* The Killing Fields, *brilliantly directed by Roland Joffé*

perspiring cotton-picker, was persuasive in a sometimes overly roseate vision of the Depression.

Perhaps the saddest omission in the 1984 awards was an Oscar for 76-year-old David Lean, nominated as Best Director, for Best Screenplay Adaptation and as Best Editor for **A Passage To India** after a 14-year absence from the screen. His consolation was that he already held two directorial awards, for **The Bridge On The River Kwai** (1957) and **Lawrence Of Arabia** (1962). In the end, it can be said that **Amadeus** waltzed it.

WINNERS 1984

Nominations Announced: February 11, 1985
Awards Ceremony: March 25, 1985
Dorothy Chandler Pavilion, Los Angeles County
Music Center

Best Picture
AMADEUS, Zaentz/Orion: SAUL ZAENTZ, Producer

Actor
F. MURRAY ABRAHAM in *Amadeus*

Actress
SALLY FIELD in *Places In The Heart*, Tri-Star

Supporting Actor
HAING S. NGOR in *The Killing Fields*, Goldcrest/Warner Bros.

Supporting Actress
PEGGY ASHCROFT in *A Passage To India*, GW Films/Warner Bros.

Directing
MILOS FORMAN for *Amadeus*

Writing
(Best Original Screenplay)
PLACES IN THE HEART: ROBERT BENTON
(Best Screenplay Adaptation)
AMADEUS: PETER SCHAFFER

Cinematography
THE KILLING FIELDS: CHRIS MENGES

Art Direction-Set Decoration
AMADEUS: PATRIZIA VON BRANDENSTEIN
Set Decoration: KAREL CERNY

Sound
AMADEUS: MARK BERGER, TOM SCOTT, TODD BOEKELHEIDE and CHRIS NEWMAN

Film Editing
THE KILLING FIELDS: JIM CLARK

Music
(Best Original Score)
A PASSAGE TO INDIA: MAURICE JARRE
(Best Original Song Score and Its Adaptation or Best Adaptation Score)
PURPLE RAIN, Purple/Warner Bros.
Original Score: PRINCE

(Best Original Song)
I JUST CALLED TO SAY I LOVE YOU from *The Woman In Red*, Orion
Music & Lyrics: STEVIE WONDER

Costume Design
AMADEUS: THEODOR PISTEK

Make-Up
AMADEUS: PAUL LeBLANC and DICK SMITH

Short Films
(Animated)
CHARADE, Sheridan College: JON MINNIS, Producer
(Live Action)
UP, Pyramid: MIKE HOOVER, Producer

Documentary
(Short Subjects)
THE STONE CARVERS, Wagner: MARJORIE HUNT and PAUL WAGNER, Producers
(Features)
THE TIMES OF HARVEY MILK, Black Sand Educational/TC Films International: ROBERT EPSTEIN and RICHARD SCHMIECHEN, Producers

Foreign Language Film Award
DANGEROUS MOVES, Cohn (Switzerland)

Visual Effects
INDIANA JONES AND THE TEMPLE OF DOOM, Lucasfilm/Paramount:
DENNIS MUREN, MICHAEL McALISTER, LORNE PETERSON and GEORGE GIBBS

Honorary Awards
JAMES STEWART for 50 years of meaningful performances, for his high ideals, both on and off the screen, with the respect and affection of his colleagues
NATIONAL ENDOWMENT FOR THE ARTS, FRANK HODSOLL, Chairman

Jean Hersholt Humanitarian Award
DAVID L. WOLPER

1985

HOLLYWOOD HAS BEEN guilty of many errors of judgment and displays of churlishness over the years, but the Academy's snubbing of Steven Spielberg at the 58th Annual Awards ceremony takes some beating. The controversy began with the nominations: eleven each for Sydney Pollack's **Out Of Africa** and Spielberg's **The Color Purple**, but with Spielberg himself ignored in the Best Director category. Warner Brothers immediately responded to what seemed like a spiteful vendetta against Hollywood's most financially successful director with a statement which read: "The company is shocked and dismayed that the movie's primary creative

force – Steven Spielberg – was not recognized." It was the first time since Sam Wood was overlooked in 1942 that a film with ten or more nominations didn't include a nod for its director. (Despite eleven chances, Wood's **Pride Of The Yankees** won only for Best Editing.)

But worse was to come for **The Color Purple**. On Oscar night, the Best Picture choice, **Out Of Africa**, totalled seven awards in all, **Witness** took two from eight nominations, **Cocoon** two from two and **Prizzi's Honor** one from eight. Spielberg's film drew a total blank, equaling the unhappy feat of the **The Turning Point** with nothing from eleven nominations in 1977. **The Color Purple's** leading lady, Whoopi Goldberg – a Best Actress nominee for her first film – perhaps best summed up the feelings in the Spielberg camp when she presented **Witness**'s Best Editing Oscar to the absentee Thom Noble and suggested that he would have wanted to thank his mother, "as some of us might have wanted to thank our mothers, too."

The Spielberg slight brought an element of farce to

BELOW *Karen Blixen (Meryl Streep) with the native Kenyans whom she befriends in the year's Best Picture,* Out of Africa, *which captured all the major awards except those for acting*

the awards. The day after the ceremony, the Hollywood branch of the National Association for the Advancement of Colored People accused the Academy of a blackout against **The Color Purple** – a moving, handsomely filmed but unsettling adaptation of Alice Walker's novel about a young black girl, Celie (Goldberg), trying to cope with patriarchal and sexual oppression in the Deep South – and its famous director. This was hotly denied, of course.

An important departure personally for Spielberg in that it represented a break from a long run of ingenious special-effects adventure movies that had turned their creator into a multi-millionaire, towards a cinema of serious social concern, **The Color Purple** – a fine achievement that is less than a masterpiece – had consciously been made, it seems, with Academy Awards in mind, although for it to lose out in eleven nominated categories doesn't look like just bad luck.

Its fate did not enhance the merit of **Out Of Africa**'s victory, which swept the board with Oscars for Pollack as Best Director and producer of the Best Film, and won, too, for Best Screenplay Adaptation, Cinematography, Best Score, Best Art Direction and Set Decoration and Best Sound.

There were, however, no acting prizes for the film, despite nominations for Meryl Streep (perhaps the Academy considered her two previous awards enough for the moment) as Best Actress and Klaus Maria Brandauer as Best Supporting Actor. But Pollack, who significantly shook hands with Spielberg on his way up to collect his statuette, made special mention of Streep in his acceptance speech. Her performance as Karen Blixen/Isak Dinesen – the Danish baroness on whose books Kurt Luedtke, working in close collaboration with associate producer and Dinesen biographer Judith Thurman, based the film – was certainly remarkable. A stylish epic of African colonial life re-created for the screen as instant golden nostalgia, Pollack's movie traces Blixen's life from her arrival in Kenya before the First World War – "I had a farm in Africa once", she recalls in voice-over – to her departure from this Eden-like country in 1931.

In many ways a modern 'woman's picture', it also depicts her struggles as an independent woman coping with a feckless husband, Baron Blixen (Brandauer), who gives her debts and syphilis; her courageous journey across the veld, where wandering bands of dangerous Masai roam, to bring supplies to the English colonials during the war; the razing of her property to the ground by fire; and, perhaps most difficult of all, her love affair with the free-spirited gentleman adventurer, Denys Finch Hatton (Robert Redford), in which she has to fight her own possessive need for him, and his death in a plane crash. Streep delivered a lilting Danish accent and coped with a script that replaces melodrama with a travelogue-style plot – vast, beautifully photographed panoramas of magnificent scenery filling out the story – and made the film her own in a way that Pollack did not stamp it as his.

The latter might be considered lucky to have won the

director's Oscar in a year in which John Huston (**Prizzi's Honor**) and the great Japanese film-maker Akira Kurosawa (**Ran** – his spellbinding adaptation of *King Lear*) were in contention, along with the Brazilian Hector Babenco (**Kiss Of The Spider Woman**) and the Australian Peter Weir (**Witness**) – although **Out Of Africa** had exactly the sumptuousness, romance and glossy charm that tends to seduce the Academy. It won the Best Picture award over **The Color Purple, Prizzi's Honor, Kiss Of The Spider Woman** and **Witness**. Apparently as the result of an unaccountable administrative error in the countries of origin, **Ran** was neither nominated in this category nor entered for Best Foreign Film, the latter won by the Argentinian **The Official Story**. Pollack was in good company then, especially when he went up to collect the top honor from an esteemed and venerable triumvirate consisting of Huston, Kurosawa and Billy Wilder.

Although Huston missed out personally, he shared in the triumph of his daughter Anjelica (as did her co-star and boyfriend Jack Nicholson), who was voted Best Supporting Actress for her funny/sad performance as

ABOVE *Whoopi Goldberg (left) and Margaret Avery in Steven Spielberg's immensely successful* The Color Purple. *The movie became the cause célèbre of the 1985 Awards, thanks to the spurning of its director, and the absence of even a single win from eleven nominations*

ABOVE RIGHT *Nominated Harrison Ford as the police investigator under threat and forced to take refuge in an Amish community in Peter Weir's* Witness. *Nominated in all major categories except Best Actress, the film won for its screenplay and editing*

a Mafia woman scorned in love. Marsha Mason and Richard Dreyfuss presented her with her award and she commented: "This means a lot to me since it was for a role in which I was directed by my father, and I know it means a lot to him." She thus became the first third-generation Oscar-winner in the Academy's history; in 1948 Huston directed her grandfather Walter Huston to the Best Supporting Actor Oscar for **The Treasure Of The Sierra Madre** and himself won the Best Director and Best Screenplay awards that year.

The winner of 1985's Best Supporting Actor award was 77-year-old Don Ameche, like Anjelica Huston and their eight fellow contenders in the supporting Oscar categories, a first-time nominee. He took it for his rejuvenated, break-dancing septuagenarian in Ron Howard's **Cocoon**. The Academy rose to the old Fox favorite (celebrating fifty years in films) and he gave the most gracious acceptance speech of the evening.

Indeed, sentiment prevailed, although Paul Newman, six times a bridesmaid but never a bride, proved one of the youngest recipients ever of an honorary Oscar. "It gives me permission to risk and surprise myself a little bit," he said. Meanwhile, 61-year-old Geraldine Page was more ebullient: "Yeah for the geriatrics!" she shouted as she collected the Best Actress Oscar, following seven previous unsuccessful nominations since 1953. She fended off Streep, Goldberg, Anne Bancroft (**Agnes Of God**) and Jessica Lange (**Sweet Dreams**), although her winning role – that of Mrs Watts, a hymn-singing pensioner who journeys from an unhappy existence in Houston to the hometown of her youth, a final odyssey, in debutant director Peter Masterson's excellent **The Trip To Bountiful** – may not necessarily go down as her best film. Still, she is superb in it – "the performance of a lifetime" said *Variety* – and the Oscar was long overdue for this outstanding American actress and leading exponent of the Method. The previous year's Best Actor, F. Murray Abraham, said, "I consider this woman the greatest actress in the English language," when he announced her win, and performed the most elaborate and adulatory bow as he welcomed her on stage.

Sally Field engagingly guyed her own over-the-top Oscar acceptance speech of a year before in presenting 1985's Best Actor award to William Hurt, who seemed a little overawed by the occasion. "I'm very proud to be

TOP *William Hurt as Molina, the South American homosexual romantic, here in a gay club after his release from prison in Hector Babenco's* Kiss Of The Spider Woman. *Hurt's skilled portrayal won him the Best Actor award*

ABOVE *Geraldine Page with her long-awaited and hard won Best Actress Oscar for* The Trip To Bountiful. *One of America's most distinguished actresses, Miss Page has a total of four Best Actress and four Best Supporting Actress nominations to her credit*

an actor," was about all he could muster. Hurt – who beat Oscar-holders Jack Nicholson (**Prizzi's Honor**) and Jon Voight (**Runaway Train**) and fellow first-time nominees James Garner (**Murphy's Romance**) and Harrison Ford (**Witness**) to the prize – became the first man to win it by playing a gay. The role was that of the effeminate and ultimately heroic homosexual prisoner in a Latin American jail in **Kiss of the Spider Woman**, and Hurt's performance was both magical and deeply moving.

The film is the story of a bizarre relationship between the sensitive, romantic Molina, who weaves imaginary movieland dreams to while away the long hours of boredom, and his cellmate Valentin (Raul Julia), a hard, stoical political prisoner who has no time for such fripperies. As a kind of love develops between them, their roles strangely reverse and Molina is issued out into the real world to take up 'the Cause'. Hurt, perhaps best-known before for his slow-witted, macho lawyer duped by a *femme fatale* in **Body Heat**, was remarkably transformed as the gentle, limp-wristed Scheherazade forced to run from an assassin in the cold light of day. The Academy didn't err in this instance. Nor in giving the television presentation of the ceremony into the capable hands of Stanley Donen, who paid stylish and entertaining homage to the past and left viewers looking forward to Oscar's future.

WINNERS 1985

Best Picture
OUT OF AFRICA, Universal: SYDNEY POLLACK,
Producer

Actor
WILLIAM HURT in *Kiss Of The Spider Woman*, H.B.
Filmes/Sugarloaf/Island Alive/Island Pictures

Actress
GERALDINE PAGE in *The Trip.To Bountiful*, Bountiful/
Island Pictures

Supporting Actor
DON AMECHE in *Cocoon*, Fox/Zanuck-Brown/
20th Century-Fox

Supporting Actress
ANJELICA HUSTON in *Prizzi's Honor*, ABC/
20th Century Fox

Directing
SYDNEY POLLACK for *Out Of Africa*

Writing
(Best Original Screenplay)
WITNESS, Feldman/Paramount: EARL W. WALLACE,
PAMELA WALLACE and WILLIAM KELLEY
(Best Screenplay Adaptation)
OUT OF AFRICA: KURT LUEDTKE

Cinematography
OUT OF AFRICA: DAVID WATKIN

Art Direction-Set Decoration
OUT OF AFRICA: STEPHEN GRIMES
Set Decoration: JOSIE MacAVIN

Sound
OUT OF AFRICA: CHRIS JENKINS, GARY ALEXANDER,
LARRY STENSVOLD and PETER HANDFORD

Sound Effects Editing
BACK TO THE FUTURE, Amblin Entertainment/Universal:
CHARLES L. CAMPBELL and ROBERT RUTLEDGE

Film Editing
WITNESS: THOM NOBLE

Music
(Best Original Score)
OUT OF AFRICA: JOHN BARRY

(Best Original Song)
SAY YOU, SAY ME from *White Nights*, New Vision/
Columbia
Music & Lyrics: LIONEL RICHIE

Costume Design
RAN, Greenwich/Nippon Herald/Herald Ace/
Orion Classics: EMI WADA

Make-Up
MASK, Universal: MICHAEL WESTMORE and
ZOLTAN ELEK

Short Films
(Animated)
ANNA & BELLA, Netherlands: CILIA VAN DIJK, Producer
(Live Action)
MOLLY'S PILGRIM, Phoenix: JEFF BROWN and
CHRIS PELZER, Producers

Documentary
(Short subjects)
WITNESS TO WAR: DR. CHARLIE CLEMENTS, Skylight:
DAVID GOODMAN, Producer
(Features)
BROKEN RAINBOW, Earthworks: MARIA FLORIO and
VICTORIA MUDD, Producers

Foreign Language Film Award
THE OFFICIAL STORY, Historias Cinematograficas/
Cinemania & Progress Communications/Almi (Argentina)

Visual Effects
COCOON: KEN RALSTON, RALPH McQUARRIE,
SCOTT FARRAR and DAVID BERRY

Honorary Awards
PAUL NEWMAN in recognition of his many memorable
and compelling screen performances and for his personal
integrity and dedication to his craft
ALEX NORTH in recognition of his brilliant artistry in the
creation of memorable music for motion pictures

Jean Hersholt Humanitarian Award
Charles (Buddy) Rogers

LEAGUE TABLE OF WINNERS

For complete and easy reference, this appendix
summarizes, in alphabetical order, the Academy's
Best Actors and Actresses throughout 58 years of Awards.
The listing includes all nominations ever received in this category
by each star, as well as any Best Supporting Oscars each might have
won. The particular film for which the award was given
is denoted in italic type. The date of each nomination follows the film title.

BEST ACTORS

F. MURRAY ABRAHAM
Amadeus, 1984
GEORGE ARLISS
The Green Goddess, 1929/30
Disraeli, 1929/30
LIONEL BARRYMORE
A Free Soul, 1930/31
WARNER BAXTER
In Old Arizona, 1928/9
WALLACE BEERY
The Big House, 1929/30
The Champ, 1931/2 (Tie with
   Fredric March)
HUMPHREY BOGART
Casablanca, 1943
The African Queen, 1951
The Caine Mutiny, 1954
ERNEST BORGNINE
Marty, 1955
MARLON BRANDO
A Streetcar Named Desire, 1951
Viva Zapata!, 1952
Julius Caesar, 1953
On The Waterfront, 1954
Sayonara, 1957
The Godfather, 1972 (Award
   refused)
Last Tango In Paris, 1973
YUL BRYNNER
The King And I, 1956
JAMES CAGNEY
Angels With Dirty Faces, 1938
Yankee Doodle Dandy, 1941
Love Me Or Leave Me, 1955
ART CARNEY
Harry And Tonto, 1974
RONALD COLMAN
Bulldog Drummond, 1929/30
Condemned, 1929/30
Random Harvest, 1942
A Double Life, 1947

GARY COOPER
Mr Deeds Goes To Town, 1936
Sergeant York, 1941
The Pride Of The Yankees, 1942
For Whom The Bell Tolls, 1943
High Noon, 1952
BRODERICK CRAWFORD
All The King's Men, 1949
BING CROSBY
Going My Way, 1944
The Bells Of St Mary's, 1945
The Country Girl, 1954
ROBERT DE NIRO
Taxi Driver, 1976
The Deer Hunter, 1978
Raging Bull, 1980
Best Supporting Actor Award:
The Godfather Part II, 1974
ROBERT DONAT
The Citadel, 1938
Goodbye Mr Chips, 1939
RICHARD DREYFUSS
The Goodbye Girl, 1977
ROBERT DUVALL
The Great Santini, 1980
Tender Mercies, 1983
JOSÉ FERRER
Cyrano de Bergerac, 1950
Moulin Rouge, 1952
PETER FINCH
Sunday, Bloody Sunday, 1971
Network, 1976 (Awarded
   posthumously)
HENRY FONDA
The Grapes of Wrath, 1940
On Golden Pond, 1981
CLARK GABLE
It Happened One Night, 1934
Mutiny On The Bounty, 1935
Gone With The Wind, 1939

ALEC GUINNESS
The Lavender Hill Mob, 1952
The Bridge On The River Kwai, 1957
GENE HACKMAN
The French Connection, 1971
REX HARRISON
Cleopatra, 1963
My Fair Lady, 1964
CHARLTON HESTON
Ben-Hur, 1959
DUSTIN HOFFMAN
The Graduate, 1967
Midnight Cowboy, 1969
Lenny, 1974
Kramer vs Kramer, 1979
Tootsie, 1982
WILLIAM HOLDEN
Sunset Boulevard, 1950
Stalag 17, 1953
Network, 1976
WILLIAM HURT
Kiss Of The Spider Woman, 1985
EMIL JANNINGS
The Last Command, 1927/8
The Way Of All Flesh, 1927/8
BEN KINGSLEY
Gandhi, 1982
BURT LANCASTER
From Here To Eternity, 1953
Elmer Gantry, 1960
Bird Man Of Alcatraz, 1962
Atlantic City, 1981
CHARLES LAUGHTON
The Private Life Of Henry VIII,
   1932/33
Mutiny On The Bounty, 1935
Witness For The Prosecution, 1957
JACK LEMMON
Some Like It Hot, 1959
The Apartment, 1960
Days Of Wine And Roses, 1962

Save The Tiger, 1973
The China Syndrome, 1979
Tribute, 1980
Missing, 1982
PAUL LUKAS
Watch On The Rhine, 1943
FREDRIC MARCH
The Royal Family Of Broadway,
    1930/31
Dr Jekyll And Mr Hyde, 1931/32
    (Tie with Wallace Beery)
A Star Is Born, 1937
The Best Years Of Our Lives, 1946
Death Of A Salesman, 1951
LEE MARVIN
Cat Ballou, 1965
VICTOR McLAGLEN
The Informer, 1935
RAY MILLAND
The Lost Weekend, 1945
PAUL MUNI
The Valiant, 1928/29
I Am A Fugitive From A Chain
    Gang, 1932/33
The Story Of Louis Pasteur, 1936
The Life Of Emile Zola, 1937
The Last Angry Man, 1959
JACK NICHOLSON
Five Easy Pieces, 1970
The Last Detail, 1973
Chinatown, 1974
One Flew Over The Cuckoo's Nest,
    1975
Prizzi's Honor, 1985
Best Supporting Actor Award:
Terms Of Endearment, 1983
DAVID NIVEN
Separate Tables, 1958
LAURENCE OLIVIER
Wuthering Heights, 1939

Rebecca, 1940
Henry V, 1946
Hamlet, 1948
Richard III, 1956
The Entertainer, 1960
Othello, 1965
Sleuth, 1972
The Boys From Brazil, 1978
GREGORY PECK
The Keys Of The Kingdom, 1945
The Yearling, 1946
Gentleman's Agreement, 1947
Twelve O'Clock High, 1949
To Kill A Mockingbird, 1962
SIDNEY POITIER
The Defiant Ones, 1958
Lilies Of The Field, 1963
CLIFF ROBERTSON
Charly, 1968
MAXIMILIAN SCHELL
Judgment At Nuremberg, 1961
The Man In The Glass Booth, 1975
PAUL SCOFIELD
A Man For All Seasons, 1966
GEORGE C. SCOTT
Patton, 1970 (Award refused)
The Hospital, 1971
ROD STEIGER
The Pawnbroker, 1965
In The Heat Of The Night, 1967
JAMES STEWART
Mr Smith Goes To Washington, 1939
The Philadelphia Story, 1940
It's A Wonderful Life, 1946
Harvey, 1950
Anatomy Of A Murder, 1959
SPENCER TRACY
San Francisco, 1936
Captains Courageous, 1937
Boys Town, 1938

Father Of The Bride, 1950
Bad Day At Black Rock, 1955
The Old Man And The Sea, 1958
Inherit The Wind, 1960
Judgment At Nuremberg, 1961
Guess Who's Coming To Dinner,
    1967
JON VOIGHT
Midnight Cowboy, 1969
Coming Home, 1978
Runaway Train, 1985
JOHN WAYNE
Sands Of Iwo Jima, 1949
True Grit, 1969

It is worth noting that the major
box-office stars listed below, in spite
of their talent, critical success and
enormous public following, did not
win – or have not, so far, won – a
Best Actor Award. The number of
nominations they received in the
category is bracketed behind their
names. Some of them did receive
honorary awards.

Warren Beatty (3)
Richard Burton (6)
Michael Caine (3)
Charlie Chaplin (2)
Maurice Chevalier (2)
Montgomery Clift (3)
James Dean (2 – Both posthumous)
Kirk Douglas (3)
Cary Grant (2)
Paul Newman (6)
Peter O'Toole (7)
Al Pacino (4)
Robert Redford (1)
Mickey Rooney (2)

BEST ACTRESSES

JULIE ANDREWS
Mary Poppins, 1964
The Sound of Music, 1965
Victor/Victoria, 1982
ANNE BANCROFT
The Miracle Worker, 1962
The Pumpkin Eater, 1964
The Graduate, 1967
The Turning Point, 1977
Agnes Of God, 1985
INGRID BERGMAN
For Whom The Bell Tolls, 1943
Gaslight, 1944
The Bells Of St Mary's, 1945

Joan Of Arc, 1948
Anastasia, 1956
Autumn Sonata, 1978
Best Supporting Actress Award:
Murder On The Orient Express, 1974
SHIRLEY BOOTH
Come Back Little Sheba, 1952
ELLEN BURSTYN
The Exorcist, 1973
Alice Doesn't Live Here Anymore,
    1974
Same Time, Next Year, 1978
Resurrection, 1980

JULIE CHRISTIE
Darling, 1965
McCabe And Mrs Miller, 1971
CLAUDETTE COLBERT
It Happened One Night, 1934
Private Worlds, 1935
Since You Went Away, 1944
JOAN CRAWFORD
Mildred Pierce, 1945
Possessed, 1947
Sudden Fear, 1952
BETTE DAVIS
Dangerous, 1935
Jezebel, 1938

Dark Victory, 1939
The Letter, 1940
The Little Foxes, 1941
Now, Voyager, 1942
Mr Skeffington, 1944
All About Eve, 1950
The Star, 1952
What Ever Happened To Baby
 Jane?, 1962
OLIVIA DE HAVILLAND
Hold Back The Dawn, 1941
To Each His Own, 1946
The Snake Pit, 1948
The Heiress, 1949
MARIE DRESSLER
Min And Bill, 1930/31
Emma, 1931/32
FAYE DUNAWAY
Bonnie And Clyde, 1967
Chinatown, 1974
Network, 1976
SALLY FIELD
Norma Rae, 1979
Places In The Heart, 1984
LOUISE FLETCHER
One Flew Over The Cuckoo's Nest,
 1975
JANE FONDA
They Shoot Horses, Don't They?,
 1969
Klute, 1971
Julia, 1977
Coming Home, 1978
The China Syndrome, 1979
JOAN FONTAINE
Rebecca, 1940
Suspicion, 1941
The Constant Nymph, 1943
GREER GARSON
Goodbye Mr Chips, 1939
Blossoms In The Dust, 1941
Mrs Miniver, 1942
Madame Curie, 1943
Mrs Parkington, 1944
The Valley Of Decision, 1945
Sunrise At Campobello, 1960
JANET GAYNOR
Seventh Heaven, 1927/28
Street Angel, 1927/28
Sunrise, 1927/28
A Star Is Born, 1937
HELEN HAYES
The Sin Of Madelon Claudet,
 1931/32
Best Supporting Actress Award:
Airport, 1970

SUSAN HAYWARD
Smash Up – The Story Of A Woman,
 1947
My Foolish Heart, 1949
With A Song In My Heart, 1952
I'll Cry Tomorrow, 1955
I Want To Live!, 1958
AUDREY HEPBURN
Roman Holiday, 1953
Sabrina, 1954
The Nun's Story, 1959
Breakfast At Tiffany's, 1961
Wait Until Dark, 1967
KATHARINE HEPBURN
Morning Glory, 1932/33
Alice Adams, 1935
The Philadelphia Story, 1940
Woman Of The Year, 1942
The African Queen, 1951
Summertime, 1955
The Rainmaker, 1956
Suddenly, Last Summer, 1959
Long Day's Journey Into Night,
 1962
Guess Who's Coming To Dinner,
 1967
The Lion In Winter, 1968 (Tie with
 Barbra Streisand)
On Golden Pond, 1981
JUDY HOLLIDAY
Born Yesterday, 1950
GLENDA JACKSON
Women In Love, 1970
Sunday, Bloody Sunday, 1971
A Touch Of Class, 1973
Hedda, 1975
JENNIFER JONES
The Song Of Bernadette, 1943
Love Letters, 1945
Duel In The Sun, 1946
Love Is A Many Splendored Thing,
 1955
DIANE KEATON
Annie Hall, 1977
Reds, 1981
GRACE KELLY
The Country Girl, 1954
VIVIEN LEIGH
Gone With The Wind, 1939
A Streetcar Named Desire, 1951
SOPHIA LOREN
Two Women, 1961
Marriage Italian Style, 1964
SHIRLEY MacLAINE
Some Came Running, 1958
The Apartment, 1960
Irma La Douce, 1963
The Turning Point, 1977

Terms Of Endearment, 1983
ANNA MAGNANI
The Rose Tattoo, 1955
Wild Is The Wind, 1957
LIZA MINNELLI
The Sterile Cuckoo (GB: Pookie),
 1969
Cabaret, 1972
PATRICIA NEAL
Hud, 1963
The Subject Was Roses, 1968
GERALDINE PAGE
Summer And Smoke, 1961
Sweet Bird Of Youth, 1962
Interiors, 1978
The Trip To Bountiful, 1985
MARY PICKFORD
Coquette, 1928/29
LUISE RAINER
The Great Ziegfeld, 1936
The Good Earth, 1937
GINGER ROGERS
Kitty Foyle, 1940
NORMA SHEARER
The Divorcee, 1929/30
Their Own Desire, 1929/30
A Free Soul, 1930/31
The Barretts Of Wimpole Street,
 1934
Romeo And Juliet, 1936
Marie Antoinette, 1938
SIMONE SIGNORET
Room At The Top, 1959
Ship Of Fools, 1965
MAGGIE SMITH
The Prime Of Miss Jean Brodie,
 1969
Travels With My Aunt, 1972
Best Supporting Actress Award:
California Suite, 1978
SISSY SPACEK
Carrie, 1976
Coal Miner's Daughter, 1980
Missing, 1982
The River, 1984
MERYL STREEP
The French Lieutenant's Woman,
 1981
Sophie's Choice, 1982
Silkwood, 1983
Out Of Africa, 1985
Best Supporting Actress Award:
Kramer vs Kramer, 1979
BARBRA STREISAND
Funny Girl, 1968 (Tie with Katharine
Hepburn)
The Way We Were, 1973

ELIZABETH TAYLOR
Raintree County, 1957
Cat On A Hot Tin Roof, 1958
Suddenly, Last Summer, 1959
Butterfield 8, 1960
Who's Afraid Of Virginia Woolf?, 1966
JOANNE WOODWARD
The Three Faces Of Eve, 1957
Rachel, Rachel, 1968
Summer Wishes, Winter Dreams, 1973
JANE WYMAN
The Yearling, 1946
Johnny Belinda, 1948

The Blue Veil, 1951
Magnificent Obsession, 1954
LORETTA YOUNG
The Farmer's Daughter, 1947
Come To The Stable, 1949

It is interesting to note that the Best Actresses seem, on the whole, to have chalked up more nominations and Oscars than the Best Actors ie more honors distributed among fewer people. Correspondingly, it is really astonishing – and in some cases, unbelievable – to note the

great actresses who failed ever to win in this category. They include, notably, those listed below. (Number of nominations in brackets after the names.)

Irene Dunne (5)
Greta Garbo (4)
Judy Garland (1)
Deborah Kerr (6)
Vanessa Redgrave (4)
Rosalind Russell (4)
Barbara Stanwyck (4)
Gloria Swanson (3)

BEST PICTURE

Below is a listing of all the Best Picture winners in chronological order. The total number of nominations for each movie is bracketed after the director. It is one of the anomalies of the Awards that the Best Director does not always direct the Best Picture! For additional interest and reference, therefore, we provide the directors of the movies and, where they failed to win, we additionally give the director who captured the Oscar and the film with which he managed it.

1927/28
WINGS, director William Wellman, not nominated (2)
Best Director: FRANK BORZAGE (*Seventh Heaven*)
1928/9
BROADWAY MELODY, director Harry Beaumont (3)
Best Director: FRANK LLOYD (*The Divine Lady*)
1929/30
ALL QUIET ON THE WESTERN FRONT, director LEWIS MILESTONE (4)
1930/31
CIMARRON, director Wesley Ruggles (7)
Best Director: NORMAN TAUROG (*Skippy*)
1931/32
GRAND HOTEL, director Edmund Goulding, not nominated (1)
Best Director: FRANK BORZAGE (*Best Girl*)
1932/33
CAVALCADE, director FRANK LLOYD (4)
1934
IT HAPPENED ONE NIGHT, director FRANK CAPRA (5)
1935
MUTINY ON THE BOUNTY, director Frank Lloyd (8)
Best Director: JOHN FORD (*The Informer*)
1936
THE GREAT ZIEGFELD, director Robert Z. Leonard (7)
Best Director: FRANK CAPRA (*Mr Deeds Goes To Town*)
1937
THE LIFE OF EMILE ZOLA, director William Dieterle (10)

Best Director: LEO McCAREY (*The Awful Truth*)
1938
YOU CAN'T TAKE IT WITH YOU, director FRANK CAPRA (7)
1939
GONE WITH THE WIND, director VICTOR FLEMING (11)
1940
REBECCA, director Alfred Hitchcock (10)
Best Director: JOHN FORD (*The Grapes of Wrath*)
1941
HOW GREEN WAS MY VALLEY, director JOHN FORD (10)
1942
MRS MINIVER, director WILLIAM WYLER (11)
1943
CASABLANCA, director MICHAEL CURTIZ (8)
1944
GOING MY WAY, director LEO McCAREY (9)
1945
THE LOST WEEKEND, director BILLY WILDER (6)
1946
THE BEST YEARS OF OUR LIVES, director WILLIAM WYLER (8)
1947
GENTLEMAN'S AGREEMENT, director ELIA KAZAN (7)
1948
HAMLET, director Laurence Olivier (7)
Best Director: JOHN HUSTON (*The Treasure Of The Sierra Madre*)
1949
ALL THE KING'S MEN, director Robert Rossen (7)
Best Director: JOSEPH L. MANKIEWICZ (*A Letter To Three Wives*)
1950
ALL ABOUT EVE, director JOSEPH L. MANKIEWICZ (13)

1951
AN AMERICAN IN PARIS, director Vincente Minnelli (8)
Best Director: GEORGE STEVENS (*A Place In The Sun*)
1952
THE GREATEST SHOW ON EARTH, director Cecil B. DeMille (6)
Best Director: JOHN FORD (*The Quiet Man*)
1953
FROM HERE TO ETERNITY, director FRED ZINNEMANN (13)
1954
ON THE WATERFRONT, director ELIA KAZAN (12)
1955
MARTY, director DELBERT MANN (8)
1956
AROUND THE WORLD IN 80 DAYS, director Michael Anderson (7)
Best Director: GEORGE STEVENS (*Giant*)
1957
THE BRIDGE ON THE RIVER KWAI, director DAVID LEAN (8)
1958
GIGI, director VINCENTE MINNELLI (8)
1959
BEN-HUR, director WILLIAM WYLER (11)
1960
THE APARTMENT, director BILLY WILDER (10)
1961
WEST SIDE STORY, directors ROBERT WISE & JEROME ROBBINS (11)
1962
LAWRENCE OF ARABIA, director DAVID LEAN (10)
1963
TOM JONES, director TONY RICHARDSON (10)
1964
MY FAIR LADY, director GEORGE CUKOR (12)
1965
THE SOUND OF MUSIC, director ROBERT WISE (10)
1966
A MAN FOR ALL SEASONS, director FRED ZINNEMANN (8)
1967
IN THE HEAT OF THE NIGHT, director Norman Jewison (6)
Best Director: MIKE NICHOLS (*The Graduate*)
1968
OLIVER!, director CAROL REED (10)
1969
MIDNIGHT COWBOY, director JOHN SCHLESINGER (7)
1970
PATTON, director FRANKLIN J. SCHAFFNER (9)
1971
THE FRENCH CONNECTION, director WILLIAM FRIEDKIN (8)
1972
THE GODFATHER, director Francis Ford Coppola (10)
Best Director: BOB FOSSE (*Cabaret*)

1973
THE STING, director GEORGE ROY HILL (10)
1974
THE GODFATHER PART II, director FRANCIS FORD COPPOLA (10)
1975
ONE FLEW OVER THE CUCKOO'S NEST, director MILOS FORMAN (9)
1976
ROCKY, director JOHN G. AVILDSEN (9)
1977
ANNIE HALL, director WOODY ALLEN (5)
1978
THE DEER HUNTER, director MICHAEL CIMINO (9)
1979
KRAMER vs KRAMER, director ROBERT BENTON (8)
1980
ORDINARY PEOPLE, director ROBERT REDFORD (6)
1981
CHARIOTS OF FIRE, director Hugh Hudson (7)
Best Director: WARREN BEATTY (*Reds*)
1982
GANDHI, director RICHARD ATTENBOROUGH (11)
1983
TERMS OF ENDEARMENT, director JAMES L. BROOKS (11)
1984
AMADEUS, director MILOS FORMAN (11)
1985
OUT OF AFRICA, director SYDNEY POLLACK (11)

The following directors have never won a Best Director Award. They include some of the most notable talents ever to have graced the art of film-making, and represent a formidable collection of famous nominated and/or winning movies. The number of nominations each received is bracketed behind their names.

Robert Altman (2)
Michelangelo Antonioni (1)
Ingmar Bergman (2)
Clarence Brown (5)
John Cassavetes (1)
Charles Chaplin (1)
Federico Fellini (4)
Howard Hawks (1)
Alfred Hitchcock (5)
Stanley Kubrick (4)
Ernst Lubitsch (2)
George Lucas (2)

Arthur Penn (3)
Roman Polanski (2)
Otto Preminger (2)
Jean Renoir (1)
Robert Rossen (2)
Martin Scorsese (1)
Steven Spielberg (3)
Josef von Sternberg (2)
François Truffaut (1)
King Vidor (5)
Orson Welles (1)
William Wellman (3)

INDEX

INDEX OF ACTORS AND OTHER PERSONNEL

308

309

INDEX OF FILM TITLES

PICTURE CREDITS

Associated Press 300 bottom; **Joel Findler** 7 8 9 10 11 12-13 14 15 16 18-19 22-23 24 27 32 35 38 44 45 48 49 54-55 57 63 67 73 80 85 87 94 98-99 103 113 114 122-123 125 127 128-29 133 134 143 145 148-149 150 155 157 158 159 160 162-163 168-169 170 172-173 174 175 179 182 184 187 188 189 195 198-199 200 202-203 204 205 206 207 208 209 210 213 214-215 217 218 219 222-223 224 225 227 229 230 233 234 235 237 240 242-243 244 245 248-249 250 252-253 257 258-259 262 263 268-269 272 273 275 277 279 280 282 283 287 288-289 292-293 294 295 300; **Kobal Collection** 4 5 7 17 21 34-35 38-39 42-43 64-65 68-69 72-73 76 78-79 83 84-85 102 108 110 115 118 120 124 130 132 135 137 138-139 140 142-143 147 149 153 154-155 163 164-165 167 177 180 183 185 188 190 192-193 194 196 212 228 232 238 239 247 249 254 259 260 264 265 267 268 269 270 274 275 278 284 285 290 292; **National Film Archives** 20 25 26 28-29 30-31 33 36 37 40 52 53 58 59 60 62 64 70 74-75 79 82-83 88-89 90 92-93 95 97 100 104-105 107 109; **Universal City Studios** 297; **Warner Bros.** 298-299; **Joel Finler** Half title; **Kobal** Contents and title page

Multimedia Publications have endeavoured to observe the legal requirements with regard to the rights of suppliers of photographic material.